The Muslim Brotherhood in Syria

Having played a role in every iteration of Syrian politics since the country gained independence in 1946, the Muslim Brotherhood were the most prominent opposition group in Syria on the eve of the 2011 uprising. But when unrest broke out in March 2011, few Brotherhood flags and slogans were to be found within the burgeoning protest movement. Drawing on extensive primary research including interviews with Brotherhood members, Dara Conduit looks to the group's history to understand why it failed to capitalise on this advantage as the conflict unfolded, addressing significant gaps in accounts of the group's past to assess whether its reputation for violence and dogmatism is justified.

In doing so, Conduit reveals a party that was neither as violent nor as undemocratic as expected, but whose potential to stage a long-awaited comeback was hampered by the shadow of its own history.

DARA CONDUIT is Associate Research Fellow in the Middle East Studies Forum at the Alfred Deakin Institute, Deakin University. She was a Visiting Scholar at the University of Cambridge, is a board member of the Syrian Studies Association and has provided advice to the UN OHCHR's Working Group on Mercenaries. Author of articles in the *Middle East Journal, Studies in Conflict and Terrorism* and *Journal of Contemporary China*, she gained her MLitt from the University of St Andrews, and her PhD from Monash University. Her thesis was a finalist for the Terrorism Research Institute's annual thesis award.

Cambridge Middle East Studies

Editorial Board

Charles Tripp (general editor)
Julia Clancy-Smith
F. Gregory Gause
Yezid Sayigh
Avi Shlaim
Judith E. Tucker

Cambridge Middle East Studies has been established to publish books on the nineteenth- to twenty-first-century Middle East and North Africa. The series offers new and original interpretations of aspects of Middle Eastern societies and their histories. To achieve disciplinary diversity, books are solicited from authors writing in a wide range of fields including history, sociology, anthropology, political science, and political economy. The emphasis is on producing books affording an original approach along theoretical and empirical lines. The series is intended for students and academics, but the more accessible and wide-ranging studies will also appeal to the interested general reader.

A list of books in the series can be found after the index.

The Muslim Brotherhood in Syria

Dara Conduit
Deakin University

CAMBRIDGE
UNIVERSITY PRESS

University Printing House, Cambridge CB2 8BS, United Kingdom

One Liberty Plaza, 20th Floor, New York, NY 10006, USA

477 Williamstown Road, Port Melbourne, VIC 3207, Australia

314–321, 3rd Floor, Plot 3, Splendor Forum, Jasola District Centre, New Delhi – 110025, India

79 Anson Road, #06-04/06, Singapore 079906

Cambridge University Press is part of the University of Cambridge.

It furthers the University's mission by disseminating knowledge in the pursuit of education, learning, and research at the highest international levels of excellence.

www.cambridge.org
Information on this title: www.cambridge.org/9781108499774
DOI: 10.1017/9781108758321

© Dara Conduit 2019

This publication is in copyright. Subject to statutory exception and to the provisions of relevant collective licensing agreements, no reproduction of any part may take place without the written permission of Cambridge University Press.

First published 2019

Printed in the United Kingdom by TJ International Ltd. Padstow Cornwall

A catalogue record for this publication is available from the British Library.

Library of Congress Cataloging-in-Publication Data
Names: Conduit, Dara, 1986- author.
Title: The Muslim Brotherhood in Syria / Dara Conduit.
Description: New York, NY : Cambridge University Press, 2019. | Series: Cambridge Middle East studies | Includes bibliographical references and index.
Identifiers: LCCN 2019004940| ISBN 9781108499774 (hardback) | ISBN 9781108731287 (paperback)
Subjects: LCSH: Jamaat al-Ikhwan al-Muslimīn (Syria) | Syria–Politics and government–21st century. | Islam and politics–Syria. | Islam–Syria–History–21st century.
Classification: LCC BP10.J383 C66 2019 | DDC 956.9104/23–dc23
LC record available at https://lccn.loc.gov/2019004940

ISBN 978-1-108-49977-4 Hardback
ISBN 978-1-108-73128-7 Paperback

Cambridge University Press has no responsibility for the persistence or accuracy of URLs for external or third-party internet websites referred to in this publication and does not guarantee that any content on such websites is, or will remain, accurate or appropriate.

To Nana, who died just weeks after this manuscript was submitted, having lovingly provided treats and a second home for every step of my life's journey

Contents

List of Tables	*page* ix
Acknowledgements	x
Note on Transliteration	xii
Glossary of Names	xiii
Introduction	1
Part I The History of the Muslim Brotherhood in Syria	**19**
1 A Brief History of Syria and the Syrian Muslim Brotherhood	21
2 The Syrian Muslim Brotherhood's Founding Ideas	40
3 The Brotherhood's Political Practice	66
4 The Syrian Muslim Brotherhood and Violence	91
5 International Relations and Survival in Exile	134
Part II The Syrian Uprising	**153**
6 The Brotherhood Re-Enters the Political Fray	155
7 Looking beyond the Opposition in Exile	173
8 Military Uprising	199
Conclusion	222

Appendix 1 Brotherhood Electoral Details 1947–1963   227
*Appendix 2 Reported Syrian Brotherhood/Vanguard Members
            and Syrians Who Travelled to Afghanistan*   232
Appendix 3 Relationships between Current and Past Leaders 238
Bibliography   240
Index   265

Tables

1.1 Status of the Syrian political system 1947–63	*page* 28
3.1 Brotherhood electoral activity 1947–63	68

Acknowledgements

This book has been many years in the making, and I have been fortunate to receive support from colleagues, family, friends and strangers throughout the journey. Although this book would not have come to fruition without this army of support, all remaining mistakes or deficiencies are wholly my own.

I am grateful to my interviewees who generously gave their own time for interviews that sometimes stretched into the early hours of the morning. Their willingness to have challenging discussions gave a much-needed human perspective on the Syrian Muslim Brotherhood and helped to fill many of the gaps in the group's history. While everyone I spoke to was united by their love for Syria, some also felt a palpable disenchantment and rage: Syrians deserved better than the government and the opposition that they had been dealt. It was a privilege to hear these stories. Many of these conversations would not have been possible without the assistance of those who kindly shared advice, documents or contacts, including Dr Andre Bank, Aron Lund, Professor Nadim Shehadi, Dr Raphael Lefèvre, Rossitza Deleva, Dr Sarah Karkour, Andrew Leber, Zaki Chehab, Ali al-Bayanouni and Samir Abu Laban, as well as a number of anonymous participants and Syrian friends whose names I will withhold. Thank you for sharing information that you could have just as easily kept to yourselves.

This book was written at and supported by Monash University and subsequently Deakin University, where I have been fortunate to have the most amazing colleagues and mentors. In particular I am indebted to Dr Ben MacQueen, whose trust in me and conceptually brilliant mind contributed immeasurably to early drafts of this book. The book also benefited from Associate Professor Pete Lentini's vast knowledge and extraordinarily nice emails, and Associate Professor Sayed Khatab and Dr Taghreed Jamal al-Deen's meticulous checking of my translations. Professor Shahram Akbarzadeh has been a constant source of support and encouragement, believing in the project and me even when I did not, while Professor Charles Tripp and Associate Professor Sarah Phillips provided nuanced and thoughtful feedback that pushed me to think harder. Day-to-day life as an Early Career Researcher would have been immeasurably harder had it not been for my peers, in particular the kindness of Steph and Sam, Will and my many Alfred Deakin Institute colleagues. I must also give thanks to the Cambridge University Press team, especially Maria Marsh, Atifa Jiwa, Robert Judkins, Elizabeth Stone, Sindhujaa Ayyappan and Cassi Roberts, and the Prince Alwaleed Bin Talal Centre of Islamic Studies at the University of Cambridge for hosting me as a Visiting Scholar in 2015.

Lastly, my family. My parents not only gave me my strong sense of social justice, but continue to support me emotionally, gastronomically (thanks for the emergency food deliveries, Mum!) and practically (Dad is my most honest proof reader) more than a decade after leaving the nest. To Ciara for the love of dogs; to Tomoko for the constant chorus of well-wishes; to Bid and my Irish aunts, who cheer so loudly that I can almost hear them from Melbourne; and to Kaye for the ongoing support. Finally, I owe much to Jackson for asking the 'simple' Middle East questions that I should have been able to answer, for feeding and watering me when the deadlines loomed, and most of all for always being unapologetically and genuinely yourself.

Note on Transliteration

This book includes a large number of Arabic words, names and place names. The transliteration of these words follows a simplified version of the *International Journal of Middle East Studies* (IJMES) system,[1] without special characters or diacritical marks.[2] The names of living people are transliterated in line with the person's preference (where known), for example Hassan al-Hachimi instead of the IJMES-styled Hassan al-Hashimi. Other names and proper nouns (including place names and political parties) are transliterated in accordance with mainstream use. Words that are included in mainstream English dictionaries such as mujahidin, ulama or shaykh are not italicised and are spelled in accordance with the IJMES word list.[3] Words that are not commonly transliterated in English texts follow IJMES's proscribed system. When the researcher refers to groups or organisations, the most commonly used name is used, so Liwa al-Tawhid is not translated after the first instance, but Farouq Brigades is translated. Finally, El- and Al- are rendered as al- throughout the work, while foreign words used in quoted works appear in their original form, even if this is in conflict with the IJMES style. The latter is most evident in the English language versions of *al-Nadhir,* which the Brotherhood itself sometimes transliterated to 'al-Nazeer'. *Al-Nadhir* is used in the text for the sake of consistency between the two publications, but 'al-Nazeer' is used in citations when appropriate so that readers can easily find the primary text.

---

[1] 'IJMES Translation and Transliteration Guide', *International Journal of Middle East Studies*, 2013, http://ijmes.chass.ncsu.edu/IJMES_Translation_and_Transliteration_Guide.htm.

[2] Special characters are only used in rare cases, such as that of the Baʿth Party, *Daʿwa* and *Baʿya* in line with mainstream use, or in the case of direct quotes or the title of references.

[3] 'IJMES Word List', *International Journal of Middle East Studies*, 5 October, https://ijmes.chass.ncsu.edu/docs/WordList.pdf.

Glossary of Names

Anas al-Abdeh	Former President of the Syrian National Coalition (SOC), son of the Brotherhood linked Muhammad al-Abdeh.
Husni Abu	Fighting Vanguard leader in Aleppo.
Ali al-Ahmad	Joined the Brotherhood's armed movement in 1981. From Idlib. Left the Brotherhood in the 2000s.
Bashar al-Assad	President of Syria 2000 – present.
Hafez al-Assad	President of Syria from 1971 until his death in 2000.
Rifaat al-Assad	Brother of Hafez al-Assad; widely seen as the architect of the 1982 Hama massacre and the 1980 Palmyra prison massacre. Has been in exile since 1984.
Issam al-Attar	Leader of the Syrian Muslim Brotherhood 1957–69,[1] exiled in 1964.
Ali al-Bayanouni	Senior Brotherhood leader during the Brotherhood-Ba'th confrontation, head of the Aleppo faction, 2011 uprising-era *Shura* Council chief. Brotherhood leader 1996–2010. Son of founding member Ahmad al-Bayanouni.
Mohammad Abu Nasr al-Bayanouni	Senior cleric, head of the Syrian Islamic Front. Head of Jamiyat Abi Dharr. Brother of Ali al-Bayanouni.
Maruf al-Dawalibi	Founding member of the Brotherhood, represented the People's Party in the

---

[1] All leadership dates used in this table are sourced from: Raphaël Lefèvre, *Ashes of Hama: The Muslim Brotherhood in Syria* (London: Hurst, 2013), p. 209.

Glossary of Names

	parliament for many years, including as Prime Minister.
Molham Aldrobi	Former head of the Brotherhood's Strategic Planning office, as a Brotherhood spokesman.
Hosam Ghadban	Deputy leader of the Brotherhood in the 2011 uprising era. Nephew of Munir Ghadban.
Munir Ghadban	Brotherhood leader 1986, uncle of the deputy Brotherhood leader Hosam Ghadban.
Burhan Ghalioun	Liberal opposition figure based in Paris. First president of the Syrian National Council.
Abd al-Fatah abu Ghuddah	Member of the Syrian parliament in the democratic era, Brotherhood leader 1972–75, 1986–91.
Hassan al-Hachimi	Former head of the Brotherhood's political office, son of Mohammad al-Hachimi.
Mohammad al-Hachimi	Chair of the Brotherhood's evaluation committee.
Marwan Hadid	Egyptian trained agronomist from Hama. Rose to prominence in the 1964 Hama riots and soon after began advocating for an armed uprising against the regime. Founder of the Fighting Vanguard.
Muhammad al-Hamid	Founding member of the Brotherhood in Hama, mentor to Said Hawwa.
Said Hawwa	Brotherhood ideologue in the 1960s and 1970s.
Hassan al-Houeidi	Leader of the Brotherhood 1980–85, 1990–96.
Fida al-Sayyid Issa	A Brotherhood youth member from a prominent Brotherhood family from Idlib. Founder of the Syrian Revolution Facebook page. Based in Sweden.
Tarif al-Sayyid Issa	Brotherhood member. Father of Fida al-Sayyid Issa. From a prominent

Glossary of Names

	Brotherhood family in Idlib. Participated in the armed uprising. Killed in a car bombing March 2018.
Abdul Halim al-Khaddam	Minister of Foreign Affairs (1970–84), Vice President (1984–2005), acting Prime Minister (June–July 2000). Formed the short-lived National Salvation Front alliance with the Brotherhood in 2005 following his defection.
Samir Abu Laban	Member of the Brotherhood's political office. Based in Austria.
Muhammad al-Mubarak	Founding member of the Brotherhood, Brotherhood representative in the Syrian parliament.
Omar al-Mushaweh	Head of the Muslim Brotherhood media office for much of the 2011 uprising era.
Adnan Saadeddine	Leader of the Hama faction in the 1970s and 1980s, Brotherhood leader from 1975 to 1980. Split from the Brotherhood in the mid-1980s.
Zuhair Salem	Brotherhood ideologue between 1986 and 2010, senior Brotherhood member.
Ayman Shorbaji	Leader of the Fighting Vanguard in Damascus.
Riad al-Shaqfeh	Leader of the Muslim Brotherhood 2010–14. Held responsibilities in the group's military command during the 1979–82 uprising. Key figure in the Hama faction.
Mustafa al-Sibai	Founder and first Brotherhood leader 1946–57.
Abu Khalid al-Suri (Mohammad al-Bahaiya)	Former Fighting Vanguard member, close associate of Abu Musab al-Suri, founding member of Ahrar al-Sham, acted as Ayman al-Zawahiri's intermediary with ISIS.
Abu Musab al-Suri (Mustafa Setmariam Nasar)	Former Brotherhood and Fighting Vanguard member, high profile jihadist strategist.

xvi   Glossary of Names

Mohammed Sarmini	Former Brotherhood member, advisor to the then Prime Minister of the Syrian Interim Government Prime Minister Ahmed Tomeh.
Farouq Tayfour	Senior Brotherhood leader in the Hama faction, Vice President of the SNC.
Adnan Uqlah	Leader of the Fighting Vanguard during the Hama uprising.
Muhammad Walid	A British trained ophthalmologist and poet, leader of the Syrian Muslim Brotherhood from 2014 - the time of writing.
Ibrahim al-Youssef (Captain)	Fighting Vanguard and Ba'th Party member, possibly Brotherhood member. Responsible for the Aleppo Artillery School massacre.
Abd al-Sattar al-Zaim	Fighting Vanguard leader who preceded Adnan Uqlah.

Introduction

As the Arab Uprisings spread across the Middle East in January 2011, the Syrian Muslim Brotherhood's leaders gathered in a town a few hundred kilometres from Istanbul for their monthly meeting. The group had been in exile for the nearly three decades since their failed previous uprising, and its leaders and members were now scattered across the world. For the first time in many years however, the Brothers had reason to be hopeful. The swift overthrow of Tunisia's long-reigning dictator, Zine El Abidine Ben Ali, and the growing protests against the Egyptian President, Hosni Mubarak, had raised the question of revolt in Syria. The Brotherhood's Strategic Planning chief, Molham Aldrobi, later recalled that up until that moment: 'none of us ... had imagined or dreamed or had that nightmare—however you want to describe it—that a revolution might happen in Syria because for the 30-plus years since 1980, nothing had happened'.[1]

A new item was quickly added to the Syrian Brothers' January meeting agenda: the leaders would discuss what to do if the wider Arab unrest spread to Syria. This was important because should the country's nearly 50-year-old Ba'thist regime be destabilised, the group's leaders and members might finally be able to return home. The group would need to be ready.

Molham Aldrobi was assigned to prepare a document overnight on what could happen. He presented the brief to the leadership the following day and later explained:

I drafted a Project Charter called the 'Bashar Leave!' project, and in that document I discussed the special situation of Syria compared to Tunisia and Egypt, and what we as the Muslim Brotherhood needed to do in case revolution erupted in Syria ...We were hopeful that something might happen in Syria that would change the situation in Syria to become a democratic country. We wanted these changes to happen peacefully.[2]

---

[1] Interview with Molham Aldrobi, 13 September 2017.   [2] Ibid.

But when the unrest finally reached Syria in March 2011, Brotherhood flags or slogans were few and far between in the burgeoning protest movement. Protesters in the town of Zabadani went so far as to formally distinguish themselves from the Brotherhood, holding a placard that declared: 'Neither Salafi nor Brotherhood, my religion is freedom'.[3] Indeed, while the Muslim Brotherhood remained Syria's best-known opposition group, it would face an uphill battle to rebuild a popular base in Syria.

The Muslim Brotherhood in Syria (*al-Ikhwan al-Muslimun fi Suriya*) has played a role in every iteration of Syrian politics since the country gained independence in 1946, including in Syria's parliament from 1947 to 1963. Syria's democratic era came to a close after the Arab Socialist Baʻth Party took power by coup in 1963, marking the beginning of the Brotherhood's long struggle to return to the corridors of Syrian political power. Initially the Syrian Brothers mounted their discontent peacefully through youth groups, study circles and popular protests inside Syria. However, as repression hardened and avenues for political opportunity narrowed over the subsequent decade and a half, the Brotherhood made the fateful decision to take up arms against the Syrian government. In the violent years that followed, membership of the group would become a capital offense. The Brotherhood–government bloodletting eventually cultimated in the bloody 1982 Hama uprising.

The uprising had begun in the early hours of 3 February 1982 in the central city of Hama, although the exact episode that sparked the conflict between the Syrian army and the militants remains disputed.[4] Whatever the cause, once the violence started, government opponents in Hama, including some Brotherhood cells, rose up against the regime, seizing government buildings, and by morning declaring the city 'liberated'. The government responded by closing all roads and communication links to the city, cutting off the up-to-200 Brotherhood militants and others

---

[3] 'Syria Live Blog - April 23', Al-Jazeera (23 April 2011), https://web.archive.org/web/20110426120021/http://blogs.aljazeera.net/live/middle-east/syria-live-blog-april-23.
Note that this page is no longer available on the Al-Jazeera website and must be accessed through a web archive.

[4] The incident that sparked the conflict is variously reported as: a Brotherhood ambush of an army patrol (see Patrick Seale, *Asad of Syria: The Struggle for the Middle East* [Berkeley: University of California Press, 1988], p. 332.), an army operation to round up individual members of the Brotherhood (see Mark A. VanderVeen, 'Showdown in Syria: An Examination of Islamist Repression and Rebellion in 1982 Hama' [American University of Paris, 2009], p. 2.), the discovery of an opposition hideout by a government patrol (see Fred H. Lawson, 'Social Bases for the Hamah Revolt', *MERIP Reports*, no. 110 (1982), pp. 24–8) or a Syrian army operation to seize a known opposition weapons cache (see Thomas Friedman, *From Beirut to Jerusalem* [London: HarperCollins, 1995], p. 82.).

inside Hama from the group's exiled leaders and outside support.[5] By the time news of the uprising reached the outside world nearly a week later, a fierce battle was underway, with the Syrian government besieging the town's population with heavy weaponry. In just three weeks, up to 25,000 people were killed, and large sections of the city's old quarters were flattened.[6] 1,000 Syrian soldiers died in the battle. As the dust settled in Hama however, it became clear that a significant further price would be exacted from the Brotherhood and its supporters for their defiance: thousands were imprisoned or disappeared, the group's support base was destroyed, and large numbers of the group's followers were forced to join their leaders in a seemingly permanent exile. Exile then created a new challenge for the Syrian Muslim Brotherhood: the struggle for relevance.

Nonetheless, the Syrian state's intolerance of almost all opposition meant that on the eve of the 2011 uprising the Brotherhood still remained one of Syria's most resilient and best-resourced opposition political actors. As one of the few groups with salaried staff, an institutional structure and funds, it was able to use its organisational strength and resources to guarantee itself a seat at the political table. Brotherhood members went on to participate in all of the opposition conferences in the first year of the uprising, and it became a 'king maker' on the new opposition political bodies the Syrian National Council (SNC) and the National Coalition for Syrian Revolution and Opposition Forces (SOC - Syrian Opposition Coalition). Although the influence of these exiled political bodies diminished as the uprising militarised, the Brotherhood's organisational skills nonetheless had endowed it with a significant advantage in early days of the revolt. The disconnect between this early advantage and the Brotherhood's subsequent limited success in the uprising as a whole would later become quite stark.

For all the Syrian Muslim Brotherhood's prominence as the uprising first unfolded however, questions were quickly raised about its ambitions and *modus operandi*. Prominent Middle East analyst Marina Ottaway

---

[5] Estimates of the number of Brotherhood members that fought in Hama vary from Brotherhood Shura council chief Ali al-Bayanouni's estimate of 20–25 members, to the US Defense Intelligence Agency's report that 200 Brotherhood fighters were within the city. See interview with Ali al-Bayanouni, London (13 September 2015); 'Syria: Muslim Brotherhood Pressure Intensifies (U)', *US Defense Intelligence Agency* (May 1982), p. 11.

[6] Estimates of casualties vary between 5,000 and 25,000 given the secretive nature of the event. Middle East Watch (part of Human Rights Watch) claimed that most credible estimates range from 5,000 to 10,000 deaths, predominantly civilians. See Middle East Watch, *Syria Unmasked* (New Haven: Yale University Press, 1991), p. 20. Nikolaos Van Dam put the death rate at between 5,000 and 25,000 – Nikolaos Van Dam, *The Struggle for Power in Syria* (London: I.B.Tauris, 1996), p. 111.

queried in April 2011: 'Has it gone underground, how quickly can it be revived, how much sympathy is there still for the Muslim Brotherhood? I have no idea and I don't think anybody else has an idea on that'.[7] This sense of uncertainty remained unresolved a year later, when *The New York Times'* David Kirkpatrick conceded that while the Syrian Brotherhood's violent history was well known, 'not much more is known about the current internal dynamics of the group'.[8] Such observations were remarkable given that the Syrian Brothers' Egyptian counterpart is one of the most thoroughly studied Islamist groups in the Middle East.

It wasn't as though good research didn't exist on the Syrian Brothers: it did, although most of it had been written prior to 1982.[9] It was that the Hama massacre remained one of the few reference points through which Syria and the Brotherhood were known and understood, with hundreds of articles published as the protests broke out reminding readers that the Brotherhood's 1982 uprising was the last major instance of anti-government revolt in Syria by members of the country's Sunni Arab majority.[10] This memory of the Hama massacre – in particular its imagery of violence, bloodshed, radicalism, Islamism, siege, destruction and tragedy – was difficult to reconcile with the group's more moderate

---

[7] Cited in: Lachlan Carmichael, 'US Hedges Its Bets on Syria: Analysts', *Agence France Presse* (3 April 2011).

[8] David D. Kirkpatrick, 'Concerns about Al Qaeda in Syria Underscore Questions about Rebels', *The New York Times* (21 August 2012), http://thelede.blogs.nytimes.com/2012/08/21/concerns-about-al-qaeda-in-syria-underscore-questions-about-rebels/.

[9] See for example: Hanna Batatu, 'Syria's Muslim Brethren', *MERIP Reports*, no. 110 (1982), pp. 12–36; Umar F. Abd-allah, *The Islamic Struggle in Syria* (Berkeley: Mizan Press, 1983); Raymond Hinnebusch, *Authoritarian Power and State Formation in Bathist Syria: Army, Party and Peasant* (Boulder: Westview Press, 1990); Hans Gunter Lobmeyer, 'Islamic Ideology and Secular Discourse', *Orient* 32, no. 3 (1991), pp. 395–415; Hans Gunter Lobmeyer, 'Al-dimuqratiyya hiyya al-hall? The Syrian Opposition at the End of the Asad Era', in *Contemporary Syria: Liberalization between Cold War and Cold Peace*, ed. Eberhard Kienle (London: British Academic Press, 1994); Alasdair Drysdale, 'The Asad Regime and Its Troubles', *MERIP Reports*, no. 110 (1982); Lawson, 'Social Bases'; Alison Pargeter, *The Muslim Brotherhood: The Burden of Tradition* (London: Saqi Books, 2010); Line Khatib, *Islamic Revivalism in Syria: The Rise and Fall of Ba'thist Secularism* (Abingdon: Routledge, 2011); Thomas Pierret, *Religion and State in Syria: The Sunni Ulama from Coup to Revolution* (Cambridge: Cambridge University Press, 2011).

[10] A Factiva search with the keywords 'Syria', 'Muslim Brotherhood' and 'Hama' and date filters 15 March 2011–15 April 2011 produced 156 results, including: Suleiman Al-Khalidi, 'Syrian Forces Kill Three Protesters in Southern City', *Reuters* (19 March 2011); 'Syrian Violence Escalates', *Financial Times* (24 March 2011); 'Syria Crackdown Leaves 15 Dead, Activists Say' (24 March 2011); Praveen Swami, 'Family in Power for 40 Years; Assad's Dynasty' (25 March 2011); James Hider and Nicholas Blanford, 'There Was a Massacre in the Streets but We Are Not Afraid, Say Witnesses', *The Times* (25 March 2011); 'Protests and Shooting in Syria as the Death Toll Climbs', *Al-Arabiya* (25 March 2011).

recent record. This led Hama to often be seen as the definitive example of the group's character, more instructive than the nearly four decades of organisational history that preceded the event and the three decades that followed. Many observers therefore assumed that the example of the group's violent behaviour in 1982 would be replicated in 2011, with an editorial in *The Australian* noting that were President al-Assad 'to be deposed, it's likely that Sunnis, possibly Muslim Brotherhood extremists, would take over', while Cook declared that the Syrian President Bashar al-Assad 'may be an implacable foe, but he is better than the Syrian Muslim Brotherhood'.[11] Schanzer too affirmed that the al-Assad regime 'is a very nasty regime. Of course, the idea of having the Muslim Brotherhood come in ... is equally unpalatable.'[12] It was as though the Brotherhood's true colours were revealed in Hama.[13]

In some ways, this was to be expected. Hama was a watershed moment in Syria's political history, with Leverett observing that, 'How a contemporary Syrian feels about Hama reveals much about his political orientation; how an outside analyst interprets Hama says much about his view of Syrian political culture and of the Asad [sic] regime.'[14] To those who supported the government, the Hama massacre served as a grave warning about the destructive and revolutionary threat that Islamists pose to their way of life; a narrative that the Assad regime itself went to great lengths to foment. Ismail found that the Hama events played a 'politicaly formative role':

> Memories of Hama are constitutive of a community of subjects of humiliation, whose lives were stifled or, in the words of Manhal al-Sarraj, "became still." The memories, muted as they have been, feed into sentiments of grievance and a deep-rooted sense of discrimination – a sense that a historical wrong remains unrecognised and that no atonement or reparation has been attempted.[15]

Indeed, for many, Hama represented a tragedy of history that demonstrated the brutality of their leaders and the lengths that they would go in

---

[11] 'Syrian Leader Must Adapt or Go', *The Australian* (2 April 2011), www.theaustralian.com.au/opinion/editorials/syrian-leader-must-adapt-or-go/news-story/ab29258aaecef4c74e8b614a832e4266, p. 15; Steven A. Cook, 'Unholy Alliance: How Syria Is Bringing Israel, Iran, and Saudi Arabia Together', *The Atlantic* (9 May 2011). www.theatlantic.com/international/archive/2011/05/unholy-alliance-how-syria-is-bringing-israel-iran-and-saudi-arabia-together/238084/.

[12] Jenna Lee, 'Interview with Jonathan Schanzer', *Fox News: Live Event* (1 April 2011).

[13] For a more detailed discussion of the development of the narrative surrounding Hama, see Dara Conduit, 'The Syrian Muslim Brotherhood and the Spectacle of Hama', *The Middle East Journal* 70, no. 2 (2016), pp. 211–26.

[14] Flynt Leverett, *Inheriting Syria: Bashar's Trial by Fire* (Washington, DC: Brookings Institute, 2005), p. 35.

[15] Salwa Ismail, *The Rule of Violence: Subjectivity, Memory and Government in Syria* (Cambridge: Cambridge University Press, 2018), pp. 133 and 157.

the name of self-preservation, and also of the huge cost that the Brotherhood was willing to inflict upon the Syrian people. To the Syrian intellectual Yassin al-Haj Saleh, the significance of 1982 went further, representing 'the end point—not to the conflict with Islamists, but to any political rights for all Syrians'.[16] The Hama massacre continued to resonate in the 2011 Syrian uprising, with opposition groups at times strategically deploying the imagery of the Hama massacre to discredit the al-Assad regime.[17]

But the roots of the Hama memory extend beyond Syria's polarised political arena, drawing too from the dominant discourses that guide the understanding of Islamist groups more broadly. Cobb noted that global narratives are often 'downloaded' into local settings, shaping the way in which sense is made of events.[18] In such narratives, Islamist groups are viewed as predisposed to violence or undemocratic behaviour. When such groups call for elections or democratic processes, it is assumed that their commitment to democracy is limited to 'one person, one vote, *one time*', as coined by US diplomat Edward Djerejian in his now famed 1992 Meridian House speech. Djerjian later explained: the comments 'reflected our concern that certain Islamist parties and groups in the region would use elections as a vehicle to come to power only to undermine the democratic electoral process in order to stay in power'.[19] Like Djerjian, Talhamy concluded in 2012 'though in many ways the [Syrian] Brotherhood's official political platform is a model of Islamist moderation and tolerance, it is less a window into the group's thinking than a reflection of its political tactics'.[20] Such behaviour is often viewed as intrinsic to the 'facts' and 'truths' of Islamists and often Islam more broadly, ensuring that many of the events that have taken place in the

---

[16] Yassin al-Haj Saleh, *Impossible Revolution: Making Sense of the Syrian Tragedy* (London: Hurst, 2017), p. 236.

[17] AFP, 'Syria Opposition Commemorates Hama Massacre', *The Telegraph* (2 February 2012), www.telegraph.co.uk/news/worldnews/middleeast/syria/9056350/Syria-opposition-commemorates-Hama-massacre.html; Phil Sands, 'Government and Protesters both Invoke Hama Massacre of 1982', *The National* (7 July 2011), www.thenational.ae/news/world/middle-east/government-and-protesters-both-invoke-hama-massacre-of-1982 (parenthesis added); Alain Gresh, '"The Bullets Killed Our Fear": Syria Waits for Ramadan', *Le Monde Diplomatique* (1 August 2011), http://mondediplo.com/2011/08/03syria.

[18] Sara Cobb, *Speaking of Violence: The Politics and Poetics of Narrative in Conflict Resolution* (Oxford: Oxford University Press, 2013), p. 6.

[19] Edward P. Djerejian and William Martin, *Danger and Opportunity: An American Ambassador's Journey through the Middle East* (New York: Simon & Schuster, 2008), p. 22.

[20] Yvette Talhamy, 'The Muslim Brotherhood Reborn: The Syrian Uprising', *Middle East Quarterly*, Spring (2012), p. 33.

Middle East are attributed to the nuances and 'irrationality' of Islamist movements. In this regard, the Hama massacre, the infamy of which probably dwarfs the renown of the Syrian Muslim Brotherhood itself, played into these expectations, becoming an Islamist event par excellence and confirming to some the group's primordial propensity to violence and rebellion, which is supposed to be common to all Islamist groups. Very few commentators considered the contra; that the Hama massacre itself may have been an aberration for an otherwise mainstream group. Although the book does not seek to understate the Brotherhood's responsibility for events, it underlines the importance of interrogating whether the Hama memory has distorted knowledge on the group.

So, as the 2011 uprising unfolded, expectations of the Brotherhood often fell into the well-worn binaries ascribed to other Islamist movements, as a group that was violent *or* democratic, secular *or* dogmatic, but rarely something in between. The Brotherhood was variously depicted as a threat to Syria's future and its secular path, or a force for good in the fledgling opposition movement, while the Syrian uprising itself was often viewed through the lens of an existential battle between the secular Assad regime and the fanatical Brotherhood. This led to the understatement of the scale and diversity of the country's existing and emerging opposition movement, the overstatement of the Brotherhood's significance, and perhaps most significantly for this book's line of enquiry: the oversimplification of the Brotherhood's history and character, limiting the ability of observers to predict how the Brotherhood would fare as the 2011 uprising developed.

Rethinking the Brotherhood

This book uses the gap in understanding, the prominence of the violence narrative and the Syrian Muslim Brotherhood's perceived significance on the eve of 2011 as a starting point to examine the ways in which the Brotherhood's past informs the choices it has made in the uprising. It observes the Brotherhood's history from its founding moments to 2011 in order to identify its formative experiences and key characteristics, and to examine how these features changed over time. The book argues that it is these historical experiences, contexts and wounds that most strongly influenced its entrance into – and subsequent underperformance in – the 2011 uprising. It builds on the early works of scholars such as Batatu, Abd-Allah and Hinnebusch, as well as Lefèvre's 2013 *Ashes of Hama* by using additional Arabic-language primary sources, interviews, recently released archival documents and the lessons of five further years of Syrian war.[21] It complements Lefèvre's chronological account by explaining the Brotherhood thematically to more closely investigate the group's core features, although takes a less optimistic view of the Brotherhood's organisation and promise.

The book employs a Constructionist qualitative research methodology[22] because the Syrian Muslim Brotherhood is a socially constituted organisation and product of the social world. Its history has been defined by the interactions between individuals, making Constructionism an important tool because of its acknowledgement of the inevitability of finding accounts that reflect slightly different truths: 'people build or construct their understanding of the external world—that is, they interpret it'.[23] The research was not expected to uncover a repository of accepted facts and 'truths' on the group. In fact, it was clear from the moment that the research was conceived that the Brotherhood's deeply contested history would preclude the discovery of an uncontested account of the past. It is not that every participant or source rewrote history (although some did), but that they have interpreted events through their own lenses, ensuring that each data set had emerged from a different set of experiences and social reality. Other methodologies – including many of those in the positivist tradition – would treat conflicting data as problematic and perhaps worthy of annulment. In contrast, the Constructionist approach enabled the use of conflicting perspectives to enrich the analysis, particularly when it came to assessing the organisational health of the Brotherhood.

The research incorporated multiple qualitative methods with a strong emphasis on primary source material. Primary documents, one-on-one interviews and archival material are the building blocks of the book. Sources were based in either Arabic or English. The three separate research methods were chosen to provide 'a confluence of evidence', enabling the triangulation of findings to enhance data integrity.[24] The three methods also enriched the data, which if left to a single method could be vulnerable to bias or agenda. Indeed, as Mouton and Marais noted, 'by employing different methods of data collection in a single

---

[21] Batatu, 'Syria's Muslim Brethren'; Abd-allah, *The Islamic Struggle in Syria*; Hinnebusch, *Authoritarian Power*; Raphaël Lefèvre, *Ashes of Hama: The Muslim Brotherhood in Syria* (London: Hurst, 2013).

[22] Herbert J. Rubin and Irene S. Rubin, *Qualitative Interviewing: The Art of Hearing Data* (Thousand Oaks: SAGE, 2012), p. 16.

[23] Ibid.

[24] Thomas R. Lindlof, *Qualitative Communication Research Methods*, 3rd edn (Thousand Oaks: SAGE, 2011), p. 274; Elliot Eisner, *The Enlightened Eye: Qualitative Inquiry and the Enhancement of Educational Practice* (Upper Saddle River: Merrill/Prentice Hall, 1998), p. 110.

Introduction

project we are, to some extent, able to compensate for the limitations of each'.[25] Where necessary or appropriate, primary sources were complemented by secondary sources.

The research initially examined official Brotherhood documents, including published political programmes, official statements issued by leaders, editions of the Syrian Muslim Brotherhood newspapers *al-Nadhir* (which was published in Arabic, with excerpts published in English across Europe and the USA) and *al-Ahd,* and Brotherhood members' own account of the Hama massacre *Hama Masaat al-Asr.* Document analysis was chosen as the first avenue of research because it provided a data set to be built on and verified through the subsequent interview process. Although official documents are vulnerable to agendas, bias and half-truths like any other source, they provide insight into the way the Brotherhood communicated with its supporters and how it wanted to be portrayed at certain important junctures. While human accounts have been modified by reflection and memory, historical documents are exactly preserved, offering a window into the Brotherhood uninfluenced by the passage of time.

The second second step of the research process drew data from human sources, including personal documents and memoirs written by Brotherhood and Fighting Vanguard members (most of whom are now dead), as well as one-on-one interviews. Efforts were made to talk to members and source documents from all three Brotherhood factions, as well as members across all three generations. The documents included memoirs written by Adnan Saadeddine (former leader), Said Hawwa (former ideologue), Ayman Shorbaji (former Fighting Vanguard leader) and Abu Musab al-Suri (former Fighting Vanguard Member/Brotherhood military trainer), and letters written by Brotherhood and Fighting Vanguard figures to their supporters and the leadership. The book also used documents found in the US raid on the al-Qaeda leader Osama bin Laden's house in Abbottabad, Pakistan, including one letter thought to be written by Bin Laden himself.[26] These personal documents were complemented by interviews given by Brotherhood leaders in both the

---

[25] Johann Mouton and H.C. Marais, *Basic Concepts in the Methodology of the Social Sciences* (Pretoria: HSRC, 1996), p. 92.
[26] Unknown author, ND 'SOCOM-2012–0000017-HT – Letter found in Osama bin Laden's Abbottabad, translated by the Combatting Terrorism Center at West Point, thought to be written by Osama bin Laden'. The letter was assessed by Lahoud et al. as being written by Osama bin Laden. See Nelly Lahoud et al., 'Letters from Abbottabad: Bin Ladin Sidelined?', Combatting Terrorism Center at West Point (3 May 2012), www.ctc.usma.edu/v2/wp-content/uploads/2012/05/CTC_LtrsFromAbottabad_WEB_v2.pdf, p. 58.

English and Arabic-language press over a period of nearly 40 years. In addition, 20 one-on-one semi-structured interviews were conducted with senior Muslim Brotherhood members (mostly from the Aleppo branch of the group), former Brotherhood members (including from the Hama and Damascus branches), non-Brotherhood Syrian Islamist opposition figures and secular Syrian opposition figures. Every person interviewed had been linked to the Brotherhood in some way, either as a member or former-member, associate, or as the child of a Muslim Brotherhood member (past or present) that had grown up in a Syrian Brotherhood community in exile. All of the non-members had worked closely with – and often competitively against – the group, either historically or as part of the 2011 uprising. Some Brotherhood members and Syrian activists generously participated on the condition of anonymity.

It is acknowledged that interviews are not without flaws. Humans can forget or repress memories, make mistakes, exaggerate or lie. Some participants will have agendas of their own.[27] These considerations formed part of the research design from the outset and garnering fact and exact truth from all participants was not expected. When information was uncovered purporting to be fact, it was triangulated with other participants from a range of backgrounds, as well as with the other data sources (as is discussed in further detail below). At times, the variation in accounts enriched the data considerably.

The research also incorpated archival material produced by Western governments working in the Levant from the early 1940s until today. Although Western archival sources require a thorough consideration of Orientalist bias,[28] the bias is of a different nature to that inherent in Brotherhood-centric sources, so acted as a balance of sorts. Archival material was found to be particularly useful in shedding light on the broader socio-political context surrounding the Brotherhood's emergence and activities. It was also helpful, because like document analysis, archival research is free from the concerns of 'reactivity' inherent in the interview process, where participants may respond differently because they know they are being observed.[29]

Significant thought was given to balance between sources and data reliability. Possible concerns that using so many Muslim Brotherhood sources could skew the research findings in line with the group's own

---

[27] Lindlof, *Qualitative Communication*, p. 173.
[28] See Edward W. Said, *Orientalism: Western Conceptions of the Orient* (London: Penguin Books, 2001).
[29] C. James Goodwin, *Research in Psychology: Methods and Design* (Hoboken: John Wiley & Sons, 2010), p. 388.

Introduction 11

narrative were mitigated to an extent by speaking to members of opposing Muslim Brotherhood factions, as well as non-Brotherhood opposition members who provided outside perspectives. Data was triangulated using Denzin's 'within-method' of data triangulation, which validates data inside a single method,[30] as well as the 'member validation' approach,[31] which involved testing hypotheses with knowledgeable Brotherhood members, and seeing whether they thought that the findings were plausible. Seale argued that this is the most effective way to establish credibility, as 'they (participants) can indicate their agreement or disagreement with the way in which the researcher has represented them'.[32] Data triangulation processes were applied across the board. All new data that is reported in this book was corroborated with another data source. At times, this process proved that data was hearsay, prompting the evidence to be discounted.

The question of author positionality is an inherent challenge. The author is a white, Western-born and educated female, whose views, contexts and privilege shape her objectivity and the way that information is presented in this book, however unintentionally. The author acknowledges that her identity may have also influenced the way that her participants perceived her and could have shaped the information that interview participants chose to divulge, particularly on issues related to violence, democracy and personal status laws. Although efforts were made to mitigate the positionality impact, including by employing vigilant self-awareness throughout the research and writing process, it is nonetheless an important point to flag.

A New Look at the Syrian Muslim Brotherhood

The book argues that the Muslim Brotherhood in Syria must be conceived as a political organisation like any other that seeks political opportunities, weighs available information to make decisions and attempts to reconcile the desires of its members with political realities. Although the group has its own ideological frame, its character and actions are strongly influenced by its historical experiences and political contexts. Too often Islamist groups are seen as a direct product of their ideology: this book argues otherwise, finding that the Brotherhood's organisational history, personnel, political experiences and operating context give a better view

---

[30] Norman K. Denzin, *The Research Act*, 2nd edn (New York: McGraw-Hill, 1978), p. 301.
[31] Lindlof, *Qualitative Communication*, p. 278.
[32] Clive Seale, *The Quality of Qualitative Research* (London: SAGE, 1999), p. 45 (parenthesis added).

into the group than any carefully planned Islamist ideological programme. Understanding the Brotherhood's mundane organisational flaws and history is the key to illuminating many of the reasons for the group's limited success after 2011.

In order to understand the Brotherhood, this book looks to the work of scholars of contentious politics under authoritarianism, political organisations and political violence. Those observing contentious politics have made an important contribution to the study of the Middle East in recent decades by examining the multiple modes of opposition political contestation that take place in authoritarian environments, as well as the often-symbiotic relationships between regimes and their oppositions.[33] Oppositions living under authoritarianism face specific challenges related to the limited opportunities and often-substantial coercive threats distributed by regimes, not to mention the significant power imbalance between rulers and the ruled. Although groups too have agency, authoritarian states are inhospitable environments for oppositions, and groups do not survive unscathed. They are shaped by a regime's processes of co-optation and repression, as well as its official narratives, and also by the way in which they decide to respond to such conditions.[34]

Indeed, by 2011 the Brotherhood had been shaped by the more than 50 years in which it had existed as an opposition group under the mantle of authoritarian regimes, most recently under the Baʿth Party, but also under the illiberal pre-Baʿth governments of Husni al-Zaim (1949), Adib Shishakli (1951–4) and the United Arab Republic (1958–61). Even in exile, the Brotherhood remained closely linked to Syrian political structures—at least in an intellectual sense—by releasing platforms, holding regular meetings and periodically negotiating with the regime. Scholars have argued that opposition decision-making in such environments exists on a skewed plane of costs and benefits because the power imbalance between regimes and oppositions is so great that vulnerable oppositions must calibrate political programmes to appeal to constituents, without prompting a regime response. These processes often manifest in distinct organisational characteristics such as a short-term modus operandi,

---

[33] See for example: Charles Tilly and Sidney Tarrow, *Contentious Politics* (Oxford: Oxford University Press, 2015); Ellen Lust-Okar, *Structuring Conflict in the Arab World: Incumbents, Opponents and Institutions* (Cambridge: Cambridge University Press, 2005); Holger Albrecht, *Raging against the Machine: Political Opposition under Authoritarianism in Egypt* (Syracuse: Syracuse University Press, 2013).

[34] Lisa Wedeen, *Ambiguities of Domination: Politics, Rhetoric and Symbols in Contemporary Syria* (Chicago: University of Chicago Press, 1999), pp. 48–9.

opportunistic decision-making and alliance volatility.[35] Such experiences can leave a lasting footprint on a group because the tactics used by those attempting to survive authoritarianism are internalised and difficult to shake after the collapse of an authoritarian regime.[36] Given that the Brotherhood endured some of the harshest repression in the Middle East, its experiences under authoritarianism, as well as the memory of repression and of the group's failed 1982 uprising, would continue to colour the group's every move after 2011.

While scholars of contentious politics acknowledge the long-term impact of authoritarianism and the role that historical repertoires of contestation play in shaping future repertoires, scholars of political organisations go further, arguing that an organisation's character should be traced back as far as a group's founding moments, which leave a clear impression on a group for life.[37] Leaders in a group's formative stages set the ideology, the identity and the institutions that determine how an organisation functions, and this impacts the way it responds to political challenges well into the future. This is not to say that organisations are incapable of change or evolution, but that it takes considerable effort for organisational change to take place.[38] Such dynamics are often even more pronounced in exiled organisations, where 'origin often determines both material resources and recruiting policies, especially during the initial period abroad'.[39] This underwrites the book's decision to trace the Brotherhood's past back to its moment of birth.

Indeed, contra to the Hama-centric descriptor of the Brotherhood as violent, dogmatic and illiberal, this book identifies three central Syrian Brotherhood characteristics that emerged in its founding decades that have shaped the group's navigation of its operating environment and

---

[35] Jack A. Goldstone and Charles Tilly, 'Threat (and Opportunity): Popular Action and State Responses in the Dynamics of Contentious Action', in *Silence and Voice in the Study of Contentious Politics*, ed. Ronald R. Aminzade, Jack A. Goldstone, Doug McAdam, Elizabeth J. Perry, William H. Sewell, Sidney Tarrow and Charles Tilly (Cambridge: Cambridge University Press, 2001). pp. 179–95.

[36] See Nancy Bermeo, 'Democracy and the Lessons of Dictatorship', *Comparative Politics* 24, no. 3 (1992), pp. 273–4; Vincent Boudreau, *Resisting Dictatorship: Repression and Protest in Southeast Asia* (Cambridge: Cambridge University Press, 2004), p. 11.

[37] Maurice Duverger, *Political Parties*, trans. Barbara North and Robert North, 3rd edn (Paris: Methuen & Co Ltd., 1967), p. xxxv; Angelo Panebianco, *Political Parties: Organization & Power*, trans. Marc Silver (Cambridge: Cambridge University Press, 1988), p. xiii.

[38] Robin T. Pettitt, *Contemporary Party Politics* (New York: Palgrave Macmillan, 2014), p. 43.

[39] Yossi Shain, *The Frontier of Loyalty: Political Exiles in the Age of the Nation-State* (Ann Arbor: University of Michigan Press, 2005), p. 30.

responses to political challenges and change ever since. The first characteristic—pragmatism—was built into the Brotherhood's DNA in its founding years and remained a defining feature of the group in the 2011 uprising. It endowed the group with a unique ability to adapt to changing political conditions, although at times the group's pragmatism bordered on opportunism. The second characteristic, individualism, has equally influenced the group's trajectory. The Syrian Brothers' founding constituency was made up of economically liberal elites who prized individual rights such as education and economic freedom and used the Brotherhood as a vehicle to achieve these goals. Although these elites often acted under the banner of the Brotherhood, they simultaneously pursued individual interests, which expanded the group's skill-base and reach enormously. Finally, the Brotherhood has always been ideologically flexible. Although the group has promulgated a lifelong commitment to democratic ideas and economic liberalism, the Syrian Brothers have demonstrated flexibility on other issues and in the way they pursue goals because it has never been a deeply ideological group. This approach has fundamentally guided the group's decision-making over its seven-decade history, enabling it to change during times of political flux and respond to new opportunities and trends. The interweaving of the group's pragmatism and flexibility however has proven a double-edged sword. On the one hand, it has endowed the group with the resilience required to remain one of the great survivors of Syrian politics. But on the other, this willingness to constantly morph alongside the political mood has led to a hollowing of its core purpose, giving outsiders the sense that the group would compromise almost anything or anyone to maximise its chances of success. This manoeuvring in relation to other Syrian opposition groups in particular has drawn its claimed democratic values into question.

The book also looks to scholars of political violence to understand the Brotherhood's violent history. While scholars of contentious politics acknowledge that the interactions between regimes and their oppositions sometimes contribute to the emergence of political violence, Martin and Perliger argue that groups have a range of political tactics (including violence) to choose from at any given time, and make the choice based on a rational analysis of threats and opportunities.[40] Recognition that political violence is a tactic provides a useful window through which to

---

[40] Susanne Martin and Arie Perliger, 'Turning to and from Terror: Deciphering the Conditions under Which Political Groups Choose Violent and Nonviolent Tactics', *Perspectives on Terrorism* 6, nos. 4–5 (2012), p. 21.

observe the Brotherhood because it underlines that searching for ideological vulnerabilities to violence obfuscates the political process that facilitated the Brotherhood's transformation. Violence was never part of the group's ideology; its dangerous (and in hindsight, foolhardy) escalation reflected a tactical response to circumstance, rather than core belief. Scholars of political violence also highlight the importance of context in understanding a group's use of violence – radicalisation is a political process that takes place over time. It can be exacerbated by authoritarian crackdowns that prompt moderate opposition members to disengage because they are unwilling to pay the cost of dissent, enabling radical members to garner more-decisive influence in the group.[41] This pattern was seen after the Brotherhood split in 1970, when the group's moderate Damascus faction resigned. Division over the legitimacy of violence as a tactic would then paralyse the group for years. In this way, the literature on how regular political actors radicalise and endorse violence provides another set of tools to understand the Brotherhood beyond the simple binaries of *good* or *bad*, violent or non-violent. Although the early chapters demonstrate that the group has never formally had a radical ideology, subsequent chapters show that it has been a violent and radical organisation at particular junctures of its history, in line with its changing political context.

The book therefore sits at the intersection of the literatures on contentious politics, political violence and political organisations, contributing new empirical data to underline the importance of context, contingency and history in understanding the political behaviour of Islamist organisations. The Syrian Brotherhood could reasonably be described at various junctures in its life as an opposition group under authoritarianism, a terrorist group or a democratic political party, but none of these formations were inherent to its Islamist ideology. The Brotherhood is an ordinary political organisation that over its 70-year history has been pulled in different directions on the basis of a variety of factors. Some of these directions were deeply destructive, but such changes took place independent of its Islamist agenda, which takes a back seat to its rational pursuit of survival and relevance. This is instructive for the study of Islamist politics more broadly, highlighting that it is through the lens of circumstance rather than ideology that understanding of an Islamist organisation is best elucidated.

---

[41] Stephen W. Beach, 'Social Movement Radicalization: The Case of the People's Democracy in Northern Ireland', *The Sociological Quarterly* 18, no. 3 (1977), p. 314.

16   Introduction

Structure of the Book

The book re-examines the Brotherhood in two parts: The first section observes the Syrian Brotherhood's history from its founding moments to 2011 in order to identify its formative experiences and key characteristics, and to examine how these features changed over time. The second section examines the Brothers' engagement in the 2011 uprising.

After a brief background on the Brotherhood in Chapter 1, Chapters 2 and 3 assess the major points of the group's political thinking and politics up until 2011. For the sake of practicality, the author has split the chapters into Ideological Development and Political Practice, although the chapters note that the two subjects are not always mutually distinct. Chapter 2 specifically examines the Brotherhood's ideological roots, official political platforms and the works of its main ideologues. It demonstrates that for the most part, the Brotherhood's official political platforms and ideas over the decades have been consistent, and absent of radical ideas. Nonetheless, subsequent chapters show that the Brotherhood has periodically adopted radical tactical changes, including using violence and behaving questionably in its relations with other opposition groups. In this regard, while the chapter's examination of its political ideas sets a necessary baseline from which the Brotherhood can be considered, one most look beyond ideology to understand the reasons for the Brotherhood's political decision-making.

Chapter 3 then examines the group's political development and practice through its behaviour in parliament in the period 1947–63, opposition to the government, internal political dynamics and interaction with other opposition groups. It traces the emergence of the Brotherhood's foundational organisational characteristics: ideological flexibility, individualism and pragmatism, making two main arguments: First, while the Brotherhood mostly remained true to its political platforms discussed in Chapter 2, the platforms have never enjoyed universal support amongst members. Second, although the group had a strong track record of democratic behaviour in its early years, its experience as an opposition group under authoritarianism changed the group, endowing it with a desperation for relevance that has made it vulnerable to opportunism. The group's behaviour between 1967 and 2011 in particular had significant consequences for the group's credibility in Syria after the 2011 uprising began.

The fourth chapter charts the Brotherhood's relationship to violence, noting that while contemplation of violence played little role in the Brotherhood's official ideology or amongst its senior members, significant diversity existed within the group's base. It argues that the confluence of political events and membership changes saw parts of

Brotherhood take on violence as a tactic, even though official platforms never wavered. Although this period of violence was relatively shortlived, the Brotherhood did not escape the violence unscathed – it was forced to evolve as an organisation, acquiring deep scars that continued to impact the group after 2011.

Chapter 5 chronicles the Brotherhood's international relations to understand the way that the group has operated outside Syria. Exploring the group's relations with foreign countries, as well as other Brotherhood wings, it paints a picture of a truly international organisation. Indeed, the group's exile forced members to disperse across the world, ensuring that by 2011 it was worldlier than most other Syrian opposition groups. This characteristic and track record proved a considerable advantage when the uprising broke out as the Brotherhood could leverage its international connections for finance, materiel, diplomatic support and manpower in a way that other Syrian groups could not do.

Part II of the book explores the Brotherhood's involvement in the Syrian uprising between 2011 and 2018, examining the way the Brotherhood's history influenced its political decision-making after 2011, and how the group evolved after the uprising began. Chapter 6 examines the Brotherhood's political activity during the uprising, showing that it was the best placed group on the eve of the uprising, and analysing its role as a member of the Syrian opposition in exile, where it has been most successful in projecting its influence. It is argued that while the group was an enthusiastic participant in the uprising, its historical political baggage prevented it from becoming a candidate for significant power in any post-Assad Syria. This saw it make opportunistic and short-term decisions to amplify power at the expense of its long-term relationships with the broader opposition. Although this closely reflected the ineffective strategies it employed during the 2000s, it highlighted that the Brotherhood lacked the political acumen required to rebuild its legitimacy.

These challenges were compounded by the reality that it was the Brotherhood's ability to rebuild a base inside Syria, rather than with the mostly elite exiled opposition, that ultimately would determine its future. Chapter 7 examines the Brotherhood's efforts to win back its support base among the Syrian population, silence its internal dissenters and leverage its international connections to strengthen its position. The chapter highlights the long shadow that history has cast over the Brotherhood, with fear of repeating past mistakes and internal paralysis preventing the group's regeneration, and subsequently preventing it from rebuilding the trust of those on the ground.

The final chapter, Chapter 8, discusses the Brotherhood's involvement in the armed uprising. It is shown that although the Brotherhood decentralised its activities significantly after 2011, the armed conflict revealed the weight of the burden the Brotherhood still carries from its earlier and unprocessed 1970s and 1980s militarisation. This has represented a major barrier to the Brotherhood participating effectively in the 2011 uprising as it has been unable to claim a significant stake in the success of those on the ground, hampering its ability to use the uprising as a vehicle to win back its base and credibility.

In short, context matters a great deal to understanding the Syrian Muslim Brotherhood. The reading of history put forward in this book shows that the Brotherhood's behaviour since 2011 bears little resemblance to that of the Hama uprising in that the group is neither as undemocratic nor as violent as the example of Hama suggests, nor is it particularly ideological. Instead, the book shows that the key to understanding the Brotherhood is the observation of how it has morphed as a result of the various political questions that it has faced. In particular, its limited success in re-engaging in the Syrian political scene after 2011 can be explained by three key factors. First, the Brotherhood was deeply scarred by its experience as an opposition group under the Syrian Baʿth authoritarian regime, meaning that while the Brotherhood's operating context changed significantly after 2011, it in many ways still behaved as a group operating within an authoritarian environment. This failed to win it friends among the burgeoning opposition landscape. Second, the book finds that the Syrian Muslim Brotherhood has acquired deep reputational flaws throughout its history including a reputation for opportunism that has prevented it from achieving its much-anticipated political rehabilitation among the political class and the broader population in the 2011 conflict. Finally, although the Hama uprising bears little resemblance to the group's contemporary self, the event remained a central influence on the group's decision-making. Indeed, the memory of 1982, including the large loss of civilian life, the deviation from the group's long-held goals and the decades of suffering that followed led to organisational paralysis that continued to diminish the Brotherhood's decision-making process through the Syrian uprising.

Part I

The History of the Muslim Brotherhood in Syria

1 A Brief History of Syria and the Syrian Muslim Brotherhood

The Syrian Muslim Brotherhood was established around 1945 or 1946 in Damascus, although accounts of its date of formation vary widely.[1] The group did not have a distinct 'hour of birth', but its establishment marked the formal amalgamation of reformist Islamic political currents and groups that had been operating in Syria since the late 1800s. Indeed, by the time the Syrian Muslim Brotherhood emerged in the 1940s, Syria had witnessed more than a century of Islamic reform. These reform trends were not isolated from regional Islamic reform debates, but the Syrian movements had a distinctively local flavour, cloaked in the Syrian cultural milieu as well as the political environment of the Ottoman Empire's last century of existence. Between the First and Second World Wars, out of these movements developed Islamic *jamiyat* (societies or associations), which were the direct organisational antecedents to the Syrian Muslim Brotherhood. This is important, because political organisation theorists note that the experiences and characteristics developed

---

[1] 'The Syrian Moslem Brotherhood was founded in 1936 at the Syrian University Law School': see Kennett Love, 'Moslem Brothers Faithful to Chief', *New York Times*, 27 February 1955, p. 30; Weismann argued that the *jamiyat* were 'united under the same name in 1944–45 by Mustafa al-Siba'i': Itzchak Weismann, 'The Politics of Popular Religion: Sufis, Salafis, and Muslim Brothers in 20th-Century Hamah', *International Journal of Middle East Studies* 37, no. 1 (2005), p. 50; Khoury and Khatib point to 1944 as the date of the Brotherhood's formation: Philip S. Khoury, *Syria and the French Mandate: The Politics of Arab Nationalism, 1920–1945* (Princeton: Princeton University Press, 1987), p. 607 and Line Khatib, *Islamic Revivalism in Syria: The Rise and Fall of Ba'thist Secularism* (Abingdon: Routledge, 2011), p. 37; Rassas, Lefèvre, Batatu, Pierret and Talhami identify 1946 as the date of formation: see e.g. Mohammad Saied Rassas, 'Syria's Muslim Brotherhood: Past and Present', *Al-Monitor*, 5 January 2014, www.al-monitor.com/pulse/politics/2014/01/syria-muslim-brotherhood-past-present.html#;
Raphaël Lefèvre, *Ashes of Hama: The Muslim Brotherhood in Syria* (London: Hurst, 2013), p. 55; Joshua Teitelbaum, 'The Muslim Brotherhood in Syria, 1945–1958: Founding, Social Origins, Ideology', *The Middle East Journal* 65, no. 2 (2011), p. 216; Hanna Batatu, 'Syria's Muslim Brethren', *MERIP Reports*, no. 110 (1982), p. 16; Thomas Pierret, *Religion and State in Syria: The Sunni Ulama from Coup to Revolution* (Cambridge: Cambridge University Press, 2011); Ghada Hashem Talhami, 'Syria: Islam, Arab Nationalism and the Military', *Middle East Policy* 8, no. 4 (2001), p. 113.

by a group during its formative years shape the way that the group navigates challenges decades later.²

Sufism, that is the mystical practice of Islam, had a major impact on the Brotherhood. Sufism has long played an important role in Sunni religious practice and thought in Syria, with much of the country's ulama (Islamic scholars) emanating from a Sufi background. Although Sufism declined in Syria in the early twentieth century, it has always enjoyed a prominent place in the Syrian Muslim Brotherhood, with many of its founding members hailing from prominent Sufi families and brotherhoods.³ By the time the Brotherhood emerged in the mid-1940s, Sufism in Syria was a modern movement actively engaged in the public sphere, having produced two significant reformist trends in the nineteenth century.⁴

The first Sufi reform movement, led by the Naqshbandiyya-Khalidiyya reformists, highlighted the umma's deviation from the path of the Sharia and advocated a society-wide return to Islamic orthodoxy. Harnessing the Naqshbandi tradition of activism, advocates such as Shaykh Diya al-Din Khalid advocated for Islam's engagement in political and social affairs.⁵ However, the Sufi reform movement was by no means homogenous, and after Shaykh Khalid's death, disagreement emerged about whether shaykhs should accept government posts. This led to a split in the order's Damascus leadership.⁶

The second Sufi reform trend, the Akbariyya, responded to the perceived threat that the West posed by partially embracing rationalism, which proponents considered the foundation of the West's substantial achievements.⁷ One of the Akbariyya trend's key figures, Abd al-Qadir al-Jazairi, became celebrated for his embrace of religious tolerance in 1860 after hiding Christians in Damascus' Christian quarter from angry mobs and negotiating with Muslim notables to prevent the outbreak of communal violence.⁸ Damascus' official ulama had up until that point

---

² Maurice Duverger, *Political Parties*, trans. Barbara North and Robert North, 3rd edn (Paris: Methuen & Co Ltd., 1967), p. xxxv; Angelo Panebianco, *Political Parties: Organization & Power*, trans. Marc Silver (Cambridge: Cambridge University Press, 1988), p. xiii.
³ Paulo G. Pinto, 'Sufism, Moral Performance and the Public Sphere in Syria', *Revue des mondes musulmans et de la Méditerranée* (December 2006), pp. 155–71.
⁴ Itzchak Weismann, 'Sufism and Salafism in Syria', *Syria Comment*, 11 May 2007, www.joshualandis.com/blog/sufism-and-salafism-in-syria-by-itzchak-weismann/.
⁵ Itzchak Weismann, *Taste of Modernity: Sufism, Salafiyya, and Arabism in Late Ottoman Damascus* (Leiden: Brill, 2001), pp. 21–140.
⁶ Ibid., p. 83.   ⁷ For an excellent discussion of these Sufi reform movements, see ibid.
⁸ Philip S. Khoury, *Urban Notables and Arab Nationalism: The Politics of Damascus 1860–1920* (Cambridge: Cambridge University Press, 1983), p. 34.

refused to criticise the riots.⁹ Although Commins argued that al-Jazairi's actions might reflect a pragmatic effort to avoid French intervention rather than a deep-seated belief in religious harmony, either way the engagement of Sufi intellectuals in the political issues of the day created a precedent for future Islamists.¹⁰

A third Islamic reform movement emerged in Syria in the 1880s in the country's Salafiyya movement, which was a competitor to Syria's Sufis. Many of the adherents of the Salafiyya movement were members of Sufi reform families, reacting to the consolidation of the Ottoman–ulama political alliance in the 1880s.¹¹ Weismann noted significant continuity between the reform movements, arguing that the Sufi reformists 'played a seminal role in the formulation and dissemination of Salafi ideas'.¹² At the time, the regional Salafiyya movement experienced an awakening through the work of Jamal al-Din al-Afghani and his pupil Muhammad Abduh, who argued that the Muslim world's malaise was caused by the distortion of the original teachings of Islam.¹³ Its proponents began to use the Quran and the Sunna as their principal sources of guidance, rather than works produced by legal scholars in the many centuries since Islam's revelation. However, the Salafiyya was by no means an anti-modern movement, with Salafists advocating the use of technology from the West and the acquisition of scientific knowledge.

Syria's Salafists also emphasised the relevance of the works of the fourteenth-century Islamic scholar Taqi al-Din Ahmad ibn Taymiyyah, expending considerable time and energy finding and republishing his work. Although Ibn Taymiyyah and his followers (particularly those in the Wahhabi branch of Islam) are renowned for their intolerance of Sufism and religious minorities, Syria's Salafists rejected his position,¹⁴ which may have reflected the familial ties between Sufis and Salafists in Syria. As a result, many of the country's early Salafist thinkers believed that Sufism offered Islam an important spiritual element.¹⁵ Although the Salafists rejected some elements of Sufi practice, as Lefèvre noted, they 'stressed the importance of building up healthy relations with religious

---

⁹ David Commins, *Islamic Reform: Politics and Social Change in Late Ottoman Syria* (New York: Oxford University Press, 1990), p. 28.
¹⁰ Ibid.
¹¹ Itzchak Weismann, 'Between Ṣūfī Reformism and Modernist Rationalism: A Reappraisal of the Origins of the Salafiyya from the Damascene Angle', *Die Welt des Islams* 41, no. 2 (2001), pp. 206–37.
¹² Weismann, *Taste of Modernity*, p. 215.
¹³ John L. Esposito, *Islam: The Straight Path*, 3rd edn (New York: Oxford University Press, 2005), p. 130.
¹⁴ Weismann, *Taste of Modernity*, p. 294.   ¹⁵ Weismann, 'Sufism and Salafism in Syria'.

minorities in Syria as well as with the popular Sufi Sheikhs'.[16] An exception to this trend was seen in 1901, when a Salafist on the fringe of the movement, Abd al-Hamid al-Zahrawi, published an essay titled 'Jurisprudence and Sufism', which condemned Sufi practices.[17] He appeared to be largely alone in his viewpoint, but the work demonstrates some divergence in the message of tolerance advocated by the leading Salafist scholars at the time. The Salafiyya's ongoing reverence for Ibn Taymiyya also meant that there was always a chance that intolerant ideas would infiltrate the future Brotherhood group.

Members of the Syrian Salafiyya movement also engaged in politics. Damascus' Salafist ulama were closely aligned to the Committee of Union of Progress (CUP) and supported the 1908 Young Turk revolution in the Ottoman Empire, arguing that the new Ottoman constitution was consistent with Islam and resembled the 'precepts of jurisprudence'.[18] This made the Damascene Salafists early proponents of parliamentary political systems. In fact, Jamal al-Din al-Qasimi stood in stark contrast to the Orthodox ulama of the day by arguing that the constitution was both consistent with Sharia and required by Islam.[19] As a result, the Salafists' political activity led to the pragmatic development of close relationships with Arabists and Young Turks in the early 1900s.

The Emergence of the *Jamiyat*

The first organisational manifestation of the reformist trends appeared in the political *jamiyat* that emerged across Syria in the early 1900s. The earliest example was Jamiyat al-Gharra founded in 1924 in Damascus. The organisation had Salafist tendencies and was established to oppose French control of the Syrian education system.[20] Other emerging groups such as Jamiyat al-Ulama aimed to restore the status that the elite ulama had enjoyed under the Ottoman system, or were formed by members of the Salafiyya such as the Damascus-based Jamiyat al-Tamaddun al-Islami.[21] The Islamic Guidance Society was founded in 1931 and published the weekly *Islamic Urbanisation* magazine, which Ziadeh noted, represented 'the views of the minor bourgeoisie, such as imams, doctors and lawyers' and was later linked to a number of key Brotherhood

---

[16] Lefèvre, *Ashes of Hama*, p. 26. [17] Commins, *Islamic Reform*, p. 56.
[18] Cited in ibid., p. 126. [19] Weismann, *Taste of Modernity*, p. 300.
[20] Pierret, *Religion and State in Syria*, p. 30.
[21] Elizabeth Thompson, *Colonial Citizens: Republican Rights, Paternal Privilege and Gender in French Syria and Lebanon* (New York: Columbia University Press, 2000), p. 105.

figures, including Muhammad al-Mubarak and Omar Bahaa al-Din al-Amiri.[22] Some *jamiyat*, such as Dar al-Arqam, had close ties to Sufi orders in Syria.[23] The *jamiyat* were frequently led by professionals and members of the petite bourgeoisie, including teachers and lawyers, although Thompson noted that 'some populists were themselves embittered former Salafis'.[24] Members of the Islamic reform movements were often directly involved in *jamiyat*. They included the important Sufi thinker Isa al-Bayanouni, who coordinated with Jamiyat al-Birr wa-l-Akhlaq to organise protests against the Italian invasion of Libya. His son Ahmed was one of the founders of Dar al-Arqam.[25] The Brotherhood's founding leader, Mustafa al-Sibai, established the *jamiyah* Shaab Muhammad in Damascus.

The diversity of *jamiyat* goals and composition led to varied political behaviour. In the early 1940s, one of the more conservative groups, Jamiyat al-Gharra, rallied against the increased visibility of women in public life. It was involved in large-scale protests in May 1942, when it joined with the al-Hidaya al-Islamiyya *jamiyah* to protest against the opening of theatres, as well as uncovered women's faces. They were also supported by al-Tamuddin al-Islami, but were unable to unify the *jamiyat* on the issue because of opposition by the influential Jamiyat al-Ulama.[26] The matter reared its head again in May 1944 when al-Gharra violently protested against a charity ball held by the political establishment, where women attended unveiled.[27] The Brotherhood's 1996–2010 leader and subsequent Shura Council chief Ali al-Bayanouni, by contrast, described the Aleppo-based Dar al-Arqam, which was founded by his father, as an organisation that 'welcomed moderates and was open to various practices: it represented an ideology of the "middle way", if you will'.[28] It was purportedly more progressive than *jamiyat* in Hama or Deir al-Zor.[29] The *jamiyat* can be considered as the direct organisational predecessors of the Brotherhood as many were amalgamated to form the new movement. This added organisational

---

[22] Radwan Ziadeh, *Power and Policy in Syria: Intelligence Services, Foreign Relations and Democracy in the Modern Middle East* (London: I.B. Tauris, 2011), p. 131.
[23] Although the extent of Sufi *jam'iyat* isn't well known, it is known that in Hama they were closely connected to the Kaylani family, and the Qadiri and Rifa'i Sufi orders. For a more detailed discussion of this, see Weismann, 'The Politics of Popular Religion', p. 47.
[24] Thompson, *Colonial Citizens*, p. 103. [25] Interview with Ali al-Bayanouni, London.
[26] Khoury, *Syria and the French Mandate*, p. 610.
[27] Sami Moubayed, 'The History of Political and Militant Islam in Syria', *Terrorism Monitor* 3, no. 15 (2005), www.jamestown.org/programs/tm/single/?tx_ttnews%5Btt_news%5D=550&tx_ttnews%5BbackPid%5D=180&no_cache=1#.VhJ-QI9Viko.
[28] Cited in Lefèvre, *Ashes of Hama*, p. 24. [29] Ibid.

complexity because individual *jamiyat* directly influenced the political inclinations and organisational make-up of members and branches. Al-Bayanouni, for example, attributed the progressive nature and flexibility of the Aleppan Brothers as a direct legacy of the Sufi-dominated Dar al-Arqam, whose moderate inclinations were briefly discussed above.[30]

Ideologically, the pre-independence Islamic movements had a significant impact on the Brotherhood. The Sufi movements endowed the group with respect for Islamic Orthodoxy and many of the spiritual elements that Sufism offered Islam. The Sufis also displayed religious tolerance and openness, and the tradition of ulama engagement in politics left a strong imprint on the group. On the other hand, the Salafiyya movement provided the Brotherhood with the foundation for its easy transition to democratic politics. The Salafiyya's experience with constitutionalism in the Ottoman era gave the group ample opportunity to reconcile its ideological principles with Syria's new political system. This prompted Lefèvre to note that Syria's Salafiyya movement 'contributed to the rise of a particularly moderate politico-religious trend instinctively favouring political pluralism and religious tolerance'.[31] Khatib pointed out that, even though the Syrian Brothers had a predominantly Salafist outlook, they also 'believed that the Sufi tariqas were an efficient tool for attracting the masses to their new, populist Islamic association'.[32] This fusing of Sufi and Salafi trends was consistent with the founder of the Egyptian Muslim Brotherhood Hassan al-Banna's thinking. Al-Banna had defined the Brotherhood as 'a *Salafiyya* message, a Sunni way, [and] a Sufi truth' and had what Mitchell described as personal ties to Sufism 'in a special way for most of his life'.[33]

Many of the founding members of the Muslim Brotherhood in Syria came directly from the Islamic activist community. Muhammad al-Hamid, who was a founder of the Hama branch and a Brotherhood parliamentary representative, was a prominent member of the Naqshbandi Sufi order.[34] Al-Hamid carried many of the beliefs of his reformist predecessors, becoming renowned as an advocate of religious tolerance and education. Many of his students went on to become prominent

---

[30] Cited in ibid.   [31] Ibid., p. 4.
[32] Line Khatib, Islamic and Islamist Revivalism in Syria: The Rise and Fall of Secularism in Ba'thist Syria (PhD thesis, McGill University, 2010), p. 47.
[33] Richard P. Mitchell, *The Society of the Muslim Brothers* (Oxford: Oxford University Press, 1991), pp. 2, 14.
[34] Itzchak Weismann, 'Sa'id Hawwa: The Making of a Radical Muslim Thinker in Modern Syria', *Middle Eastern Studies* 29, no. 4 (1993), p. 608.

Brotherhood figures, including Said Hawwa, the group's 1970s ideologue.[35] Another prominent reformist Sufi scholar, Isa al-Bayanouni, argued that Sufi leaders needed to evolve in line with modern circumstances.[36] Although al-Bayanouni died before the Brotherhood's formation, as mentioned previously, his descendants became key figures in the Brotherhood. His son Ahmed, a founder of Dar al-Arqam, became a founding member of the Brotherhood's Aleppo branch. Ahmed's sons were Ali al-Bayanouni, the 2011 uprising-era Shura Council chief, and Mohammad Abu al-Nasr, a prominent Aleppan Islamic legal scholar who became the Secretary General of the Brotherhood-dominated Syrian Islamic Front in 1980.[37] Members from the Salafiyya movement were also strongly represented in the Syrian Brotherhood. Weismann describes the founder, Mustafa al-Sibai, as a 'scion of an ulema family with Salafi inclinations'.[38] Sibai's successor, Issam al-Attar, was also a Salafist.

The Founding of the Muslim Brotherhood in Syria

As the Muslim Brotherhood in Syria emerged in the mid-1940s, it was able to borrow from Syria's vibrant Sufi and Salafi history for its intellectual foundation, and from the *jamiyat*, which provided direct organisational precursors. The Syrian Muslim Brotherhood's first General Supervisor (*al-muraqib al-amm*), Mustafa al-Sibai, had studied at Egypt's al-Azhar University and was friends with the Egyptian Muslim Brotherhood founder, Hassan al-Banna.[39] The nature of al-Sibai and al-Banna's relationship meant that personal links existed between the Syrian and Egyptian Muslim Brotherhoods, but Syria's unique geopolitical landscape and the distinct background of the group's founders and the *jamiyat* limited the tangible significance of the connection.

In contrast to its Egyptian counterpart, Syrian Brotherhood members participated in parliamentary elections from 1947, fielding members of parliament and later ministers.[40] Syria's democratic era was politically

---

[35] Itzchak Weismann, 'Sufi Fundamentalism between India and the Middle East', in *Sufism and the Modern in Islam*, ed. Martin Van Bruinessen and Julia Day Howell (London: I.B. Tauris, 2007), pp. 115–48.
[36] Itzchak Weismann, 'The Hidden Hand: The Khalidiyya and Orthodox-Fundamentalist Cooperation in Aleppo', *Journal of the History of Sufism* 5 (2006), p. 16.
[37] Pierret, *Religion and State in Syria*, p. 69.
[38] Weismann, 'The Politics of Popular Religion', p. 50.
[39] Teitelbaum, 'The Muslim Brotherhood in Syria, 1945–1958', p. 214.
[40] Mr Schrivener, 'E 7037/388/89 – The Syrian Elections', *UK Foreign Office*, 28 July 1947.

Table 1.1 *Status of the Syrian political system 1947–63*

Dates	Political system	Coups	Parliamentary Elections held	Status of Brotherhood
1947–49	Democratic	March 1949	July 1947	Minor participant
Mar–Aug 1949	Authoritarian	August 1949	-	-
Aug 1949–52	Mixed	December 1949	November 1949	Minor participant, cabinet member
1952–4	Authoritarian	February 1954	-	Banned
1954–8	Democratic	-	September 1954	Minor participant
1958–61	Authoritarian	September 1961	-	Banned
1961–3	Democratic	March 1962 April 1962 March 1963	December 1961	Minor participant, cabinet member
1963–current	Authoritarian Ba'th	February 1966 November 1970	-	Banned

tumultuous, characterised by three new constitutions (1950, 1953, 1958)[41] and at least eight military coups (as shown in Table 1.1), though none instigated by the Brotherhood. This prompted Lerner to declare in 1958 that the country was 'a case study of political instability in an area rocked by explosive politics', while Zisser dubbed it a 'fragile and very defective parliamentary democracy'.[42]

The 1947 parliament that included Brotherhood members was elected to a four-year term, but was interrupted two years later when the military officer Husni al-Za'im staged the first coup of the period. But al-Za'im's rule lasted only a matter of months; he was assassinated that August in a second coup that reinstated the democratic process with new elections held in November 1949.

Syria's democratic process was shaken once more in December 1949 when Adib al-Shishakli staged the third coup of the year.[43] The parliament sat in the first years after the coup, with parliamentary

---

[41] The constitution of 1928, implemented under the French and British mandate, was the relevant instrument at the beginning of the independence period in 1946. Sami M. Moubayed, *Steel & Silk: Men and Women Who Shaped Syria 1900–2000* (Seattle: Cune Press, 2006), p. 598.

[42] Daniel Lerner, *The Passing of Traditional Society: Modernizing the Middle East* (Glencoe: Free Press, 1958), p. 264; Eyal Zisser, 'Syria', in *Elections in Asia and the Pacific: A Data Handbook: Volume I: Middle East*, ed. Dieter Nohlen, Florian Grotz and Christof Hartmann (Oxford: Oxford University Press, 2001), p. 213.

[43] 'New Coup in Syria', *The New York Times* (15 August 1949), p. 16.

delegates drafting and enshrining the country's first post-independence constitution the following year. However, the situation deteriorated significantly in 1951 after al-Shishakli dissolved Syria's civilian government and arrested the cabinet. That year, the British Minister to Syria William Montagu-Pollock expressed concern that the army 'has developed an unhealthy appetite for politics'.[44] In 1952, al-Shishakli banned political parties (including the Brotherhood) and all opposition newspapers, marking the beginning of military rule. The Syrian Muslim Brotherhood's influence in this era, however, should not be overstated; the British Embassy noted in 1952 that the Brotherhood 'though influential, are not politically a strong party'.[45]

Adib al-Shishakli was eventually overthrown in February 1954 by an opposition coalition, with new parliamentary elections held in September the same year. The period between 1954 and 1958 became widely known as Syria's 'democratic years', in which democratic life was restored and left-wing parties including the Ba'th Party, the Communist Party and the Syrian Social Nationalist Party built large followings. Yet democracy was again halted in 1958, when the country's leaders agreed to merge Syria with Egypt, forming the United Arab Republic (UAR) under the leadership of the Egyptian President, Gamal Abdel Nasser. Syrian Brotherhood members were banned and jailed in this period.

In September 1961, Syrian officers staged another coup, leading to Syria's split from the UAR and the resumption of parliamentary life. The Brotherhood achieved its best ever electoral result at the parliamentary elections in December that year, winning ten parliamentary seats, although this made up less than 6 percent of the chamber.[46] The conservative People's Party, many of whose supporters the Brotherhood would later inherit, gained almost 20 percent of seats in the parliament, making it the largest parliamentary party. The following two years were relatively stable, with the exception of two minor coups that prompted cabinet changes. The era came to a close in March 1963 following a coup by the Ba'th Party, which marked the end of Syrian democratic life and the beginning of the regime that remains in power today.

Islamism never formed a major part of the Syrian Muslim Brotherhood's political agenda.[47] The British Embassy in Damascus in the 1940s and 1950s described the group as 'extremist' and declared its

---

[44] W. Montagu-Pollock, 1951 'EY1011/1: Syria: Annual Review for 1950', *British Embassy Damascus*, 6 January.
[45] 1952 'EY 1016/1 – Political Situation in Syria', *British Embassy Damascus*, 8 January.
[46] Zisser, 'Syria', p. 225.
[47] Patrick Seale, *Asad of Syria: The Struggle for the Middle East* (Berkeley: University of California Press), p. 31.

leader Mustafa al-Sibai to be 'a vehement ranting orator who appeals to the masses', while at the same time it acknowledged that the Brotherhood was 'allied' with the economically and socially conservative People's Party, where Brotherhood members were well represented.[48] In fact, the Brotherhood was, at its heart, a conservative political party, and from its founding moments a pragmatic group. A senior Brother characterised al-Sibai's thinking along the lines of: 'this is political life and we have to contribute to it in order to reform the society…[whether we] were able to reform it 100 percent, or [only] one percent'.[49] Brotherhood parliamentarians mobilised around the populist Arab Nationalist and anti-colonial issues of the day, while its platform largely promulgated the economic status quo. In this regard, it offered little appeal to members of the middle and lower echelons of urban and rural society, whose support was captured by socialist and communist groups, including the emerging Arab Socialist Baʿth Party.[50] In addition, the closest the group came to advocating an Islamist agenda was when it argued unsuccessfully to have Syria recognised as a 'Muslim country' in the draft 1950 constitution. Although the proposed clause was rejected, the Brotherhood achieved concessions, including retaining the 1930 Constitution's clause that the religion of the president is Islam.[51] Mustafa al-Sibai declared the compromise to be a success for the group.[52]

The Baʿth Era: Testing the Brotherhood's Ideology and Relationship with Violence when Under Pressure

If there was a sense that the Brotherhood's star was rising after the collapse of the UAR and its 1961 electoral success, its fortunes quickly soured after the 1963 coup that brought the Syrian Baʿth Party to power. Although the Baʿth was just one element of the coalition of military officers and political figures that carried out the coup, the party quickly moved to consolidate control over the state.[53] This led to widespread purges of the Baʿth Party's former allies from the military,[54] and the

---

[48] Philip Broadmead, 1948 'E 15809/2603/89 No. 136: Disturbances in Syria', *British Embassy Damascus*. EY 1012/1; W. Montagu-Pollock, 1951 'EY 1012/1 – Leading Personalities in Syria', *British Embassy Damascus*, 2 July.
[49] Anonymous interview, 2015.
[50] Khatib, 'Islamic and Islamist Revivalism in Syria', p. 45.
[51] Majid Khadduri, 'Constitutional Development in Syria: With Emphasis on the Constitution of 1950', *Middle East Journal* 5, no. 2 (1951), p. 152.
[52] Pierret, *Religion and State in Syria*, pp. 174–5.
[53] Raymond Hinnebusch, *Syria: Revolution from Above* (London: Routledge, 2001), p. 47.
[54] Raymond Hinnebusch, *Authoritarian Power and State Formation in Bathist Syria: Army, Party and Peasant* (Boulder: Westview Press, 1991), p. 121.

outlawing of major political groups such as the Syrian Communist Party.[55]

Founded in 1947 by the Christian Michel Aflaq and Sunni Salah al-Din al-Bitar, the Ba'th Party had been an active player in Syria's post-independence politics, winning the second largest number of seats in the 1954 elections.[56] The Ba'th put forward a potent populist ideological programme of secularism, socialism and Arab nationalism that appealed to the country's long-ignored rural low and middle classes, and Arab minorities.[57] Although the regime maintained a public façade of secularism and religious diversity, embodied in the position enjoyed by Sunni Muslims such as Defence Minister Mustafa Tlass and Vice President Abd al-Halim al-Khaddam, it increasingly came to be perceived as a sectarian Alawite government because minorities were overrepresented among its army support base and its leaders including President Hafez al-Assad derived from the Alawite sect. Although Van Dam argued that this happened by chance rather than as the result of active policy, it became a source of frustration among Syria's increasingly excluded Sunni majority.[58] The perceived Alawite character of the regime was probably also overstated, with Phillips noting that:

> While its enemies labelled it an 'Alawi regime' Assad's was more a regime run by 'some Alawis', specifically members of the president's family, his Numailatiyya clan and Matawira tribe… However, a significant enough number of Syrians and outsiders believed that it was sectarian.[59]

In one of the most eloquent descriptions of the regime, the Syrian intellectual Yassin Salah al-Haj argued:

> The reality of the regime is power and social privilege: not the faith of the ruler and not the society's cultural character. Sectarianism itself is not the regime's reality: it is a strategy for political control, a tool for governing, subordination, and the protection of privileges and privileged segments of society. Sectarianism is a socially divisive power that obscures the fact of political and social disparities behind the diversities of identities and religious beliefs.[60]

---

[55] David Commins, *Historical Dictionary of Syria* (London: The Scarecrow Press, 1996), p. 250.
[56] Zisser, 'Syria', p. 225.
[57] Albert Hourani, *A History of the Arab Peoples* (London: Faber and Faber, 1991), p. 409.
[58] Nikolaos Van Dam, 'Middle Eastern Political Cliches "Takriti" and "Sunni" Rule in Iraq; "Alawi" Rule in Syria. A Critical Appraisal', *Orient* 21, no. 1 (1980), p. 50.
[59] Christopher Phillips, 'Sectarianism and Conflict in Syria', *Third World Quarterly* 25, no. 2 (2015), p. 365.
[60] Yassin al-Haj Saleh, *Impossible Revolution: Making Sense of the Syrian Tragedy* (London: Hurst, 2017), p. 264.

Indeed, while it is tempting to view the Brotherhood-Baʿth conflict that emerged in years that followed the Baʿth coup through the lens of sectarianism, it is more instructive to conceive the Baʿth ascent as a massive disruption of the avenues of power and opportunity in Syria.

The Syrian political environment became increasingly difficult for the Brotherhood, which was outlawed again in 1964. The group's leader, Issam al-Attar, was forced into exile that same year, with members of the group subjected to increasing repression.[61] This marked a dramatic shift in the Brotherhood's operating environment and prompted its transition from parliamentary party to opposition group under an authoritarian regime. However, one Brotherhood member who joined the group during this period recalled,

> At that time nobody dared to do political work except for the Muslim Brotherhood, and the other political parties or ideologies did not enjoy the [same] credibility. Their words did not match their actions. They were completely different...The Communists were swimming in bribery and...were separated from the society. And so I did not find that I related to them [as I related to the Brotherhood].[62]

Nonetheless, the new political environment proved a significant challenge for the Brotherhood, with internal divisions emerging along roughly regional and *jamiyat* lines over how to respond to the political situation. Issam al-Attar remained committed to non-violent opposition, a position backed by most senior members of the Brotherhood during the 1960s.[63] However, as Baʿth repression intensified in the late 1960s, factional divisions deepened, spurred further by personality clashes, including the perception that al-Attar was aloof and nepotistic.[64] In the late 1960s, these internal tensions came to a head, manifesting in the leadership crisis of 1969–72. Shaykh Abd al-Fatah abu Ghuddah, a member of the group's Aleppo branch, was elected leader, but the Damascus wing boycotted the election, leading to a stalemate. The international Brotherhood organisation eventually intervened to confirm the legitimacy of the election, prompting al-Attar's supporters to split from the group.[65]

At the same time, Syria itself was undergoing significant change. The Baʿth regime had rewritten Syria's social contract, taking an

---

[61] Adrienne Edgar, 'The Islamic Opposition in Egypt and Syria: A Comparative Study', *Journal of Arab Affairs* 6, no. 1 (1987), n.p.
[62] Interview with Samir Abu Laban, Istanbul, 28 August 2015.
[63] Lefèvre, *Ashes of Hama*, p. 89.
[64] Umar F. Abd-allah, *The Islamic Struggle in Syria* (Berkeley: Mizan Press, 1983), p. 102.
[65] Ibid., pp. 107–8.

unprecedented role in the Syrian economy through job creation, heavy regulation, nationalisation and state-owned industry. These responsibilities would be enshrined in the constitution, which stated that '[t]he state economy is a planned socialist economy which seeks to end all forms of exploitation'.[66] However, the benefits were never evenly distributed; government scholarships, jobs and patronage disproportionately benefited the Baʿth Party's main constituents. A tight nexus was thereby developed between the state and class in Syria, developing a clear demarcation of those who were excluded. By the late 1960s, the Baʿth regime had undergone further internal purges, including of the Party's founding fathers Michel Aflaq and Salah al-Din al-Bitar, who fled the country.

In 1970 the Syrian Minister of Defense, Hafez al-Assad, led a bloodless intra-Baʿth coup dubbed the Corrective Movement that fomented more pragmatic governance. Al-Assad quickly wound back the worst excesses of his neo-Baʿth predecessors' policies, relieving some of the popular pressure against the Baʿth. He also began the important task of rebuilding Syria's relations with the Arab states, including Saudi Arabia, with whom relations had become particularly hostile.[67] To Perthes, these two strategies went hand in hand: the economic reform was aimed at attracting public sector investment from the wealthier Arab states, which would soon experience the oil boom.[68] The strategy quickly bore fruit: in 1972 Syria received just US$45 million from the Arab oil states. By 1977, that figure would reach US$1.173 billion.[69] Alongside this foreign investment, the average Syrian income grew by 271 percent in the first five years of al-Assad's rule.[70] Al-Assad also took a softer approach to religion by co-opting popular Muslim leaders into the political fold.[71] This comparatively positive political climate dampened any appetite for revolution amongst the Brotherhood's traditional base. Soon after the coup, an article in *The New York Times* rightly declared al-Assad's

---

[66] 'The Syrian Constitution – 1973–2012', *Carnegie Middle East Center* (5 December 2012), http://carnegie-mec.org/diwan/50255?lang=en.
[67] Sonoko Sunayama, *Syria and Saudi Arabia: Collaboration and Conflicts in the Oil Era* (London: I.B. Tauris, 2007), p. 31.
[68] Volker Perthes, *The Political Economy of Syria under Assad* (London: I.B. Tauris, 1995), p. 50.
[69] Ibid., p. 36.
[70] Michael Morton, 'Foreign Capital Vital to Syria's Economic Boom', *The Jerusalem Post* (10 May 1977). p. 1.; 'Syria in a Period of Economic Growth', *The New York Times* (16 November 1976), p. 35.
[71] For a full discussion of this, see Hanna Batatu, *Syria's Peasantry: The Descendants of Its Lesser Rural Notables, and Their Politics* (Princeton: Princeton University Press, 1999), pp. 260–1.

ascendance to be a 'setback for extremists'.[72] Indeed, in the first half of the 1970s, Hafez al-Assad had successfully placated major popular grievances against the Ba'th and as a result, the Brotherhood leadership change in 1971 turned out to be immaterial in the immediate aftermath of those events. Syria's economic boom, however, was not to last.

The Brotherhood did not officially take up arms against the regime until the late 1970s, but pressure was mounting throughout the decade within the group's grassroots, which was bearing the brunt of Ba'th economic reform. Indeed, while the general economic situation in Syria had improved on the basis of the Ba'th's large projects of economic redistribution, especially among the rural and urban poor, the Brotherhood's constituents from Syria's small merchant class had suffered. State-mandated minimum wages, cheap products from state-run factories, land reform and an exponential increase in foreign imports had seen business profitability plummet and livelihoods damaged, marking the end of the post-independence economic environment that had been largely endorsed by the Brotherhood and its supporters.[73] This pressure was exemplified in the rise of the charismatic Brotherhood youth member Marwan Hadid, who hailed from a wealthy family in Hama province. Hadid instigated the bloody 1964 riots in Hama, in defiance of Brotherhood leaders. He had studied in Egypt and was influenced by the Egyptian Brotherhood ideologue and leader Sayyid Qutb. Hadid advocated war against the al-Assad regime and found sympathetic ears amongst the movement's rank and file. This led to the formation of a breakaway group on the Brotherhood's periphery called the Fighting Vanguard, although the line between the two groups would remain blurred throughout the lifetime of the Vanguard, perhaps deliberately.[74] In the late 1960s, Hadid took his supporters to Jordan to receive military training in the Palestinian training camps.[75] After Hadid's death in custody in 1976, the Fighting Vanguard assassinated various regime figures and associates.[76] The Brotherhood simultaneously underwent a transformation: in 1975, the group's leadership transferred to its Hama branch under the guidance of the more tactically violent Adnan

---

[72] Eric Pace, 'Shift in Syria Is Setback for Extremists', *The New York Times* (22 November 1970), p. 171.
[73] Fred H. Lawson, 'Social Bases for the Hamah Revolt', *MERIP Reports*, no. 110 (1982), pp. 24–8.
[74] Lefèvre, *Ashes of Hama*, p. 104.
[75] Ayman Shorbaji, *The Diary of a Vanguard Combatant in Syria (in Arabic)* (publication details not known), p. 22.
[76] Ibid., p. 27.

Saadeddine.⁷⁷ As Baʻth repression hardened, the group's leadership was progressively forced into exile.

In 1979, the Fighting Vanguard carried out its most brazen attack, sending its militants into the Aleppo Artillery Academy in Ramouseh, killing up to 200 unarmed Alawite cadets.⁷⁸ The Brotherhood claimed to know nothing of the massacre.⁷⁹ Although the Brotherhood's relationship to the Vanguard was deliberately unclear, the Baʻth regime responded to the massacre by cracking down on the Brotherhood proper and its supporters. This crackdown, along with the appointment of more radical leaders in the preceding years, prompted the group to formally declare war on the regime. From mid-1979, the Brotherhood's magazine *al-Nadhir* began reporting sporadic attacks on government targets across the country under the banner of the 'Mujahidin in Syria'.⁸⁰ The Brotherhood's direct involvement in violence was probably limited, as by 1980 the group's most senior leaders had left the country and those that remained were forced to operate as part of a mostly autonomous cell structure in order to evade capture. Most of the violence carried out by Brotherhood members was therefore undertaken by decentralised cells, although this does not in any way absolve the Brotherhood for responsibility for events, as discussed later in this book.⁸¹

The Brotherhood's position continued to deteriorate over the following two years. Following a near-miss assassination attempt on President Hafez al-Assad in 1980, the Baʻth regime instituted Law No. 49, which made membership of the Brotherhood punishable by death.⁸² That same year, the Brotherhood formed an alliance called the Syrian Islamic Front alongside the Fighting Vanguard, Issam al-Attar's Damascus branch of the Brotherhood and members of the ulama.⁸³ The

---

⁷⁷ Lefèvre, *Ashes of Hama*, p. 81.
⁷⁸ Reports of the death toll in the Artillery School massacre varies widely. See Chapter Four for a full discussion.
⁷⁹ 'A statement from the Muslim Brotherhood, issued on June 24 (in Arabic)', 3 July 1979. Available in: Umar abd Al-Hakim, *The Islamic Jihadi Revolution in Syria (in Arabic)* (Peshawar: n.p., 1991), p. 574. Umar abd Al-Hakim is one of the many pseudonyms used by Mustafa bin abd al-Qadir Sitt Maryam Nasar. He is best known as Abu Musab al-Suri. The appendices of this book includes a substantial number of Brotherhood and Vanguard primary documents.
⁸⁰ The first copy of *al-Nadhir* reported news on 'the Mujahidin in Syria' See *Al-Nadhir no. 1 (in Arabic)* 9 September 1979. A copy of this document is stored in the British National Archive, with a partial translation. See Vincent Fean, 'FCO 93/2253: Syria Internal: Moslem Brotherhood', *British Embassy Damascus*, 14 November 1979.
⁸¹ Interview with Ali al-Bayanouni, London.
⁸² John Kifner, 'Syria Starts Drive to Curb Terrorism: Guard Said to Fall on Grenade Assad Introduced Death Bill "New Chapter of the Conspiracy"', *The New York Times* (4 July 1980), p. A5.
⁸³ See Abd-allah, *The Islamic Struggle in Syria*, pp. 118–28.

Front never came to much, dissolving in 1981 after the Vanguard's leader, Adnan Uqlah, discovered that the Brotherhood was secretly negotiating with secular Syrian groups to form a broader opposition alliance, which included secular parties.[84] At the same time, Brotherhood members in camps in Iraq were receiving military training from the Iraqi military, while the group's leaders were building ties with a Syrian army faction that was planning a coup inside Syria.[85] In January 1982, that faction was discovered, destroying the Brotherhood's most viable plan. Pressure increased as Ba'thist intelligence services continued rooting out the last remnants of the Brotherhood in Syria. Just weeks later, the Hama uprising, which is discussed in detail in Chapter 4, broke out, leading to the death of tens of thousands of civilians.

The Brotherhood's culpability for the Hama uprising is disputed today, even within its own ranks. While Brotherhood leaders in February 1982 acknowledged their participation, today's members prefer to downplay the Brotherhood's role, blaming unruly radical members acting without their leaders' sanction.[86] This claim of complete innocence appears as a curious and transparent attempt at historical revisionism given the closeness of the local Brotherhood cells and the Fighting Vanguard in Hama at that time, and the group's wholesale attempt to take responsibility for events once the uprising had begun.

Regrouping in Exile: 1982–2011

Within two months of the failed Hama uprising, the Brotherhood announced it was forming a new alliance with Syria's secular opposition under the umbrella of the National Alliance for the Liberation of Syria. This new alliance proved ineffective, the acuteness of which was seen in 1983–4 when it failed to take advantage of a weakening of the Ba'th regime while Hafez al-Assad was hospitalised and his brother Rifaat

---

[84] Abu Musab Al-Suri, 'Lessons Learned from the Armed Jihad Ordeal in Syria', translated and published by the Combatting Terrorism Centre (CTC), West Point, www.ctc.usma.edu/v2/wp-content/uploads/2013/10/Lessons-Learned-from-the-Jihad-Ordeal-in-Syria-Translation.pdf, p. 13.

[85] Interview with Ali al-Bayanouni, London.

[86] In an interview in 2005, the then-Muslim Brotherhood leader Ali al-Bayanouni claimed that the Muslim Brotherhood's members had withdrawn from Hama at the request of the group's leaders, leaving others to fight in the city for the three-week siege. See Mahan Abedin, 'The Battle within Syria: An Interview with Muslim Brotherhood Leader Ali Bayanouni', *Terrorism Monitor* 2013, no. July 21 (2005), www.jamestown.org/single/?no_cache=1&tx_ttnews%5Bswords%5D=8fd5893941d69d0be3f378576261ae3e&tx_ttnews%5Bany_of_the_words%5D=bayanouni&tx_ttnews%5Btt_news%5D=551&tx_ttnews%5BbackPid%5D=7&cHash=a3596e18cae2d132225d7cfe253aa2cf.

began efforts to seize power. Internally, the Brotherhood's prognosis was even worse. The group suffered mass desertions due to dissatisfaction with their leaders' deficient responses and management.[87] In addition, the group's longstanding internal factionalism resurfaced over who was to blame for Hama.

Nevertheless, many of those involved in the failed uprising remained in the group's leadership following new elections, including Adnan Saadeddine, who purportedly maintained private military camps in Iraq until the mid-1980s, and may have undertaken further attacks inside Syria.[88] The group eventually split in 1985–6 with the ousting of Saadeddine's faction, only for it to re-join the group in 1991. Saadeddine himself was not readmitted to the Brotherhood until shortly before his death in 2010. For its part, the Fighting Vanguard pledged to continue fighting the Syrian regime, although its leader Adnan Uqlah was captured when trying to re-enter Syria in late 1982 and is presumed to have died in custody. The Fighting Vanguard movement largely dissipated after Uqlah's death, except for some members who travelled to Afghanistan to continue their *jihad* against the Soviet regime. Other Vanguard members returned to Syria during a limited amnesty in 1985.[89] The Brotherhood remained active in exile, surviving largely at the pleasure of a number of Arab states including Jordan, Iraq and Saudi Arabia, and later the UK. The Brotherhood negotiated with the Syrian government on and off over the next 30 years, although never with great success.

Hafez al-Assad died in 2000, passing the Syrian presidency to his son Bashar. Bashar al-Assad was not a career military officer like his father but a doctor whom observers hoped would herald a new era of pluralism and tolerance in Syria. A civil society movement quickly emerged, and became known as the Damascus Spring. In September 2000, activists produced the 'Statement of 99', a document published in *al-Hayat* signed by 99 intellectuals, artists and professionals that called for the suspension of emergency law (which had been in place since before the Ba'th came to power), the release and pardoning of political prisoners and political reform. George noted that the Statement 'was carefully crafted to minimise annoyance to the regime ... none of the signatories had significant histories of anti-regime activism and the authorities were thereby denied the chance to condemn them as "well-known

---

[87] Interview with Ali al-Ahmad, London, 7 August 2015.
[88] Ibid.; interview with Zuhair Salem, London, 1 October 2015.
[89] Associated Press, 'Syria Offering Amnesty to Underground Group', *The New York Times* (27 January 1985), p. 5.

enemies of the state" or "agents of Israel",.[90] The Statement of 99 was followed by the January 2001 'Statement of 1,000' in which activists called for substantive reforms in Syria, questioning the Ba'th's prized monopoly of the Syrian political system and calling for the establishment of a multi-party political system.[91] The momentum building behind the fledgling movement, however, alarmed the al-Assad regime, which quickly cracked down and closed the brief Syrian political opening. Until 2011, the opposition scene inside Syria was characterised by a mix of co-optation and repression, which proved a significant barrier to opposition mobilisation.

The Brotherhood worked on rebuilding its reputation throughout the 2000s, releasing two key ideological tracts that reiterated the group's commitment to democracy and non-violence. The Brotherhood was also involved in opposition coalitions such as the Damascus Declaration in 2005, and the following year joined the National Salvation Front, a coalition led by the recently defected Syrian Prime Minister, Abdul Halim al-Khaddam.[92] In 2009 during the Gaza war, the Brotherhood suspended opposition to the regime altogether in recognition of the Syrian government's support of Hamas.[93] Although it is clear that the Brotherhood has taken steps to move on from its period of violent confrontation, senior members remained reticent to discuss those events, as many of the scars remain unhealed. The findings of an internal investigative report into Hama undertaken by the group in the 1990s have never been publicly released.[94]

Nonetheless, the broader Syrian opposition movement also remained weak. As former Syrian National Coalition (SOC) President Riad al-Turk described in 2005, 'the most appropriate adjective for the state of the opposition, society, and the regime is chaos—intellectual chaos. Indecisiveness, impotence, hopelessness—these are the most prominent adjectives of the opposition'.[95] Another activist, Ammar Qurabi, noted, 'Really, there is no such thing as "the opposition". There are [only]

---

[90] Alan George, *Syria: Neither Bread Nor Freedom* (London, Zed Books, 2003), p. 40.
[91] Joshua M. Landis and Joe Pace, 'The Syrian Opposition', *The Washington Quarterly* 30, no. 1 (2006–7), pp. 45–68; George, *Syria: Neither Bread Nor Freedom*, pp. 39–46.
[92] 'The Bayanouni – Khaddam Link-Up: Is the Opposition Real Now?', *Syria Comment* (17 March 2006), http://faculty-staff.ou.edu/L/Joshua.M.Landis-1/syriablog/2006/03/bayanouni-khaddam-link-up-_114264946582158617.htm.
[93] Fahd al-Argha Al-Masri, 'Muslim Brotherhood Chief Announces End of "Truce" with Syria', *Free Syria* (2010) (London: BBC Monitoring Middle East).
[94] Anonymous interview.
[95] Joe Pace, 'Riad al-Turk Interviewed by Joe Pace on Mehlis, the Opposition, Ghadry', *Syria Comment* (8 September 2005), http://faculty-staff.ou.edu/L/Joshua.M.Landis-1/syriablog/2005/10/riad-al-turk-interviewed-by-joe-pace.htm.

individual activists and writers.'[96] In contrast, the Syrian Brothers had been able to rebuild themselves in exile and were able to re-emerge in 2011 as the strongest political group in theory, but less so in practice.

This history meant that on the eve of the Syrian uprising, the Syrian Muslim Brotherhood had a mixed track record. While it could boast of significant experience in opposition and in interacting with the al-Assad regime, plus extensive international connections and resources, and a wealth of political experience garnered from the group's participation in Syria's fledgling parliamentary era, it also had a record of participating in the worst violence in the country's modern history prior to 2011. Nonetheless, even with limited roots on the ground, it appeared the strongest opposition group politically as the uprising unfolded and was seen to bear significant potential for Syria's future. The group failed to live up to these expectations.

---

[96] Cited in: Landis and Pace, 'The Syrian Opposition', p. 51.

2 The Syrian Muslim Brotherhood's Founding Ideas

To understand the role that the Brotherhood played in the 2011 uprising, one must take a long view of the group's history. The Brotherhood was not borne out of the political vacuum that emerged in 2011, but instead bore the marks of seven decades of political thinking and reasoning. Decade after decade it had produced detailed political documents to promote its ideals and character, and build a sympathetic support base. Although even in its founding moments it was not a deeply ideological organisation, the documents it produced conveyed a sense of how it communicated and wanted to be perceived. From the outset, the group's intellectual platforms reflected its intellectual inheritance from the Sufi and Salafiyya movements, and the *jamiyat*, as well as its pragmatic and flexible disposition.

In particular, the positions articulated in the group's early decades are pivotal because they were expressed during the formative years of the group's identity. Brotherhood leaders have since expended considerable energy to return to this original path. The contemporary Brotherhood ideologue Zuhair Salem clarified that, 'we believe that the only way forward is to oppose the regime through peaceful means on the model of the organization's historical leaders, Mustapha [sic] al-Sibai and Issam al-Attar'.[1] This is consistent with patterns seen in other political organisations, whereby the path set by a group's founders set its lifelong dispositions.[2]

The Syrian Muslim Brotherhood emphasised its history and democratic credentials throughout the 2011 uprising. In an interview in 2013, the group's former leader and by then Shura Council chief Ali al-Bayanouni argued that the Brotherhood had

---

[1] Cited in Raphaël Lefèvre, *Ashes of Hama: The Muslim Brotherhood in Syria* (London: Hurst, 2013), p. 171.
[2] Maurice Duverger, *Political Parties*, trans. Barbara North and Robert North, 3rd edn (Paris: Methuen & Co Ltd., 1967), p. xxxv; Angelo Panebianco, *Political Parties: Organization & Power*, trans. Marc Silver (Cambridge: Cambridge University Press, 1988), p. xiii.

the political experience to deal with this vacuum. Most moderate Syrians will accept democracy because it is a tool to choose, remove or appoint a leader. This does not contradict Islamic governance and exists within Islamic tradition [since] the time of the Prophet.[3]

It was clear that al-Bayanouni believed that the Brotherhood's rich ideological history bestowed it with the ideas that it needed to navigate the crisis.

1945–1963: The Formative Years

The Syrian Muslim Brotherhood was established in either 1945 or 1946 with the merger of many of the pre-independence *jamiyat* including Shaab Mohammad in Damascus, the Ikhwan al-Muslimin in Hama and Dar al-Arqam in Aleppo, among others. Scholars of political oganisations such as Eliassen and Svaasand note that groups that form via such a bottom-up amalgamation process often risk suffering ideological disunity and factionalism,[4] but Ali al-Bayanouni argued that the *jamiyat* 'all had the same aim, so there was no problem forming'.[5] This could also be attributed to the presence of the Brotherhood's charismatic first leader Mustafa al-Sibai, whose clear vision and passionate speeches quickly unified the group's disparate parts. One Brotherhood associate who was alive during the Mustafa al-Sibai era described al-Sibai's personality as 'like a magnet' for the Brotherhood's supporters,[6] which enabled the group to forge a clear political path and achieve internal discipline during its crucial founding decades. Although this proved helpful during these early years, the death of al-Sibai would have significant long-term consequences for the group's internal cohesion. Nonetheless, in the al-Sibai era, the young Brotherhood organisation advanced a series of ideological stances in line with the philosophies of its *jamiyat* membership base and the contemporary political mood.

The Syrian Brotherhood's founding constituency set it apart from the Egyptian Muslim Brotherhood, and had a defining impact on the new group's vision and political goals. The *jamiyat* had bequeathed the Brotherhood its close ulama-traditional classes relationship, ensuring that the emerging group found easy support amongst the traders and

---

[3] Tam Hussein, 'A Brotherhood Vision for Syria: In Conversation with the Former Leader of the Syrian Muslim Brotherhood', *The Majalla* (2013), http://eng.majalla.com/2013/11/article55247035.
[4] For a useful discussion of the impact of amalgamation processes, see Kjell A. Eliassen and Lars Svaasand, 'The Formation of Mass Political Organizations: An Analytical Framework', *Scandinavian Political Studies* 10, no. A10 (1975), p. 116.
[5] Interview with Ali al-Bayanouni, London.   [6] Anonymous interview.

merchants in Syria's cities. Many of these relationships were carried directly over from the *jamiyat*, with Batatu noting that Jamiyat al-Gharra had 'close ties with the city's well-to-do merchants, who helped the association financially and were strongly represented in its board of trustees'.[7] This set the foundation of the Damascus Brothers' relationship with the city's merchants in the decades to come. At the same time, *jamiyat* populism endowed the group with linkages to Syria's non-educated classes.[8]

The Brotherhood found an early constituency among residents of the old cities because, according to Batatu, urban traders and artisans were 'the most religiously oriented class in Syria [and were] akin to the religious shaikhs [*sic*] in values and way of life'.[9] Khoury noted that 'they were also literally kin to religious shaykhs, many of whom came from the same social strata and some whom also owned their own small business enterprises'.[10] This enabled the Brotherhood to easily find support for its advocacy for a greater role for Islam in public life, and wedded the group to a number of conservative policy stances that would set it apart from its more radical competitors such as the Communists or the Ba'thists. Indeed, Syria's traditional classes were losing out under Syria's new economic and political arrangements and sought political representation that would protect the status quo. Accordingly, the Brotherhood espoused a commitment to private property rights, economic liberalism and a 'constitution with "Islamic bearing"'.[11] It was not the 'extremist' or 'reactionary' group portrayed by British diplomats in Damascus, but was a thoroughly status quo and elitist organisation.[12] Indeed, Weismann argued that the 'Salafi–Sufi synthesis' advocated by some of the group's senior figures 'reflected a broader rapprochement between Syria's big landowners and its professional middle class, who following independence

---

[7] Hanna Batatu, *Syria's Peasantry: The Descendants of Its Lesser Rural Notables, and Their Politics* (Princeton: Princeton University Press, 1999), p. 261.
[8] Elizabeth Thompson, *Colonial Citizens: Republican Rights, Paternal Privilege and Gender in French Syria and Lebanon* (New York: Columbia University Press, 2000), p. 105.
[9] Hanna Batatu, 'Syria's Muslim Brethren', *MERIP Reports*, no. 110 (1982), p. 15–16, cited in Philip S. Khoury, *Syria and the French Mandate: The Politics of Arab Nationalism, 1920–1945* (Princeton: Princeton University Press, 1987), p. 609.
[10] Ibid.
[11] Line Khatib, 'Islamic and Islamist Revivalism in Syria: The Rise and Fall of Secularism in Ba'thist Syria' (PhD thesis, McGill University, 2010), p. 47.
[12] 'E 15809/2603/89 – Further Correspondence Respecting Syria Part 2', *British Embassy Damascus*, 1948; 'E 7787/171/89 – Syria: Political Summary No. 5 for July 1947', *British Embassy Damascus*, 1947, received by UK Foreign Office 25 August.

united in exploiting the new opportunities offered by the capitalist expansion of the economy'.[13]

This elite pattern was even more pronounced among the Brotherhood's senior members, who emerged from Syria's bourgeois and educated classes. In this regard, the Brotherhood's advocacy of conservative ideas was not a cynical attempt to garner votes from the broader community, but also reflected the interests of its core members. Many senior figures held tertiary or advanced degrees, which was significant given that only an estimated 30–35 per cent of the Syrian population were literate at the time.[14] Moreover, a number of members had received Western educations, including the Damascene parliamentary delegate Muhammad al-Mubarak and two founders of the Aleppan branch, Omar Baha al-Amiri and Maruf al-Dawalibi, who were all educated in France.[15] Both al-Amiri and al-Dawalibi hailed from Aleppo's upper class. Hinnebusch noted that this was part of a broader trend, observing that

Dawalibi is by no means that only scion of the old aristocracy who speaks the language of political Islam and there is much to the claim that, particularly under the Ba'th 'behind the mask of religion stands the khumasiya' – the power of capital.[16]

Likewise, those without wealth often came from respected families. Mustafa al-Sibai was born into a prominent religious family in Homs and received a doctorate from al-Azhar in Egypt.[17] Issam al-Attar had a more modest background, but hailed from a middle ulama family, taught high school Arabic literature and was a prayer leader at the Umayyad Mosque in Damascus.

Although history has shown that a direct line cannot be assumed between class and political outlook, the backgrounds of the group's early leaders appeared to have a defining impact on the organisation's character and political thinking. These men had benefited considerably from the status quo, which imbued conservative interests as fundamental to the party. This nexus between the intellectual class, power and wealth

---

[13] Itzchak Weismann, 'The Politics of Popular Religion: Sufis, Salafis, and Muslim Brothers in 20th-Century Hamah', *International Journal of Middle East Studies* 37, no. 1 (2005), p. 52.
[14] 'World Illiteracy at Mid-Century' (Geneva: UNESCO, 1957), p. 39.
[15] Mohammad Saied Rassas, 'Syria's Muslim Brotherhood: Past and Present', *Al-Monitor* (5 January 2014), www.al-monitor.com/pulse/politics/2014/01/syria-muslim-brotherhood-past-present.html#; W. Montagu-Pollock, 'EY 1012/1 – Leading Personalities in Syria', British Embassy Damascus, 2 July 1951.
[16] Raymond Hinnebusch, *Authoritarian Power and State Formation in Bathist Syria: Army, Party and Peasant* (Boulder: Westview Press, 1991), p. 279.
[17] Alison Pargeter, *The Muslim Brotherhood: The Burden of Tradition* (London: Saqi Books, 2010), p. 64.

was tightly bound, and meant that moderate economic principles were so deeply rooted that even at the height of Communist fervour the group as a whole did not question the sanctity of property and business rights, or the right to individual wealth. Although the group was by no means one of the establishment political parties that represented the post-independence political elite, it never put forward policy ideas that would seriously undermine the foundations of the Syrian state. The group's 'Islamist' agenda was muted perhaps, as Teitelbaum noted, because many of the foreign educated Brothers had received both secular and religious legal education that may have allowed 'for a greater openness to other ideas and issues that were not "Islamic"'.[18] This elite base also had practical implications by creating one of the Brotherhood's most enduring personality traits: individualism. Since many of the group's founding members enjoyed successful lives outside the Brotherhood as lawyers, university lecturers and deans, merchants and so on, many members simultaneously supported the Brotherhood while pursuing their own individual economic interests. The Brotherhood itself was never a tightly bound organisation that provided social mobility for its members; many members joined because they saw it as the best vehicle for their interests.

The group's background acted as a font of admiration and prestige for its supporters. Many 2011 uprising-era Brothers explained that they joined because of its 'cultivated' and 'educated' identity, while Ali al-Bayanouni acknowledged that it had initially been a grouping of intellectuals.[19] One member of the Brotherhood political office who joined over a decade after the 1963 Ba'th coup echoed this observation, recalling that

> [w]hen I used to sit with the men from the Muslim Brotherhood, I used to see the democracy in the way they think, and their bigger political vision that predates the whole state. [They were] educated people. When I met one of them, I would feel that I had gained something from meeting them.[20]

Pierret added that graduates of Syria's secular schools 'were more naturally attracted to the sophisticated intellectuals heading the Muslim Brothers than to the conservative mashyakha (Shaykhs)'.[21] However, while the group's urban elite base appealed to some, it was also a limitation as the Syrian Brothers struggled to compete with broad-based rural

---

[18] Joshua Teitelbaum, 'The Muslim Brotherhood in Syria, 1945–1958: Founding, Social Origins, Ideology', *The Middle East Journal* 65, no. 2 (2011), p. 226.
[19] Anonymous interview; interview with Samir Abu Laban, Istanbul; interview with Ali al-Bayanouni, London.
[20] Interview with Samir Abu Laban, Istanbul.
[21] Thomas Pierret, *Religion and State in Syria: The Sunni Ulama from Coup to Revolution* (Cambridge: Cambridge University Press, 2011), p. 63.

populist movements such as the Ba'th Party, which later leveraged its large popular base to seize power.²²

Given the Brotherhood's pedigree among Syria's middle religious class, Islam inevitably played a major role in the group's self-image. The group popularised slogans such as 'God is our End; His Messenger our Example; the Quran our Constitution; the Jihad our Path; and Death for God's Cause our Highest Desire', and they promised to reform the Syrian state in line with the teachings of Islam.²³ A *New York Times* interview with Mustafa al-Sibai in 1955 noted al-Sibai's observation that, 'the Brotherhood's program was based on trying to revive Islam from its present, wide-spread petrification', which, he said, 'resulted from the failure of the theologians and the *ulema* [sic] to maintain contact with the people'.²⁴ Al-Sibai had earlier characterised the emerging group as, 'neither a jam'iyah nor a political party but a *ruh* [spirit] that permeates the very being of the *ummah*: It is a new revolution'.²⁵ In line with the teaching of Hassan al-Banna and the *Salafiyya* movement, al-Sibai believed that Islam could provide the solution to Syria's economic, political and social malaise. He called for the spread of high-quality Islamic teaching across the country and for policies based on Islamic values. This translated to a number of vague policy stances in the Brotherhood's 1954 political platform, such as 'the combatting of ignorance, disease, want, fear, and indignity' and 'the establishment of a virtuous polity which would carry out the rules and teachings of Islam'.²⁶ This focus on Islam and social justice saw it undertake a substantial number of social and economic projects, consistent with both the group's *jamiyat* foundations and the social work undertaken by the Egyptian Brothers.

Mustafa al-Sibai made periodic reference to an 'Islamic State', which senior Brotherhood figure and former ideologue Zuhair Salem explained:

The Islamic state is not a country of Islamic clerics. When we speak about an Islamic state, we speak about a state of ideas, rather than clerics. And I emphasise that on society, Islamic ideas are the same as the Christian and Jewish ideas. Our land is the land of these three religions: Judaism, Christianity and Islam.²⁷

---

²² Umar F. Abd-allah, *The Islamic Struggle in Syria* (Berkeley: Mizan Press, 1983), p. 91.
²³ Batatu, 'Syria's Muslim Brethren', p. 12.
²⁴ Kennett Love, 'Moslem Brothers Faithful to Chief', *The New York Times* (27 February 1955), p. 30.
²⁵ Cited in Abd-allah, *The Islamic Struggle*, p. 92.
²⁶ Batatu, 'Syria's Muslim Brethren', p. 12.   ²⁷ Interview with Zuhair Salem, London.

Nonetheless, the Brotherhood's approach to Islam was always flexible, with Ziadeh arguing that the Brotherhood had never let religion define its political choices:

> Despite the centrality of religion to their interests, the Muslim Brotherhood nevertheless acted as a purely political movement. It neither considered itself the only legal representative of Islam nor monopolized the right to speak on behalf of Islam.[28]

Indeed, the Brotherhood demonstrated itself throughout its founding decades to not be driven by ideological dogmatism. It was a political party with a clear set of political goals that it channelled through Syria's existing parliamentary system. Batatu observed that for the most part, 'there is nothing characteristically Islamic' about its values.[29] This vagueness in political ideology would prove beneficial later, as it would enable the Brotherhood to make pragmatic changes to its political platforms without overtly violating previous positions. The Brotherhood's religious pedigree nevertheless proved an important point of differentiation from its Communist and Socialist rivals in both the parliament and at the ballot box, with its leaders frequently using mosque pulpits to garner support.[30]

Mustafa al-Sibai and other Brotherhood members frequently spoke about the relationship between Islam and the state in their writing, although al-Sibai and his successor Issam al-Attar's election to the Syrian parliament implied that they did not have a fundamental problem with Syria's secular parliamentary system. This is consistent with the path carved by their predecessors in Syria's Salafiyya movement during the 1908 Young Turk revolution.

Mustafa al-Sibai published a work on the relationship between Islam and the state in *al-Fath* while he was in Egypt in the 1930s. The article, titled 'Ulama and Politics', argued that the ulama needed to return to the political realm in order to 'guide the nation toward the Islamic ideals over a long period of time and to deflect much damage to Islam by evildoers from within or attacks by the enemies of its faith'.[31] He cited instances

---

[28] Radwan Ziadeh, *Power and Policy in Syria: Intelligence Services, Foreign Relations and Democracy in the Modern Middle East* (London: I.B. Tauris, 2011), p. 136.
[29] Batatu, 'Syria's Muslim Brethren', p. 13.
[30] 'E 2507/171/89 – Correspondence Respecting Syria Part 1', *British Embassy Damascus*, week ending 25 February 1947.
[31] Meir Hatina, 'Appendix: Translation of Muṣṭafā l-Sibāʿī's Essay "'Ulamāʾ and Politics" in an Earlier Sunnī Version of Khomeini's Rule of the Jurist: Muṣṭafā l-Sibāʿī on Ulamā and Politics', *Arabica* 57, no. 4 (2010), p. 470.

where the ulama had advised the Rightly Guided Caliphs,[32] arguing that the ulama had not only the authority, but also the duty to be involved in the affairs of state. However, the specific role he advocated for ulama was couched in the language of democracy and in words including 'parliament', 'chairs in the government' and 'congress', and he saw executive power as a separate function.[33] Although this political order may not be ambiguously secular, he concluded that

> [o]ur 'ulamā' are duty bound to sense their great responsibility and move forward with devotion and determination until the hall of parliament is filled with them and the branches of government are completely occupied by them and the keys to the government are in their hand.[34]

Al-Sibai repeated the language of contemporary democracies, drawing attention to the link between 'halls of parliament' and government. Indeed, to al-Sibai, the ulama's keys to government would come through the democratic process in the same way that it worked in other countries.

Perhaps the most comprehensive indication of the Brotherhood's position on Islam and democracy came from an article Mustafa al-Sibai wrote in 1950 and published in Syria in the newspaper he founded, *al-Manar*, as the Syrian constitution was being revised. Al-Sibai was a member of the parliamentary committee responsible for the amendments. The Brotherhood ran a campaign to have Islam constitutionally recognised as the religion of the Syrian state. This particular article, titled 'The Establishment of Islam as the State Religion in Syria', justified the Brotherhood's position on the grounds of its 'indispensability to national morale'.[35] Al-Sibai argued for Islam's recognition as state religion on the basis of 'democratic principles', and then in terms of the 'domestic interest', the 'national interest', the 'political interest'. He believed that becoming an officially Islamic country would also open Syria up to the large trade markets in other parts of the Islamic world.[36] He added that 'we do not for a moment want by this establishment [of Islam as the state

---

[32] The first four successors of Muhammad who were companions of Muhammad during his lifetime. See John L. Esposito, *Islam: The Straight Path*, 3rd edn (New York: Oxford University Press, 2005), pp. 35–7.
[33] Hatina, 'Appendix: Translation of Muṣṭafā l-Sibāʿī's Essay "'Ulamāʾ and Politics"', p. 475.
[34] Ibid., p. 476.
[35] R. Bayly-Winder, 'Islam as the State Religion a Muslim Brotherhood View in Syria', *The Muslim World* 44, nos. 3–4 (1954), p. 215.
[36] Mustafa Al-Sibai, 'The Establishment of Islam as the State Religion of Syria', *The Muslim World* 44, nos. 3–4 (1954), pp. 219–20.

religion] to eliminate the parliament, to reject the representatives of the nation, or to abrogate the laws'.[37]

Mustafa al-Sibai's argument was remarkable for its political pragmatism and absence of ideological or religious zeal, although this should not understate the validity of the concerns expressed by Syria's substantial minority communities. Nonetheless, al-Sibai did not cite Quranic verses or tracts from Islamic history, but rather based his justification on political realism. Indeed, his article concluded that 'the only reason for establishing a state religion is to color [sic] the state with a spiritual, moral hue so that regulations and laws will be carried out under the impetus of a deep, spiritual driving force'.[38] Al-Sibai's campaign was unsuccessful and the Brotherhood was forced to compromise and accept that Islam would not be the religion of the state, but would only be the religion of the President. Brotherhood deputies in the parliament supported the amended text, with al-Sibai declaring that the new constitution was 'a model constitution for a Muslim state'.[39] Article 3, Clause 2 of the new constitution also stated that 'Islamic law shall be the main source of legislation';[40] both clauses remained in the Syrian constitution on the eve of the 2011 uprising, and after 2012 constitutional revision. The Brotherhood's controversial ideologue Said Hawwa spoke positively of the 1950 developments in his memoir decades later, noting that the group's deputies had succeeded in 'colouring [the constitution] with the Islamic character'.[41]

The constitution campaign was significant because it provided the first substantive example of the Brotherhood's two other defining characteristics, which exist in addition to the individualism described above. First, it demonstrated the Brotherhood's pragmatism through al-Sibai's willingness to couch his goals in the language of politics in order to give his campaign a chance of succeeding. This showed that even in the Brotherhood's founding moments when it was closest to its ideological forefathers in Hassan al-Banna and Mustafa al-Sibai, and led by an *alim* (Islamic scholar), it had ideological goals and behaviours characterised by pragmatism, not dogmatism. Second, the process also highlighted the Brotherhood's ideological flexibility. Although Islam was integral to the group's name, it was willing to compromise. Thus, ideological pragmatism and flexibility in conjunction with individualism defined the

---

[37] Ibid., p. 224. [38] Ibid., p. 225.
[39] Cited in Pierret, *Religion and State in Syria*, pp. 174–5.
[40] Majid Khadduri, 'Constitutional Developments in Syria: With Emphasis on the Constitution of 1950', *The Middle East Journal* 5, no. 2 (1951), p. 153.
[41] Said Hawwa, *This Is My Experience and This Is My Testimony (in Arabic)* (Cairo: Maktabat Wahba, 1987), p. 41.

key parameters of the Brotherhood's character. In this, the Brotherhood seemed very clearly influenced by the experiences and beliefs of its predecessors in the Sufi and Salafiyya reform movements and the *jamiyat*.

Mustafa al-Sibai continued to publish prolifically on the permissibility of democracy in Islam for the remainder of his life, later arguing that every citizen has

[h]is right in supervising and advising those who are in charge because [the citizen] is responsible for the future of the nation ... This [political responsibility] comes under the generalisation of the Prophet's, "All of you are shepherds and all are responsible for his sheep."[42]

According to Zuhair Salem, Mustafa al-Sibai

practiced it (democracy) in every single way. When he wanted to suggest an article [in the constitution] saying that the religion of the country is Islam, he did not succeed. And when he did not succeed, he accepted that. He [later] joined the elections and he did not succeed either.[43]

Batatu argued that most of the Brothers' principles in this period were 'drawn from the moral armoires of classical liberalism'.[44]

The Brotherhood also advocated religious tolerance in its founding decades. Al-Sibai referred to Christianity and Judaism as 'sister religions' and the Brotherhood stated that 'the people of the book are entitled to protection and can expect to live in security under the laws of Islam'.[45] This is consistent with the teachings and practice of the Brotherhood's Sufi forefathers such as Abd al-Qadir al-Jazairi discussed in Chapter 1. A theme of tolerance was present throughout the Brotherhood's writings and platforms. Mustafa al-Sibai said, 'We want to cooperate with Muslims and Christians who hear the voice of heaven and the precepts of the Gospels and the Qur'an'.[46] In his tract on the constitution, he noted in 1950 that 'Islam respects Christianity as a revealed religion and leaves to its followers freedom of belief and worship without interfering in their affairs'.[47] He assured Christians that Muslims would never seek to intervene in areas of Christian personal status, and suggested an

---

[42] Mustafa Al-Sibai, 'Al-Takaful al-Ijtimai', in *Arab Socialism [al-Ishtirakīyah Al-'Arabīyah]: A Documentary Survey*, ed. Sami Ayad Hanna and George H. Gardner (Leiden: Brill, 1969), p. 154.
[43] Interview with Zuhair Salem, London (parenthesis added).
[44] Batatu, 'Syria's Muslim Brethren', p. 13.
[45] Al-Sibai, 'The Establishment of Islam as the State Religion of Syria', p. 223; cited in Lefèvre, *Ashes of Hama*, p. 59.
[46] Al-Sibai, 'The Establishment of Islam as the State Religion of Syria', p. 226.
[47] Ibid., p. 221.

additional constitutional article that declares 'the sacredness and the sanctity of the revealed religions and the sacredness of the personal status of the members of the other religious communities'.[48] Al-Sibai went so far as to say that the Brotherhood would prefer to 'have Christianity the state religion than to have the state atheistically secular'.[49] Zuhair Salem claimed that during this period, Brotherhood members often spoke about their political programmes in churches.[50]

Mustafa al-Sibai maintained his attitude towards non-Muslims, declaring more than a decade later in 1962 that 'Islam does not persecute non-Muslims that live in a Muslim land; it does not persecute them for their beliefs or deny them their rights'.[51] He argued that the Prophet's experience provided 'irrefutable evidence' that 'the Islamic state was based on social justice, and that the basis of relations between Muslims and others was peace'.[52] While his position never wavered towards Christians, notably his generosity of spirit towards Jews was lost by this point, who he declared 'treacherous' and 'evil'.[53] This may also have reflected broader Middle Eastern political dynamics related to the establishment of the state of Israel.

Given that sectarianism was not a significant feature of the Syrian landscape at the time, the Brotherhood did not dwell on the question of sect, although the group provided some indication of its position. 'Religion is brotherhood; sectarianism is enmity' was a key early plank of the party's platform and al-Sibai had long argued that Muslims should avoid disunity over theological matters and they should be united by their commonality.[54] In his discussion on the constitution noted above, he said that Syria should be Muslim and he did not deal with the question of sects at all. Al-Sibai also sought to spread a message of 'jihad, struggle and work ... it is not a philosophical message ... Islam is *'amal* [work and action] not *jadal* [controversial argumentation]'.[55] The absence of sectarian language in Syria's democratic era suggests that the Brotherhood was not primordially biased against the Alawite community that later became closely associated with the Ba'th regime, but that members' sectarianism developed in the context of political events in later decades.

---

[48] Ibid., p. 222.   [49] Ibid., pp. 225–6.   [50] Interview with Zuhair Salem, London.
[51] Mustafa As-Sibaa'ie, *The Life of the Prophet Muhammad: Highlights and Lessons*, trans. Nasiruddin Al-Khattab (Riyadh: International Islamic Publishing House, 2003), p. 80.
[52] Ibid., p. 79.
[53] Al-Sibai, 'The Establishment of Islam as the State Religion of Syria', p. 223; As-Sibaa'ie, *The Life of the Prophet Muhammad*, pp. 138–9.
[54] Cited in Teitelbaum, 'The Muslim Brotherhood in Syria', p. 222.
[55] Abd-allah, *The Islamic Struggle in Syria*, p. 95.

Its embrace of minorities suggests that the group's platforms went well beyond democratic participation, also extending to religious freedoms.

Nevertheless, it would be wrong to assert that the Brotherhood enjoyed total ideological harmony in its founding decades. Muhammad al-Mubarak, one of the Brotherhood's founding members and politicians, wrote *The Islamic System: The Government and the State* in which he articulated his own position on the relationship between Islam and democracy. He supported democracy in principle and argued in favour of a dual legislature that is based on the principle of the separation of powers. He further asserted that this European system of governance was allowable because 'it is permissible to adopt and benefit from anything that may help realize the goals of the Islamic state and hinder excess and tyranny ... even if it was unknown in the past'.[56] However, Mubarak's bicameral system would have seen religious figures make up an upper house and while the appointment method for those members was not specified, a serious limitation on democratic nature of the parliament may well have been the result.[57] Mubarak later wrote in *Contemporary Islamic Thought in Confronting Western Ideas* that

> [democracy] emanates from a philosophy that Islam does not accept. Indeed, democracy may conflict with Islam's philosophy and perception in many of its dimensions...In reality both are two different doctrines in their foundations, roots and philosophies and in the results of their applications.[58]

During this period it also became clear that the group had a conservative underbelly that was not represented in the language of its more liberal leadership. This was to be expected given the group's ideological diversity and its *jamiyat* foundations. A split appeared as early as 1947, perhaps due to the influences of the conservative Jamiyat al-Gharra on the Brotherhood's Damascus members, when members attacked the Roxy Theatre after the announcement of a 'ladies day' promotion for female cinemagoers.[59] There is little indication that the group opposed women's rights more broadly, given there was no record of significant Brotherhood protest against the 1949 Electoral Law when the right of suffrage was given to women.[60] Further, as Teitelbaum noted, the Brotherhood's newspaper *al-Manar* routinely printed advertisements

---

[56] Cited in Itzchak Weismann, 'Democratic Fundamentalism? The Practice and Discourse of the Muslim Brothers Movement in Syria', *The Muslim World* 100, no. 1 (2010), p. 9.
[57] Cited in ibid.   [58] Ibid., p. 28.
[59] Teitelbaum, 'The Muslim Brotherhood in Syria', p. 231.
[60] M.C. Man, 'E 11501/1018/89 – Syrian Electoral Law', *UK Foreign Office*, 19 September 1949.

that depicted men and women romantically embracing,[61] so the protest probably reflected a small albeit vocal minority.

Similar tensions appeared after the 1950 constitution vote, when some Brotherhood supporters drove cars through the Christian quarters of Damascus and Aleppo to noisily gloat at Islam now being the constitutionally mandated religion of the president.[62] Although there is little indication that such behaviour had support from the group's senior members, Teitelbaum noted that, the act 'reveals perhaps some of the latent animosity towards Syria's Christian population', at least amongst its base.[63] Indeed, even under Mustafa al-Sibai, it was clear that the Brotherhood was a diverse movement, and there was significant ideological heterogeneity among its members.

1963–1996: The Brotherhood's Ideology under the Ba'th

The period from 1963 to 1982 proved challenging for the Brotherhood ideologically as it faced a trio of new developments that would lead to the erosion of the very principles that had guided its founding decades. The Brotherhood was outlawed after the 1963 Ba'th coup, which paralysed its political activities and forced the group to go underground. In 1964 the group's new leader, Issam al-Attar, travelled to Saudi Arabia for the Hajj and was not allowed to return. Mustafa al-Sibai died the same year, although his poor health had precluded him from exerting any operational influence over the group for several years prior. Given al-Sibai's past charismatic leadership and his strong support for his protégé, al-Attar, the latter two developments levelled the group a double blow, facilitating a rise in political disunity. This was exacerbated by the rising profile of Egyptian Brotherhood member Sayyid Qutb, whose 1964 call to arms *Milestones* had an especially strong influence on the Syrian Brothers' rank and file. These factors combined to threaten the Brotherhood's original ideological path during the early years of opposition to the Ba'th regime.

The most significant threat to the Brotherhood's previously mainstream political positions came from the ascendancy of the group's new ideologue, Said Hawwa. Hawwa was a religious scholar and member of

---

[61] Teitelbaum, 'The Muslim Brotherhood in Syria', p. 231.
[62] Joshua Teitelbaum, 'The Muslim Brotherhood and the "Struggle for Syria"', 1947–1958 between Accommodation and Ideology', *Middle Eastern Studies* 40, no. 3 (2004), p. 144.
[63] Ibid.

the Hama branch of the Muslim Brotherhood who became a senior figure in the group from the 1960s until the early 1980s.[64] Although Hawwa had Salafist influences during his childhood, he received Sufi training and was a student of Muhammad al-Hamid.[65] The young Hawwa's ideological thought impressed Brotherhood leaders, and he was formally appointed to develop the group's doctrine in the mid-1960s. Parts of his thought were inspired by al-Sibai and al-Hamid, and he supported many of the group's earlier liberal economic principles, particularly those related to the group's constituency and material interests. This included the right to private property and the rights of individuals to earn and control their own wealth.[66] However, on other fronts, Hawwa was significantly more radical than his forefathers, prompting Lawson to dub him Sayyid Qutb's 'Syrian contemporary'.[67] Hawwa's considerable intellectual achievements facilitated his quick ascent to the group's leadership, which Pargeter argued gave him 'more influence than other leading figures within the Ikwhan' and enabled him to foment a seismic shift in the group.[68]

Said Hawwa shared the Brotherhood founding fathers' thinking on the legitimacy of the group's combined Sufi–Salafi model. Like his forefathers, Hawwa argued that education and *Da'wa* (proselytisation) represented the best way to revive Islam. He advocated the spread of high-quality religious education through the establishment of study circles in local mosques across the country, which eventually became important recruiting tools for new Brotherhood members. Many current Brothers joined the group after participating in these study circles in the 1970s.[69] However, Hawwa did not share his forefathers' tolerance of the non-Sunni sects and non-Muslims. Hawwa published a booklet titled *Khomeini – Deviation in Doctrines, Deviation in Positions,* which criticised the Shia worship of Imams.[70] Hawwa also hinted at an Ibn Taymiyya fatwa (religious edict) to criticise the Alawites, marking an important

---

[64] Itzchak Weismann, 'The Making of a Radical Muslim Thinker in Modern Syria', *Middle Eastern Studies* (1993), p. 602.
[65] Ibid., pp. 607–11.
[66] Fred H. Lawson, *Global Security Watch: Syria* (Denver: Praeger, 2013), p. 64.
[67] Ibid., p. 64.   [68] Pargeter, *The Muslim Brotherhood*, p. 74.
[69] Interview with Ali al-Ahmad, London; anonymous interview; interview with Samir Abu Laban, Istanbul.
[70] Geneive Abdo, 'Salafists and Sectarianism: Twitter and Communal Conflict in the Middle East', Brookings Institute (2015), www.brookings.edu/~/media/research/files/papers/2015/03/26-sectarianism-salafism-social-media-abdo/abdo-paper_final_web.pdf, p. 13.

shift from traditional Syrian Salafist thought.[71] He was not alone in his position: at the time many Brotherhood members (although not all of its leaders) began to see the merit of Ibn Taymiyyah's previously inconceivable sectarianism, as the Syrian regime became perceived as displaying increasingly direct favouritism of the Alawite sect. One former Brotherhood member explained that the Syrian regime's sectarian positions at the time were a significant factor in his decision to join the group.[72] Hawwa's positions were echoed by other Syrian thinkers at the time, including Mohammad Surur Zein al-Abideen, who left the Brotherhood in the 1960s and later became a renowned Islamic scholar highly critical of the Brotherhood movement.[73] In 1980, Surur published a book titled *Then Came the Turn of the Fire-Worshippers,* in which he dubbed all Shia as part of a 'Persian Conspiracy'.[74] Although he was not a Brotherhood member at the time, it does highlight the diversity of thinking with the group's base over time. Surur died in November 2016, prompting the Brotherhood to express 'sadness' on its Facebook page.[75]

Perhaps of most significance however was Said Hawwa's position on democracy, which differed from the Brotherhood's forefathers. In one of his most widely distributed books, *JundAllah* (Soldiers of God), published in 1977, Hawwa argued that *Shura* (consultation) and democracy were mutually exclusive terms because democracy denoted the sovereignty and rule of the people, whereas *Shura* required a leader to consult others only in regard to compliance with Islamic law.[76] He noted that

> [i]n Islam, the people do not govern themselves by laws they make on their own, as in a democracy; rather the people are governed by a regime and a set of laws imposed by God, which they cannot change or modify in any case.[77]

This was a considerable departure from the position advocated by Mustafa al-Sibai and Issam al-Attar. Al-Sibai had specifically argued that 'one of the most prominent features of Islam is *shoora* [*sic*] or consultation ... [and] one of the most prominent features of the longest-serving Muslim

---

[71] Itzchak Weismann, 'Sa'id Hawwa and Islamic Revivalism in Ba'thist Syria', *Studia Islamica* 85 (1997), p. 152.
[72] Interview with Ali al-Ahmad, London.
[73] Stéphane Lacroix, *Awakening Islam: The Politics of Religious Dissent in Contemporary Saudi Arabia* (Cambridge: Harvard University Press, 2011), p. 69.
[74] Abdo, 'Salafists and Sectarianism'.
[75] The Syrian Brotherhood Media Office, *Facebook* (13 November 2016), www.facebook.com/IkhwanSyriaMedia/photos/a.581223625263415.1073741826.555454591173652/1318636 824855421/?type=3&theater.
[76] Shukri B. Abed, 'Islam and Democracy', in *Democracy, War and Peace in the Middle East,* ed. David Garnham and Mark Tessler (Bloomington: Indiana University Press, 1995), p. 123.
[77] Ibid.

rulers in history is the fact that they would consult and not dictate, they would discuss with every specialist in every field that concerned them'.[78] Hawwa's position on democracy softened later in life – in a 1983 interview when asked about his vision for Syria should the Brotherhood seize power, he explained: 'An Islamic state could be established from the first day, provided these two principles are fulfilled: that under the constitution the state's religion is Islam, and that Islam is the source of law'.[79] When Hawwa's interviewer clarified whether Islam would be 'the principal or the only source' of law, Hawwa responded: 'With our partners, we agreed on the word "principal"'.[80] It is worth noting that the first of these requirements was consistent with Mustafa al-Sibai's own efforts in 1950, while the second already existed in the Syrian constitution as the 'main source' of legislation.

Hawwa's more radical ideas did not permeate the group's official statements. Documents, speeches and statements released in the heat of the 1979–82 conflict between the Brotherhood and the Syrian state echoed the ideas of the group's founding leaders. Hinnebusch summarised the group's thinking in this era as

reflecting its utter disaffection from populist Ba'thism, was a relatively liberal but economically anti-populist variant of Islam which expessed the anti-statist world view of the *suq*, Sunni resentment of minority domination of the state, and the need to appeal to Syria's relatively liberal educated classes.[81]

The major ideological document of this era was the 1980 'Declaration and Program of the Islamic Revolution in Syria', which was signed by the Brotherhood's senior leaders, Said Hawwa, Ali al-Bayanouni and Adnan Saadeddine. The Declaration devoted considerable space to democratic principles, directly articulating the group's desired political system, which it calls 'the system of mutual consultation (democracy)'.[82] It promised that

[t]he Islamic revolution in Syria declares its intention to adhere to the principle of mutual consultation and expresses its determination to realize the political rights of all the citizens...No nation will survive without freedom, mutual consultation and the preservation of human dignity.[83]

---

[78] As-Sibaa'ie, *The Life of the Prophet Muhammad*, p. 132.
[79] Chris Kutschera, 'Syria: Muslim Brothers: The Question of Alliances', *The Middle East* 103 (May 1983), p. 27.
[80] Ibid.
[81] Raymond Hinnebusch, *Syria: Revolution from Above* (London: Routledge, 2001), p. 94.
[82] 'Declaration of Program of the Islamic Revolution in Syria' (Damascus: The Higher Command of the Islamic Revolution in Syria, 1980), p. 14.
[83] Ibid., p. 15.

In this regard, the Declaration closely followed Mustafa al-Sibai's vision for the group and differed from the position put forward by Said Hawwa. This highlights that even with a diversity of thinking among some leaders, these were never sufficient to dent the consistency of the Brotherhood's formal platforms. The document committed to a number of fundamental democratic principles, such as freedom of expression, freedom of the press and the separation of powers, noting that 'from the beginning, Islam ordered this separation'.[84] The Declaration called for 'freedom to form political parties' and noted that it would have 'no reservation against any political party'.[85] It added that, 'the need of the nation for regaining its freedom is as important as its need for air, water and food',[86] although lacked details on the specifics of the group's desired political system. There was no mention as to whether Syria would have a presidential or a Westminster political system, and no discussion of electoral mechanics, which would be appropriate given Syria's diversity and the Lebanese experience. It noted that

> [f]rom the Islamic point of view, mutual consultation is the basis of good government. The validity of this principle has been proven by the experiments of other nations, which also proved that mutual consultation is like a life boat in storms, and that it is a protection against political and military dictatorship and a safeguard against personal ambitions and party or sectarian domination.[87]

This is remarkably similar to the position on *Shura* put forward by Mustafa al-Sibai.

This message was echoed in other documents at the height of the group's violence. In an interview with the Kuwaiti *al-Mujtamaa* in 1981, the head of the Syrian Islamic Front Abu Nasr al-Bayanouni declared that: 'we refuse the idea of one-party system. The Islamic system is a "shura" [sic] system and guarantees the freedom of all the people'.[88] Likewise, during the Hama uprising, Adnan Saadeddine gave a speech on the 'Voice of the Mujahidin' radio station directed at Syria's Alawites, reminding them that Syria's sects had once worked together to found the Syrian state 'based on tolerance, liberty, parliamentary life and economic prosperity'.[89] This suggests that the group's dramatically changed operating environment and the infiltration of radical ideas didn't erode the Brotherhood's original ideas, at least publicly. Dekmejian noted that the document also differed in important ways from the thinking of their Egyptian counterparts, lacking 'the ideological rigidity

---

[84] Ibid. [85] Ibid., p. 16. [86] Ibid., p. 13. [87] Ibid., p. 15.
[88] Cited in 'An Interview', *Abstracts from al-Nazeer no. 38 (English edition)*, 9 September 1981.
[89] See *Al-Nadhir No. 10 (in Arabic)*, 19 February 1982.

The Syrian Muslim Brotherhood's Founding Ideas 57

that has characterized the doctrines of some Egyptian Islamist groups' and reflecting 'a greater sense of pragmatism and lack the doctrinal subtleties and controversies that have been the feature of the Egyptian Islamist societies'.[90]

The Declaration and Program of the Islamic Revolution in Syria also echoed Mustafa al-Sibai's non-sectarian philosophies, promising 'equality between the citizens' and that 'civil and legal rights of all ethnic and religious minorities would be protected and their personal liberties guaranteed'.[91] Accusing the government of perpetuating sectarianism, the document discussed Syria's sectarian problems in non-emotive terms. The English edition of the Declaration specifically referred to the Alawite minority as 'Alawite', rather than '*Nusayri*', the popular derogatory term for the sect. It added that Islam was born without sects, and that in the post-Ba'th system, 'All Muslims will have a common ground which could form the foundation stone for building a new world'.[92] However, while the document offered members of the Alawite sect the opportunity to distance themselves from the Ba'th regime and join the opposition, there was also a veiled threat. It noted:

We declare without deceit or intrigue that we shall be happy to see them shake off the guardianship of the corrupt elements which drove them to this dangerous predicament. There is still sufficient time left for them and the hearts of our people are large enough to welcome those who will come back.[93]

Therefore, although the document did not reflect primordial sectarianism, it did imply a willingness to target the entire Alawite sect based on its close political ties to the al-Assad regime.

Nonetheless, it would be wrong to assert that Said Hawwa's thinking had no impact on the Brotherhood. His ideas enjoyed sympathy in some parts of the movement, especially among its youth and most radical members. One member of the Fighting Vanguard splinter group had declared: 'to set up a democratic state is not our problem',[94] while another noted 'for us, men don't have a right to govern by themselves, they must be governed through God'.[95] A third member commented that he did 'not know why and on what religious ground should reform [*sic*] be achieved through the democratic process'.[96] Hawwa's book *Jund Allah* (Soldiers of God) became popular in Syria around this time, and

---

[90] R. Hrair Dekmejian, *Islam in Revolution: Fundamentalism in the Arab World*, 2nd edn (Syracuse: Syracuse University Press), p. 111.
[91] 'Declaration of Program of the Islamic Revolution in Syria', p. 13.   [92] Ibid., p. 12.
[93] Ibid., p. 11.   [94] Kutschera, 'Syria: Muslim Brothers', p. 28.
[95] Cited in Lefèvre, *Ashes of Hama*, pp. 119–20.   [96] Ibid., p. 120.

was 'distributed widely in mosques and underground religious bookshops'.⁹⁷

Said Hawwa is also widely blamed for laying the ideological foundation for the Brotherhood's slide to violence in the late 1970s, as he made it clear that he considered Syria to be in a state of unprecedented crisis that was worthy of violent jihad. However, this may be a misreading of his writing, Hawwa set a number of hurdles that needed to be overcome before declaring jihad, including a lengthy preparation process. As Weismann noted,

> Hawwa has no doubts as to the validity of jihad in principle, but the stiff stipulations that he imposes on its implementation...indicate that in practice not only jihad against the jahili'a but also against the ridda must be postponed. Even in the extreme case of Syria, where ridda is declared, a long process of education, as well as a Sunni predominance in the army, are required before jihad can be proclaimed.⁹⁸

Hawwa's Sufi roots were also evident here, which as Hatina noted had led him to argue that '[t]he Sufi path of intensive prayer, fasting and discipline is important in an era in which materialism and hedonism are dominant, for it constitutes a necessary preparatory stage to the act of jihad'.⁹⁹ Indeed, Hawwa was critical of Brotherhood figures such as Marwan Hadid, who had taken up violence against the regime in the 1960s. While he agreed with Hadid's goals, he believed that Hadid had acted prematurely.

But Said Hawwa's ideas were complex and often difficult to understand.¹⁰⁰ During the 2011 uprising, a Brotherhood member noted that Hawwa's intended message was not nearly as radical as it was interpreted, but was instrumentalised by the Brotherhood's more radical members.¹⁰¹ Eventually it became a driver of grassroots radicalisation and was used to sanction the use of violence. Weismann argued that this slide into violence marked

> the failure of Sa'id Hawwa as a *rabbani*. His analysis of the Syrian condition was basically correct, but he failed to persuade his fellow members of the need for long preparation and restraint.¹⁰²

---

⁹⁷ Ibid., p. 98.   ⁹⁸ Weismann, 'Sa'id Hawwa and Islamic Revivalism', p. 153.
⁹⁹ Meir Hatina, 'Restoring a Lost Identity: Models of Education in Modern Islamic Thought', *British Journal of Middle Eastern Studies* 33, no. 2 (2006), p. 189.
¹⁰⁰ Weismann, 'Sa'id Hawwa and Islamic Revivalism', p. 149.
¹⁰¹ Anonymous interview.
¹⁰² Weismann, 'Sa'id Hawwa and Islamic Revivalism', p. 154.

The Syrian Muslim Brotherhood's Founding Ideas   59

Thus, while Hawwa's thinking did not infiltrate the Brotherhood's official political platforms, it had a transformative influence on the Brotherhood's grassroots, contributing to the erosion of Mustafa al-Sibai's peaceful message, facilitating an appetite for violence and eventually creating a chasm between the group's leaders and followers. These dynamics were crucial to the Brotherhood's own adoption of violence.

Hawwa died in 1989, but his ideas retain currency in the group. A senior Brotherhood leader acknowledged that while Hawwa's thinking is still taught by the Brotherhood today, the group uses his ideas selectively.[103] Zuhair Salem, the group's contemporary ideologue, explained:

> We like Said Hawwa, but we do not want to be the same way that he used to be. And you know that he has a lot of books. We don't agree with many of them. We want our way to be in Islam that develops, not goes back.[104]

Nonetheless, like the works of Ibn Taymiyyah, the group's close proximity to Hawwa's philosophies remain a vulnerability. Salem acknowledged that '[w]henever there are difficult political situations like the current one (the 2011 Syrian uprising), you find that people are [once again] interested in his (Said Hawwa's) books'.[105] In March 2016, the Brotherhood posted a eulogy to Hawwa on its Facebook page, marking 27 years since his death.[106]

1996–2011: Righting the Path

The failed Hama uprising was a watershed moment for the Brotherhood, leading to the departure of Said Hawwa from the group's leadership and the appointment of its new ideologue, Zuhair Salem, in 1985. Salem began to foment an effort to return the group to the path set by Mustafa al-Sibai, although it would take another decade for the Brotherhood to organisationally recover from Hama. The years following the Hama massacre were a time of unprecedented chaos for the Syrian Muslim Brotherhood, characterised by blame, mass resignations from the group's base and forced exile. This led to a second split in the Brotherhood in 1985–6 before a reunification in 1991, followed by a period of dormancy until Ali al-Bayanouni was elected General Guide in 1996.[107]

---

[103] Anonymous interview.   [104] Interview with Zuhair Salem, London.
[105] Ibid. (parentheses added).
[106] The Syrian Brotherhood Media Office, *Facebook* (14 October 2016), www.facebook.com/IkhwanSyriaMedia/posts/1111832078869231:0.
[107] Interview with Zuhair Salem, London, 2015.

Al-Bayanouni led the Brotherhood from 1996 until 2010, overseeing the group's efforts to rebuild, come to terms with the past and clarify its ideological positions. As Zuhair Salem recalled,

> The idea [of reform] was there and it was started by [our leader] Sheikh Abd al-Fatah [abu Ghuddah] in 1985. In the 1990s until 1995...there was nothing major happening ... [but when Ali al-Bayanouni became leader in 1996] at that time we took practical steps.[108]

It is worth noting that al-Bayanouni had not always been associated with the Brotherhood's peaceful message. He headed the group's military high command during its 1979–82 militarisation, but Lefèvre suggests that he underwent a significant intellectual shift between then and 1996, noting that 'his interaction with Islamists from other countries, such as *Ennahda's* Rashid Ghannouchi from Tunisia had a profound impact on his thinking'.[109] There was little evidence to suggest that this shift was anything short of genuine: by the time the 2011 uprising unfolded, al-Bayanouni was viewed across the opposition as both a moderate and a constructive member of the opposition.

Just four years after al-Bayanouni took over the leadership, the Brotherhood's long-term foe, President Hafez al-Assad, died suddenly and was replaced by his son Bashar. It was in this context of the new presidency, and the potential first serious political opening in Syria in 20 years, that the Brotherhood began to lay out its vision for its future in Syria. It even purportedly enlisted an Arab head of state to carry a conciliatory message on its behalf to Bashar al-Assad at his father's funeral.[110] This hope seemed well founded: in November that year President al-Assad sanctioned the release of 600 political prisoners, including 380 members of the Syrian Muslim Brotherhood, and closed the notorious Mezze prison in the western suburbs of Damascus.[111] Palmyra prison was closed the following year.

The first significant ideological document released in the Ali al-Bayanouni era was the 'National Honour Charter', which was published in May 2001. This set out general principles for Syria's future, as well as acknowledging the 1980s as a 'long-gone phase and an era

---

[108] Ibid.
[109] Raphaël Lefèvre, 'The Syrian Muslim Brotherhood's Alawi Conundrum', in *The Alawis of Syria: War, Faith and Politics in the Levant*, ed. Michael Kerr and Craig Larkin (Oxford: Oxford University Press, 2015), pp. 125–40 at p. 131.
[110] Hanlie Booysen, 'Surviving the Syrian Uprising: The Syrian Muslim Brotherhood', in *New Opposition in the Middle East*, ed. Dara Conduit and Shahram Akbarzadeh (New York: Palgrave Macmillan, 2018), p. 156.
[111] Alan George, *Syria: Neither Bread Nor Freedom* (London: Zed Books, 2003), p. 40.

buried in history, which resulted from emotional spillage as well as misinterpretation and misunderstanding'.[112] With the Brotherhood always looking for political openings, the Charter's release coincided with two significant developments in addition to Bashar al-Assad's elevation to power. First, Syrian-Jordanian relations had begun to thaw after the death of both countries' long-term leaders, Hafez al-Assad and King Hussein bin Talal. The Brotherhood's fortunes were closely tied to the Syria–Jordan bilateral relationship because large numbers of Brothers lived in Jordan. The Brotherhood had publicly welcomed the détente, with al-Bayanouni reiterating his readiness for dialogue with the Syrian regime 'on the basis of safeguarding general freedoms, releasing the detainees, guaranteeing political pluralism and revoking Law 49 of 1980'.[113] In addition, the Brotherhood was keen to take advantage of the fledgling Damascus Spring movement, which had fomented an unprecedented political opening for opposition activities.[114] The main architect of the Charter, Zuhair Salem, explained that he shared the document with the Brotherhood's other leaders in this political climate in 2001: 'I presented the National Charter [to senior Brotherhood leaders]. Nearly everyone agreed about it. And even Bashar al-Assad did not say anything about it. All national and international parties welcomed it'.[115] The momentum behind the movement, however, quickly rose beyond the limits of what the new regime would tolerate, prompting a crackdown.[116] By the time the Charter was publicly released in May 2001, the Damascus Spring had ended.

The National Honour Charter was consistent with the Brotherhood's earlier political platforms, providing a detailed account of the group's democratic credentials. It noted that 'Basic freedoms and political and civil rights are no longer matters of debate' and that freedom was 'essentially a common political and civilisational achievement and a basic right of the people'.[117] Although the Charter lacked detail, it was significant in its reiteration of the group's founding principles. The fact that it was so widely accepted by the group's leaders and base, despite the changes that the group had undergone in the 1970s and 1980s, shows how deeply

---

[112] Lefèvre, 'The Syrian Muslim Brotherhood's Alawi Conundrum', p. 131.
[113] Cited in 'Jordanian Islamist Leader Denies Mediating between Syria and Muslim Brotherhood', *Al-Sharq Al-Awsat* (London: BBC Summary of World Broadcasts, 15 May 1999).
[114] Joshua M. Landis and Joe Pace, 'The Syrian Opposition', *The Washington Quarterly* 30, no. 1 (2006–7), pp. 45–68.
[115] Interview with Zuhair Salem, London.
[116] For a good discussion of this period, see 'The Damascus Spring', *Carnegie Middle East Center* (1 April 2012), http://carnegie-mec.org/diwan/48516?lang=en.
[117] 'National Charter of Syria' (London: Syrian Muslim Brotehrood, 2002), p. 1.

democratic ideas had penetrated the group. Mustafa al-Sibai's democratic vision remained a permanent mark on the group's thinking.

The Brotherhood expanded substantially on the Charter in 2004 through its 'Political Project for the Future Syria: A Vision of the Muslim Brotherhood Group in Syria'. It was released within months of the UN Security Council passing Resolution 1559 that backed the Lebanese electoral process and calling for the withdrawal of remaining foreign forces from Lebanon. The resolution was largely directed at Syria's presence in the country, and Bashar al-Assad was looking increasingly isolated on the international stage. The timing again demonstrated the Brotherhood's continued reactivity to events and opportunities surrounding the al-Assad regime, and its desire to maximise any chance for détente.[118] Like the Charter, the Brotherhood had seen a potential shift in the strength of the al-Assad regime, on which it sought to capitalise.

Following a news conference in London to launch the Political Project, Ali al-Bayanouni gave a live interview to *al-Jazeera*, in which he clarified that the Project

> underscores the need to build a modern state. The manifestations of this contemporary state are similar to those of the Islamic state. We consider citizenship in the general sense of the word a basis for justice and equality in this state. The modern state we are demanding must be established on contractual and pluralistic bases, rotation of power and separation between the branches of power. We call for rebuilding the homeland society, institutions and state on sound and strong bases. We have proposed this through our political project. We presented it as a contribution to the process of rebuilding the country.[119]

The Project described the group as having an 'ideology steeped in tradition and methodology ever developing' and quotes Mustafa al-Sibai.[120] It briefly addressed the group's history, noting that, 'the Muslim Brotherhood is enduring a process of self-revitalisation, through reconsidering the past, pondering the present and forecasting the future'.[121] It noted its period of violence, saying that 'there can be little doubt that this (the violence) is an exceptional phase within the history of

---

[118] Ellen Lust-Okar, *Structuring Conflict in the Arab World: Incumbents, Opponents and Institutions* (Cambridge: Cambridge University Press, 2005).
[119] Khadijah Bin-Qinnah, 'Syrian Muslim Brotherhood Leader Interviewed on Proposed Reform Plan', *Al-Jazeera TV* (Doha: BBC Summary of World Broadcasts, 17 December 2004)
[120] 'A Summary of the Political Project for the Future Syria: A Vision of the Muslim Brotherhood Group in Syria' (London: Syrian Muslim Brotherhood, 2004), p. 8.
[121] Ibid., p. 8.

our group, and must not in any way taint the pure and original trend thereof, nor its shining record and unblemished history'.[122] The document stopped short of acknowledging fault. The Political Project included new discussions about the rights of women and gender equality, which highlighted its ability to mould its founding ideas with the new ideas shaping the political climate. Consistent with their previous messaging, the Political Project also reiterated the group's commitment to private property and individual rights.[123]

The Political Project put forward the most detailed discussion of democracy that the group has published, repeating the Brotherhood's commitment to tolerance, plurality and democratic principles, and specifically articulating that it wants a democratic, republican system to be established in Syria. It called for the separation of powers, limits on executive power, fixed-length and limits on the number of presidential terms, fixed parliamentary terms, an independent electoral commission and a parliament with sufficient legislative and regulatory power. It affirmed

unequivocally that the people are the source of authority and that no individual, party, group or organisation may hold claim to the right to rule, unless derived from a proper will and authority of the people.[124]

The level of detail on the group's proposed democratic system implied that the Brotherhood had devoted considerable time and discussion in articulating its ideals. Given that many Islamist groups are accused of articulating vague political goals or existing in 'grey zones' in order play their cards close to their chest,[125] the document is notable for its detail. The Political Project repeated the group's previous pledges on the importance of freedom of expression, freedom of the media and freedom to demonstrate. It pledged to guarantee legal equality and full civil and political rights for all citizens constitutionally. It further observed that Syria was comprised of 'more than 20 religious and racial groups, which the Muslim Brotherhood in Syria see as a potential source of strength and richness, rather than an element of weakness and division'.[126]

The Project also discussed Islam, which had been mostly absent from its political programmes after the al-Sibai era. Once again, the group

---

[122] Ibid., p. 11.   [123] Ibid., p. 20.   [124] Ibid., p. 18.
[125] Nathan J. Brown, *When Victory Is Not an Option: Islamist Movements in Arab Politics* (Ithaca: Cornell University Press, 2012), p. 2.; Nathan J. Brown, Amr Hamzawy and Marina Ottaway, 'Islamist Movements and the Democratic Process in the Arab World: Exploring the Grey Zones' (Washington, DC: Carnegie Endowment for International Peace/Herbert-Quandt-Stiftung, 2006).
[126] 'A Summary of the Political Project for the Future Syria', p. 13.

made heavy use of Quranic verses, including in its legitimation of democracy. It noted that the

> principles of constitutional governance within the modern state generally agrees with the teachings of Islam and its general principles of equality, justice and shura. These principles are the most elementary within the Islamic political system and the most prominent amongst the main objectives of Islamic Shari'ah. The Group believes that the electoral parliamentary system which derives its credibility from free and fair ballot boxes, is one of the practical means through which the objectives of Shari'ah and its general rules within the political system can be attained.[127]

In this way too, the group's tone had softened, including the statement that, 'we in no way suggest nor imply that we consider ourselves to be the group that represents all Muslims, or that we are guardians over people in the name of Islam'.[128] However, it specified that the official religion of Syria should be Islam, which should also provide 'the main and highest source of reference for all legislation, whilst the people are the source of authority'.[129]

The Political Project was regularly referred to throughout the 2011 uprising by Brotherhood leaders as the essential guide to the group's plans. It in some ways seemed a sense of pride for the group's members in that it reflected the strong and consistent lineage of democratic thought articulated by the group's founding leaders, while also demonstrating its capacity to innovate and respond to new political developments. In the half century following Mustafa al-Sibai's death, the group demonstrated that the philosophies of its founding fathers had left a deep imprint. Its political platforms had not wavered in their commitment to democracy even in the face of Said Hawwa's influential ideology, pressure from its membership base or in the changing political environment. As a result, while some observers interpreted the Brotherhood's 2000s documents as an innovation, democratic thought can be observed in every Brotherhood political platform over six decades, starting with Mustafa al-Sibai's message and example. This stands in stark contrast to the Hama-centric view of the Brotherhood that ascribes violence, undemocratic philosophy and dogmatism as core group features. It is remarkable given that for much of its life, the Brotherhood has existed in Syria under largely non-democratic regimes. Indeed, its political aspirations were in many ways aligned more with its conservative secular political opponents than to other Islamist movements.

---

[127] Ibid., p. 16. [128] Ibid., p. 4. [129] Ibid., p. 18.

However, as Chapter 3 shows, the Muslim Brotherhood was never a particularly ideological organisation. While its political decision-making rarely contradicted its stated principles, those decisions were more shaped by three other factors: (1) The group's founding organisational characteristics of individualism, pragmatism and ideological flexibility; (2) the group's operating context; and (3) political opportunities. Nonetheless, the written documents discussed in this chapter are significant because they reflect the way that the Muslim Brotherhood communicates with its audience and how it would like to be perceived. The Political Project in particular, as the beneficiary of the Brotherhood's lengthy ideological work and close ties to its base proved particularly important, as it was the group's last official word before the 2011 uprising.

3 The Brotherhood's Political Practice

As the 2011 uprising unfolded, it became clear that the Brotherhood's political history, rather than its platforms, was standing in the way of its popular rehabilitation. Ideology and practice invariably intermingle, sometimes guiding or producing political outcomes. This was true to an extent in the Brotherhood's case, in that its largely conventional ideological views supported mainstream political decision-making, or at least never stood in its way. However, the Brotherhood's political behaviour has been even more strongly coloured by interaction between its founding characteristics of individualism, pragmatism and flexibility, and the environment in which it found itself. While Syria's fledgling democratic system in the post-independence era saw the Brotherhood act as a democratic political group, this shifted under the Ba'th as its traits of pragmatism and flexibility helped it negotiate the new authoritarian operating environment, and produced behaviours different to its previous formations and also at times distant from its stated principles.

Brotherhood members in the uprising remained certain that its history was a source of strength that underlined its democratic ambitions. Senior Brotherhood figure Farouq Tayfour argued:

We have existed in Syria well before the Ba'ath [Party]. Since 1945, our history has been one of participation. The Muslim Brotherhood acted as a real partner during the free era. In the free era, we were partners in democracy. In the era of dictatorship, we were imprisoned for [voicing] objection to [the regime].[1]

From a policy perspective, the Brothers' participation in democracy was not a major stretch, as it was consistent with their early political documents. This was embedded and put into practice by the group's first two leaders, Mustafa al-Sibai and Issam al-Attar, who led by example by

---

[1] Hazim al-Amine, 'Leader of Syrian Muslim Brotherhood Discloses Secret Offer from Iran', *Al-Monitor* (originally published in *al-Hayat*, translated by Naria Tanoukhi) (20 January 2012), www.al-monitor.com/pulse/politics/2012/01/tayfour-to-al-hayat-iran-offered.html#ixzz47rSW2vW2.

participating in parliament during their leadership tenures. The group's future leader Shaykh Abd al-Fatah abu Ghuddah was also represented in parliament during this time,[2] signalling that the group's participation in secular processes enjoyed sanction from the highest echelons of the Syrian organisation across three generations of leaders. Syria's democratic era was a foundational period for the Brotherhood. Although politically tumultuous, it is widely remembered by members as the group's halcyon era because it was the only time that the Brotherhood has ever enjoyed any semblance of political freedom.[3]

The Brotherhood, starting in a small way, contested the 1947 elections by endorsing an electoral list with the Rabitat al-Ulama (The League of the Ulama) in Damascus, as well as a series of independent candidates across the rest of the country. The group backed its most senior members for election, including Mahmud al-Shaqfeh in Hama, Muhammad al-Mubarak in Damascus and Maruf al-Dawalibi in Aleppo.[4] The Damascus list included three further Brotherhood candidates, Abd al-Hamid al-Tabba, Ahmad Mazhar al-Azma and Arif al-Taraqji. Al-Tabba and al-Azma were close to Jamiyat al-Gharra and al-Tamaddun al-Islam and therefore commanded significant personal followings. The remaining list was made up of high-profile secular independents such as Zaki al-Khatib and Ali Buzu, the latter whose Kurdish background did not appear to discourage the group's support.[5] The list also included Nuri al-Ibish and Faris al-Khuri, two candidates whom Teitelbaum dubbed 'assured of victory'.[6] In line with the electoral system, which allocated seats for Syria's religious sects and minorities, the list endorsed four Christians and one Jew.[7] Although the endorsement of minorities in itself is not significant in the context of the electoral rules, the Brotherhood's decision to choose high-performing minority candidates who could actually exercise significant influence in parliament should they be elected suggests that the group took its stated pluralist principles seriously.

---

[2] Abu Ghuddah won an Aleppan seat in the 1961 parliament. For full results of the 1961 election, see: Yitzhak Oron, *Middle East Record*, vol. 2 (Jerusalem: Tel Aviv University, 1961), pp. 503–5.
[3] Interview with Hassan al-Hachimi, Istanbul, 30 August 2015.
[4] R. Bayly-Winder, 'Islam as the State Religion a Muslim Brotherhood View in Syria', p. 216; Robert G. Rabil, 'The Syrian Muslim Brotherhood', in *The Muslim Brotherhood: The Organization and Policies of a Global Islamist Movement*, ed. Barry Rubin (New York: Palgrave Macmillan, 2010), p. 74.
[5] 'The List of the Umma', *Al-Manar*, 7 July 1947; John Gardener, 'NY 1012/1 – Leading personalities in Syria', UK Foreign Office, 15 January 1955.
[6] Joshua Teitelbaum, 'The Muslim Brotherhood and the "Struggle for Syria"', 1947–1958: Between Accommodation and Ideology', *Middle Eastern Studies* 40, no. 3 (2004), p. 137.
[7] M.C. Man, 'E 11501/1018/89 – Syrian Electoral Law', UK Foreign Office, 19 September 1949; 'The List of the Umma', *Al-Manar*, 7 July 1947.

Table 3.1 *Brotherhood electoral activity 1947–63*[8]

Year	Total seats	Total Brotherhood seats won	Brotherhood seats won in Damascus
1947	136	≥3 (≥2.2 %)*	≥1
1949	114	3 (2.6 %)–4 (3.5%)**	3 (23 %)
1954	141	5 (3.5 %)	3 (18.7 %)
1961	173	10 (5.8 %)	3 (17.6 %)

* Plus at least four from the *Rabiṭat al-Ulama* list
** Possible two others from the Islamic Socialist Front list
For a more detailed table of the Brotherhood's political engagement, including available candidate lists, see Appendix One.

The candidate choices spoke volumes about the Brotherhood's political priorities more broadly. Its endorsement of three high-profile founding members as candidates suggests that parliamentary activity was core to the group's interests and that it wanted to be taken seriously by both constituents and the parliament. Its decision to also endorse well-known *jamiyat* members and non-Brotherhood candidates indicated that the group's leaders gave meticulous consideration to local realpolitik, with the aim of maximising electoral outcomes. Indeed, from its earliest political interaction, the Brotherhood showed itself as an astute, rational and pragmatic actor, with significant political ambitions.

The group's 1947 election results (Table 3.1) were modest, but voters elected several senior Brotherhood figures. Mustafa al-Sibai welcomed the outcome, telegramming Hassan al-Banna in Cairo to tell him that

> The election ended with the victory of three candidates from the Muslim Brotherhood: Dr. Ma'ruf al-Dawalibi, Muhammad al-Mubarak and Mahmud al-Shaqafeh [sic]. This marks the first time official representatives of the Islamic idea were elected to parliament in any Islamic or Arab State.[9]

Despite the leadership's enthusiasm, the group's integration into the parliamentary scene was not without challenges. One of the Brotherhood's

---

[8] Table 3.1 addresses all parliamentary elections (excluding by-elections) held between 1946 and 1963. Owing to the lack of complete electoral data and the need to harvest the best possible information from multiple sources, entries in this table may not be entirely accurate. The table uses the best possible data sources. Where results are unclear or disputed, the table uses the symbol '≥' to depict that some sources report higher numbers. The data is collated from a combination of: Hanna Batatu, 'Syria's Muslim Brethren', *MERIP Reports*, no. 110 (1982), p. 17; Patrick Seale, *The Struggle for Syria* (London: Oxford University Press, 1965), p. 182; Eyal Zisser, 'Syria', in *Elections in Asia and the Pacific: A Data Handbook: Volume I: Middle East*, ed. Dieter Nohlen, Florian Grotz and Christof Hartmann (Oxford: Oxford University Press, 2001), p. 225.

[9] Cited in Teitelbaum, 'The Muslim Brotherhood and the "Struggle for Syria"', pp. 137–8.

founding members, Mahmud al-Shaqfeh, resigned from his elected position that same year, declaring that he 'saw the sharia of Islam crying'.[10]

Nonetheless, the group's calculus on well-known non-Brotherhood candidates paid off – according to the British Embassy in Damascus, Nuri al-Ibish won the largest number of votes.[11] Other *Rabitat al-Ulama* list candidates were elected, including the Jewish Wahid Mizrahi,[12] Christian Faris al-Khuri,[13] and Zaki al-Khatib.[14] Some took up executive positions, including al-Ibish, who became the Minister of Agriculture in two cabinets. Al-Khuri became Parliamentary Speaker from 1947 to 1949, continued his role as the Syrian Representative on the UN Security Council (1946–8) and was the head of the Syrian delegation to the UN General Assembly in 1947.[15] Zaki al-Khatib would later become the Minister of Justice and Ali Buzo the People's Party Minister of Agriculture in the 1950 cabinet.[16] Indeed, the Brotherhood's electoral alliances suggested that the group had a serious interest in the political process.

This would not be the last time the Brotherhood formed short-term alliances with other political groups. The group later worked with Akram al-Hourani's Socialist Party to oppose the proposed unification of Syria and Iraq,[17] allied with the communists to organise anti-government protests after opposition was banned under the Shishakli dictatorship and joined with Nasserites in student union elections.[18] At times, the Brotherhood even allied with Syria's independence-era elite – Mustafa al-Sibai enjoyed the backing of National Party figures during his 1957 by-election campaign in Damascus, while in 1961 the Islamic Cooperative Bloc (headed by Issam al-Attar) included at least one National Party member.[19] By the end of the democratic era, the relationship between the Brotherhood and the popular conservative People's Party was so close that the Brotherhood absorbed many People's Party members after

---

[10] Thomas Pierret, *Religion and State in Syria: The Sunni Ulama from Coup to Revolution* (Cambridge: Cambridge University Press, 2013), p. 173.
[11] M.C. Man, 'E 11904/1012/89 No. 16 – Leading Personalities in Syria', *UK Foreign Office*, 1949.
[12] "Letter dated January 12', *American Minister at Damascus*, 1949.
[13] Man, 'E 11904/1012/89 No. 16'. UK Foreign Office.
[14] Sami M. Moubayed, *Steel & Silk: Men and Women Who Shaped Syria 1900–2000* (Seattle: Cune Press, 2006), p. 275.
[15] Man, 'E 11904/1012/89 No. 16'. UK Foreign Office.
[16] William Montagu-Pollock, 'EY 1015/31 No. 11 – Political Situation', *British Embassy Damascus*.
[17] Fred H. Lawson, *Global Security Watch: Syria* (Denver: Praeger, 2013), p. 62.
[18] Walter Z. Laqueur, *Communism and Nationalism in the Middle East* (London: Routledge & Paul, 1956), p. 160.
[19] Naum al-Suyufi, who became the Minister of Planning in the al-Dawalibi cabinet. See Yitzhak Oron, *Middle East Record*, vol. 2, p. 507.

the latter's dissolution following the 1963 coup.[20] One Brotherhood associate argued that the People's Party's function as a mainstream conservative party 'was taken over by the Brotherhood' after 1963.[21] The willingness of other groups to work with the Brotherhood underlined the mainstream nature of its political behaviour and positions.

Domestically, the group showed itself to be closely attuned to political trends, especially in relation to the language *du jour* – socialism. The Brotherhood's main competitors at the ballot box were the Ba'th and Communist parties who both espoused potent left-wing positions that appealed to Syria's lower and middle classes. The sense that the group was adapting its policies in response to its competition was evident in a dispatch from the British Embassy in Damascus in 1947 that showed the Brotherhood attempting overtly to appeal to the workers. The dispatch reported *al-Manar* publishing an article that urged 'workers to abandon foreign doctrines, to rally to the Moslem [sic] Brotherhood, and to follow the teachings of Mohammad, rather than those of Stalin, Lenin and Molotov'.[22] The Brotherhood applied this thinking in policy, with the US Legation in Damascus noting in 1947 that the socially focused ideological and policy principles outlined in a Brotherhood policy statement were 'in line with the thinking of advanced social security advocates'.[23]

At the next election in November 1949, the group ran under the banner of the 'Islamic Socialist Front' in Damascus, giving further momentum to its efforts to mould its own principles with a socialist flavour. The group supported Brotherhood candidates across the country, with Mustafa al-Sibai elected to the parliament for the first time and becoming a member of the committee charged with drafting Syria's new constitution.[24] Although the Brotherhood's leaders distinguished themselves from the atheistic ideology of their competitors, Brotherhood member and a leader of the Islamic Socialist Front parliamentary coalition Muhammad al-Mubarak described the Front's ideology as a 'Marxist drink in a Moslem [sic] cup'.[25] The Front's 1949 political manifesto supported land and tax reform, workers' rights and social equality.[26]

---

[20] Interview with Ali al-Bayanouni, London. [21] Anonymous interview.

[22] 'E 12267/213/89 – Weekly Political Summary No. 241', *UK Foreign Office*, week ending 3 December 1947.

[23] Cited in Joshua Teitelbaum, 'The Muslim Brotherhood in Syria, 1945–1958: Founding, Social Origins, Ideology', *The Middle East Journal* 65, no. 2 (2011), p. 229.

[24] W. Montagu-Pollock, 'EY 1012/1 – Leading personalities in Syria', *British Embassy Damascus*, 2 July 1951.

[25] Andrew Rathmell, *Secret War in the Middle East: The Covert Struggle for Syria 1949–1961* (London: I.B. Tauris, 2013), p. 11.

[26] Teitelbaum, 'The Muslim Brotherhood and the "Struggle for Syria"', p. 140.

The Brotherhood's merging of Islam and socialism may seem cynical, but it was accompanied by one of Mustafa al-Sibai's best-known ideological tracts *The Socialism of Islam*, which interpreted socialism through the lens of humanism, rather than class struggle, and therefore articulated parallels in Islamic thought.[27] Al-Sibai argued that, while the world had recently embraced socialist calls for *al-Takaful al-Ijtimai* (mutual or joint responsibility) in societies,

> Islam recognised this fourteen centuries ago. After legislating for each citizen the Five Rights, without which human dignity and happiness could not be fulfilled, it [Islam] looked at those whose circumstances prevented their enjoyment of [the Five Rights] and held society responsible for making them possible.[28]

Sibai described these five rights as *haq al-hayat* (The Right to Live), *haq al-hurriyah* (The Right of Freedom), *haq al-ilm* (The Right of Education), *haq al-tamalluk* (The Right of Ownership) and *haq al-karamah* (The Right of Dignity).[29] This translated into advocacy for economic equality, which would require improving the conditions of workers, placing small limitations on land ownership, free education for all Syrians and a strong and independent economy.[30] However, it notably preserved the Brotherhood's commitment to private property, prompting Teitelbaum to declare the model 'little more than classical liberalism; it was at most a vaguely articulated form of social democracy'.[31]

The Brotherhood's relationship to socialism exemplified the intertwined and often contradictory influence of its organisational characteristics. The group's willingness to engage in meaningful debate about socialism and how this related to its own goals demonstrated the scale of its pragmatism and ideological flexibility. Although on the face of it, socialism contradicted everything the Brotherhood stood for, the group was able to morph its own positions to adopt socialism's main lessons of equality. In many ways, this demonstrated a sponge-like quality, whereby the group could absorb any political mood and adapt as necessary. This proved a significant strength in the parliamentary era, as it enabled the Brotherhood to be

---

[27] *Ishtirakiyyat al-Islam* (The Socialism of Islam) was published as a book, and remains one of the most authoritative attempts by an Islamist to take on the socialism question. The book was later adopted by Abd al-Nasser's regime in Egypt despite its crackdown on the Egyptian Brothers.
[28] Mustafa Al-Siba'i, 'Mutual Responsibility', in *Islamism: A Documentary and Reference Guide*, ed. John Calvert (Westport: Greenwood Press, 2008), p. 83.
[29] Mustafa Al-Sibai, 'Al-Takaful al-Ijtimai', in *Arab Socialism [al-Ishtirakīyah Al-'Arabīyah]: A Documentary Survey*, ed. Sami Ayad Hanna and George H. Gardner (Leiden: Brill, 1969), pp. 149–71 at p. 169.
[30] Umar F. Abd-allah, *The Islamic Struggle in Syria* (Berkeley: Mizan Press, 1983), p. 94.
[31] Teitelbaum, 'The Muslim Brotherhood in Syria', p. 223.

a modern and responsive representative of the will of its constituents. Some members' rejection of this socialist veneer also underlined the ongoing significance of individualism and ideological diversity in the group's operation. Brotherhood founding member Muhammad al-Hamid left the group in the 1950s in opposition to these socialist positions.[32] In 1964, al-Hamid published a lengthy rebuttal of Sibai's *The Socialism of Islam*.[33]

The December 1949 parliament was important because the Brotherhood gained its first executive experience, with two members appointed to the cabinet. From December 1949 until May 1950 (when the entire cabinet resigned), Muhammad al-Mubarak was the Syrian Minister of Public Works, while Maruf al-Dawalibi (a Brotherhood member elected to the parliament as a member of the People's Party) was the Minister of National Economy.[34] Al-Dawalibi became Parliamentary Speaker in 1951 and briefly served as the Prime Minister.[35] The Brotherhood's approach to executive participation was facilitated by the pragmatism that guided its ideological thinking and political behaviour. Islamist representatives in executive positions often favour responsibilities in the *awqaf* (endowments), culture or justice ministries related to their own reform agendas. In some cases, members of groups such as the Islamist Islah in Yemen complained about being given technical cabinet positions (such as Health, Electricity and Water, and Supply and Trade) that curbed their cultural influence and 'political space', and forced them to make difficult decisions that would be unpopular with their constituency.[36] This contrasted sharply with the Brotherhood, which appeared to prize its technocratic positions. In fact, the importance of its cabinet presence was reportedly a factor in the group's decision to compromise on the role of Islam in the state's new constitution in 1950. Reissner argued that the Brotherhood's decision was coloured by the group's awareness that failing to resolve the constitutional issue could trigger early elections in which the Brotherhood may have lost Muhammad al-Mubarak's ministerial post.[37]

---

[32] Itzchak Weismann, 'The Politics of Popular Religion: Sufis, Salafis, and Muslim Brothers in 20th-Century Hamah', *International Journal of Middle East Studies* 37, no. 1 (2005), p. 52.
[33] Ibid., p. 53.   [34] Montagu-Pollock, 'EY 1012/1 – Leading personalities in Syria'.
[35] Moubayed, *Steel & Silk*, p. 221.
[36] For a discussion of this, see Jillian Schwedler, *Faith in Moderation: Islamist Parties in Jordan and Yemen* (Cambridge: Cambridge University Press, 2006), p. 104. See also: 'The Islah Party in Yemen: Politics Opportunities and Coalition Building in a Transitional Society', in *Islamic Activism: A Social Movement Theory Approach*, ed. Quintan Wiktorowicz (Bloomington: University of Indiana Press, 2004), p. 208.
[37] Cited in Thomas Pierret, *Religion and State in Syria: The Sunni Ulama from Coup to Revolution* (Cambridge: Cambridge University Press, 2011), p. 174.

The Brotherhood's fortunes waned during Adib al-Shishakli's dictatorship between 1949 and 1954, when at one point the group was formally banned. To survive, the Brotherhood adopted a low profile, which Abd-Allah described as turning 'toward politically neutral areas concerned with the "religious and moral education" of the people'.[38] Notably, it did not mobilise violent protests, even though some of the Brotherhood youth received a level of paramilitary training in the 1940s and many members participated in the 1948 Palestine war. Such skills could have been used to agitate against the Shishakli regime should the Brotherhood have considered it a worthy choice. The fact that this tactical option was not taken suggests that there was something unique about the period post-1963 that led the group to sanction violence.

The Syrian Brothers did not contest the 1954 election, which was the first free poll after the Shishakli regime. However, they continued to support individual candidates. Mustafa al-Sibai wrote in the group's newspaper *al-Manar* that the Brotherhood had withdrawn from the electoral process because the 'political arena had enough activists, while the area of social reform lacks activists'.[39] More broadly, as Rabil noted, President Gamal abd al-Nasser's populist rise in Egypt created a serious conundrum for the group: 'How to reconcile their opposition to "imperialist" plans with support for Nasser, whose popularity had surged within the ranks of the Baʿth and the Communist parties in Syria?'[40] In 1957, al-Sibai ran in a by-election, but narrowly lost to Baʿth candidate Riad al-Malki, who was the brother of the high-profile Syrian Army Lieutenant Colonel Adnan al-Malki who had been assassinated in 1955.[41] Although al-Sibai received 47 percent of the vote, Roded noted that 'Malki's victory was a harbinger of the rising power of the Baʿth party and Arab socialism rather than Islamist socialism'.[42] That same year, al-Sibai had a debilitating stroke and was forced to hand the Brotherhood's leadership over to Issam al-Attar. The group's position then worsened after Syria and Egypt merged to form the United Arab Republic (UAR) in 1958, when it was again banned.

The Brotherhood returned to politics in the first post-UAR parliament in 1961, achieving its best ever election result. The group won ten

---

[38] Abd-allah, *The Islamic Struggle in Syria*, p. 100.
[39] Cited in Teitelbaum, 'The Muslim Brotherhood and the "Struggle for Syria"', p. 151.
[40] Robert G. Rabil, 'The Syrian Muslim Brotherhood', p. 76.
[41] Raymond Hinnebusch, *Authoritarian Power and State Formation in Bathist Syria: Army, Party and Peasant* (Boulder: Westview Press, 1991).
[42] Ruth Roded, 'Lessons by a Syrian Islamist from the Life of the Prophet Muhammad', *Middle Eastern Studies* 42, no. 6 (2006), p. 863.

seats, more than doubling its pre-UAR record. Seven of these seats were outside Damascus, implying what Hinnebusch observed as 'a broadening of its geographic base'.[43] The Brotherhood's new leader, Issam al-Attar received the second-largest number of votes in Damascus[44] and became 'one of the most influential personalities in Syrian politics'.[45] Muhammad al-Mubarak and a number of leading Syrian political figures had signed the National Charter prior to the elections, which committed Syria to Arab unity, Arab socialism, agrarian reform and the principles of democratic rule.[46] This period marked the apex of the group's political career, with the Brotherhood again returning to cabinet. Mustafa al-Zarqa was appointed to the positions of Minister of Justice and Minister of *Awqaf*, while Maruf al-Dawalibi became Prime Minister again from December 1961 to March 1962. The group enjoyed four seats in Khalid al-Azm's 1962 cabinet.[47] Said Hawwa later argued in his memoir that the Syrian Muslim Brotherhood's participation in ministries 'enriched the Islamic experience'.[48]

The Brotherhood's pragmatism towards its ministerial positions was seen again in 1962. Issam al-Attar mounted a scathing criticism of the government's perceived closeness to the Soviet bloc through the Brotherhood's two Damascus-based newspapers *al-Manar* and *al-Liwa*, even though the Brotherhood had three cabinet members at the time. In embassy communication that underlined both the British government's failure to understand the Brotherhood, as well as the Orientalist lens through which it was viewed, the British Ambassador to Syria Thomas Blomley dryly noted:

A westerner might be forgiven for expecting that a public attack on the government by the head of a politico-religious group such as the Moslem [*sic*] Brotherhood would have as its logical consequence the resignation of that group's ministers from the cabinet. That this has not happened is probably because Issam [al-]Attar realised that the withdrawal of the three Ministers of his persuasion would not achieve a change in the Prime Minister's policies, let along unseat him, but it would inevitably leave the field open to the Baathists and Socialists, who would then dominate the cabinet.[49]

---

[43] Raymond Hinnebusch, 'Syria', in *The Politics of Islamic Revivalism: Diversity and Unity*, ed. Shireen T. Hunter (Bloomington: Indiana University Press, 1988), p. 49.
[44] Yitzhak Oron, *Middle East Record*, vol. 2, p. 503.
[45] Abd-allah, *The Islamic Struggle in Syria*, p. 101.
[46] Yitzhak Oron, *Middle East Record*, vol. 2, p. 503.
[47] Thomas Mayer, 'The Islamic Opposition in Syria 1961–1982', *Orient* 24, no. 4 (1983), p. 591.
[48] Said Hawwa, *This Is My Experience and This Is My Testimony (in Arabic)* (Cairo: Maktabat Wahba, 1987), p. 67.
[49] FO 371/164385. *British Embassy Damascus*. 27 November 1962.

Al-Attar's strategy further underlined the Brotherhood's pragmatism in relation to cabinet positions; the group was willing to loudly voice its criticisms, but it would not sacrifice its own position by resigning from cabinet. In this way, the Brotherhood's early leaders considered achieving incremental reform to be preferable to being locked outside the political game.

This pragmatism had limits, though, with the group demonstrating that it would not accept political power at any price. The Brotherhood boycotted the run-off elections in 1949 after it emerged that a number of National List ballots had been forged,[50] and the group's Islamic Socialist Front declared in May 1950 that it would no longer participate in cabinet following army interference in the political process.[51] This was seen again in 1962, when Issam al-Attar refused to participate in a coup organised by Syrian military officer Abd al-Karim al-Nahlawi, even though it would have guaranteed him more influence. Al-Attar later justified the decision by saying: 'I am a man of principles and I never thought that military involvement into [sic] politics could bring any good to democracy'[52] Months later, when President Nazim al-Qudsi offered al-Attar the prime ministership in exchange for supporting al-Qudsi's planned crackdown on his political opponents, al-Attar again refused on the grounds of 'the principles of liberty and justice which I have always cherished in my heart'.[53] Indeed, despite the tumult, the Brotherhood was committed to upholding the rules and principles that guided Syria's democratic era.

The Brotherhood's political behaviour over its founding decades therefore conveyed a picture of a party that was a rational and strategic political actor. Although it never enjoyed significant electoral success, it demonstrated a willingness to adapt policies, participate in government and form pacts with other parties across the ideological spectrum to maximise its influence and bring it into the political mainstream. Like other groups, the Brotherhood was moulded by its experiences, given that its very formation and institutionalisation took place in the context of Syrian parliamentary politics. In this regard, the group's foundational democratic experience may go some way to explaining its contemporary pluralist sympathies, which seem more deeply embedded in the group's psyche than those of many other movements in the region. This

[50] Man, 'E 11904/1012/89 No. 16'. UK Foreign Office.
[51] M.C. Man, 'EY 1015/18 No. 5 – Formation of a Cabinet under Nazim al-Qudsi', *UK Embassy Damascus*, 5 June 1950.
[52] Cited in Raphaël Lefèvre, *Ashes of Hama: The Muslim Brotherhood in Syria* (London: Hurst, 2013), p. 87.
[53] Ibid.

parliamentary period might also provide a useful indicator of the Brotherhood's future electoral appeal. Considering the group's limited record of electoral success between 1946 and 1963, and its subsequent exile and poor reputation, it could be expected to struggle to build a significant electoral base should free and fair elections ever be reintroduced in Syria.

Opposition to the Ba'th: 1963–2011

The Brotherhood's operating environment changed drastically after the Ba'th coup in 1963, ending Syria's democratic era and heralding a level of authoritarianism unprecedented in the country. Although the Brotherhood never renounced its stated democratic principles, the experience of Ba'th authoritarianism had a profound impact on the group, creating significant physical and cultural changes that impeded its ability to operate, and that shaped every subsequent political decision. As already noted, the Brotherhood underwent significant external and internal change during this period. Soon after the 1963 coup the Brotherhood was outlawed, causing an immediate reduction in the group's opportunities for political engagement. The leadership was then substantially weakened with Mustafa al-Sibai's death and Issam al-Attar's forced exile in 1964. The years that followed were characterised by weakness in leadership, which led to a failure to mobilise against the regime, the progressive erosion of core operating principles and growing disillusionment among its base. This first manifested in the violent 1964 Hama riots, which are discussed in Chapter 4, but of equal significance was the gradual decline of the group's ability to respond to the small political opportunities that came its way under Ba'th rule.

The Brotherhood faced a significant political crisis on the eve of the Six-Day War with Israel in April 1967, when Alawite army officer Ibrahim al-Khallas penned an article in *Jaysh al-Shaab* (The People's Army) magazine, calling for the creation of 'A New Arab Man'.[54] He declared that 'God, religions, feudalism, capitalism, imperialism, and all other values that prevailed in previous society are nothing but embalmed toys in the museum of history'.[55] The article provoked furore in Syria, with thousands taking to the streets in Damascus. The Ba'th Party later condemned the article and jailed both al-Khallas and the magazine's

---

[54] The Brotherhood's first violent confrontation with the Ba'th regime took place during the Hama riots in 1964, discussed in depth in Chapter Four.
[55] '3 in Syria Sentenced to Life for an Article Attacking Religion', *The New York Times* (12 May 1967), p. 14.

editor,[56] but tensions continued to build, particularly after Syrian security forces arrested and seized the property of the popular Damascene shaykh Hassan al-Habbanaka and 45 other religious figures. An estimated 70 percent of traders in the Midan quarter of Damascus, many of whom would have been Brotherhood supporters, closed their shops in protest.[57] The regime arrested 3,000 members of the ulama, merchant and notable class over the following three weeks, and used the People's Militia and members of the labour unions to force shops to open,[58] effectively mounting a direct assault on the Muslim Brotherhood's constituency. These tensions were worsened by the country's humiliating defeat in the Six-Day War less than two months later.

Despite the Ba'th's weakness, the Brotherhood did not mobilise for a number of reasons, including the new leader Issam al-Attar's fear of bloodshed. Even had the Brotherhood possessed the political appetite, it was also organisationally ill prepared for revolt. The group's 1948 Palestine War military capacity was outdated, and by the 1960s it had little opportunity to take advantage of the political vacuum. It drew its support from the bourgeois classes and had few links to the Syrian armed forces, whose senior ranks were constituted largely of minorities and those personally loyal to President Hafez al-Assad and his brother Rifaat.[59] These were sections of the community to whom the Brotherhood had little connection. Urban Sunnis, who made up much of the Brotherhood's constituency, could usually afford to pay out their military service, and had little recent exposure to military thinking or experience.[60] As one Syrian activist close to the Brotherhood noted: 'I don't think the Brotherhood was ready then. I don't think they had the right leadership, I don't think they had the military capability, even organisationally.'[61] Indeed, the group had neither the capacity nor the political will to seriously challenge the regime during the 1960s, although, as noted in Chapter 4, some members began to take matters into their own hands.

---

[56] 'Syria Averts Protest by Jailing Writer of an "Atheistic" Article', *New York Times* (7 May 1967), p. 16.
[57] 'Syria Ousts 2 Saudi Diplomats as Active in "Anti-State Plot"', *The Jerusalem Post* (10 May 1967), p. 1.
[58] Thomas F. Brady, 'Syrians Using Force to Break a Protest Strike by Merchants', *The New York Times* (9 May 1967), p. 7.
[59] Eyal Zisser, 'The Syrian Army: Between the Domestic and the External Fronts', *Middle East Review of International Affairs* 5, no. 1 (2001), p. 3.
[60] Hanna Batatu, 'Some Observations on the Social Roots of Syria's Ruling Military Group and the Causes for Its Dominance', *Middle East Journal* 35, no. 3 (1981), p. 342.
[61] Anonymous interview.

Nonetheless, a sense of frustration and blame began to infiltrate the group's ranks. The late senior Brotherhood figure Mohamed Hansawi recalled that 'self-criticism started spreading as to how the Ba'thists had managed to take power whilst we the stronger group couldn't manage it. All that criticism was channelled towards Issam al-Attar because he was the guide.'[62] These sentiments and the sense of frustration were echoed by Said Hawwa, who noted that between the 1961 collapse of the UAR and the March 1963 coup, the Brotherhood had 'become a strong force at all levels. The Islamists were supposed to inherit' the post-UAR political era that had been potentially within their grasp.[63] A contemporary Brotherhood associate was more overt in his comments, noting that Issam al-Attar 'must be held responsible historically speaking for not saving the nation ... or not acting decisively'.[64] He added:

> There were decisive moments in which he could have done something, but he didn't. For instance, he could have stopped the Ba'th Party coup. In fact ... he was unwittingly complicit in the Ba'th coup because [when in parliament he applied pressure that] toppled the government of Khalid al-Azm who was suspected of being a closeted communist. But al-Azm was a strong prime minister, and when he fell, al-Attar kept whipping up a frenzy, Friday sermon after Friday sermon ... and that set the stage for the Ba'th party to assume control.[65]

In addition to this, as Ali al-Bayanouni reflected, al-Attar 'was always strong when it came to public speaking, but in organisational skills he wasn't as good'.[66] These latent tensions finally came to a head in the Brotherhood's 1969–71 leadership crisis, which drew the lines of a battle for power that would change the group fundamentally over the next decade. In 1971, the international wing of the Brotherhood intervened to support Aleppan members over Issam al-Attar. Al-Attar's Damascus faction left the Brotherhood soon after.

The next crisis emerged in February 1973 when the country's new president Hafez al-Assad attempted to implement a secular constitution for Syria. He proposed removing the Brotherhood's hard-fought 1950 clause that required the country's president to be Muslim.[67] The draft provoked outrage across Syria, with the Brotherhood working closely with the ulama to foment a response. Said Hawwa was one of the key opposition organisers, who Pierret noted:

> Immediately understood that the draft constitution provided the Muslim Brothers with a unique opportunity to mobilise (and shield themselves

---

[62] Cited in Alison Pargeter, *The Muslim Brotherhood: The Burden of Tradition* (London: Saqi Books, 2010), p. 67.
[63] Hawwa, *This Is My Experience*, p. 69. [64] Anonymous interview. [65] Ibid.
[66] Interview with Ali al-Bayanouni, London. [67] Lefèvre, *Ashes of Hama*.

behind) both the ulama, on religious grounds, and secular opposition parties, which were de jure marginalised.[68]

Again, the Syrian population took to the streets, with the ulama leading demonstrations across the country, particularly in Hama and Homs.[69] The British Embassy in Beirut recorded strikes by Brotherhood youth in Aleppo.[70] Hawwa collected signatures from ulama across the country with the goal of 'exploit[ing] the religiously driven anger of the clergy in pursuit of an eminently political endeavour, the destabilisation of the regime'.[71] In response, President al-Assad asked the parliament to consider 'the wishes of the people' by returning the constitutional article that proscribes Islam as the religion of the Syrian head of state. This satisfied many of the ulamas' concerns and de-escalated the crisis, much to the Brotherhood's chagrin. Al-Assad then doubled down these efforts, undertaking the Umrah in 1974 and regularly attending Friday prayers in Damascus.[72] In this regard, while Hawwa's campaign was successful insofar as al-Assad compromised on some of his demands, it both failed to improve the Brotherhood's political position and drove a wedge between the Brotherhood the ulama.[73] Several of the Brotherhood's leaders were imprisoned in the following years.[74]

These political failures were not without consequence, giving momentum to the emerging militant trend within the group that would eventually manifest as the Fighting Vanguard – a splinter faction that was prepared to confront the Ba'th. By contrast, the Brotherhood's official leaders remained committed to their original path, exemplified in their decision to pragmatically back conservative candidates in the 1972 governorate elections and the 1973 national election, which could have been construed as endorsing Ba'th rule. This increasing chasm between leadership and support base would lead to the group's near ruination the following decade.

Of equal importance to the physical and membership changes, however, was the sharp cognitive shift that began to permeate the Brotherhood. The experience of persecution and failure endowed the group with a deep-seated sense of frustration and desperation that would colour the way it interpreted political opportunities in the decades to come. Morale

---

[68] Pierret, *Religion and State*, p. 185.   [69] Hinnebusch, *Authoritarian Power*, p. 292.
[70] P.W. Ford, 'FCO 93/301 – Letter to MLH Hope – Disturbances in Syria', *British Embassy Beirut*, 26 February 1973.
[71] Pierret, *Religion and State in Syria*, p. 185.
[72] R. Hrair Dekmejian, *Islam in Revolution: Fundamentalism in the Arab World*, 2nd edn (Syracuse: Syracuse University Press), p. 108.
[73] Ibid., p. 187.   [74] Abd-allah, *The Islamic Struggle in Syria*, p. 111.

had been low in the group before, with Abd-Allah noting that after the fall of the United Arab Republic in 1961,

> The spirit of the Brotherhood had been broken, many members who had survived the nightmare of direct governmental oppression lacked their earlier self-confidence and in many cases, no doubt, felt alienated from the people themselves who had done so little to aid them or abate the oppression.[75]

This disillusionment once again became entrenched in the group. The former Brotherhood ideologue Zuhair Salem acknowledged that in later years, 'Whenever there was a national [event]... for example Independence Day, or anything that has to do with the country, we used to write something to say to the Syrian people and get them involved and convince them of our plans',[76] but the Brotherhood was able to achieve very few wins. This cumulative decades-long failure and disillusionment became an impediment to the group's thinking, evolving into a quest for survival under authoritarianism that increasingly exhibited the hallmarks of desperation and opportunism.

Negotiating with the Ba'th

One of the first areas in which the Brotherhood's changing political character was evident was in its direct negotiations with the Syrian regime. Although the Brotherhood and the regime had long been at loggerheads, the two parties engaged in both public and secret talks for decades. This became an important survival tactic, underwritten by the pragmatism the Brotherhood developed in its founding years. However, this pragmatic behaviour had become increasingly opportunistic by the 2000s, with the Brotherhood making choices with little regard for the longer-term cost.

The first Brotherhood negotiations with the Ba'th regime took place in 1978. The Fighting Vanguard had undertaken a campaign of assassinations against high-level Ba'thists, Alawites and regime officials over the preceding years, prompting increasing alarm within government ranks. Negotiations were initiated by President al-Assad while the Brotherhood's leaders were in prison. Issam al-Attar's deputy from the 1960s, Amin Yegen, led the negotiations on the Brotherhood's behalf. The group was reportedly offered a position in the regime-loyal National Progressive Front parliamentary coalition in return for a cessation of hostilities,[77] but the deal fell apart. Ali al-Bayanouni, who participated in the negotiations explained:

---

[75] Ibid., pp. 103–4. [76] Interview with Zuhair Salem, London.
[77] Anonymous interview.

The Brotherhood made the condition that everyone should be released [from prison]. All the members should be released. They released some. But after that in April 1980, they stopped releasing people and they brought them back, saying that the operation had stopped.[78]

Al-Bayanouni maintained that the negotiations collapsed because the regime had not held up its side of the bargain. Yet a Brotherhood associate with knowledge of the events claimed that the Brotherhood overplayed its hand, pretending to have more control over the Fighting Vanguard and the armed events than it really did in practice. This episode demonstrated the utility of the deliberately blurred boundaries between the Brotherhood and the Vanguard, which could be used to the Brotherhood's political advantage. According to that same Brotherhood associate:

> The Brotherhood in a very opportunistic way didn't say: 'we've got nothing to do with it' [the violence]. They decided that this is an opportunity that we can take advantage of. So they went back to Hafez al-Assad while they were still in prison and told him: 'fine, but we're not going to negotiate while we're being held in prison, and we need to speak to our base to convince them that the idea of negotiations is a good one', so he [al-Assad] said: 'Fine I will release you.' And this was the understanding: that they would come out and that they would then lay the foundation for some kind of resolution.
>
> Now, whether Hafez al-Assad was serious about this or if it was just some kind of tactical ploy ... they came out of prison, they then went to Jordan and they must have met some regional actors, Jordanian intelligence, people like that, and they reached the conclusion that the best course of action would be to declare jihad against Hafez al-Assad and join the uprising.[79]

For this associate, the Brotherhood interpreted Hafez al-Assad's overtures as a sign of weakness and an opportunity to strike. And when al-Assad realised, the deal was annulled. It has not been possible to determine which account is true, but it is known that the Brotherhood sanctioned a violent strategy against the regime in mid- to late 1979, months before April 1980 when Ali al-Bayanouni claimed that the regime had stopped releasing prisoners. Given the timeframe, the Brotherhood itself may have therefore precipitated the collapse of the deal. Another senior Brotherhood figure privately acknowledged that separate negotiations continued secretly to take place throughout the armed uprising.[80]

The group negotiated with the regime again in the mid-1980s when it was battling the sidelined status of exile. Representatives of the group met the head of Syrian military intelligence, Ali Duba, in West Germany

---

[78] Interview with Ali al-Bayanouni, London.
[79] Anonymous interview (parentheses added). [80] Ibid.

at least twice. Ali al-Bayanouni reportedly justified the decision to the Brotherhood leadership in 1984, declaring that 'we have to re-evaluate our resources and facilities. Do they permit us to achieve our goal of overthrowing the regime? If they don't, we have no alternative but to talk.'[81] These meetings were backed by the international Brotherhood, but the group subsequently concluded that the regime was not interested in rapprochement. Former Prime Minister Abdul Halim al-Khaddam later confirmed the Brotherhood's suspicions, agreeing that,

[t]here never was any serious intent on the part of the regime to actually settle the dispute with the Muslim Brotherhood, these negotiations were doomed in advance ... in reality, the regime did not wish to see any form of agreement being reached with the Muslim Brotherhood.[82]

In fact, the regime may have been attempting to exploit known divisions within the Brotherhood as it had become clear that those in the group's Hama faction did not support the talks. Former leader and head of the Hama faction, Adnan Saadeddine declared: 'There is nothing to discuss with these criminals; they are not a government, they are a mafia.'[83] The Brotherhood thus became increasingly isolated.

In the 1990s, the Brotherhood re-engaged in negotiations with the regime, often with Amin Yegen's assistance. A deal that met the group's bottom line of resuming political activity in Syria was never achieved. Nonetheless, an agreement was reached that allowed 3,000 Brothers to return to Syria as private citizens in the 1990s, including former leader Shaykh Abd al-Fatah abu Ghuddah, who returned to Aleppo in 1995.[84]

There were strong signs by the 2000s, however, that the group was becoming desperate to engage with the regime when it unilaterally suspended opposition to the al-Assad regime during the 2008–9 Gaza war. In a statement, al-Bayanouni explained:

On the occasion of the Zionist aggression against Gaza, we adopted a position of solidarity with our people in Palestine. We called on all our brothers to fulfil the call for supporting them by donating money and blood. On the occasion of this aggression, we decided to suspend our opposition activities in Syria so that all efforts will be pooled in this battle and resistance against this aggression.[85]

---

[81] Cited in Chris Kutschera, 'When the Brothers Fall Out', *The Middle East Magazine* 162 (1988), p. 21.
[82] Cited in Lefèvre, *Ashes of Hama*, p. 166.
[83] Cited in Kutschera, 'When the Brothers Fall Out', p. 21.
[84] Lefèvre, *The Muslim Brotherhood Prepares for a Comeback in Syria*, (Washington, DC: Carnegie Endowment for International Peace, 2013), p. 6.
[85] Lina Zahr-al-Din, interview with Ali Sadr-al-Din al-Bayanuni, Controller General of the Syrian Muslim Brotherhood Movement, via satellite from London, *Al-Jazeera* (London: BBC Monitoring Middle East, 4 April 2009).

The Brotherhood has long had a complex relationship with the Palestinian Hamas, which is another Brotherhood offshoot that paradoxically enjoyed the patronage of the Syrian regime. As Lefèvre noted:

> For a long time Bashar al-Assad in Syria was a fairly consensual figure in the Middle East because he was supporting the so called 'Islamic Resistance' agenda against Israel, so that meant that a lot of Muslim Brotherhood branches in the region actually supported the Syrian regime because of its fight against Israel. That put the Syrian Muslim Brotherhood on the margins of the regional Muslim Brotherhood network.[86]

Ironically, Hamas's leaders had lived safely in Syria for years, despite that membership of the Syrian group remained a capital offence. For these reasons, the Syrian Brothers had to tread carefully on the Palestine issue.

The group's opportunistic decision provoked uproar among the Brotherhood's base, and purportedly fomented the factional shift that sidelined Ali al-Bayanouni's Aleppo faction in favour of the Hama wing the following year.[87] A Brotherhood associate who was highly critical of the Brotherhood's decision stated:

> They are opportunistic … they don't stick to their word or their principles; they see where the wind is going. So at that time the flavour of the month was Hamas and Gaza … [As a result, I] lost all respect for them, because I thought, 'you guys led thousands of young men to their deaths including relatives of mine, so you have a duty at least to those to people keep fighting the regime … Even if the battle isn't going to go anywhere, at least people will recall that they [the Brotherhood] died in exile against the regime', but instead they changed. They backed down.[88]

This dramatic change in stance signalled a new level of policy pragmatism that saw the Brotherhood publicly violate one of its long-standing positions: opposition to the Baʿth regime. It went well beyond the group's previous policy of secret bilateral negotiations and was a clear legacy of its accumulated experiences as an opposition group under authoritarianism. It is worth noting that such decision-making is common among exiled groups, which often operate with a sense of urgency because of their fear of irrelevance.[89] This can at times manifest

---

[86] From 8:04: Raphaël Lefèvre, 'POMEPS Conversations 46 with Raphaël Lefèvre ~ 2/10/15 [Video]', *POMEPS* (10 February 2015) http://pomeps.org/2015/02/10/pomeps-conversations-46-with-raphael-lefevre-21015/.
[87] Aron Lund, 'The Syria Muslim Brotherhood: Leadership Transition from Bayanouni to Shaqfa', *Syria Comment* (21 August 2010), www.joshualandis.com/blog/the-syria-muslim-botherhood-leadership-transition-from-bayanouni-to-shaqfa-by-aron-lund/.
[88] Anonymous interview.
[89] Yossi Shain, *The Frontier of Loyalty: Political Exiles in the Age of the Nation-State* (Ann Arbor: University of Michigan Press, 2005), pp. 31–2.

in short-term thinking and erratic decision-making. But the Brotherhood's exaggerated flexibility and perceived willingness to pander to the Ba'th Party caused embarrassment for the group and a loss of support, leading to further political marginalisation.

The group's decision had tangible outcomes, leading to the emergence of a new splinter faction called the National Action Group (NAG) in 2010, which was made up of younger Brotherhood figures who did not wish to be part of a Hama faction-dominated Brotherhood. The NAG was founded by Ali al-Bayanouni associate Obeida Nahas, purportedly with al-Bayanouni's blessing. Al-Bayanouni acknowledges that NAG has close Brotherhood connections, noting that 'some of the Brotherhood's members came together and formed this group', but says that it is not part of the Brotherhood.[90] According to Nahas, 'there is a generational break with the Ikhwan [Brotherhood] ... the National Action Group represents a new generation of conservative technocrats working on national projects for the future of Syria ... the ideological component [in the new generation] is almost nonexistent'.[91] This was not the first formal manifestation of intergenerational tension in the group. During the 2000s, members on the Brotherhood periphery formed the Movement for Justice and Development, led by Anas al-Abdeh, whose father was close to the Muslim Brotherhood's Damascus wing.[92]

The second and perhaps more damaging impact of the 2009 decision was its ambiguity on the eve of the uprising, which became a source of suspicion for many opposition figures. The Brotherhood's then-leader Riad al-Shaqfeh ended the suspension in August 2010, saying that 'this war in Gaza is over now ... Therefore, our opposition to the regime has been reinstated.'[93] But this was purportedly contradicted in a subsequent interview, as well as by a statement on the Brotherhood's website. This prompted senior Syrian activist Najib Ghadban to conclude: 'The new Brotherhood leadership seems still undecided whether to resume opposition officially.'[94] The Brotherhood appeared to be once again leveraging

---

[90] Interview with Ali al-Bayanouni, London.
[91] Cited in Lefèvre, *Ashes of Hama*, p. 197 (parenthesis added).
[92] 'Syria in Crisis – The Damascus Declaration', *Carnegie Middle East Center* (1 March 2012), http://carnegie-mec.org/diwan/48514?lang=en.
[93] Fahd al-Argha Al-Masri, 'Muslim Brotherhood Chief Announces End of "Truce" with Syria', *Free Syria* (London: BBC Monitoring Middle East, 2010).
[94] Najib Ghadbian, 'New Syrian Brotherhood Leader: Continuity or Change?', *Carnegie Endowment for International Peace* (8 September 2010), http://carnegieendowment.org/sada/?fa=41527.

the 'grey area' in order to hedge its bets. This represented a significant sore spot in intra-opposition relations in 2011 because the Brotherhood was seen to have appeased the Baʿth on the eve of the uprising, even though Syrians inside the country continued to suffer under the tyranny of Baʿth rule.

Alliance-Making in the Context of Authoritarianism

The Brotherhood's newfound opportunism became pronounced even earlier in its alliance-making. The group continued to engage with opposition groups from across the political spectrum while in exile, but these alliances became short-lived and tumultuous, in contrast to the group's electoral alliances in the democratic era. This is consistent with patterns seen in other authoritarian jurisdictions such as Morocco, in which opposition coalitions are rarely long lasting because they are founded on a narrow base.

The Brotherhood's first significant opposition alliance under the Baʿth emerged in 1980 in the Syrian Islamic Front (SIF), an umbrella group consisting of the Brotherhood, the Fighting Vanguard and the Brotherhood's former Damascus wing. The SIF was a single-issue alliance, with the three parties having little more in common than their joint hatred of the Baʿth.[95] One Brotherhood official privately admitted that the Front was formed largely as an 'attempt [by the Brotherhood leadership] to contain the Fighting Vanguard'.[96] It suffered from a number of flaws, including the fact that its leadership was based in exile, whereas the majority of its followers languished inside the country. It was also crippled by intergroup tension, and was therefore never particularly effective.

Nonetheless, the SIF disintegrated in 1981 when a draft of the terms of agreement for a new alliance between the Brotherhood and secular parties was leaked.[97] The document showed that the Brotherhood had been secretly negotiating a new alliance with other parties without the knowledge of its SIF partners. Controversially, the new alliance included exiled secularists such as Syrian Baʿthists based in Iraq, Riad al-Turk's

---

[95] Francesco Cavatorta, '"Divided they Stand, Divided They Fail": Opposition Politics in Morocco', *Democratization* 16, no. 1 (2009), pp 147–56 at p. 141.
[96] Anonymous interview.
[97] Muslim Brotherhood, 'Text of the project offered by Adnan Saad al-Din and Ali Sadr al-Din al-Bayanouni as Part of a National Alliance with Opposition Political Parties and Groups for Rule in Syria (in Arabic)', 1981,. Available in Umar abd Al-Hakim, *The Islamic Jihadi Revolution in Syria (in Arabic)* (Peshawar: Unknown, 1991), p. 598.

Communist Party, Akram al-Hourani's Arab Socialist Party and the Socialist Union. It enjoyed Iraq's backing.[98] The leak immediately prompted both Issam al-Attar's Damascus group and the Fighting Vanguard to split from the SIF. The Vanguard leader Adnan Uqlah furiously declared:

> The Muslim Brotherhood and anyone who agrees with or supports the alliance [with secular parties], or anyone who is aware of this alliance yet remains loyal to those leaders and organizations, is a heretic, blasphemer and infidel![99]

A Fighting Vanguard official later explained:

> An agreement for a unified leadership was signed to group all forces against the regime, but it went the opposite way. Our forces were frozen because the others are not trained and are not ready to fight. We made three conditions for joining the leadership: that we would not lay down our arms or give up jihad, that we would never negotiate with the regime and that there would be no alliance with the political parties. They did not stick to their word and made a secret alliance with the political parties.[100]

A third Vanguard member complained that the Brotherhood 'traded a good son for someone pretending to be friendly'.[101]

Nonetheless, the Brotherhood swiftly recovered, announcing the formation of the National Alliance for the Liberation of Syria with its new partners in March 1982. An article in *al-Nadhir* discussed the alliance on 27 March, declaring it 'a natural development and outcome of the struggle between [*sic*] our people and the criminal sectarian regime of Syria'.[102] It further explained:

> Al-Mujahideen [*sic*] have – right from the beginning of the struggle realized that the most effective weapon against Assad's regime (after relying on Allah's help) is a unified struggle of all the people. This was declared by al-mujahideen [*sic*] in the 'Programme of the Islamic Revolution' which was issued more than two years ago. The continuity of the struggle has proved the validity of this view as the revolution is daily gaining more people and new groups to its side. The Islamic Front of Syria which united most of the Islamic groups under the banner of jihad came into existence following the first phase of the struggle,

---

[98] Tareq Y. Ismael and Jacqueline S. Ismael, *The Communist Movement in Syria and Lebanon* (Gainesville: University Press of Florida, 1998), p. 197.

[99] Abu Musab Al-Suri, 'Lessons Learned from the Armed Jihad Ordeal in Syria', translated and published by the Combatting Terrorism Centre (CTC), West Point, www.ctc.usma.edu/v2/wp-content/uploads/2013/10/Lessons-Learned-from-the-Jihad-Ordeal-in-Syria-Translation.pdf, p. 13.

[100] Kutschera, 'Syria: Muslim Brothers', p. 28. [101] Al-Suri, 'Lessons Learned', p. 32.

[102] 'Editorial: The Declaration of the National Alliance for the Liberation of Syria', *Al-Nadhir No. 45 (English edition)*, (27 March 1982), p. 2.

and it is now necessary for all the national groups to unite in order to save the country from Assad's gang. This is the reason for the formation of the national alliance.[103]

Although the Brotherhood painted the decision as a next logical step for the SIF, in reality the SIF had dissolved before the Alliance was formalised. This breakup marked an early example of the Brotherhood's evolution from a pragmatic to an opportunistic group. It was no longer a reliable alliance partner because its emerging utilitarian tendency prioritised short-term gains out of fear for its survival. Desperation for relevance had eroded some of the political aptitude that once defined the group's modus operandi. This proved particularly short sighted: Rabinovich observed soon after that 'despite the breadth of its membership, the Alliance has been unable to generate a new wave of effective opposition or even to create the impression abroad that the Asad [sic] regime faced a serious challenge'.[104]

This pattern of alliance opportunism worsened with time, with the Brotherhood at one point even purportedly reaching out to Hafez al-Assad's brother Rifaat, whose leadership of the defence companies during the Hama uprising had earned him the moniker 'Butcher of Hama'. After attempting to seize power in 1984, Rifaat had been forced into exile, and at some point made contact with the Brotherhood.[105] The process hastened after Bashar al-Assad's came to power in 2000 and consolidated his regime against the odds, leaving the Brotherhood in exile with little prospect of return. Under these circumstances, the Brotherhood transgressed to embrace any political opportunity, no matter the cost. This was in stark contrast to the principled pragmatism that it displayed between 1946 and 1963.

The Brotherhood became a signatory to the Damascus Declaration, a broad-based opposition statement released in October 2005 that condemned the regime and put forward a model for Syria's future. The Declaration pledged to

> work to end the stage of despotism. We declare our readiness to offer the necessary sacrifices for that purpose, and to do all what is necessary to enable the process of democratic change to take off, and to build a modern Syria, a free

---

[103] Ibid., p. 2 (parenthesis added).
[104] Itamar Rabinovich, 'The Syrian Arab Republic (al-Jumhuriyyat Suriyya al-'Arabiyya)', in *Middle East Contemporary Survey, Vol. IX 1984–5*, ed. Itamar Rabinovich and Haim Shaked (Boulder: Westview Press, 1987), p. 648.
[105] Ahmad al-Masri, 'Al-Banayuni Rejects Foreign Help Despite Opposition to Regime in Syria', *Al-Quds al-Arabi* (London: BBC Monitoring Middle East, 2008).

homeland for all of its citizens, safeguard the freedom of its people, and protect national independence.[106]

The Declaration united a number of opposition groups under the one umbrella, and was signed by secular and religious parties, as well as Arab and Kurdish groups. The Syrian intellectual Yassin al-Haj Saleh applauded the Declaration, dubbing it a 'historic initiative' and 'a huge development for the opposition within Syria ... For the first time we're seeing a blueprint for reconstituting Syria's political process.'[107] The Brotherhood's then-leader Ali al-Bayanouni reassured observers of the Brotherhood's position, declaring that the group was 'ready to accept others and to deal with them. We believe that Syria is for all its people, regardless of sect, ethnicity or religion. No one has the right to exclude anyone else.'[108]

But only months later, the Brotherhood decamped for a better offer, forming the National Salvation Front with the newly defected Syrian Vice President Abdul Halim al-Khaddam.[109] This new alliance represented the peak of the group's alliance opportunism, built on the hope that al-Khaddam's defection would undermine al-Assad by breaking the nexus between Sunni regime supporters and the Baʻth Party and. The National Salvation Front was controversial because al-Khaddam had sat among the highest echelons of the al-Assad regime for decades and his defection may merely have reflected his frustration at being politically marginalised by Bashar al-Assad's government.[110] Yet, Ali al-Bayanouni demonstrated remarkable pragmatism, later explaining that al-Khaddam 'wasn't a military ruler. He was a political ruler ... We believed that we could make a difference by going hand in hand with him. It was all for Syria.'[111] Although this may seem like splitting hairs, there appeared an

---

[106] 'The Damascus Declaration for Democratic National Change (translated by Joshua Landis)', *Syria Comment* (1 November 2005) http://faculty-staff.ou.edu/L/Joshua.M.Landis-1/syriablog/2005/11/damascus-declaration-in-english.htm.

[107] Yassin al-Haj Saleh, 'From Damascus, an Appeal for Salvation', *The Daily Star* (2005), www.dailystar.com.lb/Opinion/Commentary/2005/Oct-28/98244-from-damascus-an-appeal-for-salvation.ashx.

[108] Anthony Shadid, 'Inside and Outside Syria, a Debate to Decide the Future', *The Washington Post* (9 November 2005) www.washingtonpost.com/wp-dyn/content/article/2005/11/08/AR2005110802070_pf.html.

[109] Reuters, 'Syria Opposition Forms United Front to Oust Assad', *Hurriyet Daily News* (18 March 2006), www.hurriyetdailynews.com/syria-opposition-forms-united-front-to-oust-assad.aspx?pageID=438&n=syria-opposition-forms-united-front-to-oust-assad-2006-03-18.

[110] For a good discussion of this, see Joshua Landis, 'Khaddam Damns Bashar al-Asad', *Syria Comment* (1 January 2006), http://faculty-staff.ou.edu/L/Joshua.M.Landis-1/syriablog/2006/01/khaddam-damns-bashar-al-asad.htm.

[111] Interview with Ali al-Bayanouni, London.

increasing sense that for the Brotherhood, the ends could justify almost any means.

Like the SIF, the al-Khaddam decision had a rational foundation, but it did little to endear the Brotherhood to its opposition counterparts, creating a widely held perception that the group was power hungry and unprincipled. As Damascus Declaration member Hasan Abdel-Azim remarked, Ali al-Bayanouni 'made two big mistakes: first in meeting Khaddam and launching the National Salvation Front, and then by not consulting [opposition figures inside the country]'.[112] The US Embassy in Damascus noted in a cable that the Brotherhood's 'recent flirtation with former Syrian VP Khaddam has reinforced this widely shared perception of their opportunism'.[113]

The al-Khaddam interaction also created internal problems for the Brotherhood. Farouq Tayfour published a statement online criticising 'those who forsake their homeland in these difficult and critical times, cannot respect the issues they set forth, and cannot be designated as opposition'.[114] He added that Abdul al-Halim al-Khaddam had no right to discuss Syrian reform. Ironically, the National Salvation Front, which represented the peak of Brotherhood alliance opportunism, collapsed in 2009 when the Brotherhood decided to suspend opposition against the Baʿth.[115]

In this way, while the Brotherhood had been an astute and principled political actor in its founding decades, the 1963 Baʿth coup had precipitated significant change in the group's behaviour. Although the Brotherhood never renounced its stated democratic principles, the experience of Baʿth authoritarianism had a profound impact on the group's political character, creating physical and cognitive changes that impeded its ability to operate, and which coloured every political decision. The cumulative burden of history, including the Brotherhood's failure to mobilise at critical times, futile negotiations and the collapse of alliances, resulted ultimately in a diminution in the stature, influence and ability of the group. The progressively more opportunistic tactics reached a damaging peak in the years prior to the uprising with the National Salvation Front

---

[112] 'Internal Syrian Opposition Claims No Ties to Exile Group', *The Daily Star* (21 March 2006), www.dailystar.com.lb/News/Middle-East/2006/Mar-21/69201-internal-syrian-opposition-claims-no-ties-to-exile-group.ashx.

[113] US Embassy Damascus, 'The Muslim Brothers in Syria; Part 1: Could They Win an Election Here?', *Wikileaks* (8 February 2006), www.wikileaks.org/plusd/cables/06DAMASCUS517_a.htm.

[114] Badra Bakhus Al-Fagali, 'Dissent Continues among Syrian Opposition', *Al-Diyar* (London: BBC Monitoring Middle East, 2006).

[115] Lina Zahr-al-Din, interview with Ali Sadr-al-Din al-Bayanuni.

and the 2009 suspension of opposition, creating a track record of bungled political decisions and reputation as an unreliable opposition partner that the Brotherhood took with it into the 2011 uprising. This highlighted the importance of context and political opportunity in shaping the Muslim Brotherhood. By 2011, it was not its political platforms that had failed it; it was its tendency to jump at any political opportunity, regardless of the cost.

4 The Syrian Muslim Brotherhood and Violence

The Brotherhood has enjoyed a long and often productive political history, but it is important to also acknowledge and examine its substantial violent record. Violence itself is a tactical choice that is sometimes used by groups to achieve their goals. Scholars of political violence argue that groups choose from a range of political tactics (including violence) at any given time, and that they make the choice based on a rational analysis of threats and opportunities.[1] To Weinberg, Pedahzur and Perliger, 'the entire distinction between the concepts "political party" and "terrorist group" might not be clear-cut'.[2] Members of Japan's Aum Shinrikyo contested elections in the years before its deadly sarin attack on the Tokyo subway, while some members of the Islamic Salvation Front in Algeria turned to violence in the civil war that followed the Algerian army's cancellation of the 1991 election results. In El Salvador, the Nationalist Republican Alliance group participated in elections while simultaneously running anti-communist death squads.[3] Political organisations choose to act as a political party or a terrorist group for tactical reasons, depending on political conditions.[4] Recognition of the possibility of a duality of character provides a useful window through which to observe the Brotherhood, locating change as part of a continuum or an evolution rather that a schizophrenic phenomenon. It also explains how the Brotherhood could undertake violence even though its ideological documents and political history gave no indication of such capacity.

The Brotherhood witnessed significant political change after 1963, including shifting tactical preferences among its base, the dwindling of opportunities for legitimate political activity and changes in the broader Syrian political environment. This political process facilitated the group's

---

[1] Susanne Martin and Arie Perliger, 'Turning to and from Terror: Deciphering the Conditions under which Political Groups Choose Violent and Nonviolent Tactics', *Perspectives on Terrorism* 6, nos. 4–5 (2012), p. 21.
[2] Leonard Weinberg, Ami Pedahzur and Arie Perliger, *Political Parties and Terrorist Groups*, 2nd edn (London: Routledge, 2009), p. 2.
[3] Ibid.   [4] Martin and Perliger, 'Turning to and from Terror', p. 21.

transformation and led the Brotherhood to adopt violence as a result of circumstance and tactic, rather than core belief. These dynamics did not take place in a vacuum, but reflected the extreme end of the country-wide popular response to the significant social changes that the Ba'th regime had imposed on Syria. The Brotherhood, as a group whose leaders derived from the same social strata as its base, came to personify the atmosphere of frustration and polarisation. Nonetheless, this brief flirtation with violence was catastrophic, contributing further to the cumulative emotional and political baggage that weighed on the group by 2011.

1947–1963: Violence in the Brotherhood's Founding Decades

The Brotherhood did not use violence against the formal institutions of state during its founding decades, although the group was involved in some military-like activities.[5] In 1943, Brotherhood members formed a youth organisation called the Futuwwa (youth), which was a scouts-like group. Youth activities have always formed an important part of Brotherhood movements, with the Egyptian Brotherhood founder Hassan al-Banna characterising the group as 'a political organisation, an athletic club, a cultural and scientific society, a company, and a social doctrine'.[6] The Egyptian Brothers' youth movement was called the Jawwala (Rover Scouts).[7]

The Brotherhood's first leader Mustafa al-Sibai, who had scouts experience himself, described the Futuwwa as one of the most important Ikhwan bodies, dubbing it a 'school for creating a strong generation, imbued with manliness [rujula], to spread the message of the Ikhwan in a spirit of sacrifice, obedience, and order [nizam]'.[8] The group held annual summer camps for the Futuwwa in the mid-1940s, which may have included paramilitary training.[9] Teitelbaum claimed that it was used 'as a force during a strike in 1946', and noted that a number of its rules 'suggest that the Ikhwan were planning to use the Futuwwa as a tool of

---

[5] Ishak Musa Husaini, *The Muslim Brethren: The Greatest of Modern Islamic Movements* (Beirut: Khayat's College Book Cooperative, 1956), p. 76.
[6] Cited in Richard P. Mitchell, *The Society of the Muslim Brothers* (Oxford: Oxford University Press, 1991), p. 2.
[7] See Christine Sixta Rinehart, *Volatile Social Movements and the Origins of Terrorism: The Radicalization of Change* (Lanham: Lexington Books, 2013), pp. 40–2.
[8] Cited in Joshua Teitelbaum, 'The Muslim Brotherhood in Syria, 1945–1958: Founding, Social Origins, Ideology', p. 228.
[9] 'E 9383/213/89: Extract from the Weekly Political Summary no 230 Syria and Lebanon (Secret)', *British Embassy Damascus*, 1946.

subversion should the need arise'.[10] Yet the Futuwwa was never used in a significant way in Syrian domestic politics, even when the Brotherhood was outlawed under the Shishakli dictatorship in the early 1950s. This leaves some ambiguity about the purpose of the group, which may just have been a discipline-centric cadets programme aimed at recruiting youth into the broader movement. In 1946, the Syrian government established its own Futuwwa paramilitary programme for high schools, suggesting that the principle had some mainstream acceptance.[11]

Of greater long-term significance was the Brotherhood's relationship to the 1948 Palestine War. The partition of Palestine was an important issue in Syria and particularly to the Brotherhood: in 1947, the British Foreign Office reported receiving a telegram from the Brotherhood 'protesting that the failure of the London Conference (on Palestine) proved that the British viewed the Palestine problem through Zionist spectacles' and pledging to fight for Palestine's return.[12] This is consistent with the group's 1947 National Charter, which declared that the Arab states must not rely upon the West to provide justice for Palestine.[13] The British Embassy in Damascus reported in 1947 that 'The efforts of Mustafa Sebai (el Ikhwan el Muslimeen) [sic] to recruit an Arab "Army of Liberation" ... have been favourably commented upon'.[14] Accounts by Brotherhood figures suggest that many members heeded this call. According to Said Hawwa, in 1948 the 'Islamic movement ... opened volunteer centres [for the War] everywhere, and many Islamic movement brigades left for the land of *jihad*'.[15] Hawwa claimed that dozens of the group's members were killed.[16] Adnan Saadeddine maintained that al-Sibai himself had 'led the mujahidin brigades in Palestine', although this claim could not be verified.[17]

The Brotherhood's participation in the Palestine War was unremarkable in the context of the post-WWII Syrian political environment where many actors were mobilising, but it later had a tangible impact on the group.[18] Ayman Shorbaji, the leader of the Fighting Vanguard's

---

[10] Teitelbaum, 'The Muslim Brotherhood in Syria', pp. 228–9.   [11] Ibid., p. 227.
[12] 'E 2101/171/89 – Syria: Weekly Summary No. 7', *UK Foreign Office*, week ending 18 February 1947 (parenthesis added).
[13] Umar F. Abd-allah, *The Islamic Struggle in Syria* (Berkeley: Mizan Press, 1983), p. 149.
[14] 'E 10404/171/89 – Syria Political Summary No 7 for September 1947', *British Embassy Damascus*, received 7 November 1947.
[15] Said Hawwa, *This Is My Experience and This Is My Testimony (in Arabic)* (Cairo: Maktabat Wahba, 1987), p. 40.
[16] Ibid., p. 41.
[17] Adnan Saadeddine, *The Muslim Brotherhood in Syria: Notes and Memories (in Arabic)*, vol. 3 (Dar al-Amar, 2006), p. 55.
[18] See newspaper reports from 1947. For example, in September 1947, a conference of 52 Shaykhs representing all the Syrian tribes declared that Palestine's partition would

Damascus cells, noted decades after that 'many [in his ranks had] fought in the battles on the land of Palestine, and acquired military experience. The benefits of this were broadly reflected on the [Fighting Vanguard] organisation later on.'[19] Indeed, it meant that when the Baʿth regime took over Syria and there was an upsurge of militarism among the Brotherhood's members, the some group members had a baseline of military experience (albeit significantly outdated).

1963–1979: The Brotherhood's Path to Violence

The 1963 Baʿth coup was a watershed moment in the Brotherhood's history. Although Syria was no stranger to military regimes by that time, the Baʿth coup proved tangibly different, leading to a momentous shift in the group's operating environment and precipitating significant changes in its behaviour. Its political plans and visions quickly became pipe dreams. However, the Brotherhood's conflict with the Baʿth was not as much ideological as it was political. As Lobmeyer observed:

> All the regimes in power in Syria from independence in 1946 to 1963 had already implicitly pursued a secular policy ... But the opposition was never as militant and compromising as it is against the Baʿth regime. This indicates that the secular ideology of the Baʿth is not the underlying cause of the conflict.[20]

In fact, Perthes went so far as to describe the subsequent post-1970 regime under Hafez al-Assad as ideologically moribund: 'There is no all-encompassing ideology, which state and regime would offer to try to enforce on the population. Baʿthism and Arab nationalism have been watered down so as not to stand in the way of the pragmatic realpolitik of the regime.'[21] Indeed, in contrast to the Hama-centric view of the Muslim Brotherhood that depicted the group as fanatical enemies of secularism, the group's frustration stemmed mostly from the Baʿth's exertion of power and the rapid shrinking of its political space. Authoritarianism had changed the rules of the Brotherhood's game.

'stimulate Arabs to liberate her finally by arms and red blood' – 'Syria Sheiks See Bloodshed in U.N. Partitioning Proposal', *The Washington Post* (11 September 1947), p. 4. Reports emerged that an Arab army of 50,000, including retired army officers from across the Middle East, was mobilising in Damascus: Reuters, 'Big Arab Army under Training to "Save Palestine"', *The Times of India* (21 September 1947), p. 3.

[19] Ayman Shorbaji, *The Diary of a Vanguard Combatant in Syria (in Arabic)* (Unknown: Unknown, n.d.), p. 22.

[20] Hans Gunter Lobmeyer, 'Islamic Ideology and Secular Discourse', *Orient* 32, no. 3 (1991), pp. 401–2.

[21] Volker Perthes, *The Political Economy of Syria under Assad* (London: I.B. Tauris, 1995), p. 193.

Scholars of authoritarian regimes note that political tactics morph in line with the regime in which a group operates. They would therefore anticipate a potential shift in Brotherhood strategies given the suspension of Syria's democratic system in 1963. This can often manifest in violence as a tactical response to authoritarian regimes.[22]

A Shift in the Group's Grassroots

The Brotherhood's path to formally adopting violence took more than one and a half decades after the Baʿth seizure of power, underlining its leaders' reticence about the strategy. But while the Brotherhood's leaders took years to change their thinking, the group's new operating environment had quickly impressed the need for a change in strategy on junior members. Ideas of violence emerged within the Brotherhood's grassroots soon after the Baʿthist coup, as evidenced by a violent confrontation between the regime and the organisation's youth just one year later. This marked the Brotherhood's first step towards violence.

The political situation across Syria was volatile by 1964,[23] with tension building across the country in reaction to the new regime's crackdown on political freedoms, as well as its imposition of socialist policies, including land reform and the threat of nationalisation. Shopkeepers in Homs, Hama and Damascus went on strike in April 1964, and subsequently met with government officials to demand a relaxation of import restrictions and to receive assurances that the country's retail trade would not be nationalised.[24] Lawyers also joined the movement against the Baʿth, with what the Iraqi Baʿth-backed Baghdad Radio reported as a demand that 'democratic life be restored in the country'.[25] The Brotherhood actively encouraged the protests across Syria,[26] although it was supported by dissident Baʿthists and small numbers of what were left of the Nasserite groups.[27] As Seale noted, in its first year 'the Baʿth had not given Syria good government, or indeed much government at all'.[28]

---

[22] Charles Tilly and Sidney Tarrow, *Contentious Politics* (Oxford: Oxford University Press, 2015), pp. 174–5; Ehud Sprinzak, 'The Process of Delegitimation: Towards a Linkage Theory of Political Terrorism', *Terrorism and Polical Violence* 3, no. 1 (1991). p. 63.
[23] Dana Adams Schmidt, 'Nasserite Riots in Syria Quelled by Martial Law', *The New York Times* (2 April 1963), p. 1.
[24] 'Syrian Pressure Continues', *The New York Times* (29 April 1963), p. 8.
[25] 'Syria Quells Revolt, Arrests 19', *The Washington Post* (16 April 1964), p. A28.
[26] 'Damascus Suffering War Nerves: Hama Rebellion Fans Discontent in Syrian Capital', *The Washington Post* (20 April 1964), p. A1.
[27] 'Syria Isolates City Following Uprising', *The New York Times* (17 April 1964), p. 7.
[28] Patrick Seale, *Asad of Syria: The Struggle for the Middle East* (Berkeley: University of California Press, 1988), p. 92.

It was in this context of broad frustration that the 1964 riots in Hama broke out. This provided the first indication that the Brotherhood's base was edging towards the adoption of violence.

Said Hawwa, who played an important role in organising the strikes but was not involved in the subsequent violence, recalled that political pressure had mounted in the city of Hama on the eve of the event, noting that 'the atmosphere was tense, especially in the ranks of the students'.[29] Protests began following a Baʿth government decision to transfer two popular teachers from Hama, leading to a strike by Hamawi students. Security forces and police attempted to arrest students protesting at the Uthman al-Hourani school. Protesters then descended on the school, prompting Hama's governor Abdul Halim al-Khaddam to order army intervention. A young Brotherhood member, Marwan Hadid and a number of Brothers then moved to the Sultan Mosque, where they staged fiery speeches, prompting more of Hama's residents to 'flock' to the mosque.[30]

Osama bin Laden's mentor Abdullah Azzam, who is often considered the 'father of modern Islamic terrorism',[31] was studying in Damascus at the time, and developed a close relationship with Marwan Hadid. Azzam described the next stage of the Hama riot:

> He (Hadid) went to Masjid as Sultan [the Sultan Mosque] and gathered them [his supporters], each one of them carrying a grenade and a gun. Some of the youth were still in high school! They began saying 'Allahu Akbar!' and announcing their fight against the state. So, the tanks came to Masjid as Sultan and fired on it, with the youth standing on the minaret. The minaret fell with the youth in it, and the mosque was demolished with them inside.[32]

Estimates of the death toll varied, with reports of between 40 and 100 people killed.[33] Baghdad Radio reported that more than 400 houses were destroyed in the government's response, although the source is linked to the Iraqi Baʿth, so the exact figures must be taken with a pinch of salt.[34] The government arrested at least 25 of those involved in the riots, including Marwan Hadid. A minimum of 21 of these, including Hadid and Said Hawwa (who had not been involved in the violence) received

---

[29] Hawwa, *This Is My Experience*, p. 70.
[30] For a detailed account of the event, see ibid., pp. 69–78.
[31] Bruce Riedel 'The 9/11 Attacks' Spiritual Father' *Brookings Institute* (2011), www.brookings.edu/research/opinions/2011/09/11-riedel.
[32] Abdullah Azzam, 'The Soul Shall Rise Tomorrow: The Story of Marwan Hadid', From Dhilal Surat at-Tawbah, published on *Milestones on the Road to Firmness in Faith*, https://iskandrani.wordpress.com/2008/02/09/the-soul-shall-rise-tomorrow-the-story-of-marwan-hadid/ (parentheses added).
[33] 'Hafez Meets Hama Citizens', *The Jerusalem Post* (19 April 1964), p. 1.
[34] 'First Hama "Plotter" Sentenced to Death', *The Jerusalem Post* (21 April 1964), p. 1.

death sentences, although Brotherhood founding member Muhammad al-Hamid successfully appealed for clemency on Hadid's behalf.[35] Hawwa fled the country, but was able to return soon after following a regime amnesty.

Senior Brotherhood leaders condemned Hadid's actions and called for the protesters to stand down. Issam al-Attar, who inherited leadership from Mustafa al-Sibai, reportedly first heard of the violence on the radio while in Mecca in Saudi Arabia. Al-Attar maintained that he 'had no knowledge of this [the mosque sit in] and I did not approve it, but since I was the commander of the group, I was considered responsible'.[36] It represented the first significant case of the Brotherhood's leaders losing control of their base. Syrian state media blamed the events on 'feudalists'.[37]

This early period under authoritarian rule was significant because it demonstrated the increasingly bold pattern of ideological entrepreneurialism that was emerging from among the Brotherhood base. While individualism had always been a core group feature, it began to take on a life of its own once it became clear that the Brotherhood's leaders would not directly challenge the regime.

This trend was exemplified in Marwan Hadid's rise as a key youth member of the Syrian Muslim Brotherhood. Although Hadid was an agronomist by training and did not hold an official role in the Brotherhood or have formal Islamic qualifications, he was a charismatic and zealous individual who commanded a significant following. Hadid became close friends with Sayyid Qutb and the 'activist wing' of the Egyptian Brotherhood while he was studying in Egypt during the early 1960s.[38] He was respectfully dubbed 'Shaykh Marwan' by his followers. Hadid introduced segments of the Brotherhood's base to jihadist ideas, arguing that 'the regime will disappear only when armed groups ... kill its members'.[39] Khatib described Hadid and his followers as advocating

---

[35] 'Court in Syria Dooms 21 for Part in Riots in Hama', *The New York Times* (31 May 1964), p. 49.; Itzchak Weismann, 'Sa'id Hawwa: The Making of a Radical Muslim Thinker in Modern Syria', *Middle Eastern Studies* 29, no. 4 (1993), p. 616.

[36] Ahmad Zidan, 'Issam al-Attar...The Islamic Movement in Syria (in Arabic)', *Today's Meeting, Al-Jazeera Arabic* (1 July 2007), www.aljazeera.net/programs/today-interview/2007/7/1/%D8%B9%D8%B5%D8%A7%D9%85-%D8%A7%D9%84%D8%B9%D8%B7%D8%A7%D8%B1-%D8%A7%D9%84%D8%AD%D8%B1%D9%83%D8%A9-%D8%A7%D9%84%D8%A5%D8%B3%D9%84%D8%A7%D9%85%D9%8A%D8%A9-%D9%81%D9%8A-%D8%B3%D9%88%D8%B1%D9%8A%D8%A7 (parenthesis added).

[37] 'Syria Quells Revolt, Arrests 19' (16 April 1964), p. A28.

[38] Hanna Batatu, *Syria's Peasantry: The Descendants of Its Lesser Rural Notables, and Their Politics* (Princeton: Princeton University Press, 1999), p. 262.

[39] Cited in Raymond Hinnebusch, *Authoritarian Power and State Formation in Bathist Syria: Army, Party and Peasant* (Boulder: Westview Press, 1991), p. 281.

radical Salafi discourse, and [that he] relied on the writings of Sayyed Qutb, especially his book Ma'alem fi al-Tariq, and the writings of Sa'id Hawwa ... Marwan Hadid dismissed Syrian Sufism in all its aspects, and believed in the radical Sahwa (Awakening) of the Muslims, which necessitated an obligatory reinforcement of Islamic law. He ordered a militant opposition at all costs.[40]

More practically, he believed that the fight had to be taken to the Ba'th immediately. To Moubayed, Hadid's approach 'was the opposite of Mustapha al-Sibaii's [sic] gentleman policies'.[41] It also differed significantly from even the ideas of the Brotherhood's most radical leader, Said Hawwa.

With time, Marwan Hadid began to prosecute his military approach, with Ayman Shorbaji recalling that 'the Islamic leaders' rejection of military work did not discourage Shaykh Marwan from his ideas'.[42] As Abdullah Azzam noted, after being granted clemency following the 1964 riots, Hadid 'knew no rest. He was basically a bomb about to explode.'[43] However, since the Brotherhood leadership refused to review their position, Hadid was forced to look internationally for assistance, building ties with the head of the Jordanian Muslim Brotherhood Ishaq al-Farhan and undertaking training in the Qawaid al-Shuyukh (The Shaykhs' Bases) in northern Jordan. The camps were Islamist Palestinian training camps operated by the Jordanian Muslim Brotherhood that were shut down in the 1970–1 Black September strife.[44] At least 30 of Hadid's supporters undertook military training at the camp, including Abd al-Sattar al-Zaim, who later became the leader of the Fighting Vanguard.[45] Husni Abu, a future leader of the Aleppo branch of the Fighting Vanguard, claimed during a forced confession on Syrian television to have visited one of these camps in Jordan for a week in 1969.[46]

Marwan Hadid returned to Syria in the early 1970s, making his presence felt during the 1973 constitutional crisis. By the middle of the

---

[40] Line Khatib, 'Islamic and Islamist Revivalism in Syria: The Rise and Fall of Secularism in Ba'thist Syria' (PhD thesis, McGill University, 2010), p. 68.
[41] Sami Moubayed, *Under the Black Flag: At the Frontier of the New Jihad* (London: I.B.Tauris, 2015), p. 31.
[42] Shorbaji, *The Diary of a Vanguard Combatant*, p. 22.
[43] Abdullah Azzam, 'The Soul Shall Rise Tomorrow: The Story of Marwan Hadid', From Dhilal Surat at-Tawbah, published on *Milestones on the Road to Firmness in Faith*, https://iskandrani.wordpress.com/2008/02/09/the-soul-shall-rise-tomorrow-the-story-of-marwan-hadid/.
[44] Ibrahim Ghusheh, *The Red Minaret: Memoirs of Ibrahim Ghusheh (ex-spokesman of Hamas)* (Beirut: Al-Zaytouna Centre, 2013), p. 95.
[45] Shorbaji, *The Diary of a Vanguard Combatant*, p. 22.; Khatib, 'Islamic and Islamist Revivalism in Syria', p. 56.
[46] 'FCO 93/2253: Letter from Vincent Fean to Douglas Gordon on Husni Abo's Televised Confession', *British Embassy Damascus* (7 September 1979).

decade however, Hadid could no longer preach openly and was forced into hiding in Damascus. According to the Fighting Vanguard's Damascus chief Ayman Shorbaji, Hadid's followers continued their military training in the coastal mountains and forest area in Syria's northwest.[47] Between 30 and 40 individuals were trained by Abd al-Sattar al-Zaim.[48] Training would later also take place in the mountains near Damascus.[49] Hadid was eventually arrested in 1975, and died in prison the following year after undergoing severe torture.[50] Hadid's life is celebrated in radical circles, including during the 2011 uprising.

Marwan Hadid's legacy is complex for mainstream Muslim Brothers, who to this day are unsure of how to deal with his immense popularity, even though his path diverged dramatically from their own principles. Many senior members express respect for Hadid, referring to him as 'Shaykh'.[51] Former leader Riad al-Shaqfeh described Hadid as

a brave Islamic militant; he had the temper of a true leader and had much influence on Hama's youth ... Sheikh Marwan was an enthusiastic member of the Ikhwan but he was not very respectful of the organization's rule; he wanted the Brotherhood to think less and act more ... In other words, he had ambitions to revolutionize our organization.[52]

Members asked whether Hadid was evicted from the Brotherhood before his death (in line with the Brotherhood's policy on the Fighting Vanguard) gave sharply contradictory responses, and senior figures remained reluctant to publicly criticise him.[53] Herein lies the Brotherhood's challenge: how can it reconcile the legacy of a man who initiated the group's

---

[47] Shorbaji, *The Diary of a Vanguard Combatant*, p. 23. [48] Ibid. [49] Ibid., pp. 24–5.
[50] Abu Musab Al-Suri, 'Lessons Learned from the Armed Jihad Ordeal in Syria', translated and published by the Combatting Terrorism Centre (CTC), West Point, www.ctc.usma.edu/v2/wp-content/uploads/2013/10/Lessons-Learned-from-the-Jihad-Ordeal-in-Syria-Translation.pdf, p. 2.
[51] Hazim al-Amine, 'Leader of Syrian Muslim Brotherhood Discloses Secret Offer from Iran', *Al-Monitor (originally published in al-Hayat, translated by Naria Tanoukhi)* (20 January 2012). www.al-monitor.com/pulse/politics/2012/01/tayfour-to-al-hayat-iran-offered.html#ixzz47rSW2vW2.
[52] Cited in Raphaël Lefèvre, *Ashes of Hama: The Muslim Brotherhood in Syria* (London: Hurst, 2013), p. 82.
[53] Ali al-Bayanouni told the author that Hadid never left the group, but this contradicts what he earlier told Alison Pargeter. Adnan Saadeddine maintained that the Brotherhood never excommunicated Hadid and that he never disengaged from the group. By contrast, Farouq Tayfour claims to have personally asked Hadid to leave. See interview with Ali al-Bayanouni, London; Alison Pargeter, *The Muslim Brotherhood: The Burden of Tradition* (London: Saqi Books, 2010), p. 77; Ahmed Mansour, 'Adnan Saadeddine – The Brotherhood's Time in Syria, Episode 4', *Al-Jazeera* (3 October 2012), www.aljazeera.net/home/print/0353e88a-286d-4266-82c6-6094179ea26d/2c67f0e3-02ac-4bd9-b2c5-d050bad6ab5d; al-Amine, 'Leader of Syrian Muslim Brotherhood'.

turn to violence and the organisation's near total destruction, with the reality that he remains popular among radical Syrians and parts of the Brotherhood today? This is an example of the political baggage that the Brotherhood collected during the violence era. By 2011, the Brotherhood was still walking a tightrope on the question of Marwan Hadid.

The clearest legacy of Marwan Hadid's thought and efforts manifested in the formation of the Fighting Vanguard, a violent splinter faction that attracted many Brothers. This posed a significant risk for the Brotherhood as there was a chance that the Vanguard's radical ideas would cross-pollinate into the Brotherhood's base.[54] Indeed, the two groups were cognitively so close that the Vanguard's full name was: al-Talia al-Muqatila min al-Ikhwan al-Muslimin fi Suriya (The Fighting Vanguard of the Muslim Brotherhood in Syria).[55] Brotherhood/Vanguard member and later al-Qaeda strategist Abu Musab al-Suri went as far as to dub the Vanguard 'holders of the real ideas of the Brotherhood', while Adnan Uqlah claimed: 'We in the Fighting Vanguard of the Muslim Brotherhood led by the Mujahid martyr, Brother Marwan Hadid, [are] the true representatives of the Muslim Brotherhood on the path of [Hassan] al-Banna and [Sayyid] Qutb.'[56] It is unclear whether Hadid founded the Fighting Vanguard or if it was founded in his name,[57] but his ideological positions were closely echoed by his Vanguard followers. Most members of the Fighting Vanguard were expelled from the Brotherhood,[58] although there remained significant crossover within the Hamawi membership base.[59]

---

[54] For a discussion of this phenomenon, see Stephen W. Beach, 'Social Movement Radicalization: The Case of the People's Democracy in Northern Ireland', *The Sociological Quarterly* 18, no. 3 (1977), p. 316.

[55] For example, see the following letter: The Media Office of the Fighting Vanguard of the Muslim Brotherhood, 'Untitled letter' (11 May 1979). Available as an appendix in Umar abd Al-Hakim, *The Islamic Jihadi Revolution in Syria (in Arabic)* (Peshawar: Unknown, 1991), pp. 599–600. In another letter, the Vanguard leader Adnan Uqlah signed off as a soldier' from 'the Fighting Vanguard, the true representative of the Muslim Brotherhood'. See Adnan Uqlah, 'Letter from Adnan Uqlah' (11 June 1980). Also available as an appendix in Al-Hakim, *The Islamic Jihadi Revolution*, pp. 575–90.

[56] Uqlah, 'Letter from Adnan Uqlah', p. 1. Available in Al-Hakim, *The Islamic Jihadi Revolution*, p. 576.

[57] Today, Muslim Brotherhood leaders claim that Marwan Hadid did not undertake violence of form the Fighting Vanguard, but instead, his followers established it in his name after his death. Ali al-Bayanouni asserts that Hadid, 'just had this ideology, but he wasn't actually involved' in violence. In contrast, a senior Vanguard figure said that Hadid created the Vanguard. See anonymous interview; Shorbaji, *The Diary of a Vanguard Combatant*, p. 19. It may be the case that Hadid undertook violence under another name prior to incarceration.

[58] Interview with Ali al-Bayanouni, London.   [59] Lefèvre, *Ashes of Hama*.

Hadid's military training programmes recommenced after his death, with the Fighting Vanguard's future leader Adnan Uqlah a member of the first cohort to complete the training.[60] Many Vanguard members who rose to prominence in the Vanguard or subsequent organisations also had military experience through mandatory conscription or voluntary service in more senior parts of the Syrian army, including Adnan Uqlah,[61] Ibrahim al-Youssef (responsible for the 1979 Artillery Academy massacre),[62] Abu Burhan (later became a key trainer of the Afghan Arabs in the Soviet Afghan conflict),[63] and Radwan Nammous (later became a senior Jabhat al-Nusra figure during the 2011 conflict).[64] According to Seale, either the Brotherhood or Vanguard had at least one supporter within the highest echelons of the regime's intelligence apparatus: an agent based in Air Force Intelligence who handed over car registration numbers for many of the Syria's top intelligence officials.[65]

The Vanguard began its campaign of violence following the death of Hadid under the leadership of Abd al-Sattar al-Zaim on 8 February 1976, launching a series of targeted assassinations against regime officials and allies. Members of the Alawite sect were often specifically targeted, although anyone linked to the regime was considered a legitimate objective. The group's first target was the head of the Hama branch of the Mukhabarat (intelligence services) Muhammad Ghazah, a cousin of Hafez al-Assad. The Vanguard's Ayman Shorbaji claimed that the incident 'had a significant impact on the morale of the regime, as it was the first retaliatory operation carried out by the armed organisation against criminal regime personalities'.[66] The group declared the event to be 'the first bullet for the sake of God, opening the gate to organized jihad'.[67]

The assassinations continued over the following three years, targeting individuals such as the Rector of the University of Damascus and senior Ba'thist Dr Muhammad al-Fadel (both 1977), and the Vice President of the Syrian–Soviet Friendship Association Dr Ibrahim Naama (1978).[68]

---

[60] Shorbaji, *The Diary of a Vanguard Combatant*, p. 28.
[61] Abd-allah, *The Islamic Struggle in Syria*, pp. 127–8.
[62] Leah Farrall and Mustafa Hamid, *The Arabs at War in Afghanistan* (London: Hurst, 2015), p. xii.
[63] 'A Statement from the Muslim Brotherhood, Issued on June 24 (in Arabic)' (3 July 1979). Available in Al-Hakim, *The Islamic Jihadi Revolution*, p. 574.
[64] Hassan Abu Haniyeh, 'Who's Who in the Nusra Front?', *The New Arab* (15 December 2014), www.alaraby.co.uk/english/politics/2014/12/15/whos-who-in-the-nusra-front.
[65] Seale, *Asad of Syria*, p. 327.   [66] Shorbaji, *The Diary of a Vanguard Combatant*, p. 27.
[67] Cited in Khatib, 'Islamic and Islamist Revivalism in Syria', p. 66.
[68] Ibid., p. 67; Seale, *Asad of Syria*, p. 317.

Former Brotherhood and Vanguard member Abu Musab al-Suri described the time as the 'golden period' of the group's activities.[69] The campaign caused a huge sense of fear and tension among the government and its supporters that was amplified by the regime's confusion over who was responsible for the assassinations. Blame had initially been pinned on Iraq.[70] Interestingly, Adnan Saadeddine claimed that the Brotherhood too was in the dark, recalling: 'We did not know anything about who was behind these assassinations.'[71] Given the close links between the Vanguard and Saadeddine's own Hama faction of the group, this claim may be a deliberate untruth.

The assassination campaign took place in the context of a strengthening regime crackdown in Syria. Large numbers of Brothers were imprisoned and Brotherhood leaders were increasingly forced to leave the country. The Fighting Vanguard's Ayman Shorbaji explained that the departure of the Brotherhood leadership left 'the armed apparatus of Shaykh Marwan to confront the regime alone'.[72] The exile of moderate Islamist leaders therefore opened the door for more radical opposition forces to dominate the confrontation with the Ba'th. This is another consequence of authoritarianism, because when opposition members undertake a cost–benefit analysis of their activity in the face of repressive conditions, only the most radical will be willing to bear the cost.[73] Rarely do moderates see challenging brutal repression to be worthwhile, and so often retire from political activism.

This withdrawal of moderates was a significant factor in the empowerment of the Fighting Vanguard and in the erosion of the Brotherhood's control over its cadre. Remarkably many of the dynamics in this period of flux went unnoticed by foreign legations in Damascus. The British Embassy wrote to the Foreign and Commonwealth Office (FCO) in 1979, asking whether they had any information on Marwan Hadid. Embassy official T.V. Fean wrote:

> The name of Marwan Hadid appears frequently in the confessions of the alleged 'Moslem [sic] Brothers' executed in Damascus on 28 June. We know that Hadid was a Sunni Sheikh from Hama who died in police custody sometime between 1975 and early 1977. He was probably arrested several months before then.
>
> He is regarded as a martyr to the extremist Sunni cause, and has attracted a number of dedicated followers prepared to kill in their efforts to overthrow the Ba'th and Assad.

---

[69] Al-Suri, 'Lessons Learned', p. 19.   [70] Anonymous interview.
[71] Saadeddine, *The Muslim Brotherhood in Syria*, vol. 3, p. 378.
[72] Shorbaji, *The Diary of a Vanguard Combatant*, p. 45.
[73] Beach, 'Social Movement Radicalization', p. 314.

Our internal political files for 1974 and 1975 have been [examined] ... and we can find nothing since to tell just the story of Hadid's life and influence. I should be most grateful if you could send us anything you have on Hadid.[74]

The FCO research department responded, noting 'I am afraid I can add nothing to the information in your teleletter, except that he died in 1977'.[75] It is worth adding that most sources cite Hadid's death as having taken place in 1976.[76]

The Syrian Muslim Brotherhood Undergoes Change

At the same time that the Fighting Vanguard was prosecuting its assassination campaign, the Brotherhood underwent significant internal changes. The Brotherhood's factionalism, which was characterised mostly by jostling between its various city branches over access to power, began to play out. The pressure of authoritarianism had shrunk the group's political opportunities and disrupted interactions between the branches, accentuating long-standing divides and bringing the group's latent internal conflicts to the surface. Many of the conflicts had their foundation in the Mustafa al-Sibai era, and were a legacy of the group's failure to fully assimilate each city-based *Jamiyat* into a unified national organisation.

These tensions first emerged following Mustafa al-Sibai's death, as his successor Issam al-Attar lacked the charisma and popularity of his predecessor. Although al-Attar was a close associate of al-Sibai, his unwavering commitment to non-violence became contentious among members of the Brotherhood's base who wanted to mount a more active opposition to the Syrian regime.[77] The chasm between al-Attar's moderation and the ideas emerging from the Brotherhood base was evident in a letter al-Attar purportedly wrote to his supporters immediately after the Syrian government assassinated his wife in Germany in 1981. On 17 March 1981, al-Attar penned this to his supporters:

I call upon the loyal Syrian people and Arabs and Muslims in all places: Nobody should proceed in any act of revenge for my wife, the martyr Banan al-Tantawi ... [she] is just one of thousands of martyrs on our holy ground and we call for

---

[74] 'FCO 93/2253: Letter from From Vincent Fean', *British Embassy Damascus*, 18 September 1979.
[75] 'FCO 93/2253: Letter from From CJS Rundle, FCO Research Department', *British Embassy Damascus*, 1 October 1979.
[76] Abu Musab Al-Suri, *Call to Jihad against the Syrian Regime* (translated and published by the Combatting Terrorism Centre (CTC), West Point), p. 24.
[77] Abd-allah, *The Islamic Struggle in Syria*, p. 103.

justice, not vengeance, and to rid all of our people from the restraints and injustice and humiliation.[78]

This moderation towards the Alawite sect was quite remarkable given the increasingly sectarian political climate, in which language such as 'Nusayri' (a derogatory term for Alawites) and 'Kufar' (infidel) had become commonplace throughout the literature of the Fighting Vanguard, as well as within some parts of the Brotherhood at the time.[79] Pargeter argued that al-Attar 'represented perhaps the last voice of the old-style Syrian Ikhwan before it evolved into a more militant organization'.[80]

Intercity rivalry was not unique to the Brotherhood, and was in fact a long-standing feature of the broader Syrian political landscape. Both Damascus and Aleppo were important cities under the Ottoman Empire, but the carving up of Greater Syria and Turkey's annexation of Alexandretta province transformed Aleppo into Syria's second city, subordinate to the new capital in Damascus. Khoury noted that after independence, 'Damascus leaders continued to feel more comfortable in Beirut or Jerusalem than in Aleppo, let alone Latakia, while Aleppo leaders looked to Iraq (and even Turkey) as much as they did to Damascus'.[81] Syria's two post-independence elite political parties, the National Party (which drew its support base from Damascus) and the People's Party (which was strongest in Aleppo) reflected these parochial dynamics, with Seale going so far as to dub the People's Party 'essentially an Aleppo Party'.[82] Van Dam commented that this pattern even pervaded the army officer corps, which was 'polarised on a Damascene/Non-Damascene basis'.[83] The Brotherhood had a profound stake in the changes taking place in Syria because it was by definition a pragmatic and flexible group with deep and genuine ties to its base, while many of its leaders hailed from the same socio-economic background as their supporters. The group therefore inevitably reflected these broader Syrian political dynamics.

Some attribute the Brotherhood's factional problems completely to these intercity dynamics. One Brotherhood associate remarked:

---

[78] Issam Al-Attar, *Words*, vol. 2 (Aachen: Dar al-Islamiya l-l-Alam, 2008), p. 23.
[79] For example, see Shorbaji, *The Diary of a Vanguard Combatant*, p. 27.
[80] Pargeter, *The Muslim Brotherhood*, p. 65.
[81] Philip S. Khoury, *Syria and the French Mandate: The Politics of Arab Nationalism, 1920–1945* (Princeton: Princeton University Press, 1987), p. 622.
[82] Patrick Seale, *The Struggle for Syria: A Study of Post-War Arab Politics, 1945–1958* (Oxford: Oxford University Press, 1965), p. 30.
[83] Nikolaos Van Dam, *The Struggle for Power in Syria: Politics and Society under Asad and the Ba'th Party*, 4th edn (London: I.B.Tauris, 2011), p. 30.

Fundamentally it goes back to Damascus versus Aleppo, and people from those two cities, generally speaking, don't like each other, and they don't like to be under the rule of the other ... this problem will never go away because it is just a feature of bourgeois thinking.[84]

Ali al-Bayanouni confirms this, explaining that 'Aleppo and Damascus always had competition between them, considering that the two big parties were in Damascus and Aleppo'.[85] This may have become more entrenched after the Brotherhood absorbed members from the Aleppo-based People's Party after 1963. Intercity rivalries were exacerbated by the Ba'th regime's co-optation of many of the Brotherhood's Damascene allies, including members of the merchant community who had benefited from Hafez al-Assad's political and economic strategies. Seale explained that al-Assad 'had learned from [his predecessor Salah] Jadid's difficulties that to give his regime a stable base he must conciliate, or at least not wholly alienate, the Damascus commercial class'.[86] By the 1970s, members of Jamiyat al-Gharra were in charge of the prestigious Institute of Sharia Sciences in Damascus,[87] while Pierret noted that some 'old families from the "upper merchant middle class" – the traditional silent partners of the mashyakha (Shaykhs) – had got their hands on large parts of domestic and foreign trade and developed medium-sized industries.'[88] This combination of carrots as well as sticks, which came in the form of threats from those close to the government, meant that repression in Damascus was less than in other parts of the country. In the late 1970s and early 1980s when unrest was stirring across the country, Damascus remained comparatively quiet. Al-Assad's strategy had paid off.

A third Brotherhood faction emerged in the city of Hama in the 1970s. The group's Hama centre was built from the Jamiyat Ikhwan al-Muslimin, an organisation that Adnan Saadeddine described as deeply engaged in its local community in Syria's pre-independence years, even working alongside Christians.[89] Although the Hama centre is routinely depicted as more radical, religious and sectarian than the other city branches, these beginnings as a tolerant *jamiyah* suggest a similar base to the Brotherhood's other organisational predecessors. Nonetheless, one senior Brotherhood figure from Aleppo said that the group's Hamawi members were different to other parts of the group because

---

[84] Anonymous interview.   [85] Interview with Ali al-Bayanouni, London.
[86] Seale, *Asad of Syria*, p. 326.   [87] Batatu, *Syria's Peasantry*, p. 261.
[88] Thomas Pierret, *Religion and State in Syria: The Sunni Ulama from Coup to Revolution* (Cambridge: Cambridge University Press, 2011,) p. 149 (parenthesis added).
[89] Adnan Saadeddine, *The Muslim Brotherhood in Syria: Notes and Memories (in Arabic)*, vol. 1 (Dar al-Amar, 2006), p. 69.

'everyone [in Hama] has a gun'.[90] Another non-Hamawi Brotherhood member cited the crossover of membership between the Brotherhood and the Vanguard as being due to 'the special nature of the Hamawi people'.[91] Although such primordial assessments have little academic credence, it does show that the group had never fully integrated its city bases; each city remained an 'other'. This meant that central leadership control was dissipated. Hama was also home to several influential personalities, such as Muhammad al-Hamid, Marwan Hadid, Said Hawwa and Adnan Saadeddine. Given the comparatively small size of the city, such individuals were able to have a significant impact on the thinking of the Hama centre. In addition, one Brotherhood leader argued that the Hama centre was more cohesive and disciplined than other factions, claiming that 'you will find that all of Hama [supported the use of violence during this period], but Aleppo was more mixed'.[92]

Hama's socio-economic background also meant that the Brotherhood's Hamawi members had felt the impact of Ba'th Party policies and Syria's economic restructure more deeply than those in other cities. When the Ba'th came to power, Hama was a hub of small-scale manufacturing and agricultural processing. Its major industries were weaving, leather working, cotton ginning, tobacco processing and sugar refining, and the city's economy was predominantly driven by small-scale artisanal traders.[93] This was indicated in a government census carried out in the late 1970s that found that 31.5 percent of Hamawis were 'self-employed', compared to 20 percent of Damascus residents. Small-scale industry was thus integral to the city's economy.[94] The wider province was also home to some of the largest landholdings in the country in the 1960s,[95] and this is reflected in the backgrounds of many Hamawi Brotherhood members. Marwan Hadid hailed from a wealthy cotton farming family.[96] Senior figure Farouq Tayfour was born into the Tayfour family, one of the four main landowning families in Hama province.[97] This pattern was described by a 2011 uprising-era member of the Brotherhood's political office, Samir abu Laban, who hailed from neighbouring Homs: 'At the beginning of the 1970s, my father was one of the big industrialists in Syria. After Assad arrived, the trade and industrial situation of my father started to decline, he suffered a lot and this aroused my interest in politics.'[98] These broader socio-economic changes appeared to have a

[90] Anonymous interview. [91] Ibid. [92] Ibid.
[93] Fred H. Lawson, 'Social Bases for the Hamah Revolt', *MERIP Reports*, no. 110 (1982), p. 25.
[94] Ibid. [95] Ibid., p. 27. [96] Moubayed, *Under the Black Flag*, p. 28.
[97] Khoury, *Syria and the French Mandate*, p. 10; interview with Molham Aldrobi.
[98] Interview with Samir Abu Laban, Istanbul.

tangible impact on the Brotherhood. According to Adnan Saadeddine, the most militant members of the Brotherhood were the youth offspring of craftsmen and small traders.[99] This was one of the demographics that suffered the most under the Ba'th's statist policies.

Hama had been a key recipient of the new government's push to develop heavy industry in the late 1970s, with a glut of factories established in the city and surrounding villages. Although the factories turned Hama into a hub of employment for rural Syrians, it had significant consequences for the city's long-term traders, who struggled to compete with the cheap factory-made products that began to flood the *souq*. Hama's state-run factories paid workers in line with the new state-mandated minimum wage, but urban traders struggled to uphold these wage conditions in the increasingly tight economy.[100] Subsequent public-sector pay-rises added inflationary pressures and created a significant divide between private-sector workers and their better-paid public-sector counterparts. The mass influx of rural workers into the cities for factory work also led to the decline of cotton farming in Hama province, which led to higher cotton prices for small manufacturers. This pattern was seen across Syria's north, but was most pronounced in Hama.[101] Lawson went so far as to argue that the 1982 Hama uprising 'was primarily a reaction by small manufacturers and tradespeople in Hamah [*sic*] to the regime's program of large-scale industrial development'.[102] In addition, much of Hama's land was redistributed under the Ba'th to rural Alawites from the Alawi mountains, which may have given a sectarian hue to the socio-economic tensions.[103] As a result, members of the group's Hama branch were among the worst affected by Hafez al-Assad's policies, and had the least to lose from mobilising against the regime. Although the Hama group is often depicted as more ideological than other factions, in practice Hama was also the city where Ba'thist authoritarian conditions proved most oppressive. Remarkably, this pattern of discontent spurred by the government's reconfiguration of the country's economy and social contract emerged again decades later as a root cause of the 2011 uprising.[104]

Following the intervention of the international Muslim Brotherhood organisation in 1971, Shaykh Abd al-Fatah abu Ghuddah from Aleppo

---

[99] Cited in Batatu, 'Syria's Muslim Brethren', p. 15. [100] Lawson, 'Social Bases', p. 25.
[101] Hinnebusch, *Authoritarian Power*, p. 288. [102] Lawson, 'Social Bases', p. 24.
[103] Hanna Batatu, 'Some Observations on the Social Roots of Syria's Ruling Military Group and the Causes for Its Dominance', *Middle East Journal* 35, no. 3 (1981), p. 338.
[104] Dara Conduit, 'The Patterns of Syrian Uprising: Comparing Hama in 1980–1982 and Homs in 2011', *British Journal of Middle Eastern Studies* 44, no. 1 (2017), pp. 73–87.

took the leadership. Abu Ghuddah was a well-respected scholar of the Hadith and former member of the Syrian parliament. He was no radical. The Brotherhood leadership change in 1971 did not lead to immediate changes in Brotherhood policy, as it coincided with Hafez al-Assad's ascent to power. Al-Assad fomented a short-lived calming of the Syrian political climate, by softening the country's new economic policies and reaching out to a number of Muslim leaders.[105] In practice, the ideological and tactical differences between the Damascus and Aleppo factions were also minor.

Nonetheless, Abu Ghuddah's elevation to the leadership saw many moderate Damascene Muslim Brothers sever ties to the movement. The formal marginalisation of Issam al-Attar and the Damascus wing failed to completely remove the tension, as he continued to speak on behalf of the group and sign off correspondence as the group's leader well into the 1980s.[106] This caused significant confusion among foreign diplomatic representatives in Damascus, who continued to consider al-Attar as the Brotherhood leader.[107] In the British Embassy in Damascus's 1981 profiles of 'leading personalities in Syria', al-Attar was the only Brotherhood member listed.[108] Al-Attar's behaviour irritated the Brothers remaining in Syria so much that *al-Nadhir* accused him of not being genuinely opposed to the Ba'th because his sister Najah al-Attar had been appointed the Syrian Minister of Culture (later becoming Vice President).[109] In reality, this development said more about the Ba'th's mastery of psychological warfare than al-Attar's loyalties, but it was nonetheless a sore spot for the group.

The Brotherhood leadership changed again in 1975 with the ascent of Adnan Saadeddine. This marked the transfer of the leadership to the

---

[105] For a full discussion of this, see Batatu, *Syria's Peasantry*, pp. 260–1.
[106] For example, Issam al-Attar gave a lengthy interview with *an-Nahar* in 1980 in which he spoke on behalf of the Brotherhood. See 'An interview with Issam al-Attar, leader of Syria's Muslim Brothers', *An-Nahar Arab Report and Memo* (18 February 1980), pp. 3–5. Likewise, he issued a 'statement from the Muslim Brotherhood in Syria' on 9 July 1980, as the 'head of the Muslim Brotherhood in Syria' – see Issam Al-Attar, 'Statement from the Muslim Brotherhood in Syria', 9 July 1980. Available in Al-Hakim, *The Islamic Jihadi Revolution*, p. 597.
[107] The British Embassy in Damascus described al-Attar in 1981 as: 'Controller-General of the Syrian Muslim Brotherhood since 1961, though reportedly replaced by Adnan Saadeddine in 1981', even though al-Attar had lost the leadership in 1971. 'FCO 93/2943: Leading Personalities in Syria', *British Embassy Damascus*, 1981.
[108] See ibid.
[109] Michael Morton, 'Foreign Capital Vital to Syria's Economic Boom', *The Jerusalem Post* (10 May 1977), p. 1; 'Syria in a Period of Economic Growth', *The New York Times* (16 November 1976), p. 35; Thomas Mayer, 'The Islamic Opposition in Syria 1961–1982', *Orient* 24, no. 4 (1983), p. 596.

Hama faction, which tilted the group towards violence as the Hama branch's preferred tactical option to counter the Ba'th. A senior Brotherhood official noted that in contrast 'most Aleppo people thought it (violence) was suicidal'.[110] The group did not formally endorse violence during this period, largely leaving its long-standing position intact. Former Brotherhood political office chief Hassan al-Hachimi recalled that the group was still 'struggling to understand how to respond', particularly in relation to the Vanguard.[111]

The rise of the Hama leaders hastened the cross-pollination of ideas between the Brotherhood and the Fighting Vanguard. Saadeddine acknowledged that a relationship existed between Hadid's group and the Hamawi Brotherhood, which 'continued for years ... Sometimes the relationship was harmonious, but sometimes there was discord.'[112] Saadeddine had offered Hadid financial support for 'living expenses',[113] but it is important not to overstate the significance of these ties. When asked in an interview about these connections, al-Bayanouni declared:

Of course [there was communication because] he (Saadeddine) was concerned that they were members. And he was the leader of the group at the time ... He used to help them, but he was doing it separately to keep them away from the Brotherhood. [The money] was mainly for the families of people who had been captured or in prison.[114]

As a further indicator of the leadership's complexities and machinations, the Vanguard's Damascus leader Ayman Shorbaji reported that from 1977 to 1980, 'There was not any contact for us (the Damascus branch of the Fighting Vanguard) with the leadership of the Muslim Brotherhood on the outside.'[115]

Against this backdrop, several developments took place that undermined the Brotherhood's ability to influence events in Syria. The Syrian economy began to stagnate, foreign capital dried up and the long-term negative impact of the Ba'th's social reforms became pronounced, particularly among urban dwellers in the late 1970s.[116] This led to large-scale unemployment and spurred questions about the wisdom of Hafez al-Assad's economic strategies as well as the merits of the Brotherhood's

---

[110] Anonymous interview (parenthesis added).
[111] Interview with Hassan al-Hachimi, Istanbul.
[112] Saadeddine, *The Muslim Brotherhood in Syria*, vol. 3, p. 386.   [113] Ibid., p. 387.
[114] Interview with Ali al-Bayanouni, London (parenthesis added).
[115] Shorbaji, *The Diary of a Vanguard Combatant*, p. 95 (parenthesis added).
[116] For a detailed discussion of these dynamics, see Fred H. Lawson, *Why Syria Goes to War: Thirty Years of Confrontation* (Ithaca: Cornell University Press, 1996).

passive opposition. Although these pressures were particularly pronounced in Hama, they also directly impacted the Brotherhood's support base in other cities. Decades after the group's founding, the Brotherhood remained closely tied to Syria's merchant, professional and religious classes. Dekmejian described the group's leaders as continuing to fall into 'two clusters of occupational patterns: liberal professionals and *"ulama'"*', while the 1,384 government opponents arrested between 1976 and 1981 were made up of students (27.7 percent), teachers (7.9 percent) and professionals (13.3 percent, including 79 engineers, 57 doctors, 25 lawyers and 10 pharmacists).[117] Even senior members of the Fighting Vanguard shared this background – as noted above, Marwan Hadid was from a wealthy Hamawi family, while its Aleppan leader Husni Abu hailed from an Aleppan business family and married into a prominent Aleppan religious family alongside Adnan Uqlah.[118]

Other factors compounded domestic tensions, including President Hafez al-Assad's unpopular intervention on the side of Lebanese Christians against the Palestinians in the Lebanon war in 1976.[119] In June 1978, a resolution by the Damascus Bar Association called for the Emergency Law (enacted in 1962) to be lifted and criticised the government's use of torture against political prisoners. It also warned its members that those providing legal services to support the regime's unlawful activities could face sanction from the Bar. Similar resolutions were passed by the Syrian Bar Association a week later, and by the Aleppo Bar Association in November.[120]

At the same time, the Vanguard's assassination campaign was becoming increasingly brazen and enjoyed successes against Hafez al-Assad's inner circle, including in the 1978 murder of the Ministry of Interior's Director of Police affairs Colonel Ahmad Khalil, and the 1979 killing of both the Public Prosecutor of the Supreme State Security Court Adil Mini, and al-Assad's personal doctor Dr Muhammad Shahada Khalil.[121]

Finally, the Brotherhood experienced a massive influx of members. The grassroots were radicalising, with books such as Hawwa's *JundAllah* being widely distributed in mosques. Saadeddine reported that during this period,

---

[117] R. Hrair Dekmejian, *Islam in Revolution: Fundamentalism in the Arab World*, 2nd edn (Syracuse: Syracuse University Press), pp. 112–13.
[118] Raymond Hinnebusch, *Syria: Revolution from Above* (London: Routledge, 2001), p. 90.
[119] Ibid., p. 20; Hinnebusch, *Authoritarian Power*, p. 293.
[120] Alan George, *Syria: Neither Bread Nor Freedom* (London, Zed Books, 2003), p. 103.
[121] Khatib, 'Islamic and Islamist Revivalism in Syria', p. 67; Seale, *Asad of Syria*, p. 317.

A significant number of students and learned people and the sons of rural areas joined the Muslim Brotherhood organisation. So, the number increased in a way that we have not expected and even more than what we were expecting, especially in the provinces of Aleppo, Idlib and Hama.[122]

He claimed that this saw an 800 percent increase in membership numbers in the Aleppo governorate.[123] According to Pierret, many of these recruits came from 'the study circles of the ulama, particularly those whose da'wa was aimed at young educated members of the middle class, which constituted the majority of Islamic militants at the time'.[124] But many recruits rejected the Brotherhood's traditional positions, with one Syrian Brother recalling that '[t]his radical *Jihadiya* in the Ikhwan wanted to assassinate the approach of al-Sibai. We were studying [Sayyid Qutb's book] "Milestones on the Road" at that time, rather than [the Egyptian Brotherhood's General Guide Hassan al-Hubaidi's book] "Preachers, not Judges"', which reflected radical versus traditional Brotherhood ideological positions respectively.[125] According to former Brotherhood ideologue Zuhair Salem, Said Hawwa's ideas also played a role in changing the group. He 'presented views and people accepted them. Some people kind of worshipped him.'[126] Compounding this problem, Ayman Shorbaji claims that a third of the Brotherhood's members joined the Vanguard as the former's leadership trickled into exile.[127]

This combination of factors meant that by 1979, both the Brotherhood and the broader Syrian political arena had undergone a series of political changes in line with the patterns of anti-authoritarianism radicalisation. The Ba'th's time in power had fundamentally changed Syria and tensions were palpable across the country. This new operating environment had altered the costs of political activity and for many of the Brotherhood's moderates the risk of remaining active had become too high. This caused the departure of al-Attar's moderate supporters, soon to be followed by others, including Aleppan moderates.[128] The leadership balance then tilted and empowered those who favoured violent tactics. Authoritarianism had stimulated a dramatic shift in the group's political structure and provided conditions conducive to the sanction of violence.

---

[122] Saadeddine, *The Muslim Brotherhood in Syria*, vol. 3, p. 370.   [123] Ibid.
[124] Pierret, *Religion and State in Syria*, pp. 66–7.
[125] Pargeter, *The Muslim Brotherhood*, pp. 77–8.
[126] Interview with Zuhair Salem, London.
[127] Shorbaji, *The Diary of a Vanguard Combatant*, p. 45.   [128] Anonymous interview.

1979–1982: The Brotherhood Sanctions Violence against the Ba'th

The sense that the Brotherhood was losing control of its operating environment reached a peak in 1979 following the Fighting Vanguard's brazen Aleppo Artillery Academy massacre. This event marked an escalation of the Fighting Vanguard's violence and prompted a massive and unprecedented counter-mobilisation by the Ba'th. The massacre was one of the most appalling incidents of sectarian violence to have taken place up to that time in post-independence Syria.

The massacre took place on 16 June 1979 when the Fighting Vanguard launched an attack on Alawite cadets at the Aleppo Artillery Academy. The attack was masterminded by the Vanguard's Aleppan leader Husni Abu and Captain Ibrahim al-Youssef who was a Ba'th Party member and senior army officer stationed at the Academy. Vanguard sources claim that al-Youssef had participated in many previous operations in Aleppo.[129] Al-Youssef allegedly summoned the school's cadets into a hall before asking all Sunni Muslims to leave the room. Owing to the nature of the Ba'th regime and senior armed forces by this time, there were a disproportionate number of Alawites in the officer class. Fighting Vanguard militants then entered the room and opened fire, killing scores of unarmed cadets. Estimates of the death toll of cadets vary widely, from 32 (Batatu and Mayer),[130] to more than 50 (Hinnebusch),[131] to 83 (Lefèvre).[132] Some Fighting Vanguard and Brotherhood members estimate that the death toll of cadets was in excess of 200.[133] Within days, the Syrian Interior Minister Adnan Dabbagh took to Syrian radio to blame the Syrian Muslim Brotherhood.[134]

The Brotherhood, whose entire leadership was in exile by this point, claimed to have had no prior warning of the massacre, having only become aware of the attack after the Fighting Vanguard leader Adnan

---

[129] Shorbaji, *The Diary of a Vanguard Combatant*, p. 48.
[130] Batatu, *Syria's Peasantry*, p. 266; Mayer, 'The Islamic Opposition', p. 589.
[131] Hinnebusch, *Authoritarian Power*, p. 293.   [132] Lefèvre, *Ashes of Hama*, p. 73.
[133] Abu Musab al-Suri claims that 255 people were killed – Al-Hakim, *The Islamic Jihadi Revolution*, p. 95; Ayman Shorbaji claimed that more than 200 were killed: Shorbaji, *The Diary of a Vanguard Combatant*, p. 48; former Brotherhood member Ali al-Ahmad estimated that 'about 300 students from the minority', see interview with Ali al-Ahmad, London, although none of these individuals appears to have been involved in the attack.
[134] Attack at Syrian Army Barracks, text of statement by Syrian Interior Minister and Deputy Martial Law Governor, Adnan Dabbagh, *Damascus Home Service* (Damascus: BBC Monitoring Middle East, 22 June 1979).

Uqlah issued a statement of responsibility.[135] It immediately released a statement in the Kuwaiti Muslim Brotherhood's newspaper denying involvement. The statement expressed 'surprise' at both the massacre and the government's decision to blame the Brotherhood, declaring that Ibrahim al-Youssef was an 'active member' of the Ba'th Party and had no connection to the Brotherhood.[136] Issam al-Attar also issued a letter denying the group's involvement:

> The accusation that Moslem [sic] Brothers in Syria were responsible for the Artillery School incident is an open invention contradicted by the facts. Suffice it to say that the leader of the operation was a Ba'thist officer of long standing. Indeed he was the Party officer responsible for security in the school. The regime in Syria made this accusation against the Brotherhood to cover up the violent differences and contradictions existing in its own ranks, or to prepare the ground for the annihilation of the elements of Islamic forces one after the other.[137]

Ibrahim al-Youssef's membership status is disputed by Fighting Vanguard sources who maintain that he was a member of both the Fighting Vanguard and the Brotherhood.[138] But the truth in the end was immaterial: the regime had decided the Brotherhood's culpability. As Saadeddine later recalled, 'the Artillery event was an act of catastrophic proportions for the organisation of the Muslim Brotherhood'.[139]

The Syrian government responded to the massacre with a level of fury and repression not previously seen in the country. Hafez al-Assad announced soon after:

> We are now facing a conspiracy against our country and a criminal act [by the Muslim Brotherhood] ... That gang would have adopted the same position even

---

[135] Adnan Saadeddine, *The Muslim Brotherhood in Syria: Notes and Memories (in Arabic)*, vol. 4 (Dar al-Amar, 2006), p. 77.
[136] 'A Statement from the Muslim Brotherhood, Issued on June 24 (in Arabic)' (3 July 1979). Available in Al-Hakim, *The Islamic Jihadi Revolution*, p. 574.
[137] Issam Al-Attar, 'Untitled Letter in Response to the Artillery Massacre, Translated by the British Embassy Damascus' (28 June 1979). This document was found among archival material at the British National Archive. It can be located within the following folder: Vincent Fean, 'FCO 93/2253: 014/1 Correspondence to Douglas Gordon titled "Moslem Brothers"', *British Embassy Damascus*, 15 August 1979.
[138] For example, Adnan Saadeddine maintained that: 'We had not heard of Captain Ibrahim al-Youssef before the artillery incident. He was never a member of the Brotherhood, but he had been a member of the Ba'th for a long time.' See Saadeddine, *The Muslim Brotherhood in Syria*, vol. 4, p. 78; Shorbaji maintains that al-Youssef was secretly a member of both the Brotherhood and the Vanguard. See Shorbaji, *The Diary of a Vanguard Combatant*, p. 48.
[139] Saadeddine, *The Muslim Brotherhood in Syria*, vol. 4, p. 76.

if we were angels. It considers a third of the people to be non-Moslems [*sic*]. Its members want to monopolize Islam for themselves.[140]

Statements about the Brotherhood in the aftermath of the artillery massacre often took on a chilling tone. Hafez al-Assad's brother Rifaat al-Assad, who headed the elite paramilitary defence companies, declared at the Baʿth Party Regional Congress in January 1980:

Stalin sacrificed ten million to preserve the Bolshevik Revolution and Syria should be prepared to do the same ... [I am personally] willing to fight a hundred years, demolish a million strongholds, and sacrifice a million martyrs [to end the Brotherhood].[141]

The Syrian regime had matched its statements with a massive crackdown on the Brotherhood and its supporters. Thousands were arrested across the country and Syrian television broadcasted hours of confessions from alleged Brotherhood members, including the Fighting Vanguard's Aleppan leader involved in the Artillery massacre, Husni Abu.[142] Walid Saffour, a future Brotherhood member (but not one at the time), recalled:

Life became hell: I was arrested several times between June 1979 and October 1980 and tortured so severely by the Military Intelligence that I would later need to undergo three surgeries, leaving my back disabled until today.[143]

In March 1980, an army operation in the northern town of Jisr al-Shughour left more than 200 dead. The distance that the regime was willing to go became even clearer that June following the attempted assassination of Hafez al-Assad (it is uncertain which of the Vanguard or the Brotherhood was responsible). In retaliation, Rifaat al-Assad dispatched units from the defence companies to Palmyra Prison at dawn, where large numbers of Brotherhood members were incarcerated. The units were instructed to kill all prisoners in sight. Between 600 and 1,000 unarmed prisoners were slaughtered in their cells that morning;[144] many were Brotherhood members. The regime escalated its crackdown the

---

[140] Hafez Al-Assad, 'Asad's Remarks about the Moslem Brotherhood', *Damascus Home Service* (Damascus: BBC Monitoring Middle East, 30 June 1979); Issam Al-Attar, 'Statement from the Muslim Brotherhood in Syria' (9 July 1980).
[141] Seale, *Asad of Syria*, p. 327
[142] 'FCO 93/2253: Letter from Vincent Fean to Douglas Gordon on Husni Abo's Televised Confession', *British Embassy Damascus*, 7 September 1979; Vladimir Bilyakov, 'Muslim Brotherhood's "Aggressive Campaign against Syrian Regime"' (London: BBC Summary of World Broadcasts, 20 October 1980).
[143] Cited in Lefèvre, *Ashes of Hama*, p. 88.
[144] R. Shareah Taleghani, 'Breaking the Silence of Tadmor Military Prison', *Middle East Report* 45, no. 275 (2015), pp. 21–5.

following month when it introduced Law No. 49, legislation that made membership of the Brotherhood punishable by death.

In October 1981, Hafez al-Assad declared: 'We must completely eliminate any trace of this gang by effective revolutionary means, no matter how long it takes us.'[145] Although it was not clear at the time what 'effective revolutionary means' entailed, Brotherhood members could be sure that it would not bode well for their future. The Hama massacre just months later made this a certainty. In hindsight, Abdul Halim al-Khaddam, who was Syrian Foreign Minister at the time, acknowledged:

> The regime made a mistake by increasing the repression after the Aleppo Artillery incident [of June 1979], as it only further radicalized many Brothers who came to feel they had no option but to use violence.[146]

It had become abundantly clear to the Brotherhood that Ba'th retribution would know no bounds.

The Brotherhood Declares Violence on the Regime

The Ba'th crackdown represented an existential threat to opposition in Syria and the final step on the Brotherhood's path to violence. By June 1979, violence had reached the Brotherhood's doorstep. Not only could it no longer control its former (and some current) members, but the 'grey zone' was no longer a safe place to exist. It also had no ability to withstand the government crackdown. In this context, the Brotherhood endorsed violence against the regime in an act that was less a deliberate policy turn than an admission of failure and an act of survival. Although the Fighting Vanguard's use of violence in previous years on the margins had already weakened the Brotherhood's claim to innocence, large numbers of senior members purportedly still thought the formal decision to opt for violence would lead to catastrophe.[147]

The exact date of the decision to fight is unclear, but there was a significant uptick of violence from mid-1979 in Syria that was tangibly different to the targeted campaign of assassinations previously led by the Vanguard. This included large bombings.[148] The first issue of the Brotherhood's new newsletter *al-Nadhir* (The Warner) was released on

---

[145] Hafez Al-Assad, excerpts from recording of speech made at graduation of paratroopers in Latakia, *Damascus Home Service* (Damascus: BBC Monitoring Middle East, 1 October 1981).
[146] Cited in Lefèvre, *Ashes of Hama*, p. 111.   [147] Anonymous interview.
[148] 'Explosions in Aleppo Work of Muslim Brotherhood', *Damascus Home Service* (Damascus: BBC Summary of World Broadcasts, 25 August 1980).

6 September 1979.[149] It catalogued the latest attacks across Syria, including assaults on Mukhabarat vehicles on 18 and 21 July, the 12 August assassination of an Alawite Major General in Hama and the explosion at an arms depot in the Damascus suburb of Harasta.[150] Zuhair Salem, a member of the Aleppo faction and later group ideologue, acknowledges being a founding editor of *al-Nadhir*.[151] While the Brotherhood's violence is regularly blamed on the Hama faction (particularly by members of the Aleppo clique), it is important to note that Aleppan members were also prominent in it. Indeed, at the time violence was endorsed by the Brotherhood, the leader of the Aleppan faction, Ali al-Bayanouni, was deputy Brotherhood leader and he purportedly supported the tactical decision.[152] He later led the group's military high command.

Senior Brotherhood officials today remain reluctant to discuss the group's use of violence and many maintain that the group has no connection to the events that took place inside Syria during this time. Of those that acknowledge that violence did take place, most claim that the decision followed Law No. 49, even though the legislation was instituted nearly a year after the violence increased.[153] Nonetheless, Brotherhood historical documents confirm the group's slide into violence, with the 1980 Declaration and Program of the Islamic Revolution declaring:

> We strongly believe that it is not absolutely necessary for problems to be resolved by violence. On the contrary, the natural thing is for such problems to be solved through constructive dialogue and mutual confidence. But nothing could be done if one side insists on ignoring the other and refusing to deal with it except by force. Due to this, and because of our belief that the present regime has reached the point of no return, and that it is now impossible for it to undergo a radical revision, we declare that there will be no truce, no laying down of arms and no negotiation.[154]

The Brotherhood's connection to the Declaration is indisputable given that it was signed by Ali al-Bayanouni, Adnan Saadeddine and Said Hawwa. The Brotherhood logo appears on the Declaration's front page. In this regard, while many of the Brotherhood's current leaders exploit

---

[149] *Al-Nadhir* no. 1 (in Arabic) (9 September 1979). A copy of this document is stored in the British National Archive, with a partial translation. See Vincent Fean, 'FCO 93/2253: Syria Internal: Moslem Brotherhood', *British Embassy Damascus*, 14 November 1979.

[150] *Al-Nadhir* no. 1 (in Arabic) (9 September 1979). Cited in 'FCO 93/2253: Syria Internal: Moslem Brotherhood', *British Embassy Damascus*, 14 November 1979.

[151] Interview with Zuhair Salem, London.

[152] Interview with Ali al-Bayanouni, London.

[153] al-Amine, 'Leader of Syrian Muslim Brotherhood'.

[154] 'Declaration of Program of the Islamic Revolution in Syria', Damascus: The Higher Command of the Islamic Revolution in Syria, p. 11.

historical ambiguities and gaps to create a sense of uncertainty, primary source material from the period appears to disprove the group's claims to have no link to violence.

In tandem with the Brotherhood's use of violence was the continuing deterioration of the Syrian political and economic climate. By 1980, popular unrest had broken out across the country. The wider protest movement was broad based and backed by a secular opposition including lawyers, merchants, professional syndicates, Nasserites, communists and dissident Ba'thists.[155] This followed another Damascus Bar Association Resolution in August 1979 calling for the suspension of the Emergency Law and for democratic freedoms. This was echoed in a resolution passed by the Engineers' Association national congress in February 1980.[156] The Syrian government faced further crisis in Hama in that same month when residents enforced a 'near-total' strike for six days in opposition to government brutality against protesters.[157] By March, many shops were still closed.[158] The Syrian Arab Army Third Division's commander General Shafiq Fayadh purportedly stood on his tank in Aleppo and told those watching that he was willing to kill 1,000 people a day in order to root out the Muslim Brotherhood. The Third Division occupied Aleppo for the following year, and according to Seale stationed a tank on almost every street.[159] Following the March Jisr al-Shughour massacre mentioned above, the Syrian Bar Association, Medical Association and Engineers' Association called for a national strike on 31 March. On 9 April, the regime dissolved the restive professional associations, declaring them to have been 'infiltrated by reactionary elements'.[160] But this too failed to halt the rising protest movement – by the end of April, Hama was once again 'rocked by strikes and riots aimed at bringing down the government in Damascus'.[161] The regime for its part remained in no mood for conciliation: In a particularly brazen move, Rifaat al-Assad sent the 'Daughters of the Revolution' into Damascus to tear hijabs off religious women on the street.[162] Given the scale of anti-Ba'th discontent, Hinnebusch observed that support for the Islamic movement at its peak during the early Ba'th decades 'faithfully reflected

---

[155] Shyam Bhatia, 'Situation in Syrian Town Fluid Despite Army Step', *The Times of India* (29 April 1980).
[156] George, *Syria: Neither Bread Nor Freedom*, p. 104.
[157] 'New Violence Erupts in Two Syrian Cities Despite Assad Action', *The Globe and Mail* (10 April 1980).
[158] Marvine Howe, 'Syria Concedes Wide Unrest over Policies', *The New York Times* (28 March 1980).
[159] Seale, *Asad of Syria*, p. 328.   [160] George, *Syria: Neither Bread Nor Freedom*, p. 104.
[161] Bhatia, 'Situation in Syrian Town Fluid'.
[162] Hinnebusch, *Syria: Revolution from Above*, p. 101.

the interests and values of the roughly half of society effectively excluded by the Baʿth state'.[163] Although the Brotherhood's use of violence may not have enjoyed universal support, its challenging of the Baʿthist state was but the extreme end of the broad-based anti-authoritarian protest movement that was engulfing Syria.

Western diplomats based in Beirut reported in April 1980 that 6,000 people had been arrested in Aleppo and Hama alone.[164] Protests took place primarily in the *souqs* and commercial districts of the old cities, rather than in the countryside. In Damascus, the government had to send its own militias into the *souqs* to force shops open. But the trend was even more noticeable in Hama, where shops were closed for months.[165] Ever cognisant of the political mood, the Brotherhood's magazine *al-Nadhir* gave regular updates on economic developments in Syria throughout the armed uprising.[166] Pargeter described that by 1980, 'the whole country was like a powder keg waiting to go up'.[167] For Tripp, the Brotherhood's violence therefore served a dual purpose: to mount a challenge to the regime while in the process spurring a country-wide popular anti-government mobilisation.[168]

Mounting a Violent Response

The Brotherhood's embrace of violent activities bore many of the hallmarks of its political decision-making under authoritarianism, which was characterised by pragmatism, short-term thinking and strategic naivety. The Brotherhood's leadership and its elite base remained unchanged from its earlier form. The group's militants were made up of the youth of Syria's bourgeois classes which had few ties with the country's military, and it quickly became clear that it had very few capabilities or structures that could be quickly activated to prosecute its new cause.

The group formed a military high command, with its leaders taking on the role of military commanders and strategists, despite having no background in such activities. Abu Musab al-Suri accused the group's new military committee of being 'dead on arrival; just like all their other

---

[163] Ibid., p. 93.
[164] Steve K. Kindy, 'Unrest Mounts in Syria against Assad's Regime', *Boston Globe* (28 March 1980).
[165] Fred H. Lawson, *Global Security Watch: Syria* (Denver: Praeger, 2013); Hinnebusch, *Authoritarian Power*, p. 291.
[166] See Marcin Kaczmarski, *Russia–China Relations in the Post-Crisis International Order* (Abingdon: Routledge, 2015).
[167] Pargeter, *The Muslim Brotherhood*, p. 81.
[168] Charles Tripp, *The Power and the People: Paths of Resistance in the Middle East* (Cambridge: Cambridge University Press, 2013), p. 53.

institutions it was run by incapable leaders lacking the determination and qualifications to bring this idea into fruition'.[169] The backgrounds of the high command's leaders suggest that al-Suri's criticism may have had solid foundations; no member of the group's military apparatus had significant recent military experience. Ali al-Bayanouni, the head of the high command, was a lawyer. His Brother Abu Nasr al-Bayanouni was a cleric. Said Hawwa was a religious scholar, Hassan Houeidi was a doctor and Muhammad Hawary was a professor of pharmacology. Although neither higher education nor wealth have been barriers to participation in violence (and have in fact been positively associated with such participation in groups such as Hamas),[170] experience matters, particularly when leading an asymmetric campaign against such a violent foe at short notice. The Brotherhood's leaders had little connection to the armed forces, so members had to rely on their limited experience garnered during compulsory military training or acquired in the Palestine War some three decades prior. Al-Suri added that 'the new structure was closer to a board of directors for a financial institution than a leadership council for gang warfare'.[171] This proved a significant barrier to the leaders' ability to plan and direct a strategic confrontation with the Ba'th. It was hardly a recipe for success.

The decision to pursue military activities without preparation or qualifications proved foolhardy and conveyed a sense of arrogance and naivety on the part of the Brotherhood. Saadeddine acknowledged after Hama that 'none of us studied guerrilla warfare like Castro or Ho Chi Minh. Our normal field of struggle would be parliament or the ideological arena.'[172] Former Brotherhood member Ali al-Ahmad agreed, noting that the Brotherhood

> are not a fighting group, they are peaceful. They are people from the mosques. Imagine in the 1970s or 1980s, never in their lives had they carried a weapon to go out and fight. Their mentality is not fighting. It is teaching people, preaching in the mosques, so they were not prepared for this ... They are educated people. Not people who can carry weapons.[173]

This lack of preparedness led to catastrophe on the battlefield, and it quickly became clear that the Brotherhood was not good at waging war.

---

[169] Al-Suri, 'Lessons Learned', p. 8.
[170] Claude Berrebi, 'Evidence about the Link between Education, Poverty and Terrorism among Palestinians', *Peace Economics, Peace Science and Public Policy* 13, no. 1 (2007), pp. 1–36.
[171] Al-Suri, 'Lessons Learned', p. 12.
[172] Cited in Chris Kutschera, 'When the Brothers Fall Out', *The Middle East Magazine* 162 (1988), p. 27.
[173] Interview with Ali al-Ahmad, London.

The subsequent human cost and denting of the group's confidence made recovery particularly difficult.

The Brotherhood's military campaign unfolded through two parallel strategies. This involved formal involvement in the conflict while leveraging the individualist tendencies of members to empower those inside Syria to respond on their own. The Brotherhood's most significant formal contribution to the conflict was the military training it organised for members in camps established in Iraq and Jordan.[174] The Brotherhood's Iraqi camps were based in existing Iraqi military facilities near Baghdad, including at the al-Rassheed and Taji air bases.[175] The training was operated by senior members of the Iraqi armed forces, and according to one Brotherhood member who trained at the camps, the Iraqi government was generous in its provision of military equipment.[176] Fighting Vanguard and Brotherhood figures were trained at separate camps, although a number of other smaller groups were apparently present in the Brotherhood camp. The training included a *Da'wa* program run by the Brotherhood.[177] Some elite groups were also sent to Egypt to receive training from the Egyptian authorities.[178]

Serious questions were raised about the quality and scale of the Brotherhood's military programme. Abu Musab al-Suri claims that less than 1,000 people were trained in total, arguing that no more than 200 graduates were battle ready.[179] It is not clear whether any graduates were dispatched to Syria. The Brotherhood was also heavily criticised for failing to make a tangible impact on the ground. In one letter, Vanguard leader Adnan Uqlah charged: 'Do you think that by sending a handful of the large money that you receive and waste carelessly, that you are the leaders of the mujahidin?'[180] Another Vanguard member echoed these complaints: 'The leadership beyond the border (a reference to the Brotherhood) did not represent anyone except for themselves.'[181] He added that the Brotherhood leaders spent large sums of money on international travel and conferences, living affluently while those inside Syria struggled to afford the armed campaign.[182] According to Lefèvre, the Brotherhood–Vanguard relationship was so poor by 1981 that Uqlah

---

[174] Interview with Ali al-Bayanouni, London.
[175] Al-Hakim, *The Islamic Jihadi Revolution*, p. 212; interview with Ali al-Ahmad, London.
[176] Ibid. [177] Ibid.
[178] Brynjar Lia, *Architect of Global Jihad: The Life of Al-Qaida Strategist Abu Mus'ab al-Suri* (London: Hurst & Company, 2007), p. 44.
[179] Al-Hakim, *The Islamic Jihadi Revolution*, pp. 200–1.
[180] Uqlah, 'Letter from Adnan Uqlah' (11 June 1980), p. 8. Available as an appendix in Al-Hakim, *The Islamic Jihadi Revolution*, pp. 575–93.
[181] Ibid., p. 109 (parenthesis added). [182] Ibid., p. 137.

attempted to convince a member of the Syrian ulama to issue a *fatwa* (religious edict) that would permit Brotherhood leaders to be kidnapped and imprisoned.[183]

The Brotherhood's formal involvement in the conflict also included operational planning. Abu Musab al-Suri was purportedly appointed deputy commander of a unit planning a large operation in Aleppo in 1982 that never came to fruition.[184] The group's leaders were also involved in a coup plot with dissident Syrian army officers in the period late 1981 to early 1982, which was discovered in January 1982, only weeks before the uprising in Hama. Details of this plan remain scanty, but Ali al-Bayanouni confirmed that the Brotherhood 'had connections with the officers'.[185] This coup plot appears to have been the group's best opportunity during that period due to the substantive link to the Syrian armed forces. The plot's discovery was therefore a significant setback.

The Brotherhood exercised more impact on the ground through its decentralised cells inside the country. This decentralisation was an expected outcome of the group's repression given that groups under such pressure are often forced to devolve to evade capture.[186] Those on the outside of the country were now spread out across the Middle East, and although the Brotherhood's central leadership structure remained intact in Jordan and Iraq, it had little formal communication with the semi-autonomous cells inside Syria. Chapter 2 noted that Brotherhood members have always had a tendency towards individualism. Thus, while enjoying the implicit sanction of the Brotherhood's leadership, most of the Brotherhood-linked violence in Syria appears to have been carried out by affiliates as individuals and by non-Brotherhood members without the direct instruction of the leadership. When Ali al-Bayanouni was asked which attacks the Brotherhood was responsible for, Bayanouni claimed:

It was just groups of Brotherhood and non-Brotherhood ... The Brotherhood never adopted or took responsibility for any of the attacks, but the Brotherhood members were part of the groups [that undertook attacks] ... Those fighting groups inside, the majority were not Brotherhood, but they might be supporting the Brotherhood.[187]

These cells often worked with, or included members from the Fighting Vanguard, as well as other smaller groups such as Jamiyah Abi Dharr,

---

[183] Lefèvre, *Ashes of Hama*, p. 121.   [184] Lia, *Architect of Global Jihad*, p. 47.
[185] Interview with Ali al-Bayanouni, London.
[186] For further information on this trend, see Ellen Lust-Okar, *Structuring Conflict in the Arab World: Incumbents, Opponents and Institutions* (Cambridge: Cambridge University Press, 2005), p. 87.
[187] Interview with Ali al-Bayanouni, London.

which was a Brotherhood-linked *jamiyah* operated by Mohammad abu al-Nasr al-Bayanouni (Ali al-Bayanouni's brother). Abd-Allah cited an edition of *al-Nadhir* that reported that Jamiyah Abi Dharr had produced a cadre of 'strong youth, well trained in the use of various types of weapons'.[188]

The Brotherhood's magazine *al-Nadhir* carefully catalogued incidents carried out by the 'mujahidin' throughout this period. A late 1980 edition claimed: 'Al Mujahideen [sic] carried out a successful operation where 23 security elements were killed and 40 others wounded Adnan'.[189] Further editions recorded the likes of 'attacks on a security patrol that was firing from the roof and had killed two women and a child'.[190] *Al-Nadhir* also published news of large-scale incidents, including an assault on a cabinet office that purportedly killed 200 'regime agents'.[191] Major attacks took place throughout 1981, including the detonation of car bombs outside the Prime Minister's office and the Air Force headquarters, the latter of which killed 20 people and wounded 50.[192] In November 1981, a massive car bomb killed 64 in the busy Azbakiya residential district of Damascus, where a number of Syrian intelligence facilities were located.[193] Other regime symbols such as newspaper headquarters were attacked, as well as Soviet targets because the Soviet Union was a close military supporter of the al-Assad regime.[194] Seale described a tense atmosphere among government supporters by late 1982:

Hardly anyone dared stir after dark and even during the day few party members ventured out on foot. Some even stayed away from work until warned that they risked expulsion from the party. Asad [sic] was little seen in those months.[195]

By early 1982, however, there was an increasing sense that the regime was winning the battle. Both the Brotherhood and the Vanguard had sustained massive losses in the regime counter-offensive, while Aleppo and Hama had been under on-and-off military rule for nearly two years. The 8 January 1982 edition of *al-Nadhir*, the last English edition before the Hama uprising, presciently reported that 'The blood

---

[188] Abd-allah, *The Islamic Struggle in Syria*. [189] Kaczmarski, *Russia–China Relations*.
[190] Al-Mujahideen in Syria, 'News', *Abstracts from Al-Nazeer No. 36 (English edition)* (14 July 1980), p. 4.
[191] 'The News', *Abstracts from Al-Nazeer, No. 38 (English edition)* (1981), p. 4.
[192] Associated Press, 'Bomb Explosion in Syria Kills 64 and Hurts 135 in Crowded Area', *The New York Times* (30 November 1981), www.nytimes.com/1981/11/30/world/bomb-explosion-in-syria-kills-64-and-hurts-135-in-crowded-area.html.
[193] Ibid.
[194] Al-Mujahideen in Syria, 'The News', *Abstracts from Al-Nazeer, No. 38* (English edition) (1981), p. 4.
[195] Seale, *Asad of Syria*.

is flowing in Hama'.[196] Indeed, by February 1982, tensions in the city were at unprecedented levels.

The Hama Uprising

It was in this context of Brotherhood decentralisation and deteriorating security conditions that the Hama uprising broke out in February 1982. The Fighting Vanguard leader Adnan Uqlah purportedly visited Hama in late January of that year and found Brotherhood and Fighting Vanguard members in perilous conditions plotting their last stand.[197] The regime had substantially increased repression of the city, which had led to the arrest of large numbers of members and the discovery of hideouts, ammunition and weapons.[198] The remaining Hamawi fighters were at risk of being discovered and so were planning a last-ditch assault against Syrian forces. The British Embassy in Damascus characterised the thinking of those who were left: the leaders were 'afraid of being picked off one by one from the information gained from the captured members [and] decided to go on the offensive'.[199]

Precisely what happened in Hama in February 1982 will probably never be fully known. Brotherhood leaders deny all responsibility for the events, and claim to have had no involvement. An accurate account is unlikely to ever be released by the Syrian government.[200] Even in memoirs, Brotherhood leaders from this period did not discuss Hama. Both Saadeddine and Said Hawwa catalogued the Brotherhood's history in great detail up to February 1982, but glossed over the event itself,[201] underlining the difficulty that even Brotherhood leaders faced in reconciling themselves to the catastrophic events.

The uprising began less than a fortnight after Adnan Uqlah's visit to Hama. Uqlah had urged the city's members to wait for him to mobilise outside support and left Hama immediately to meet with Brotherhood leaders in Iraq and Jordan. Uqlah had previously met with Taha Yaseen Ramadan, an Iraqi government representative who was head of the Iraqi Popular Army and who acted as the intermediary between Saddam Hussein's government and the Brotherhood and the Vanguard.

---

[196] 'Editorial', *Al-Nadhir no. 42 (English edition)* (8 January 1982), p. 2.
[197] Al-Hakim, *The Islamic Jihadi Revolution*, pp. 208–11.   [198] Ibid., p. 208.
[199] 'FCO 93/3280: FM Damascus 081040Z FEB 82: TELNO u25/43', *British Embassy Damascus*, 8 February 1982.
[200] Anonymous interview; according to Ali al-Bayanouni, the regime 'surrounded them. [but] the Brotherhood told the fighters not to fight the regime.' Interview with Ali al-Bayanouni, London.
[201] See Saadeddine, *The Muslim Brotherhood*, vol. 4; Hawwa, *This Is My Experience*.

Ramadan purportedly promised Iraq's full support for any action against Hafez al-Assad.[202] Uqlah then met with Brotherhood leaders in Amman to get their support. According to Vanguard sources, the Brotherhood's leaders agreed to support the plan on the condition that Uqlah pledged *baya* (allegiance) to the Brotherhood,[203] although Brotherhood sources claim that no such agreement was demanded, and that they had refused the request because they lacked the resources.[204] In the meantime, Said Hawwa purportedly sent a message to Hamawi members urging them to stand down, but the message never arrived. Al-Bayanouni maintains that the message instructed those in the town 'to not have conflict with the regime at the time'.[205]

According to the Brotherhood's official account of events, the Hama uprising began when the Syrian government stormed a number of Brotherhood and Vanguard hideouts in the early hours of 3 February.[206] This forced the cells into action before Uqlah had returned with additional resources. Brotherhood sources claim that those in the town believed the discovery would lead to a massacre if they did not act.[207] Thus, overnight, militants in Hama rose up against the government, putting out a call for a general mobilisation of the population over the minarets of the city's mosques. They were joined by many civilians. Syrian regime forces quickly mobilised thousands of troops to Hama, shutting off the city in all directions and laying siege with what the Brotherhood later described as 'scorched earth tactics'.[208] The battle unfolded over the following three weeks, largely in the old quarters of the city. The Brotherhood had initially taken control of several quarters, but the Baʿth's superior materiel, capabilities and desire to win at any cost meant that those opposing were fighting a losing battle. Three weeks later, with little ammunition remaining and catastrophic casualties, the militants were defeated. The regime had killed tens of thousands of Hamawis in the process of uprooting the militants from their hideouts.

Given the nature of the conflict and the Baʿth's swift response, claims by the Brotherhood's current leadership that the organisation had little involvement bears some credence. Most of the hostilities were carried out by Brotherhood and Vanguard cells inside Hama, who probably received little direction from the leadership of the Brotherhood outside the country. Claims by Brotherhood members that 'very few people'

---

[202] Al-Hakim, *The Islamic Jihadi Revolution*, p. 208.   [203] Ibid., p. 210.
[204] Interview with Ali al-Bayanouni, London.   [205] Ibid.
[206] Muslim Brotherhood, *Hama: The Tragedy of the Times (in Arabic)* (Beirut: al-Maktab al-Ilami, 1982), p. 51.
[207] Ibid., p. 52.   [208] Ibid., p. 115.

were able to provide reinforcements seem plausible given that the regime had blocked all entries to the city.[209] In addition, the regime maintained total control over Syria's skies and cultivated close ties to the Hadidiyin tribe, which had acted as the regime's 'ears and eyes in the countryside of Hama and Aleppo'.[210] During the uprising, the tribe purportedly established checkpoints across Hama province, capturing fleeing Brotherhood members.[211] This made it impossible for Brotherhood militants to infiltrate the country across the desert from Iraq.[212]

In total, assessments of the number of Brotherhood members that fought in Hama vary from Ali al-Bayanouni's estimate of 20–25, to the US Defense Intelligence Agency's report that 200 Brotherhood fighters were active within the city.[213] It is even unclear when the Brotherhood leadership first heard about the uprising. An edition of *al-Nadhir* dated 4 February made no mention of Hama, so it is likely that there was a multi-day delay.[214] The group first publicly acknowledged the uprising on 9 February, nearly a week after the events had begun.[215] Ali al-Bayanouni claims that the group knew 'after two or three days when the people started to come back'.[216] Zuhair Salem explained the challenges the Brotherhood faced in obtaining reliable information:

There was confusing news and we did not have real [information. It was] ... contradictory as well ... We used to wait for a truck driver to come and give us such information [but] sometimes al-Assad used to send among these [drivers] a lot of liars [to cause further confusion].[217]

This paints a picture of a group with no command and control influence over events.

Nonetheless, the Brotherhood mounted a remarkable rhetorical response to the Hama uprising, with the group's leadership immediately taking ownership of the events, even though it knew little about what was happening on the ground. As Pargeter noted, the Brotherhood may have been attempting to ride the coat-tails of revolution in Syria.[218] That is, if the uprising in Hama was going to be successful, then the Brotherhood

---

[209] Interview with Ali al-Ahmad, London; Ali al-Bayanouni said that no one entered Hama from the outside once the uprising was underway – interview with Ali al-Bayanouni, London.
[210] Haian Dukhan, *State and Tribes in Syria: Informal Alliances and Conflict Patterns* (New York: Routledge, 2019), p. 82.
[211] Ibid.   [212] Interview with Ali Ahmad, London, 7 August 2015.
[213] Interview with Ali al-Bayanouni, London; 'Syria: Muslim Brotherhood Pressure Intensifies (U)', US Defense Intelligence Agency (May 1982), p. 11.
[214] *Al-Nadhir no. 43 (English edition)*, 4 February 1982.
[215] 'Syria: Muslim Brotherhood Pressure Intensifies', p. 6.
[216] Interview with Ali al-Bayanouni, London.
[217] Interview with Zuhair Salem, London.   [218] Pargeter, *The Muslim Brotherhood*, p. 51.

wanted to be part of it. This might be cynical, but it was consistent with the Brotherhood's other behaviour under authoritarianism, where the group felt that it had to take advantage of any small opening it was offered.

The Brotherhood announced a *Nafeer* (call to arms) that summoned Brotherhood members from around the world to Iraq for military training. Approximately 1,000 men heeded the call and began to undergo training in the group's camps in Iraq in preparation for entering Syria to back the Brothers in Hama.[219] *Al-Nadhir* began publishing grandiose claims about the 'mujahidin's' successes and printed transcripts of speeches of Brotherhood leaders that had been broadcast across Syria on the Iraq-based Voice of Arab Syria radio, calling for general strikes across Syria.[220] In one such speech, Said Hawwa declared that 'the day has come ... to set the record straight, to recover the time of your destiny'.[221] Another reported that on 14 February 'morale was high' among fighters, while the group published a call on 20 February for the residents of Damascus to commence civil disobedience.[222] On 27 February, another edition of *al-Nadhir* reported that two days earlier, 'al-Mujahideen continue[d] their attacks against the regime's forces seeking to liberate new areas'.[223] These reports were supplemented by statements released by Brotherhood members around the world who attempted to further amplify the Brotherhood's role. Members in Vienna reported in early February that the 'fighting had spread to Damascus, Latakiyah [sic], Aleppo and the eastern part of the country'.[224] Indeed, even when the conflict was all but over in late February, Islamic Front sources in New York reported incorrectly that rebels had seized a naval base in Baida.[225]

Here too the Brotherhood may have overplayed its hand. In an opportunistic bid to claim ownership of the uprising, it overstated its position, and not for the first time. Abu Musab al-Suri had accused the Brotherhood of previously 'taking credit for the military activities of the [Fighting Vanguard] mujahidin, claiming them as its own, bragging and exaggerating ... they used the blood of our martyrs to claim fictitious

---

[219] Interview with Ali al-Ahmad, London.
[220] 'Said Hawwa Speech on the "Voice of Arab Syria" Radio (transcript, in Arabic)', *Al-Nadhir No. 7* (17 February 1982). This is available as an appendix in Al-Hakim, *The Islamic Jihadi Revolution*, pp. 605–6.
[221] Ibid. [222] *Al-Nadhir no. 11 (in Arabic)*, 20 February 1982.
[223] The voice of the Islamic Revolution in Syria, 'Editorial: Army and People Unite against the Tyrant', *Al-Nadhir no. 44 (English edition)*, 27 February 1982.
[224] Shukri B. Abed, 'Syria: Muslim Brotherhood Pressure Intensifies', Defense Intelligence Agency report (1982), p. 6.
[225] 'Syrian Navy Base Reported Seized by Rebel Troops', *Christian Science Monitor* (26 February1982), p. 2; 'Syria: Muslim Brotherhood Pressure Intensifies', p. 11.

glory and collect donations in their name'.[226] It is worth considering how the Brotherhood's opportunistic claims to ownership at the time may have lead to the disproportionate blame that the group now bears for the incident.

The Brotherhood called off the *Nafeer* abruptly in March 1982, reflecting its leaders' realisation that the plan would only lead to further slaughter. According to Ali al-Bayanouni, proceeding 'wasn't an option. We didn't have any choice. The resistance stopped by itself because it couldn't keep going.'[227] Although this decision was reasonable in the face of the regime's massive military superiority, the Brotherhood's leaders in Iraq handled the situation poorly, avoiding the training camps and leaving members to wallow alone in their devastation. Ali al-Ahmad, who was in the camp at the time, recalled that in March they had been

ready to go. Start the car and go. But at the last minute it was stopped. They (the Brotherhood) said Hama is finished; it has been destroyed, and we can't go because we don't have cover from the aircraft, so if we go in the *sahara* (desert) we may be killed.[228]

He described immense anger and sadness in the camps, adding:

When they said take out the cars, empty the cars and get everything, put into storage ... I will never forget that moment ... He (my battalion leader) sat there, and he cried. He said I have been waiting for the day that I can go back to my village. I am waiting.[229]

A Vanguard member reported that very quickly 'more than 1,200 Brotherhood fighters returned to their previous residences in Saudi Arabia, the Gulf, Jordan and Europe, carrying with them the miserable image they saw'.[230] Given that most of the group's cadre were now on Syrian government blacklists because of the Brotherhood's adventurism, many would never be able to return home. This led to a mass exodus of members from the Brotherhood's ranks.[231] Thus, while the Brotherhood's decision to end hostilities after Hama may have been politically pragmatic, the group's poor handling of the aftermath showed little strategic sense as it cost the group much of its base. The group's subsequent March 1982 announcement of the formation of the National Alliance for the Liberation of Syria alliance publicly put this adventurism at Hama behind it, but caused further frustration and sowed the seeds of its future woes.

---

[226] Al-Suri, 'Lessons Learned', p. 33.   [227] Interview with Ali al-Bayanouni, London.
[228] Interview with Ali al-Ahmad, London (parenthesis added).   [229] Ibid.
[230] See Al-Hakim, *The Islamic Jihadi Revolution*, p. 269.   [231] See ibid., p. 268.

The Aftermath of Hama, 1982–2011

The failure of the Hama uprising shook the very core of the Brotherhood, precipitating a split between the Aleppo faction (united behind Shaykh Abd al-Fatah abu Ghuddah) and the Hama faction (who remained united in support of Adnan Saadeddine). Saadeddine's group formally split from the rest of the Brotherhood in the mid-1980s.[232] The two factions went in drastically different tactical directions. The Aleppan faction re-entered negotiations with the Syrian regime in the mid-1980s in an effort to secure their return to Syria.[233]

By contrast, Saadeddine's group attempted to continue their violent confrontation, retaining the group's military camps in Iraq until at least 1987.[234] The September 1982 edition of *al-Nadhir* published a statement attributed to 'an official spokesman of the Muslim Brotherhood in Syria' dated 11 September 1982:

> The claim that the Brotherhood has decided to terminate its military operation in Syria is truthless. It is a mere plot by irresponsible elements that meet with the sectarian regime in its political aspiration and its deviation from the path of the Muslim Brotherhood.
>
> The tactical pause experienced at the moment is because of the appreciation of the Command of the Islamic Revolution in Syria of the conditions which are dictated by the ultimate wellbeing of the Syrian people and the Revolution. ...
>
> The Brotherhood movement is strong enough to not act in reaction or to respond to provocation. Its determination to achieve its aim is solid and shall be directed as it may deem in its timing, place and means.
>
> The talk about splits and differences within the Brotherhood and the mujahideen ranks is a clear indication of the nature of the source and its mischievious intents. It is not strange at all that the enemy tries to spread doubts about the unity and the firmness of the movement in order to erode the support of our people to the blessed Islamic revolution.[235]

Given their critique of 'irresponsible elements that meet with the sectarian regime', the official can be assumed to be aligned with Saadeddine's faction. In an interview published in May 1983, Saadeddine explained that 'there is no alternative to military struggle to overthrow the regime;

---

[232] 'A Meeting with the Comptroller General Mohammad Riad al-Shaqfeh (in Arabic)', *The Association of Syrian Writers* (30 October 2010) www.odabasham.net/%D9%85% D9%82%D8%A7%D8%A8%D9%84%D8%A7%D8%AA/43355-%D9%84%D9% 82%D8%A7-43355.

[233] Cited in Kutschera, 'When the Brothers Fall Out', p. 21.

[234] Interview with Ali al-Ahmad, London.

[235] 'Official Statement', *Al-Nadhir no. 49 (English edition)* (15 February 1982), p. 10.

any means is legitimate'.²³⁶ Saadeddine became associated with violence in Syria in 1984 and 1985, including train bombings in Latakia that killed significant numbers of Alawite civilians. Zuhair Salem (who is a member of the Aleppo faction) recalled:

> We [in the Aleppo branch] did not support what happened ... Adnan Saadeddine's [group] were responsible for these explosions ... and we with the international organization ... did not accept this ... it killed innocent people.²³⁷

In February 1985, *al-Nadhir*, which at that stage was in the hands of Saadeddine's supporters,²³⁸ declared: 'The Moslem [sic] Brotherhood in Syria has started to resume operations since Hafez Asad attempted to strike at them in Hama in 1982.'²³⁹ In September of that year, it issued the first communiqué of the 'Syrian Liberation Army', which stated:

> Our people have decided to liberate Syria from the treacherous and perfidious regime in Damascus – from the regime that has slaughtered its citizens in Palmyra, Hama, Aleppo, Homs, Damascus, Jebel El-Zawiya, the Euphrates Basin and other regions of the country.²⁴⁰

The statement made claims to responsibility for no fewer than 24 incidents, including explosions of key power stations, oil refineries and oil pumping stations. Rabinovich noted that while a number of opposition groups claimed attacks during 1985, 'some of the explosions might actually have taken place, but they certainly did not amount to a sustained and effective action'.²⁴¹ The Syrian Liberation Army took responsibility for several large-scale attacks the following year.²⁴² Nonetheless, the momentum behind these activities lessened by the end of the decade. Following events described by Zuhair Salem as an intra-factional 'coup', the Hama faction reintegrated into the Muslim Brotherhood in 1991, without Saadeddine.

The Brotherhood has demonstrated no inclination for violence since. Given that violence was a tactical rather than an ideological choice that reflected leaders' judgement of the best way forward, retracting the

---

²³⁶ Cited in Chris Kutschera, 'Syria: Muslim Brothers: The Question of Alliances', *The Middle East* 103 (May) (1983), p. 27.
²³⁷ Interview with Zuhair Salem, London.   ²³⁸ Ibid.
²³⁹ 'News', *Al-Nadhir No. 77–78 (English edition)* (3 February 1985).
²⁴⁰ Published by the Freedom Fighters in Syria Damascus, 'Commmunique No. 1 Issued by the Syrian Liberation Army' (1 September 1985).
²⁴¹ Itamar Rabinovich, 'The Syrian Arab Republic (al-Jumhuriyyat Suriyya al-'Arabiyya)', in *Middle East Contemporary Survey*, vol. IX, 1984–5, ed. Itamar Rabinovich and Haim Shaked (Boulder: Westview Press, 1987), p. 648.
²⁴² Yosef Olmert, 'The Syrian Arab Republic'" in *Middle East Contemporary Survey*, vol. X, 1986, ed. Itamar Rabinovich and Haim Shaked (Boulder: Westview Press, 1988), p. 609.

decision was also an option. This required no ideological shift, but merely a recalculation of the opportunities, costs and tactical options available to the group.

Coming to Terms with Hama

While the Muslim Brotherhood showed little difficulty in recalibrating its political path and returning to non-violence, its experiences from 1979 to 1982 have bestowed the group with significant emotional baggage. This surrounds the questions of how the group diverged so far from its traditional path, the massive human cost of its violent turn and how the group can prevent itself from repeating such mistakes. In practice, this presents the Brotherhood as a group now afflicted by leadership paralysis, which refuses to fully assimilate and acknowledge the history and potential learnings from its period of violence.

In the period immediately following the uprising, Saadeddine and Uqlah were widely blamed for it, acting as scapegoats to divert attention from broader Brotherhood culpability. Today, Brotherhood members publicly maintain that they bear no responsibility for the violence. Farouq Tayfour claimed:

What happened in Hama was that our leadership [and our followers] were forced to decide between either leaving [the country] or defending themselves. The Vanguard Fighters had been preparing themselves [for the task], but we thought this was impermissible. Adnan Aqlah [sic], commander of the Vanguard Fighters at the time, was the one who dragged the city into confrontation which [elicited] a response of the regime's violence and wrath. But I assure you that the Brotherhood's decision was to spare the city from massacre.[243]

This position was also articulated by another senior member when asked whether the Brotherhood made any mistakes in Hama:

No. On the contrary they were victims of violence in the worst way possible ... but due to the pressure that was put on Hama some took up weapons in self-defence ... [But] The Fighting Vanguard has committed some mistakes.[244]

Another senior member claimed: 'In Syria, some Brotherhood members used arms for self-defence, like in Hama when they attacked him ... Whoever takes up arms in Syria from the Muslim Brotherhood are considered self-defence.'[245] The collapse of the Fighting Vanguard following Uqlah's capture in late 1982 fortuitously gave the Brotherhood

---

[243] al-Amine, 'Leader of Syrian Muslim Brotherhood'. [244] Anonymous interview.
[245] Ibid.

carte blanche to control this narrative.²⁴⁶ However, this has been a double-edgd sword, also preventing the Brotherhood from asking itself the necessary difficult questions about its own culpability for the violence.

The painful memories were exacerbated by the foolhardy and unprepared nature of the Brotherhood's confrontation, which left the Syrian population open to unparalleled retaliation from the Baʿth regime. This aspect of the confrontation has been widely condemned by outside parties. A letter found in the raid on Osama bin Laden's house in Abbottabad, probably written by bin Laden himself, summed up the problem:

> The failure of the Brotherhood in Syria was not surprising, and that was the view of many experts ... The Brotherhood, on the other hand, was in a dream world [and it] ... lost an entire generation ... The Brotherhood became serious, and it called for the removal of the regime ... The Brotherhood never bothered to calculate, however, what it needed to accomplish all of that. The Brotherhood had not been realistic about its own resources, and capabilities, in comparison to what the opponent Syrian regime had ... [and they] did not have enough personnel who had the expertise or prudence to lead their military operations.²⁴⁷

Osama bin Laden may have had ties to the Syrian Muslim Brotherhood prior to his involvement in the Afghan conflict. Such criticisms were also echoed by the Fighting Vanguard's leader in Damascus, Ayman Shorbaji: 'The Brotherhood did not take concrete steps to protect their organisation and its members from the clutches of the regime.'²⁴⁸ He added:

> If the leadership of the Muslim Brotherhood had committed to a practical plan, it would have been able to uproot the regime before it controlled the necks of the people ... Large numbers of the Brotherhood's youth followers were left without leadership after the departure of the leadership of the Syrian Muslim Brotherhood from Syria. Those youths found themselves in a battle that they had not planned for and were not capable of prosecuting and lost the advice of the Leader during the battle.²⁴⁹

---

²⁴⁶ The Vanguard's rebuttal has largely manifested in personal memoirs of members, such as: Shorbaji, *The Diary of a Vanguard Combatant*.
²⁴⁷ Unknown author, ND 'SOCOM-2012–0000017-HT – Letter found in Osama bin Laden's Abbottabad, translated by the Combatting Terrorism Center at West Point, thought to be written by Osama bin Laden', p. 25. The letter was assessed by Lahoud et al. as being written by Osama bin Laden. See Nelly Lahoud et al., 'Letters from Abbottabad: Bin Ladin Sidelined?', Combatting Terrorism Center at West Point (3 May 2012), www.ctc.usma.edu/v2/wp-content/uploads/2012/05/CTC_LtrsFromAbottabad_WEB_v2.pdf, pp. 57–8.
²⁴⁸ Shorbaji, *The Diary of a Vanguard Combatant*, p. 45.   ²⁴⁹ Ibid., p. 73.

The Brotherhood's negligent approach to the violence also did untold damage to its membership base and would become a serious hurdle to its reintegration in 2011.

The Brotherhood eventually assembled an evaluation committee to investigate the events surrounding Hama. However, the process of forming the committee was fraught with tension. According to Saadeddine:

> Hama was like an earthquake for the Muslim Brotherhood. The differences among us surfaced and some of us started looking for scapegoats ... We thought that we should evaluate what went wrong. We all supported that idea. The Brothers in the leadership agreed to nominate some people but when someone was appointed to head the committee others protested. This evaluation continued for twelve years.[250]

The committee was chaired by the Aleppan Mohammad al-Hachimi, who was the father of the group's 2011 uprising-era political chief Hassan al-Hachimi.[251] In 1998, the committee finally presented its 'Evaluation Report' to the *Shura* Council,[252] but the findings were never shared with the group's members. One senior Brotherhood member who has seen the report privately admitted that it 'concluded by saying it (the escalation) was wrong, [and] very aggressive'.[253] Ali al-Bayanouni, the group's leader when the report was completed, acknowledged that 'the evaluation committee have admitted that it was a mistake to be dragged into violence'.[254] A Brotherhood associate who had not seen the report added: 'What I hear is that it was very frank. In the sense that it put the blame on the people that deserved blame. But it was very blunt, which is why the report was never published.'[255] The report is rumoured to implicate current senior Brotherhood figures in criminality.[256] Al-Bayanouni is thought to have 'quite liked the report', but the Hama group rejected the findings.[257] Saadeddine (who purportedly struggled to access a copy) later published a formal response to the report titled 'Mesirat Jama'at al-Ikhwan al-Muslimeen fi Suria' (The Journey of the Muslim Brotherhood in Syria).[258]

It is worth noting, however, that even if the report is as forthright as is speculated, it did not significantly change the thinking of senior Brotherhood officials. Throughout interviews, Brotherhood members

---

[250] As told to Alison Pargeter. See Pargeter, *The Muslim Brotherhood*, pp. 85–6.
[251] Anonymous interview. [252] Ibid. [253] Ibid. (parenthesis added).
[254] Interview with Ali al-Bayanouni, London. [255] Anonymous interview.
[256] Pargeter, *The Muslim Brotherhood*, p. 85. [257] Anonymous interview.
[258] Cited in Pargeter, *The Muslim Brotherhood*, p. 86. The author was unable to obtain a copy of this response.

put forward contradictory, revisionist and often farcical accounts of the Hama incident and the group's period of violence. At best, this demonstrates arrogance and negligence in provoking the regime while taking no steps to protect the physical safety of its own supporters. At worst, it is a total fabrication. Either way, it is clear that the decision to endorse violence was catastrophic and remains ever present in the leadership's thinking, continuing to impact the Brotherhood's reputation and interactions even three decades later. Having failed to fully understand the reasons for their catastrophic choices and how to prevent such mistakes in the future, the Brotherhood entered the 2011 uprising scarred and cautious.

The Brotherhood's decision to adopt violent strategies was a tactical response to developments in the broader Syrian political milieu. The group's violence was not a rejection of Ba'thist secularism or Alawite domination, but merely the apex of the broader anti-authoritarian protest movement to which large numbers of Syrians at the time subscribed. However, many inside and outside the Brotherhood would spend the following decades harassed by Syrian intelligence services, incarcerated or isolated outside the country, often with bitter memories of the Brotherhood's adventurism. Indeed, while the violence was a historical tactical anomaly – temporary and foolhardy by its nature – the decision inflicted a huge cost on the Syrian population and the Brotherhood's members. These events were the Brotherhood's last substantive actions inside Syria, in many ways setting the scene for how the group would be remembered by ordinary Syrians upon its return in 2011.

5   International Relations and Survival in Exile

As the Brotherhood adjusted to life in exile, its international relationships became key to its survival. The group had worked with states such as Iraq and Jordan during its 1979-82 armed confrontation with the Syrian regime, while some of its members had left the country decades earlier. Its ability to leverage these connections and develop new ones would determine whether it could rebuild organisationally, support its members and prepare for return to Syria. Groups such as South Africa's African National Congress were strengthened through the experience of exile by finding sanctuary and powerful external backers, which facilitated a level of organisational development that the opposition left inside South Africa could not achieve.[1] To survive and rebuild, the Brotherhood would need to do the same.

On the surface, Muslim Brotherhood organisations in other countries may seem the reason for the Syrian Brothers' survival in exile, but in practice such ties were quite limited. The Muslim Brotherhood was created in Egypt by the Egyptian Hassan al-Banna as an international movement.[2] Brotherhood branches in the region included Syria, Jordan, Lebanon, Kuwait, Palestine and Saudi Arabia. Yet from the outset, the Syrian Brothers' cooperation with the other movements was informal and limited, with al-Sibai explaining: 'The Ikhwan of Syria is administratively and financially independent and receives no instruction or orders from other organizations with the same name in Egypt or elsewhere.'[3] This was corroborated in a report by the US Damascus

---

[1] For a discussion of these dynamics in the ANC, see Tom Lodge, 'State of Exile: The African National Congress of South Africa, 1976–86', *Third World Quarterly* 9, no. 1 (1987), pp. 2–3.
[2] Richard P. Mitchell, *The Society of the Muslim Brothers*. (Oxford: Oxford University Press, 1991), p. 269.
[3] Cited in Raphaël Lefèvre, *Ashes of Hama: The Muslim Brotherhood in Syria* (London: Hurst, 2013), p. 25.

Legation in 1947, which found little evidence of formal financial cooperation, even though the Syrian group had only just been established.[4]

Former leader Ali al-Bayanouni described the relationship as largely based on 'counselling and liaising. It isn't a direct organisational relationship and it isn't organised ... We just counsel each other because each country's circumstances are different.'[5] This was further limited by the restrictions imposed on exiled Syrian Brothers by their host countries, who often forbade interaction with that country's own Brotherhood movement.[6] As such, the Brotherhood was forced to look further afield to support its survival in exile. The international capacities that developed were not inherited from its international Brotherhood affiliation, but a by-product of its lifelong pragmatism and individualism.

Relationships with Foreign States

There are few areas where the Syrian Brotherhood's pragmatism has been more overt than in its relationships with foreign states. Unlike other Syrian opposition actors that found themselves isolated in exile, the Brotherhood has throughout its history leveraged its foreign state ties to secure sanctuary for its members and to garner much-needed resources and political power. The Brotherhood consistently selected and developed these relations on strategic rather than ideological grounds, as evidenced by its close and productive relationship to Baʿthist Iraq. This flexibility enabled the Brotherhood to enjoy relatively stable sanctuary for over three decades of exile in the lead-up to 2011. The group has, however, consistently denied receiving financial support from states – during the height of the confrontation with the Baʿth, the Syrian Islamic Front leader Abu al-Nasr al-Bayanouni declared: 'I assure you that the only source for our money is from the ordinary Muslims all over the world.'[7] Indeed, the nature and extent of its relations with foreign states remain one of its most closely guarded secrets, with few members willing to discuss the issue at all.

Iraq became a close friend of the Syrian Muslim Brotherhood during the 1970s. While Saddam Hussein's Iraq may seem an ideologically incompatible partner for the Brotherhood, pragmatism guided the relationship and enabled Iraq to become an important lifeline. Relations between Syrian and Iraqi Baʿthists had been poor since the 1960s on

---

[4] Cited in Joshua Teitelbaum, 'The Muslim Brotherhood in Syria, 1945–1958: Founding, Social Origins, Ideology', *The Middle East Journal* 65, no. 2 (2011), p. 218.
[5] Interview with Ali al-Bayanouni, London.   [6] Anonymous interview.
[7] 'An Interview', *Abstracts from al-Nazeer no. 38 (English edition)* (9 September 1981).

the basis of mutual suspicion, an ideological divide and tensions over the collapse of the Iraqi Baʿthist regime in 1963.[8] The bilateral relationship deteriorated further following Iraq's decision to provide sanctuary to exiled Syrian Baʿthists, including founding member Michel Aflaq.[9] In 2000, Moussali described the Iraq–Syria relationship as 'one of those Arab conflicts that do not seem amenable to finding a solution'.[10] The relationship was particularly poor during the 1970s, with Syria routinely blaming Iraq for the Fighting Vanguard's assassination campaign, as well as accusing it of harbouring and supporting anti-regime militants.[11] This tension had worsened by the turn of the decade after Syria backed Iran in the bloody Iran–Iraq war. In 1982, soon after the Hama uprising, Syria closed its border with Iraq, cutting off trade routes and blocking the pipeline that Iraq used to pump oil to the Mediterranean.[12] The decision reportedly cost Iraq US$17 million per day.[13] It was in this context that Iraq welcomed Syrian dissidents in the 1970s. The Brotherhood was given a direct connection to Saddam Hussein through his intermediary, the future Iraqi Vice President Taha Ramadan.

Iraq's support for the Syrian Muslim Brotherhood was extensive, encompassing military training camps, as well as the provision of arms, money and intelligence support. Camps were permitted in the country for years after the Hama uprising. In fact, the Taji base where some of the Brotherhood training camps were located was proximate to sites later accused of being linked to Iraq's chemical weapons programme, suggesting a level of trust in the Syrian Brothers based in Iraq.[14] Iraq also allowed the Brothers to use the dissident *Voice of Arab Syria* radio station, which was established in 1976 during the Arab Summit in Cairo, to broadcast their messages across Syrian airwaves.[15] This was one of a few ways that the exiled Brotherhood communicated with its cadre and supporters inside Syria.[16]

---

[8] Charles Tripp, *A History of Iraq* (Cambridge: Cambridge University Press, 2007), p. 202.
[9] Ibid.
[10] Ahmad S. Moussalli, 'The Geopolitics of Syrian-Iraqi Relations', *Middle East Policy* 7, no. 4 (2000), p. 100.
[11] 'Syria Hangs 2 Alleged Iraqi Agents', *The New York Times* (14 June 1977), p. 4.
[12] AP, 'Syria Cuts Off Iraqi Pipeline', *The Globe and Mail* (20 April 1982), p. 13.   [13] Ibid.
[14] Thomas Powers, 'Burdened in Proof in Claiming Detailed Knowledge of Iraq's Illegal Weapons, US Officials May Have Jeapordized the Credibility of American Intelligence and Policy-Making for Years to Come', *Boston Globe* (15 June 2003); CIA, 'Iraq's Chemical Warfare Program' (2004), www.cia.gov/library/reports/general-reports-1/iraq_wmd_2004/chap5.html.
[15] Colin Legum and Hakim Shaked, *Arab Relations in the Middle East: The Road to Realignment* (London: Holmes & Meier Publishers, 1979), p. 16.
[16] See for example: 'Said Hawwa Speech on the "Voice of Arab Syria" Radio (Transcript, in Arabic)', *Al-Nadhir No. 7* (17 February 1982). This is available as an appendix in:

Iraq's support for the Brotherhood continued long after the 1980s armed confrontation, and included ongoing security provisions. Such provisions were important given the Syrian regime's continued pursuit of extraterritorial assassinations. The former leader Riad al-Shaqfeh, who spent decades living in exile in Iraq, disclosed:

> Beyond money and weapons, we were also provided with security help. Safe houses were at our disposal in the Iraqi capital and the local *mukhabarat* [intelligence services] strove to foil any assassination attempts aimed at us. On a personal level, out of four assassination attempts I suffered at the hands of the Syrian security services, three were foiled by the Iraqi *Mukhabarat*.[17]

This was no small contribution given that the Syrian intelligence services were successful in assassinating individuals linked to the Brotherhood in countries including Germany and Spain.[18] The British Embassy in Amman reported in 1981 that 13 Brotherhood members had been assassinated in Jordan alone.[19] Many from the Brotherhood's Hama faction therefore lived in relative safety in Iraq for decades, including prominent Brothers such as Adnan Saadeddine and Farouq Tayfour. Lefèvre reported that the relationship was so close by the 1990s that Adnan Saadeddine had become 'Saddam Hussein's personal envoy to the Islamic world'.[20]

Syrian Brothers were given access to Iraqi universities and resources that assisted many members to build new lives. As a former Brother who lived in Iraq in the 1980s explained:

> [Saadeddine] had a very good relationship with the leadership in Iraq, with Taha Ramadan, he helped so many Brothers to graduate from the university ... I am one myself. I studied French at university for four years in Iraq. I graduated in 1991.[21]

He added: 'there are now hundreds [of graduates] in Yemen, Saudi Arabia, working because they had studied in Iraq [to be] Engineers [and] doctors'.[22] The experience in Iraq also enabled the group to remain cohesive, as Brothers often lived near to their leaders, allowing the group to retain some aspects of its institutional structure.

Umar abd Al-Hakim, *The Islamic Jihadi Revolution in Syria (in Arabic)* (Peshawar: Unknown, 1991), pp. 605–6.
[17] Cited in Lefèvre, *Ashes of Hama*, p. 130.
[18] See Reuters, 'Wife of Syrian Dissident Is Slain in West Germany' (18 March 1982); 'FCO 93/2944: Syria Internal: Muslim Brotherhood – Damascus Telno 404', *British Embassy Damascus*, 3 December 1981.
[19] Ibid.   [20] Lefèvre, *Ashes of Hama*, p. 127.
[21] Interview with Ali al-Ahmad, London.   [22] Ibid.

The relationship underlined the depth of Brotherhood pragmatism. The Syrian and Iraqi Ba'th drew from the same ultra-secular ideological foundation, yet the Syrian Brothers had no difficulties dealing with the Iraqi government. This both gives credence to the argument that the Brotherhood–Syrian regime conflict was non-ideological, and highlights the Brothers' willingness to accommodate the Iraqi regime's flaws, even though the latter evinced a similar disregard for religion, democratic principles and human rights. Saadeddine explained: 'We do not interfere in Iraqi affairs. We keep our ideology and we fight for it. But we are unable to fight for others.'[23] This thinking was also evident in comments made by Farouq Tayfour when he was asked by an interviewer how the Brotherhood could justify maintaining 'relations with the Iraqi Ba'ath [Party] during a time when the latter used to persecute the Iraqi people?' Tayfour answered: 'In Iraq, we were simply guests. [It is not appropriate for] guests to publicize their opinions about their hosts'.[24] The Syrian Brothers in Iraq also accepted limitations on their political interactions. As one Brother described:

We don't have a real relationship [with the Iraqi branch of the Muslim Brotherhood] because the regime of Saddam Hussein forbade us from making any connection, and if they discovered any connection, they would kill them. They told us this 'don't have any connection with them', so we didn't have relationships inside Iraq.[25]

This meant sacrificing relations with its international counterparts but was deemed worthwhile in the name of sanctuary and the opportunity to rebuild.

The Brotherhood also enjoyed close relations with Jordan, where many of the group's Aleppan leaders, such as Ali al-Bayanouni, lived for decades. The group retained a large membership base in the country during the 2011 uprising. Jordan also had poor relations with Syria in the early 1970s after Jordan's decision to evict the Palestinian movement from its territory.[26] Although the two countries enjoyed a temporary détente during the middle of the decade, tensions quickly re-emerged over certain issues, including Jordan's perceived support of the

---

[23] Chris Kutschera, 'Syria: Muslim Brothers: The Question of Alliances', *The Middle East* 103 (May) (1983), p. 27.

[24] Hazim al-Amine, 'Leader of Syrian Muslim Brotherhood Discloses Secret Offer from Iran', *Al-Monitor (originally published in al-Hayat, translated by Naria Tanoukhi)* (20 January 2012), www.al-monitor.com/pulse/politics/2012/01/tayfour-to-al-hayat-iran-offered.html#ixzz47rSW2vW2.

[25] Anonymous interview.

[26] Laurie A. Brand, 'Economics and Shifting Alliances: Jordan's Relations with Syria and Iraq, 1975–1981', *International Journal of Middle East Studies* 23 (1994), p. 395.

Brotherhood. Syrian state media regularly carried stories of Jordanian conspiracy, including accusing the Jordanian Prime Minister Mudar Badran of overseeing a Brotherhood military camp.[27] Syria later blamed Jordan for training those involved in the deadly 1981 bombing in the Abkaziya quarter of Damascus.[28] Jordan paid a heavy price for its tacit support for the Brotherhood – in November 1980 the Syrian army stationed 50,000 troops on the Jordanian border to demand an end to support for the group.[29] Syria later sent Syrian officers across the border in an unsuccessful attempt to assassinate Prime Minister Badran,[30] and as noted above, killed a number of Syrian Brothers within Jordanian territory.[31]

Jordan proved a different ally to Iraq in its more cautious support for the Brotherhood, which consisted mostly of providing a sanctuary for exiled Brotherhood members and their families, and possibly some low-profile training.[32] These dynamics were captured in a 1980 *New York Times* piece, which reported that 'although there is a measure of sympathy here at Government level with the Brotherhood, there is no material support of any significance given to its subversive efforts in Syria'.[33] A 1985 US intelligence report noted that while Jordan had allowed a safe haven and maintained intelligence connections to the Syrian Brothers 'it would be extremely nervous about any operation against Syria, which was seen to be planned or take place from Jordan. It apparently gives little active assistance'.[34] This differed significantly from the Iraqi position on the Brotherhood.

Brotherhood members living in Jordan did not enjoy rights as equal citizens. The Syrian Brothers were kept isolated from the remainder of the Jordanian community and forced to live together in siloed Syrian exile neighbourhoods. The Brothers were kept under close watch and were limited in their ability to rebuild their lives. As one Brotherhood associate noted:

---

[27] 'Damascus Radio Broadcast: Syrian Allegation of Jordanian Aid for Muslim Brotherhood' (London: BBC Monitoring Middle East, 1980).
[28] 'FCO 93/2944: Syria Internal: Muslim Brotherhood'.
[29] John Yemma, 'Both Sides Seek Face-Saving Device in Syria-Jordan Confrontation', *The Christian Science Monitor* (4 December 1980).
[30] 'Top Syrian Officers Confess Plot to Murder Jordan's PM', *The Jerusalem Post* (26 February 1981), p. 1.
[31] 'FCO 93/2944: Syria Internal: Muslim Brotherhood'.
[32] Brynjar Lia, *Architect of Global Jihad: The Life of Al-Qaida Strategist Abu Mus'ab al-Suri* (London: Hurst & Company, 2007), p. 45.
[33] Youssef M. Ibrahim, 'Syria and Jordan Still Poised on Border', *The New York Times* (8 December 1980), p. 16.
[34] US Embassy Damascus, 'The Syrian Muslim Brotherhood', *Wikileaks* (16 February 1985), www.wikileaks.org/plusd/cables/85DAMASCUS1314_a.html.

We had no political status or citizenship status ... Jordan accepted the Syrians that escaped from Syria, but there were restrictions that you should live with each other, that you should not get involved with much ... you cannot get involved in the Islamic movements in Jordan.[35]

Jordanian *mukhabarat* closely monitored those linked to the Brotherhood. Driver's licences, for example, were purportedly sometimes denied on the grounds of real or perceived Brotherhood allegiance.[36] This is consistent with a US intelligence report which commented that Jordan 'is suspicious of all Muslim Brotherhood activity'.[37]

The Brotherhood's decision to work with Jordan was again a pragmatic choice. The Brotherhood had been highly critical of Jordan's monarchical system during the post-independence era,[38] but the relationship with Jordan reflected many of the patterns seen in the Iraq–Brotherhood relationship, in that the group flexibly accepted to live in a political system with which it did not agree. This saw the group tolerate its conditions and make no efforts to incite discontent within Jordan, or to seriously network with Jordanian opposition movements. Indeed, it pragmatically understood that as a guest in Jordan, it had little choice but to try to make the most of a situation that was less than ideal. Exile, after all, was to be temporary.

The Brotherhood–Jordan relationship, however, also highlighted that the Brotherhood was vulnerable to external changes beyond its control. This is a common challenge of exile, whereby a group's survival depends on their host state's policy landscape, which can be subject to unpredictable change.[39] The fragility of the Syrian Brothers' status in Jordan became clear in 1985 when King Hussein publicly acknowledged that the Brotherhood had used Jordanian territory to stage 'bloody incidents in Syria with the help of Jordanians using Islam as a cover for their activity'.[40] He declared that the Syrian Brothers were 'outlaws committing crimes and sowing seeds of dissension among people' and expressed his desire to warn 'against the evil designs of this rotten group and urge all citizens to prevent them from implementing their evil designs'.[41] That same year, Jordan was reported to have arrested 250 Brotherhood

---

[35] Anonymous interview.   [36] Ibid.
[37] US Embassy Damascus, 'The Syrian Muslim Brotherhood'.
[38] 'The Brotherhood's 1947 National Charter criticised the Jordanian King Abdullah's "imperialistic Greater Syria plan"'. Cited in Umar F. Abd-allah, *The Islamic Struggle in Syria* (Berkeley: Mizan Press, 1983), p. 174.
[39] Lodge, 'State of Exile', p. 1.
[40] Ihsan A. Hijazi, 'Jordanian Prime Minister to Visit Syria', *The New York Times* (12 November 1985), p. A3.
[41] Charles P. Wallace, 'Visit to Damascus Moves Jordan, Syria Closer', *Los Angeles Times* (13 November 1985), p. 22.

members.[42] One Brotherhood associate who was living in Jordan at the time recalled:

> Jordan made peace with Hafez al-Assad in 1985, so you were allowed to stay in Jordan, but you were at their mercy. In fact that is one of the reasons that many people left, because they realised that Jordan wasn't a safe place and the Jordanians were handing over Syrians to the regime.[43]

This pattern was repeated again in 2000, when the Jordanian authorities formally normalised relations with President Bashar al-Assad. In line with that decision, Jordan asked Ali al-Bayanouni (General Guide at the time) and Mohammad al-Hasnawi (a member of the Brotherhood's executive office) to leave the country.[44] Although Iraq had proved considerably more reliable an ally, the Brotherhood's sanctuary there too eventually fell victim to international politics, with the relationship largely dissipating after the 2003 Iraq War when many Brotherhood members fled the country.

Nonetheless, the Brotherhood's time in both Jordan and Iraq allowed the group to rebuild and consolidate, to maintain its institutional structure and to live as a cohesive community in exile. This proved a major asset once the 2011 uprising began. The first Syrian National Council president Burhan Ghalioun noted that, by contrast, 'the others in the opposition are completely without organisational tradition or organisational hierarchy'.[45]

Syrian Brotherhood Exiles as International Actors

The Brotherhood's survival in exile was also supported by its individualist and entrepreneurial streak, which proved a significant asset in helping the group to broaden its financial base and develop the important international ties that became critical to its role in the 2011 uprising.

The Syrian political environment has been hostile to the Brothers for most of the group's lifetime. Members began fleeing Syria during the 1950s under the Shishakli dictatorship, and emigration peaked during Ba'thist repression in the late 1970s and early 1980s. The experience of exile was defining for the Syrian Brotherhood's organisational capacity, endowing it with cosmopolitan and often wealthy backers around the

---

[42] Ihsan A. Hijazi, 'Jordan, Joining Trend, Curbs Islamic Militants', *The New York Times* (9 December 1985), p. 6.
[43] Anonymous interview.
[44] Al-Majd', 'Jordan Reportedly Bans Syrian Muslim Brotherhood Leaders from Returning' (London: BBC Monitoring Middle East, 2000).
[45] 'Interview with Burhan Ghalioun, Paris' (3 August 2015) (parenthesis added).

world. Lefèvre estimated that the number of Syrian Brothers living in wealthy countries such as Saudi Arabia could have been in the 'low thousands' by 2013.[46]

Since the Brotherhood's members and leaders mostly hailed from Syria's educated and entrepreneurial classes, many had strong educational or business skills before leaving Syria. These Brothers quickly reaped the benefits of this in exile, becoming senior professionals or businesspeople in their adopted countries. This pattern appeared particularly pronounced among exiles in Saudi Arabia. Brotherhood founding member Maruf al-Dawalibi became a senior advisor to King Faisal and forged himself a prominent position in the Saudi textile industry,[47] while Muhammad al-Mubarak designed courses at the request of the Saudi authorities for the Sharia and Education faculties in Mecca.[48] He chaired King Abd al-Aziz University's Sharia Department from 1969 to 1973, where Ali al-Tantawi and Abd al-Rahman Habannaka also taught.[49] Said Hawwa himself spent time in Saudi Arabia in the 1960s, where he wrote his seminal book *JundAllah*.[50] Likewise, former leader Abd al-Fatah abu Ghuddah and Abu al-Nasr al-Bayanouni taught at Imam Muhammad bin Saud University.[51] Both Mohammad al-Abdeh (who was close to the Brotherhood, but may not have been a member) and former member Mohammad Surur Zein al-Abideen[52] taught Islamic law in Saudi Arabia before emigrating to the UK.[53] They both became renowned independent scholars and commanded significant followings of their own.[54] According to one senior Brotherhood figure, some of the members in this 'first migration' to Saudi Arabia had accrued significant wealth by the 1980s.[55]

Some Syrian Brothers also influenced the politics of their host countries, including playing an important role in providing the intellectual foundations of the Saudi *Sahwa* (Awakening).[56] Brotherhood delegate in the 1961 parliament Zuhayr al-Shawish was active in the education sector in Qatar.[57]

---

[46] Raphaël Lefèvre, 'Saudi Arabia and the Syrian Brotherhood', *Middle East Institute* (27 September 2013), www.mei.edu/content/saudi-arabia-and-syrian-brotherhood.
[47] Nabil Mouline, *The Clerics of Islam: Religious Authority and Political Power in Saudi Arabia*, trans. Ethan S. Rundell (New Haven: Yale University Press, 2014), p. 144.
[48] Stéphane Lacroix, *Awakening Islam: The Politics of Religious Dissent in Contemporary Saudi Arabia* (Cambridge, MA: Harvard University Press, 2011), pp. 45–6.
[49] Ibid., p. 43.   [50] Ibid., p. 44.   [51] Ibid.
[52] Mentioned briefly in Chapter 2 for his hardline positions on the Shi'a.
[53] Lefèvre, *Ashes of Hama*, p. 96.   [54] Ibid.   [55] Anonymous interview.
[56] Lacroix, *Awakening Islam*, p. 44.
[57] Courtney Freer, *Rentier Islamism: The Influence of the Muslim Brotherhood in Gulf Monarchies* (Oxford: Oxford University Press, 2018), p. 57.

Others forced to leave Syria in the 1970s and 1980s arrived in their new countries without money or resources, and became reliant on modest Syrian Brotherhood stipends that were dispersed across the region. As noted above, connections were leveraged to enable Brotherhood members to earn university degrees and rebuild their lives in exile. According to Ali al-Bayanouni, 'the Brotherhood never stopped supporting these people. They supported people whether they were from the Brotherhood or not ... Anyone that was affected.'[58] He estimates that the number of those supported by the group stretched well into the thousands.[59] Another well-connected Brother added:

They used to help other people who were in need of money. And in fact they have [still] got a very heavy (financial) burden ... [from] supporting the families of the victims and the families of the detainees. Thousands [of them] ... The families of those who have no resources, especially now they became very old, many people became very old, the family of the victims, or the family of the detainee, they are still supporting.[60]

The group also purportedly gave money to members to assist them in starting new businesses outside Syria.[61] One Brotherhood member who was exiled in Iraq recalled receiving a different type of assistance when his father was hospitalised in Jordan. He spoke of the social support provided by Muslim Brotherhood members:

My Dad had a problem in Jordan with his heart and I was in Iraq at that time. The Brotherhood helped him. They took him to hospital and stayed with him in hospital. They dealt with him like he was their own father ... they stayed with him in the hospital until he was discharged.[62]

This built a sense of camaraderie and gratitude among Brotherhood members in exile over decades. It meant that even though members were dispersed across the world, they retained an important formal link to the central Syrian Brotherhood organisation, both as clients and as loyal backers. Because of this the thousands of Brotherhood members who did not become wealthy were nonetheless politically wedded to the Brotherhood for life via their essential monthly stipends or community connections.

The pathways of these members had a tangible impact on the Brotherhood, which benefited enormously from the growing wealth of its base. Donations from members have always been the Brotherhood's primary source of funding. Every Syrian Brotherhood member is obliged to donate on average 2.5 percent of their annual income to the group, or

---

[58] Interview with Ali al-Bayanouni, London. [59] Ibid. [60] Anonymous interview.
[61] Ibid. [62] Interview with Ali al-Ahmad, London.

more during times of crisis if they have the means.[63] This percentage varies by country and can be more in wealthier states. As Brotherhood salaries increased, the donation size also increased and so this became more lucrative for the group.

Exiled Muslim Brotherhood wealth initially began to benefit the group during its first confrontation with the Syrian regime. Sunayama noted that the Brotherhood's most significant Saudi donors

> came from the Syrian community in Saudi Arabia who had immigrated in thousands since the 1960s. It consisted mainly of traditional landowners and entrepreneurs who had not only suffered material losses under the Ba'thi nationalisation measures but also political persecution for their affiliation to the Muslim Brotherhood.[64]

As noted, this demographic had always been the Brotherhood's key constituency. Maruf Dawalibi, originally from a wealthy Aleppan family, exemplified this as one of five Syrian industrialists who became major players in the Saudi textile industry, and who later used his wealth to support the Brotherhood and influence Syrian politics.[65] Hinnebusch went so far as to suggest that Dawalibi 'engineered several conspiracies' against the Ba'th from exile.[66] Ali al-Bayanouni believes that Saadeddine may have also used personal funds that he earned while working as an engineer in the UAE to finance armed cells.[67]

Ali al-Bayanouni maintained that Brothers during the 2011 uprising were paying 15 percent of their salaries to the group in recognition of the crisis.[68] Senior Brotherhood figure Samir abu Laban explained that 'Some pay 40 percent [of their salaries to the Brotherhood]. I know people that spent ten years of their savings on the [2011] revolution. I know many who sold their homes and gave [all of] their money.'[69] The accrual of significant wealth by members in exile has proven very valuable to the Brotherhood, enabling it to make investments, maintain a paid staff, continue to pay aid, and to hold meetings and events to showcase its work. Lefèvre reported that this support is so extensive that some members that 'have made a fortune working in the Gulf ... now form the financial backbone of the group's charity and military

---

[63] Interview with Samir Abu Laban, Istanbul.
[64] Sonoko Sunayama, *Syria and Saudi Arabia: Collaboration and Conflicts in the Oil Era* (London: I.B.Tauris, 2007), p. 92.
[65] Ibid.
[66] Raymond Hinnebusch, 'Syria', in The Politics of Islamic Revivalism: Diversity and Unity, ed. Shireen T. Hunter (Bloomington: Indiana University Press, 1988), p. 42.
[67] Interview with Ali al-Bayanouni, London.   [68] Ibid.
[69] Interview with Samir Abu Laban, Istanbul.

activities'.⁷⁰ These successful Brothers' connections to other wealthy Syrian families in the Gulf is also significant.⁷¹

Other Brothers and their affiliates had close diplomatic connections to governments in the West through organisations they set up in their host countries. Former Brotherhood political office chief Hassan al-Hachimi was heavily involved in Arab and Muslim organisations in his adopted country of Canada, at one time becoming Treasurer of the Muslim Association of Canada.⁷² This gave the Brotherhood experience in interacting with the international community, and endowed it with government connections that it could leverage in the wake of 2011.

These opportunities stood in stark contrast to the experiences of most of the domestic opposition. The first Syrian National Council president, Burhan Ghalioun, explained that since the Brotherhood had

> lived in exile for many years, they had more organisation, they had their own finances because many of them work in Gulf countries and send money to others ... [They are the only Syrian party with] persons who work, who are professional, who are paid to work [for the party]. Other Syrian political parties have no money.⁷³

This internationalisation of Brotherhood members through exile became a key aspect of the group's survival. It accrued resources, political connections and power that would not only sustain the group, but also bolster its return in 2011. These individual connections provided a platform for the Brotherhood's strong entrance into the conflict and an opportunity for the realisation of its long-term goals.

The Afghan War and the Emergence of the Global Jihad Movement

The international arena also gave exiled Syrian combatants the opportunity to continue their violent conflict. Although most of the Brotherhood's leaders and members had ended their battle against the Syrian regime in the first half of the 1980s, some former Brotherhood and Vanguard members spent much of the decade attempting to revive the

---

⁷⁰ Raphaël Lefèvre, 'Can Syria's Muslim Brotherhood Salvage Its Relations with Riyadh?', *Carnegie Middle East Center* (28 March 2014), http://carnegie-mec.org/diwan/55052?lang=en.
⁷¹ Aron Lund, 'Struggling to Adapt: The Muslim Brotherhood in a New Syria' (Washington, DC: Carnegie Endowment for International Peace, 2013), p. 7.
⁷² Hassan Hassan, 'How the Syrian Muslim Brotherhood Hijacked Syria's Revolution', *Foreign Policy* (13 March 2013), www.foreignpolicy.com/articles/2013/03/13/how_the_muslim_brotherhood_hijacked_syria_s_revolution.
⁷³ 'Interview with Burhan Ghalioun, Paris' (3 August 2015).

confrontation.[74] As these efforts waned, the Soviet Afghan war gained traction as a new battle for the Muslim world. On the surface, the Syrian Brothers had little in common with those fighting in Afghanistan, who were fighting a foreign enemy far divorced from the nationalist ideals espoused by the Syrian Muslim Brotherhood.[75] Nonetheless, small but important personal links developed between Syrian Muslim Brotherhood members and the Afghan jihad, further underlining the individualistic nature of Brotherhood members and associates.

The exact number of Syrians who travelled to Afghanistan is unknown, although the figure is smaller than recruits from other Arab countries.[76] Senior Brotherhood figure Zuhair Salem estimated that around 20–30 Syrians travelled to Afghanistan, with three or four of these later joining al-Qaeda.[77] Abu Musab al-Suri said that the number of Syrian recruits was in the tens, but fewer than 100.[78] The latter seems more likely given that this research readily identified the names of 25 Syrians in Afghanistan (see Appendix Two). One Pakistani source listed the names of at least seven Syrians who were killed in combat.[79] Syrians were purportedly welcomed to Afghanistan because of their military experience, which most of the Afghan Arabs lacked.[80] As a former Fighting Vanguard member recalled, officials at Maktab al-Khadimat (the Afghan Services Bureau)

> wanted to hear everything about us and did not hide their smiles when I said that I had carried arms with the *mujahideen* [sic] in the weeks ahead of Hama. My stint with the Vanguards was my passport to Abdullah Azzam.[81]

This was corroborated by Lia, who noted that the Syrian recruits were flattered on 'their possession of significant military skills, which, after all, were in great shortage in the Arab-Afghan movement at the time'.[82] Other Syrians may have also mobilised in support, rather than combat roles.[83]

---

[74] Lia, *Architect of Global Jihad*, pp. 51–3.
[75] Leah Farrall and Mustafa Hamid, *The Arabs at War in Afghanistan* (London: Hurst, 2015), p. 23.
[76] Lia, *Architect of Global Jihad*, p. 90.   [77] Interview with Zuhair Salem, London.
[78] Cited in Lia, *Architect of Global Jihad*, p. 74.
[79] Muhammad Amir Rana and Mubashar Bukhari, *Arabs in Afghan Jihad* (Lahore: Pakistan Institute for Peace Studies, 2007), pp. 142–5.
[80] Thomas Hegghammer, 'The Rise of Muslim Foreign Fighters: Islam and the Globalization of Jihad', *International Security* 25, no. 3 (2010), p. 63.
[81] Cited in Sami Moubayed, *Under the Black Flag: At the Frontier of the New Jihad* (London: I.B.Tauris, 2015), p. 47.
[82] Lia, *Architect of Global Jihad*, p. 73.
[83] Cerwyn Moore, 'Foreign Bodies: Transnational Activism, the Insurgency in the North Caucasus and "Beyond"', *Terrorism and Political Violence* 27, no. 3 (2015), pp. 395–415; Darryl Li, '"Afghan Arabs", Real and Imagined', *Middle East Report* 41 (2011), 2–7.

The Afghan conflict appeared to be particularly attractive to Vanguard members; of the nine Syrians who fought in Afghanistan with an alleged Brotherhood or Vanguard affiliation, eight were known Vanguard members. This suggests that the Afghan conflict internationalised opportunities for some of the most radical members of the Brotherhood and Vanguard. Most of the Syrians that joined the Afghan conflict arrived between 1986 and 1991, at least four years after the failed Hama uprising.[84]

There are two key aspects of the Brotherhood's relationship with the Afghan war worth noting: (1) the limited extent of official links between the Syrian Muslim Brotherhood and the Afghan conflict, as well as (2) the extensive individual involvement of some Syrian Brothers in the war. For the most part, the engagement of Syrians in the Afghan war took place separate to the Syrian Muslim Brotherhood as an institution: Brotherhood leaders did not interact substantially with the conflict. This is not surprising given the situation that the group had found itself in during the 1980s. By 1982, the Syrian Brotherhood had suffered a catastrophic loss and was imploding. Large numbers of its members had been killed or were languishing in Syrian prisons, and the group was now responsible for the welfare of a community of thousands of exiles. The Afghan conflict would never be a top priority. Ali al-Bayanouni later explained that the Brotherhood 'gave their priority to Syria ... Some [members] may have gone as individuals, but [this had] nothing to do with the Brotherhood'.[85] This was corroborated by senior Egyptian *mujahid* and Afghan war veteran Mustafa Hamid, who reported that the involvement of Syrians in the Afghan conflict 'was not an organisational decision on the part of the Syrian Ikhwan [al-]Muslimin'.[86]

The Syrian Brotherhood's institutional ties to the Afghan jihad appear limited to acknowledgement in its 1980 political manifesto, and later token outreach by those in the estranged Hama group. The by then Hama-controlled[87] *al-Nadhir* directed an editorial at the Afghan mujahidin, declaring:

Your hardships are severe, and the enemy gloats over his misdeeds and is blind to GOD [*sic*]. But GOD willing, and by His witness, victory shall be yours. You have been fighting the true fight of GOD, who says that if you let Him triumph He will give you victory and set your steps firm. For despite the numbers of your enemies and the tyranny that they practice, your steps remain firm,

---

[84] Farrall and Hamid, *The Arabs at War*, p. 23.
[85] Interview with Ali al-Bayanouni, London.
[86] Farrall and Hamid, *The Arabs at War*, p. 32.
[87] Interview with Zuhair Salem, London.

your blows remain grievous, and your victories along the path of Jihad go on being more glorious than faith demands.[88]

Notably, the editorial did not call for readers to join the mujahidin, nor did it attempt to raise funds. This is despite the fact that other foreign Brotherhood branches were actively fundraising for Afghanistan at the time.[89] Said Hawwa gave lectures to recruits at the Afghan Services Bureau in the late 1980s,[90] and wrote an endorsement in Abdullah Azzam's book *The Defence of Muslim Lands*,[91] in effect supporting Azzam's seminal call to arms. However, the importance of this should not be overstated given that the Afghan conflict was widely celebrated across the Muslim world at the time.[92] This limited nature of these official ties between the Syrian Muslim Brotherhood and the Afghan war meant that events in Afghanistan in the decades between 1982 and 2011 had little impact on the Brotherhood's leadership.

The Afghan war did, however, impact the Brotherhood by internationalising the path of individual Muslim Brotherhood and Fighting Vanguard members. Much of this travel was facilitated by Abdullah Azzam, who became 'the single most important individual behind the mobilisation of Arab volunteers for Afghanistan', particularly through his position as Emir of the Afghan Services Bureau.[93] As noted in Chapter 4, Azzam had interacted with the Syrian Brothers during his time in Damascus. He is thought to have later provided sanctuary in his own home in Jordan for fleeing Brotherhood members.[94] The Azzam connection is crucial in terms of recruitment, even though Azzam was no longer a Muslim Brotherhood member. In fact, he purportedly attempted to dissuade Fighting Vanguard member Abu Musab al-Suri from renewing the Syrian confrontation in 1987, arguing that it 'had its chance; people no longer believed in it and wished to support it ... [today, the conflict with the Baʻth appears more] like a political project than a jihadi cause'.[95] It is possible that the Brotherhood also had links to Azzam's better-

---

[88] The Voice of the Islamic Revolution in Syria, 'Letter to the Freedom Fighters in Afghanistan', *Al-Nadhir No. 75–6 (English edition)* (1 December 1984), p. 16.
[89] Barnett R. Rubin, 'Arab Islamists in Afghanistan', in *Political Islam: Revolution, Radicalism, or Reform?*, ed. John L. Esposito (London: Lynne Rienner, 1997), p. 189.
[90] Said Hawwa, *This Is My Experience and This Is My Testimony (in Arabic)* (Cairo: Maktabat Wahba, 1987), p. 154.
[91] Abdullah Azzam, 'The Defence of Muslim Lands: The Most Important Individual Duties' (c. 1985), https://archive.org/stream/Kklkkkk/20#page/n0/mode/2up, p. 4.
[92] Li, '"Afghan Arabs"'.
[93] Thomas Hegghammer, *Jihad in Saudi Arabia: Violence and Pan-Islamism since 1979* (Cambridge: Cambridge University Press, 2010), p. 39; Leah Farrall, 'Revisiting al-Qaida's Foundation and Early History', *Perspectives on Terrorism* 11, no. 6 (2017), p. 17.
[94] Lefèvre, *Ashes of Hama*, p. 142.   [95] Cited in Lia, *Architect of Global Jihad*, pp. 72–3.

known Afghan war contemporary, Osama bin Laden, whose mother and first wife were Syrian. Jocelyn wrote that 'Osama bin Laden was reportedly instructed by Brothers at a young age and may have entered the global jihad through the Brotherhood's Syrian chapter' – although these claims could not be corroborated.[96]

These ties to the Afghan conflict may seem a risk factor for the Brotherhood's future ideological cohesion, but they inadvertently aided the group by drawing key radical figures away from its ranks. Most of the Brotherhood members who went to Afghanistan were Brotherhood discontents, described by Mustafa Hamid as 'angry at the corruption in the Syrian jihad led by Ikhwan [al-]Muslimin and the events that had taken place there'.[97] This was the reverse of the phenomenon that the Brotherhood witnessed in the 1970s, when Syria's deteriorating political climate led moderates to disengage. In contrast, the Afghan war attracted the attention of some of the Brotherhood's most radical and frustrated members, and therefore led to the departure of a problematic Brotherhood cohort, enabling the Brotherhood's leaders to reconsolidate around their traditional moderate base.

This trend was exemplified in Abu Musab al-Suri (Mustafa bin abd al-Qadir Sitt Maryam Nasar), who was the most senior and best-known Syrian Brotherhood member to mobilise in Afghanistan. He was a member of the Brotherhood and later Fighting Vanguard, participating in the military high command in the early 1980s.[98] Al-Suri purportedly employed a Brotherhood training manual in his work during the Afghan war.[99] However, he left the Brotherhood after the Hama uprising, dissatisfied with the group's military and leadership performance, and then became one of the Brotherhood's harshest critics. Al-Suri published several books including the nearly 1,000-page *The Islamic Jihadi Revolution in Syria*,[100] which levelled a devastating critique of the group. The book became a key source among jihadists, but its impact on Syrian Brothers was probably muted by the considerable time and distance that existed between Abu Musab al-Suri and the group's base when it was published in 1991. Nonetheless, al-Suri's travel to Afghanistan was

---

[96] Thomas Jocelyn, 'Osama bin Laden on the Muslim Brotherhood', *The Long War Journal: Threat Matrix* (10 May 2012), www.longwarjournal.org/archives/2012/05/osama_bin_laden_on_the_muslim.php.
[97] Farrall and Hamid, *The Arabs at War*, p. 32.   [98] Lia, *Architect of Global Jihad*, p. 47.
[99] Cited in ibid., p. 42.
[100] For example, see Al-Hakim, *The Islamic Jihadi Revolution*; Abu Musab Al-Suri, 'Lessons Learned from the Armed Jihad Ordeal in Syria', translated and published by the Combatting Terrorism Centre (CTC), West Point, www.ctc.usma.edu/v2/wp-content/uploads/2013/10/Lessons-Learned-from-the-Jihad-Ordeal-in-Syria-Translation.pdf.

significant for the key impact that he had in Afghanistan, and because his absence removed a source of potential intra-Brotherhood tension. Al-Suri later became a high-profile jihadist strategic thinker closely associated with al-Qaeda, and was arrested in Pakistan in 2005 before being extradited to Syria. Rumours circulated in 2011 that al-Suri had been released from prison, although there is little evidence that this took place.[101]

A second important figure drawn to Afghanistan was Abu Burhan (full name unknown), who was a former member of the Muslim Brotherhood as well as a colonel in Syria's intelligence apparatus.[102] Abu Burhan ran the Afghan Services Bureau's Sadda and Khaldan training camps. According to Mustafa Hamid:

> The arrival of the Syrian officer Abu Burhan in the summer of 1986 resulted in a transformation in the level of training of Arabs at Sadda. Abu Burhan was one of the two most important individuals who affected the course of Arab-Afghan training after 1985 when volunteer numbers began to increase.[103]

Abu Burhan also compiled an encyclopedia of the training courses that were operated or planned in the camp. To Hamid, 'it was a unique work, and no work of its kind or anything similar appeared for that stage of the jihad in Afghanistan between 1979 and 1992'.[104] Abu Burhan was listed by Abu Musab al-Suri as one of his heroes and a 'martyr of hijra and ribat',[105] and was mentioned in meeting minutes pertaining to al-Qaeda's founding as a member of the new organisation's advisory board,[106] as well as in al-Qaeda associate Jamal al-Fadl's testimony in the 2001 United States v. Osama bin Laden trial as a founding member of al-Qaeda.[107]

These trends form an important part of the Syrian Brotherhood's history, in particular highlighting the way that the failed Syrian conflict in the 1980s reverberated across the region. The Afghan war also acted as a pressure valve that pulled up to 100 of the Brotherhood's most radical

---

[101] Bill Roggio, 'Abu Musab al Suri Released from Syrian Custody: Report', *The Long War Journal* (6 February 2012), www.longwarjournal.org/archives/2012/02/abu_musab_al_suri_re.php.
[102] Aiman Dean, Paul Cruickshank and Tim Lister, *Nine Lives: My Time as MI6's Top Spy Inside al-Qaeda* (London: Oneworld, 2018), p. 62.
[103] Farrall and Hamid, *The Arabs at War*, p. 84.   [104] Ibid., p. 85.
[105] Cited in Mark Long, 'Ribat, al-Qa'ida, and the Challenge for US Foreign Policy', *Middle East Journal* 63, no. 1 (2009), p. 39.
[106] See Peter Bergan and Paul Cruickshank, 'Revisiting the Early Al Qaeda: An Updated Account of Its Formative Years', *Studies in Conflict and Terrorism* 35, no. 1 (2012), p. 20.
[107] 'United States v. Osama Bin Laden – Day 2 Transcript', *United States District Court: Southern District of New York* (6 February 2001), p. 194.

away from its ranks. This meant that while the Brotherhood would go on to face many challenges during the 2011 conflict, none related to its former radical jihadist cadre. By 2011, the group had no meaningful connections with the international jihadist movement, and in fact many jihadists ridiculed the Syrian Muslim Brotherhood.[108]

Reaping the Benefits of Exile

The Brotherhood's period in exile was therefore a seminal time for the group, with its relationships with Iraq and Jordan proving key to its survival because they provided sanctuary, education and resources that would help sustain and rebuild the group in exile, and enabled it to build and preserve its institutional structure. The achievements of individual members in Saudi Arabia and other places endowed the group with a broad financial base, expert skillsets and important political connections. Finally, the Afghan war drew more radical elements away from the Brotherhood, providing it with a more moderate environment in which to reconsolidate.

These relationships and new international operating domain endowed the group with significant resources to rehabilitate. This meant that the Brotherhood was the most organised opposition group on the eve of the 2011 uprising. Burhan Ghalioun argued that this gave the Brotherhood a major advantage over other Syrian opposition members:

They have a network, which the others don't have ... And they have [people and connections] in the Arab countries and Saudi Arabia and other places which gives them a kind of autonomy which is very important in the confrontation. The others have nothing like this.[109]

Although the group's international connections are often attributed to its links to the broader Muslim Brotherhood movement, it is clear that the international movement has provided few tangible benefits to the Syrian Brothers. Instead, it has been members' willingness to form their own connections and paths internationally that has facilitated its

---

[108] See, for example, a letter thought to be written by Osama bin Laden: Unknown author, ND 'SOCOM-2012-0000017-HT – Letter found in Osama bin Laden's Abbottabad, translated by the Combatting Terrorism Center at West Point, thought to be written by Osama bin Laden', p. 25. The letter was assessed by Lahoud et al. as being written by Osama bin Laden. See Nelly Lahoud et al., 'Letters from Abbottabad: Bin Ladin Sidelined?', Combatting Terrorism Center at West Point (3 May 2012), www.ctc.usma.edu/v2/wp-content/uploads/2012/05/CTC_LtrsFromAbottabad_WEB_v2.pdf.

[109] 'Interview with Burhan Ghalioun, Paris' (3 August 2015).

strengths. In no area has the group's flexibility, pragmatism and sense of individualism been more pronounced, acting as the essential ingredients of the group's post-1982 survival and rehabilitation. Exile and its associated internationalism therefore gave the Brotherhood an unparalleled advantage in 2011. This left the Brotherhood as the best placed of the opposition movement to respond to the new crisis. But time would show that it lacked much-needed political legitimacy on the ground in Syria.

Part II

The Syrian Uprising

6 The Brotherhood Re-Enters the Political Fray

The spread of the Arab uprisings to Syria in 2011 caught many observers off guard.[1] Syria was stable, President Bashar al-Assad seemed reasonably well liked and the country lacked the overt structural problems that dogged Tunisia and Egypt.[2] Bashar al-Assad himself remarked to the *Wall Street Journal* in January that year that 'Syria is stable. Why? Because you have to be very closely linked to the beliefs of the people.'[3] However, al-Assad's assessment was drawn into question weeks later when Syria experienced large-scale protests following a government crackdown in Deraa.[4] By June and July, protests were taking place across the country, while some members of the opposition began turning to violence. By the time the conflict had reached its fifth anniversary in 2016, the UN Special Envoy to Syria estimated that 400,000 people had been killed.[5] The UN had stopped formally counting the dead two years prior because the brutality of the war meant that it could no longer confidently verify the data.

The March 2011 protests provided the Brotherhood with the catalyst it had long hoped would lead to the popular overthrow of the al-Assad regime. The Brotherhood, as one of Syria's oldest, best-known and best-resourced political parties, should have been well placed to benefit from any redrawing of the political system in Syria. It had been preparing for its return to Syria politically, institutionally and financially for three decades. However, the Brotherhood's recent political track record was

---

[1] Gregory F. Gause, 'Why Middle East Studies Missed the Arab Spring: The Myth of Authoritarian Stability', *Foreign Affairs* 90, no. 4 (2011), 81–90.
[2] David W. Lesch, *Syria: The Fall of the House of Assad* (New Haven: Yale University Press, 2012), chapter 3.
[3] Jay Soloman and Bill Spindle, 'Syria Strongman: Time for "Reform"', *Wall Street Journal* (31 January 2011), http://online.wsj.com/articles/SB10001424052748704832704576114340735033236.
[4] 'Deaths in Syria as Protests Continue', *Al Jazeera* (2 April 2011), www.aljazeera.com/news/middleeast/2011/04/201141132440493496.html.
[5] John Hudson, 'U.N. Envoy Revises Syria Death Toll to 400,000', *Foreign Policy* (22 April 2016), http://foreignpolicy.com/2016/04/22/u-n-envoy-revises-syria-death-toll-to-400000/.

mixed, ensuring that while the group would be an enthusiastic participant in the uprising, its history prevented it from achieving the influence it had expected among the opposition political landscape. Indeed, a chasm quickly emerged between expectations of the Brotherhood's triumphant return to Syria, and its very limited success after 2011. It turned out that a strong institutional structure and superior resources did not easily translate into rebuilding its popular base.

The Syrian uprising spread across the country in mid-March 2011 after the Baʻth regime arrested teenagers who had spray-painted anti-regime graffiti on a wall in the southern city of Deraa. The Arab uprisings began in Tunisia four months earlier after a frustrated fruit-seller, Mohamed Bouazizi, self-immolated in protest at poor economic conditions and local government corruption.[6] Within months, protests had spread across the Middle East, toppling the long-reigning presidents of Tunisia and Egypt. Until March 2011, Syria had seemed impervious to the regional unrest, with the self-immolation of Hassan Ali Akleh in Hasakah, a 1,500-strong protest in Damascus's al-Hareeqa neighbourhood and a small protest outside the Libyan embassy in Damascus all failing to inspire further activity.[7] However, within days of the arrests in Deraa, protests spread across the country, buoyed by the calls of nascent Facebook groups to mobilise for a 'Day of Rage'. Protests continued to build for the next fortnight, with al-Assad addressing the country for the first time on 30 March to declare that 'conspirators' were pushing an 'Israeli agenda'.[8] It was clear from early on that al-Assad did not take the protesters' demands seriously, and although he made a nod to reform through initiatives such as Decree number 161, which ended the half-century old Emergency Law, and Decree number 61, which granted amnesty to 'all members of the Muslim Brotherhood and other detainees belonging to political movements', al-Assad simultaneously sent Syrian security services onto the streets.[9] This proved a gross misjudgement by the regime – tokenistic reform and brute force would not easily quell the burgeoning movement. Nine months later in December,

---

[6] Peter Beaumont, 'Mohammed Bouazizi: The Dutiful Son whose Death Changed Tunisia's Fate', *The Guardian* (21 January 2011), www.theguardian.com/world/2011/jan/20/tunisian-fruit-seller-mohammed-bouazizi.

[7] Robin Yassin-Kassab and Leila al-Shami, *Burning Country: Syrians in Revolution and War* (London: Pluto Press, 2016), pp. 35–7.

[8] Katherine Marsh and Martin Chulov, 'Assad Blames Conspirators for Syrian Protests', *The Guardian* (30 March 2011), www.theguardian.com/world/2011/mar/30/syrian-protests-assad-blames-conspirators.

[9] Rania Abouzeid, 'The Jihad Next Door: The Syrian Roots of Iraq's Newest Civil War', *Politico* (23 June 2014), www.politico.com/magazine/story/2014/06/al-qaeda-iraq-syria-108214.

demonstrations in the central city of Homs were still mobilising 70,000 protesters at a time.¹⁰

Within days of the first protests, the by-then Brotherhood Shura Council chief Ali al-Bayanouni told *Asharq al-Awsat*:

> The people are demanding the fall of the regime, the abolition of the emergency law that has been in place in Syria since March 1963, the granting of general freedoms, and an end to people being arrested for their political views or affiliations, as well as the abolition of laws and special courts, and the confrontation of corruption in a serious and effective manner.¹¹

He added that 'all Syrian governorates will revolt, and there is an almost unanimous view that this regime is not viable, as the people do not want it'. However, the Brotherhood went to significant lengths to distance itself from the early protest movement, even though some of its members were integrally involved. Senior Brotherhood figure Molham Aldrobi claimed that the Brotherhood was 'one of the components of the Syrian street; it is not the entire Syrian street'.¹² While such distance may seem unusual for a group desperate to re-enter Syria, past experiences of repression often shape future political decisions, encouraging caution in groups that have previously overstepped.¹³ Former National Coalition for Syrian Revolution and Opposition Forces (the SOC – Syrian Opposition Coalition) Vice President and Brotherhood ally Hisham Marwah agreed with this assessment, arguing that the group's caution stemmed from safety concerns:

---

[10] Julian Borger, 'Arab Monitors Visit Restive Syrian City: Protest in Homs Over Fears of "Whitewash Inspection" Claims of Tanks Hidden after Army Withdrawal', *The Guardian* (28 December 2011); Melissa Block, 'In Syria, Homs Emerges as Center of Protest', *NPR* (30 August 2011) www.npr.org/2011/08/30/140070135/in-syria-homs-emerges-as-center-of-protest-movement; Roula Hajjar and Borzou Daragahi, 'At Least 18 Killed in Syrian Crackdown; An Assault is Launched in the City of Homs, Activists Say, to End Demonstrations and Detain Protest Leaders', *Los Angeles Times* (12 May 2011), http://articles.latimes.com/2011/may/11/world/la-fg-syria-protests-20110512; Ian Black, 'Homs: The story Behind Mani's Extraordinary Images from the Frontline', *The Guardian* (25 November 2011), www.theguardian.com/world/2011/nov/25/homs-mani-images-frontline; Patrick J. McDonnell, 'Syria Says Troops Have Overrun Rebel Enclave in Homs', *Los Angeles Times* (2 March 2012), http://articles.latimes.com/2012/mar/02/world/la-fg-syria-opposition-20120302.

[11] 'Syrian MB: Uprising Will not Stop until Demands Are Met', *Asharq al-Awsat* (23 March 2011), https://english.aawsat.com/theaawsat/news-middle-east/syrian-mb-uprising-will-not-stop-until-demands-are-met.

[12] Joshua Landis, 'Syrian Revolution 2011 Facebook Page Administrator, Fidaaldin Al-Sayed Issa, Interviewed by Adam Almkvist', *Syria Comment* (11 May 2011), www.joshualandis.com/blog/syrian-revolution-2011-facebook-page-administrator-fidaaldin-al-sayed-issa-interviewed-by-adam-almkvist/.

[13] Nancy Bermeo, 'Democracy and the Lessons of Dictatorship', *Comparative Politics* 24, no. 3 (1992), pp. 273–4.

Even though they (the Brotherhood) had a lot of members involved in the revolution's activities in the beginning, they tried not to say that it is ours to protect the people from being dealt with as Muslim Brotherhood [members] according to that law (No. 49).[14]

It proved a prudent strategy, as the Syrian government would go to considerable lengths to tie the group to the unrest. Less than two weeks into the uprising, Syrian presidential adviser Bouthaina Shaaban told *Agence France Presse*:

These are fundamentalists [behind the violence] who hate to see Syria as an example of peaceful coexistence. We trust our people. They were the ones who defeated the Muslim Brotherhood in 1982. Without the help of the Syrian people, we never could have defeated them ... The Muslim Brothers never forgave, and they want to do it again. But they will fail again.[15]

In April, state television began broadcasting the confessions of individuals who claimed to have received funds and weapons from a Muslim Brotherhood official.[16] This eerily echoed the forced television confessions of Brotherhood members during the 1970s and 1980s confrontations.[17] By December, the government's efforts to denigrate and defame the Brotherhood took a turn for the farcical when it built a fake website in the Brotherhood's name that took responsibility for two Damascus suicide bombings.[18]

It would be wrong to say, however, that the Brotherhood had no connection to the events surrounding the protests, even though Brotherhood supporters were few and far between on the streets. The Brotherhood played a key role in 'The Syrian Revolution Against Bashar al-Assad' Facebook page, which had 138,000 followers by April 2011.[19] Although the page does not declare a Brotherhood connection, it was

---

[14] Interview with Hisham Marwah (31 August 2015) (parenthesis added).
[15] Natacha Yazbeck, 'Syria Accuses Fundamentalists of Stirring Unrest', *Agence France Presse* (28 March 2011).
[16] Mahmud al-Jaza'iri, 'Al Jazeera Interviews Syria's Muslim Brotherhood Official on Recent Protests', *Al Jazeera* (Doha: BBC Monitoring Middle East, 13 April 2011).
[17] See 'FCO 93/2253: Letter from Vincent Fean to Douglas Gordon on Husni Abo's Televised Confession', *British Embassy Damascus*, 7 September 1979; Vladimir Bilyakov, 'Muslim Brotherhood's "Aggressive Campaign against Syrian Regime"' (London: BBC Summary of World Broadcasts, 20 October 1980).
[18] 'Syrian Muslim Brotherhood claims Damascus bombings', *Agence France Presse* (24 December 2011).
[19] Joshua Landis, 'The Man behind "Syria Revolution 2011" Facebook-Page Speaks Out', *Syria Comment* (24 April 2011), www.joshualandis.com/blog/the-man-behind-syria-revolution-2011-facebook-page-speaks-out/. Note that the name of the Facebook page has changed since the beginning of the uprising. Today it can be found online at: Labib Al-Nahas, 'I'm a Syrian and I Fight Isil Every Day. It Will Take More Than Bombs from the West to Defeat this Menace', *The Telegraph* (21 July 2015), www.telegraph.co.uk/

founded by a network of activists that included Fida al-Sayyid Issa, who is a Brotherhood youth member from a prominent Brotherhood family. The Brotherhood's link to the page exemplified the group's long-standing individualist streak, where members often engaged in political activities extraneous to the group. The page called for Syrians to rally for (unsuccessful) February 2011 protests, as well as the 15 March 'Day of Rage'. This Facebook page was declared to be 'the most influential social networking tool in the mobilisation of protestors against the Syrian regime'.[20]

Fida al-Sayyid Issa explained that his participation in the page was an individual decision, rather than one taken by the Brotherhood leadership:

We worked hard to establish the Syrian Revolution page to be for everyone. Some people focus on the page's affiliations or constituents, but we pursued a policy with everyone. We formed working teams consisting of all Syrian components, visions and ideas. They were independent at the level of media discourse or administration and we succeeded in this, thanks be to God. Regardless of my personal affiliation and the thought that I hold as a Muslim Brotherhood youth member, I was working on a Syrian issue.[21]

This gives credence to Ali al-Bayanouni's claim that the Brotherhood was not officially involved in the page. He explained: 'Some of the members got involved in different activities, but they were not actually [official Brotherhood activities].'[22] This trend of individual involvement in the uprising was also seen in the Shaam News Network, an opposition platform established in February 2011 by Abdulhassan Abazeed and Bilal Attar, who both grew up in Brotherhood families in Jordan, although they were not Brotherhood members themselves. Attar's brother was involved in the Syrian Revolution Facebook page.[23]

Brotherhood members or associates acting in an individual capacity often had a more significant impact on the conflict than the group as a whole. The Syrian Muslim Brotherhood was never a tightly structured party, even in the days of Mustafa al-Sibai. This pattern had become more pronounced during the group's exile, where the dual forces of repression and financial opportunity meant that the group became a decentralised network dispersed across the world. As one Brotherhood associate noted, 'you have to understand, the Muslim Brotherhood, like

news/worldnews/islamic-state/11752714/Im-a-Syrian-and-I-fight-Isil-every-day.-We-need-more-than-bombs-from-the-West-to-win-this-battle.html.
[20] Landis, 'Syrian Revolution 2011 Facebook Page Administrator, Fidaaldin Al-Sayed Issa, Interviewed by Adam Almkvist'.
[21] 'Knocking on the Doors of Freedom: The Founders of the Syrian Revolution Facebook Pages Speak to al-Ahd', *Al-Ahd No. 2* (15 March 2013), p. 12.
[22] Interview with Ali al-Bayanouni, London.
[23] Rania Abouzeid, *No Turning Back: Life, Loss and Hope in Wartime Syria* (London: Oneworld Publications, 2018).

any Muslim Brotherhood organisation, is a network primarily. Not a political party. It is a network of people.'[24] In practice, this means that the Brotherhood umbrella encompasses hundreds of different approaches to the uprising. At times it appeared that there was not one single Brotherhood, but many Brotherhoods in the uprising. Although this is often interpreted as a sinister means of extending power, it is in reality the ordinary behaviour of a group with individualist instincts that was forced to decentralise in order to survive decades of repression.[25]

The Brotherhood was the most organised opposition group on the eve of the uprising. It was, as Pierret dubbed, 'the grandfather of Islamist politics in Syria', which afforded it name recognition across the country, even though it had lacked a formal presence in Syria for 30 years.[26] The Brotherhood participated in all of the major opposition conferences that took place abroad at the beginning of the uprising, many that were organised by individual Brotherhood members. The first president of the Syrian National Council (SNC), Burhan Ghalioun, attributed the group's high level of engagement to its superior resources: members of the Brotherhood were 'in every meeting. No other Syrian party had the same means to attend ... They (the Brotherhood) didn't leave any meeting. They were everywhere.'[27] The group gained representation on early opposition bodies, including on the Antalya conference's 31-member Consultative Council, as well as its Executive Council.[28] Such ability and eagerness to engage with the broader opposition is not surprising given the group's lifelong willingness to build relationships with parties across the ideological spectrum in order to achieve political outcomes. This early conference participation further evidenced the advantage of the Brotherhood's organisational sophistication, size and international connections. But when it came to the local coordination committees and grassroots organising inside Syria, the Brotherhood was noticeably thin on the ground.

Nonetheless, in the early days of the uprising, the Brotherhood's media office expanded to include up to ten paid staff, many of whom had

---

[24] Anonymous interview.
[25] For further discussion of this pattern, see Ellen Lust-Okar, *Structuring Conflict in the Arab World: Incumbents, Opponents and Institutions* (Cambridge: Cambridge University Press, 2005).
[26] Thomas Pierret, 'Syria: Old-Timers and Newcomers', in *The Islamists Are Coming: Who They Really Are*, ed. Robin Wright (Washington, DC: Woodrow Wilson Center Press), p. 71.
[27] Interview with Burhan Ghalioun, Paris (3 August 2015) (parenthesis added).
[28] The Thawra Foundation, 'The Antalya Conference – A Brief Report', *POMED* (23 June 2011), http://pomed.org/wp-content/uploads/2011/06/The-Antalya-Conference.pdf, pp. 3–4.

qualifications or a background in media and communications.[29] At its peak, it would employ 30 people and host a slick, professionally designed website, social media accounts in Arabic and English and publish a newspaper.[30] The group also demonstrated a firm understanding of how international politics operates: within a month of the uprising's beginning, Ali al-Bayanouni penned an article in the influential London-based newspaper the *Guardian* aimed at the international community, titled 'No one owns Syria's uprising'.[31] He declared:

> We, along with many others from across the political spectrum, called for the formation of a national coalition to support the youth, but in no way do we claim ownership of these historic events ... It is time that all Syrians – men and women alike, regardless of ethnicity or religion – enjoy equal citizenship.

The group was also able to mobilise dormant members, particularly those that were successful in business. These people played key roles in fundraising and enabled the Brotherhood to amplify its influence on the ground to position it as something of a kingmaker. Yet, as one member of the SOC noted, the group's organisation and 'discipline does not mean their power and their abilities'.[32] Indeed, while it appeared to offer the most promising leadership on the eve of the Syrian uprising, it failed to deliver on this advantage in a substantial way.

Reintegrating into the Syrian Political Sphere

The success of Brotherhood's political rehabilitation was always going to depend on its level of acceptance by other opposition figures and the Syrian public. The Brotherhood had a long track record of interaction with other political groups, dating back to its engagement in the Syrian parliament from 1947 to 1963. Ali al-Bayanouni described the period in his 2011 *Guardian* piece: 'The Muslim Brotherhood won some rounds and lost others, and accepted each outcome.'[33]

However, it quickly became clear that the group's more recent track record of political opportunism had soured relations with the Syrian opposition. This dates all the way back to the 1980s – Ismail spoke to opposition activists who argued that the Brotherhood's lack of transparency

---

[29] Anonymous interview.
[30] Interview with Omar Mushaweh, Skype (19 September 2017).
[31] Ali Al-Bayanouni, 'No One Owns Syria's Uprising', *The Guardian* (16 April 2011), www.theguardian.com/commentisfree/2011/apr/16/syria-uprising-assad-blames-extremists.
[32] Abdullah Raja 'SOC Member Muhammad al-Dandal Tells Zaman al-Wasl: The Muslim Brothers Will not Rule Syria; the Interim Government is Negative', *Zaman al-Wasl* (Doha: BBC Monitoring Middle East, 14 October 2013).
[33] Al-Bayanouni, 'No One Owns Syria's Uprising'.

over its role in Hama in 1982 should disqualify it from playing a role in the post-2011 political machinations.[34] In the course of this research, however, it was the breaches of trust in the previous decade that appeared to weigh most heavily on opposition minds throughout the uprising. This was reflected in comments made by a senior opposition member, who recalled:

> The Damascus Declaration [in 2005] rejected continued [government] legal action against Brotherhood [members] ... Although many Damascus Declaration members were prosecuted [for their stances], the Brotherhood quickly left the party on its own. They joined Abdul Halim Khaddam's [National Salvation Front] when he defected in 2005 ... Then, in 2008, before the war on Gaza, they put their opposition to the Syrian regime on hold.[35]

The group's decision to freeze opposition to the regime during the 2008–9 Gaza war proved particularly damaging. The impact of this decision was also echoed in comments made by one opposition figure, who voiced concern that the Brotherhood might again suspend its opposition to al-Assad in return for a politically favourable deal: 'I don't trust them ... At any minute they could change their mind' about the uprising.[36] This lack of trust became a theme throughout the uprising, whereby the flexibility and pragmatism that enabled the Brotherhood's longevity against the odds also catastrophically damaged its relations with others. Many opposition figures were genuinely concerned that if the al-Assad regime made an advantageous offer, the Brotherhood would accept it at the expense of all other opposition members. This question of trust was further compounded by the behaviour of the Egyptian Muslim Brotherhood following the 2011 revolution, although the Syrian Brothers were critical of their colleagues, with Zuhair Salem explaining:

> I am criticizing [the Egyptian President Mohammad] Mursi [sic] – and maybe they are upset with me for that ... Where we differ is in our policies. For example, Egypt wants to have a fatwa council, which Al-Azhar approves; we don't want that. We say that what is permissible and what is forbidden is clear. We don't want to enter the realm of theocracy. Syrian society is different from Egyptian society. The political experience in Egypt is different from ours, and I believe personally that the Egyptian Brotherhood made a tactical mistake.[37]

---

[34] Salwa Ismail, *The Rule of Violence: Subjectivity, Memory and Government in Syria* (Cambridge: Cambridge University Press, 2018), p. 136.
[35] Cited in Ayman Sharrouf, 'The Destructive Ascendancy of Syria's Muslim Brotherhood', *Now* (3 December 2014), https://now.mmedia.me/lb/en/commentaryanalysis/564483-the-destructive-ascendancy-of-syrias-muslim-brotherhood (parenthesis added).
[36] Anonymous interview.
[37] Cited in Tam Hussein, 'The Brotherhood's Man in London', *Majalla* (23 April 2013), https://web.archive.org/web/20171129085905/http://eng.majalla.com/2013/04/article55240699.

Nonetheless, the Syrian Brothers would struggle to shake the suspicion that they too were power hungry. As a result, while the group was organisationally in a position of strength at the beginning of the uprising, its behaviour in the 2000s had left it with a much less favourable political reputation. The group had a significant credibility problem.

The first substantive test of the Brotherhood's ability to work alongside opposition groups came through the Syrian National Council, which was established in October 2011. At its peak, the SNC enjoyed the support of much of the international community, with a handful of countries and the European Union declaring it the legitimate representative of the Syrian people.[38] The Brotherhood took its involvement in the body seriously, backing the liberal candidate Burhan Ghalioun as the body's first president. Ali al-Bayanouni explained: 'we chose this face, accepted by the West and by the inside. We don't want the regime to take advantage if an Islamist becomes the Syrian National Council's head.'[39] Ghalioun claimed to have not been the Brotherhood's first preference,[40] but its decision to work with him regardless was consistent with the group's pragmatism. The Brotherhood's engagement with the SNC proved successful, with its members gaining almost one quarter of the Council's 310 seats as well as executive positions. Farouq Tayfour became the SNC Vice President and the head of the SNC's Relief and Development Bureau.

The SNC was soon accused of being dominated by the Brotherhood, and was replaced by the National Council for Syrian Revolution and Opposition Force (SOC) following a withdrawal of support from the USA, Saudi Arabia and Qatar in late 2012.[41] The Brotherhood was purportedly unenthusiastic about the establishment of the SOC because the wider membership and different structure would curb its influence.[42] Nonetheless, the group's pragmatism and survival instinct saw it embrace the new arrangements and set about achieving its goals through the new body. As Hassan acknowledged: 'The Brotherhood knew it could not insist on the survival of the SNC, so they started to build a

---

[38] 'EU Recognises Syria Opposition Bloc', *Al Jazeera* (20 November 2012), www.aljazeera.com/news/europe/2012/11/20121119195737909518.html.
[39] Khaled Yacoub Oweis, 'Syria's Muslim Brotherhood Rise from the Ashes', *Reuters* (6 May 2012), www.reuters.com/article/us-syria-brotherhood-idUSBRE84504R20120506.
[40] Interview with Burhan Ghalioun, Paris (3 August 2015).
[41] Scott Stearns, 'Clinton: SNC No Longer Leads Syrian Opposition', *VOA* (31 October 2012), www.voanews.com/a/brahimi-seeks-chinese-support-for-syria-solution/1536429.html.
[42] Rania El-Gamal and Andrew Hammond, 'Mistrust of Syria's Muslim Brotherhood Lingers', *Reuters* (12 November 2012), www.reuters.com/article/us-syria-crisis-brotherhood-idUSBRE8AB1CQ20121112.

place for themselves in the coalition – and succeeded.'⁴³ The group's pragmatism, programmed into its DNA during the Mustafa al-Sibai era again proved an asset. The Brotherhood enjoyed significant influence on the SOC, over the years holding several executive posts. As of early 2019, the Brotherhood-linked Nazir Hakim was Secretary General (and previously Vice President), while the political office included the Brotherhood-linked Haitham Rahma and Ahmad Ramadan. The Brotherhood's Farouq Tayfour and Salem Mislat had previously been vice presidents, while former Brotherhood Political Office chief Hassan al-Hachimi remained a member of the SOC political office.⁴⁴ Formally, the Brotherhood had only five members on the Coalition.

The group's political success on paper did not, however, reflect a successful reconciliation with other opposition parties, and the Brotherhood stood repeatedly accused of attempting to maximise power, often in an underhanded way. The first significant accusations levelled at the Brotherhood surrounded the issue of power monopolisation in the early days of the SNC. Although the Brotherhood bloc had more than 70 official members in 2012,⁴⁵ at least nine other senior Brotherhood members or former members sat on the SNC as 'independents' or members of other blocs. As of February 2012, this included former leadership and Shura Council member Abdulatif al-Hachimi (listed as an independent), his brother and the group's former political chief Hassan al-Hachimi (National Bloc), the group's 2011 uprising-era media chief Omar Mushaweh (independent), the group's spokesman and former ideologue Zuhair Salem (National Figures), Walid Saffour (independent) and Mohammed Sarmini (National Bloc) who was a member at the time.⁴⁶ Others included former Brotherhood members Ahmad Ramadan, Haitham Rahmeh and Obeida Nahas (all National Bloc).⁴⁷ This practice extended the group's formal membership in the SNC by at least 10 percent, with Becker adding that 'repeated restructurings and an ever-changing composition meant that even insiders find it impossible to assess the Brotherhood's real weight within the SNC'.⁴⁸ This behaviour was probably shaped by the group's deep-seated fear of irrelevance

---

⁴³ Ibid.
⁴⁴ 'Political Committee', *National Coalition of Syrian Revolution and Opposition Forces* (2017), http://en.etilaf.org/coalition-components/general-body/political-committee.html.
⁴⁵ For a full list of the SNC's membership as of February 2012, see an archived version of the SNC website: 'Members', *Syrian National Council* (11 February 2012), http://web.archive.org/web/20120207234952/www.syriancouncil.org/en/members.html.
⁴⁶ Ibid.   ⁴⁷ Ibid.
⁴⁸ Petra Becker, 'Syrian Muslim Brotherhood: Still a Crucial Actor', *SWP Comments 34* (Berlin: German Institute for International and Security Affairs, 2013), p. 2.

following its long exile and many failed political efforts, although it did little for its credibility. Ghalioun acknowledged the frustrations among the group's ranks, noting that historically

> they were a very big political party and had a lot of influence. Now, they feel frustrated and want to be visible. They want to be visible more than they are in reality ... [and] they want to redress this frustration by being recognised as a big party.[49]

Samir Nashar was harsher, declaring: 'The Brotherhood insisted on taking political leadership of the Syrian opposition and [clung] to the fantasy that it was the biggest and most influential faction.'[50]

Despite the criticism, one Brotherhood member explained that the Brotherhood had been central to the success of the opposition political institutions:

> When the Syrian National Council was established, it ... was only successful when the Muslim Brotherhood helped them to be successful ... [but] one or two people are jealous of an institution (the Brotherhood) [that] is 70 or 80 years old.[51]

Such self-assured language has done little to endear the Brotherhood to its opposition compatriots. One liberal Syrian activist went so far as to describe 'arrogance' as a hallmark of the Brotherhood's behaviour towards other opposition members.[52] This has at times manifested in a 'born to rule' mentality, with senior member Samir abu Laban suggesting that the Brotherhood's dominance of Syrian opposition bodies stemmed from the reality that other opposition members were

> not politically trained, so whenever there is a problem ... at the Syrian National Council at the beginning everyone would jump and say something quickly, until they realised that the views expressed by the Muslim Brotherhood carried more political weight and sounded also wiser than the others.[53]

Indeed, it seemed the events of 2011 were not the watershed moment the Brotherhood needed to unshackle itself from the ineffective political practices and attitudes that had characterised its previous political engagement from exile.

The Brotherhood's behaviour caused furore within the broader opposition in 2012, prompting some members to resign their posts. One such member, Walid al-Bunni, complained that 'the Brotherhood took the

---

[49] Interview with Burhan Ghalioun, Paris (3 August 2015).
[50] Sharrouf, 'The Destructive Ascendancy'.
[51] Anonymous interview (parenthesis added). [52] Ibid.
[53] Interview with Samir Abu Laban, Istanbul.

whole council ... we became like extras'.⁵⁴ Another Syrian dissident, Amr al-Azm, said: 'they are trying to make sure they have a finger in every pie and a hand on every lever of power that they can'.⁵⁵ The group's behaviour was also purportedly a source of discomfort within Brotherhood circles. An open letter published on the Facebook account of opposition figure Riad Durar, claiming to be written by the 'sons of the Muslim Brotherhood', noted:

> The group was involved in emerging Syrian national institutions after the revolution, and displayed much political realism, which is a necessary aspect of political work. But the group overreached in this plan until it became an example of a group inconsistent in its positions and uncommitted to principles. Such self-interest is abhorrent and is not befitting of the representatives of the largest political group in Syria ... Do not let history show that your representatives were working to divide up positions and small spoils while the Syrian people are being slaughtered by the thousands and rivers are flowing with the blood of their sons.⁵⁶

The Brotherhood denied the message's authenticity, with Molham Aldrobi dryly responding: 'When they voice concerns, Muslim Brothers are usually brave enough to mention their names.'⁵⁷ He later complained that the Brotherhood's critics 'do not differentiate between good Muslims and Muslim Brotherhood. There are many good Muslims on those bodies, practicing Muslims, but they are not Muslim Brotherhood' members.⁵⁸

Many hoped that the formation of the SOC would dilute the Brotherhood's influence, but in reality the new coalition's structure replicated the group's existing patterns of political engagement. The SNC is the largest bloc on the SOC, with 22 representatives. SOC members have no influence over how these 22 members are appointed, so the Brotherhood's power in the SNC was de facto carried across to the SOC (even though officially the Brotherhood only has five seats).⁵⁹ Other

---

[54] Anne Barnard, 'Syria Opposition Group Is Routed and Divided', *The New York Times* (14 March 2012), www.nytimes.com/2012/03/15/world/middleeast/syria-torture-report-military-maintains-assaults.html.
[55] Liz Sly, 'Syria's Muslim Brotherhood Is Gaining Influence over Anti-Assad Revolt," *Washington Post* (22 May 2012), www.washingtonpost.com/world/syrias-muslim-brotherhood-is-gaining-influence-over-anti-assad-revolt/2012/05/12/gIQAtIoJLU_story.html.
[56] Riad Durrar, 'Letter from a Group of the Sons of the Muslim Brotherhood', Facebook (12 January 2014), www.facebook.com/riaddrar/posts/337902093014536.
[57] Cited in Raphaël Lefèvre, 'A Revolution in Syria's Muslim Brotherhood?', *Carnegie Middle East Center* (23 January 2014), http://carnegie-mec.org/diwan/54287?lang=en.
[58] Interview with Molham Aldrobi.
[59] Yusra Ahmed, 'Syria's Muslim Brotherhood Leader Highlights Reforms, Future Plans – Interview', *Zaman Al Wasl* (20 March 2015), https://en.zamanalwsl.net/news/9402.html.

Brotherhood members or former members are represented in non-aligned groups on the SOC. As one senior SOC figure described, 'some people are members, some are probably members, and then they have allies ... They do this because they don't want it to be said that they are dominating.'[60] A Brotherhood associate estimated that this could mean that the Brotherhood has influence over 40 percent of SOC members, although this was denied by senior Brotherhood figures.[61]

The Brotherhood's reputation was further compromised by its links to so-called front groups that are perceived to further extend its influence. According to Hassan, these include the National Union of Free Syrian Students, the Levant Ulema League, the Independent Islamic Democratic Current, the Syrian Ulema League, the Civil Society Organizations' Union, the Revolution Council for Aleppo and its Countryside, the Commission for the Protection of Civilians, the National Work Front, the Kurdish Work Front, the Hama Revolution Gathering, the National Coalition for Civilian Protection, and the Syrian Society for Humanitarian Relief.[62] Others include the Syrian Human Rights Committee (SHRC). Such groups have obtained political representation or represented themselves as independent NGOs, without declaring their ties to the Brotherhood. For example, Walid Saffour, a Brotherhood member who represents the SHRC on the SNC was appointed the SOC's ambassador to London, giving the Brotherhood an important formal diplomatic link to the UK through an undeclared member.[63] A Brotherhood associate was highly critical of the decision, arguing that Saffour was unqualified for such an important diplomatic role and that the Brotherhood's push to have one of their own represented amounted to 'gross incompetence' on the group's part.[64]

It is important, however, to not overstate the impact of these patterns of engagement. While it is difficult to observe longitudinal SOC voting patterns because voting is secret,[65] opposition figures with knowledge of voting dynamics say that the Brotherhood bloc does not always vote in unison.[66] In fact, senior Brotherhood members have been known to vote in contravention of Brotherhood policy on the SOC. This was seen when senior figures broke with party position by voting in favour of the Geneva 2 conference, as well as when Farouq Tayfour argued in favour of Ahmed Jarba's presidency of the SOC in 2013, even though Mustafa Sabbagh

---

[60] Anonymous interview. [61] Ibid.
[62] Hassan Hassan, 'How the Syrian Muslim Brotherhood Hijacked Syria's Revolution', *Foreign Policy* (13 March 2013), www.foreignpolicy.com/articles/2013/03/13/how_the_muslim_brotherhood_hijacked_syria_s_revolution.
[63] Anonymous interview. [64] Ibid. [65] Interview with Hisham Marwah.
[66] Anonymous interview.

was the Brotherhood's preferred candidate.[67] In fact, even SOC members widely seen as Brotherhood stooges, such as Ahmad Ramadan or Obeida Nahas regularly vote against the Brotherhood bloc, and have been known to publicly and substantially criticise the group.[68]

The final area in which the Brotherhood's political behaviour has been controversial is in the way it has managed resources. Farouq Tayfour's role as head of the SNC's Relief and Development Bureau gave the Brotherhood control of much of the SNC's financial resources. The Relief Bureau is responsible for distributing aid and resources inside Syria, to both civilians and armed groups, but the group's critics accuse it of using the resources selectively to rebuild Brotherhood influence and networks in the country. It is also accused of favouring Brotherhood supporters in the distribution of aid. Prominent Damascus Spring activist and SNC member Kamal al-Labwani accused Muslim Brotherhood members of 'trying to monopolize aid and weapons to gain popular influence on the ground'.[69] Molham Aldrobi later clarified:

When we give support, say humanitarian aid, we do not differentiate between who is Muslim Brotherhood and who is not, because ... Those who are Muslim Brotherhood inside Syria are very minimal. The majority of the Syrian people are not Muslim Brotherhood ... for the humanitarian aid, for the educational aid, for the health and medical support, we do not differentiate between people.[70]

These criticisms also extend to the Brotherhood's apparent tendency to parachute its own members into key positions, with the group purportedly achieving control of the Council of Syrian Tribes through the appointment of Brotherhood member Shaykh Salem Abdul-Aziz al-Mislat as president.[71] Al-Mislat later took on a vice presidency position on the SOC through a seat allocated to the Council of Syrian Tribes. The trend has at times bordered on the absurd: a 60-year old Brotherhood member was appointed as the SNC's 'youth envoy' to Idlib, which has one of the most important opposition areas. The chief of the Revolutionary Council in Idlib, Mazem Arja, complained: 'The guy had not been

[67] Raphaël Lefèvre, 'Saudi Arabia and the Syrian Brotherhood', *Middle East Institute* (27 September 2013), www.mei.edu/content/saudi-arabia-and-syrian-brotherhood.
[68] 'The Syrian Opposition Coalition Accuses Sides of Thwarting the Interim Government, and 13 Military Factions Withdraw from it', *Al-Sharq al-Awsat* (Beirut: BBC Monitoring Middle East, 2013).
[69] 'Syrian Opposition Coalition Formed Without the SNC', *Al-Akhbar* (17 March 2012), http://english.al-akhbar.com/node/5319.
[70] Interview with Molham Aldrobi.
[71] Haian Dukhan, 'Tribes and Tribalism in the Syrian Uprising', *Syria Studies* 6, no. 2 (2014), p. 14.

there for 32 years ... If you dropped him at the edge of town, I doubt he could find his old house.'[72]

To some extent, this behaviour relates to the Brotherhood's decades of survival under authoritarianism, which deeply penetrated the group's psyche and created path-dependent behaviour that has proven difficult to shake.[73] Groups socialised into such an environment rarely fully surrender themselves to the democratic process because of their distrust of the system and fear that the post-authoritarian political arrangements will fail.[74] In the same regard, the front groups are a legacy of the harsh repression the Brotherhood faced over decades. Although Ghalioun accused the group of having 'the mentality of a closed club. They don't trust others and others don't trust them', he acknowledged:

> When they were persecuted in 1982, they received no support from the other opposition groups. They were totally excluded, which forced them to [turn inward and] live inside with themselves. For three, four decades ... To protect themselves. And they created their own organisations for help, relief, etc.[75]

Groups such as the SHRC were initially founded to track and advocate for those incarcerated in Syria in the 1980s. While this pragmatism was key to its survival for years in exile and proved a major strength in the initial uprising by positioning the Brotherhood to seize many opportunities that came its way, as the uprising progressed, the pragmatism evolved into opportunism and desperation, leading to perceptions that the group stood for nothing but its own political gain. Although such behaviour may have a historical justification and reflect the mark of decades under authoritarianism, in the context of the uprising it was a further source of intra-opposition suspicion.

Failing to Convince even the Exiled Elite

It was clear that history had cast a long shadow over the Brotherhood's ability to reintegrate among Syria's elite exiled political class, dealing it a dual blow that both deprived it of the political nous required to stage a successful comeback and which created a level of distrust among its opposition compatriots that would prove possibly insurmountable. The

---

[72] Neil MacFarquhar, 'Syrian Opposition Meets to Seek Unity', *The New York Times* (8 November 2012), www.nytimes.com/2012/11/09/world/middleeast/syria-war-developments.html.

[73] Vincent Boudreau, *Resisting Dictatorship: Repression and protest in Southeast Asia* (Cambridge: Cambridge University Press, 2004).

[74] For a discussion of this more broadly, see Nathan J. Brown, *When Victory Is Not an Option: Islamist Movements in Arab Politics* (Ithaca: Cornell University Press, 2012), p. 2.

[75] Interview with Burhan Ghalioun, Paris (3 August 2015).

Brotherhood began the uprising from a position of relative strength, underwritten by its lifelong characteristics of pragmatism, flexibility and individualism. But the group continued to favour opportunistic and short-term decisions, with a serious cost to its credibility. Seven years into the uprising, the group had failed to rebuild the trust of the exiled opposition. In fact, in many ways, the problem had been compounded. As one liberal activist noted:

> They (Brotherhood members) are diplomatic (unlike the Salafists). They treat you well to your face, but I have always had the feeling they were not honest with what they say ... They have an agenda that has to be realised, regardless of the price.[76]

As a former Brotherhood member remarked, the group 'might have repaired this if they dealt with [the opposition and the uprising] it in a good way, but they didn't'.[77] History had left a mixed legacy for the group, endowing it with the resources to play the political game, but without the political aptitude required to make sustainable gains.

The Brotherhood for its part saw no issue with the way it had engaged politically. When asked about the accusations of monopolisation, the group's uprising-era Strategic Planning chief Molham Aldrobi stressed:

> This is totally not true. We were always part of the Syrian national bodies. We were always helpful to others. We always tried to be as positive and as productive within these national bodies. Now of course we do have probably more organisational skills than others ... And due to the fact that we are an organisation, individuals belonging to the Muslim Brotherhood have behind them a group supporting them. So compared to individuals who do not have these groups supporting them, our productivity on those national bodies becomes more effective and more efficient. But this is by no means controlling the political power.[78]

Indeed, the Brotherhood's senior leaders believed that the group was being unfairly maligned. Its influence stemmed from the weakness of other opposition groups rather than a cynical plan on the Brotherhood's part.

To an extent, it is true that weakness of the broader political opposition enabled the Brotherhood to take on an exaggerated role. Nobody has been able to seriously challenge the group, as Karl Sharro observed:

> The Muslim Brotherhood cannot be blamed for being more effective at political lobbying within a system that the entire opposition subscribed to. There's been

---

[76] Anonymous interview (parenthesis added).
[77] Interview with Ali al-Ahmad, London (parenthesis added).
[78] Interview with Molham Aldrobi.

no self-critique whatsoever by the opposition for its complicity in creating this environment in the first place.[79]

Others agree that the group's engagement itself was not undemocratic, and that it demonstrated a high regard for the processes built into the political bodies and never tried to undermine a decision that it lost. When asked how the Brotherhood interacted on the Council, Ghalioun acknowledged that '[t]hey respected the president and the posts and the hierarchy because they have a tradition of organisation' within their own group.[80] He added: 'They are not violent like others [but] ... They are not cooperative with others ... [This being said] they are not anti-democratic.'[81] The Brotherhood may have regularly exploited loopholes, but they also respected the system's boundaries.

But in the end, this all proved immaterial to the Brotherhood's real challenge, which required it to build a popular and legitimate base for itself inside Syria, rather than obtain early numerical strength among the comparatively weak opposition outside the country. While it was trying and failing to win the elite politics game in Istanbul, Doha and Riyadh, those inside Syria languished in war. The exiled opposition existed in something of a 'bubble', with many of its parts far divorced from events on the ground. As Abouzeid described, exiled voices 'did not travel far across the border. Syrians were deaf to those claiming to represent them from the safety of elsewhere. Inside, other voices prevailed.'[82] Those inside Syria derided the SNC and SOC as the opposition of 'the hotels' or the 'hotel revolutionaries' who lived in luxury while those inside Syria paid the price for the population's defiance in 2011.[83] Yassin al-Haj Saleh expanded:

The problem lies specifically in the unnecessary, unjustifiable, and persistent infighting, which is most likely driven by attempts at self-promotion; and the deeply mediocre standing of most opposition spokepersons, manifest in their lack

---

[79] Karl Sharro, 'Did the Muslim Brotherhood Hijack Syria's Revolution?', *Karl reMarks* (14 March 2013), www.karlremarks.com/2013/03/did-muslim-brotherhood-hijack-syrias.html.
[80] Interview with Burhan Ghalioun, Paris (3 August 2015). [81] Ibid.
[82] Rania Abouzeid, *No Turning Back: Life, Loss and Hope in Wartime Syria* (London: Oneworld Publications, 2018).
[83] 'The Syrian National Coalition: The Rebel Hotels Club', Orient-Net (7 July 2013), http://orient-news.net/ar/news_show/4300/0/%D8%A7%D9%84%D8%A7%D8%A6% D8%AA%D9%84%D8%A7%D9%81-%D8%A7%D9%84%D9%88%D8%B7%D9% 86%D9%8A-%D8%A7%D9%84%D8%B3%D9%88%D8%B1%D9%8A%D9%86% D8%A7%D8%AF%D9%8A-%D8%AB%D9%88%D8%A7%D8%B1%D8%A7% D9%84%D9%81%D9%86%D8%A7%D8%AF%D9%82; Rania Abouzeid, 'Syrian Opposition Groups Stop Pretending', *New Yorker* (26 September 2013), www.newyorker.com/news/news-desk/syrian-opposition-groups-stop-pretending.

of discipline and a clear, shared vision. Consequently, trust in the broader opposition has collapsed, resulting in a nearly indiscriminate public repudiation. The opposition has been found ineffective and worthless at best, disrespectful and despicable at worst.[84]

Indeed, while the Brotherhood had expended much of its energy and political resources on unsuccessfully building influence and legitimacy within the exiled opposition, the SNC and SOC enjoyed little respect and credibility among those inside Syria. As its reputation soured with every passing year, it became clear that for all the Brotherhood's struggles among the exiled opposition, that challenge would pale in comparison to its struggle to win the support of those on the ground.

---

[84] Yassin al-Haj Saleh, *Impossible Revolution: Making Sense of the Syrian Tragedy* (London: Hurst, 2017), pp. 122–3.

7   Looking beyond the Opposition in Exile

The 2011 uprising in Syria quickly transformed from nascent demonstrations into a civil war, encompassing many parts including civilians left inside the country as well as the international powers that began exercising definitive influence on the shape of the conflict. With the Syrian opposition in exile far divorced from the broader conflict, rebuilding trust with the Syrian population would be a separate task. To survive and thrive, the Brotherhood would need to articulate a clear vision for Syria to win back its support base, silence its internal demons and develop its international connections. Ultimately, the Brotherhood's failure to rebuild this support would become the defining feature of its experience in the 2011 uprising.

Making the Case to Be Part of Syria's Future

If the Brotherhood was to enjoy a future in Syria, it would need to convince the Syrian population that it was a trustworthy political actor that would represent their interests. The Brotherhood seemed to understand the importance of its messaging from the outset, with Molham Aldrobi explaining that, when the Brotherhood was planning for the uprising at its leadership meeting in January 2011 months before the uprising began

> We identified four strategic frameworks for the revolution: it would be (1) a national revolution, (2) a peaceful revolution, (3) the preservation of the unity of the nation, and (4) the rejection of any (non-Arab and non-Muslim) foreign military intervention.[1]

Those at the meeting purportedly agreed that the Brotherhood 'would not have any specific demands, but that our demands would correspond

---

[1] 'Muslim Brotherhood Leader Molham al-Droubi Exclusively Opens Up his Papers to al-Ahd', *al-Ahd no. 1* (1 March 2013), p. 8.

to those of the people'.² The group expended significant energy at the beginning of the uprising to depict itself as in step with the will of the Syrian population.

The Brotherhood released a formal statement of intent in 2012 in the form of a two-page document titled the 'Covenant and Charter' in which the group declared its intentions:

> In this crucial stage of the history of Syria, where the dawn is born from the womb of suffering and pain, on the hands of the Syrian heros [sic], men and women, children, youth and old men, in a national overwhelming revolution, with the participation of all components of the Syrian people, for all the Syrians. We 'the muslim brotherhood [sic] in Syria' ... present this covenant and charter, to all of our people, committed to it in the letter and sprit [sic], a covenant which safeguards the rights, and a charter which dispels fears as a source of reassurance and satisfaction.³

The document declared itself 'a new social contract, establishing a modern and safe national relationship, among the Syrian society components'.⁴ It closely resembled the group's previous outlook, replicating the ideological consistency that the Brotherhood has maintained in its written documents over a 70-year period. It referred directly to Mustafa al-Sibai, the 2001 National Honour Charter and the 2004 Political Project in its closing paragraphs. The document promised

> a civil modern state with a civil constitution, coming from the will of the Syrian people, based on national harmony, written by a freely and impartially elected constituent assembly, protecting the fundamental rights of individuals and groups of any abuse or override, ensuring an equitable representation to all components of society.⁵

It declared the country's diversity to be 'an enriching factor, an extension to a long history of co-existence'.⁶ Although, as noted in Chapter 2, the Brotherhood has never been particularly ideological, the Covenant was nonetheless an important indication of how the group wished to be perceived by the Syrian population. Its mention of religion was subtle, but nonetheless there, manifesting in language such as a 'civil modern state', 'a state committed to human rights as dictated by divine law and international conventions', and the decision to close the document with a Quranic verse.

The Covenant's message was echoed by the Brotherhood's members in other fora throughout the uprising. As a senior leader explained: 'we

---

² Ibid.
³ 'Covenant and Charter' (Istanbul: The Muslim Brotherhood in Syria, 2012), p. 1.
⁴ Ibid. ⁵ Ibid. ⁶ Ibid.

are Islamists who believe in the theory of the modern state in all aspects and still we don't see that it contradicts Islam'.[7] Likewise, Shura Council chief Ali al-Bayanouni wrote in the *Guardian* in the same year the Covenant was released:

> After 50 years of autocratic rule, our national position and political record emphasises that we will not move towards autocracy, be that religious, political or social. The Muslim Brotherhood is committed to a Syria in which citizenship is the basis of rights and duties, and Syrians can reconstruct their unified civil society where the concept of majority and minority gradually disappears. Women must be given ample opportunity to assert themselves so future generations can play their crucial part in this national project.[8]

Then-Brotherhood spokesman Zuhair Salem explained the Brotherhood's concept of a 'civil state':

> We want a civil state and not a theocratic one, because Islam does not have a clergy that runs the state in the first place. For us, religion is a framework that does not enter into the details; the rules of religion with respect to the public law [make up] only five percent [of all rules]. The rest of it pertains to the private individuals' conduct in the Shari'a ... We will not bring laws which are not agreed on by the citizens; Shari'a can be expressed within the framework of democracy. So if we say that extra-marital relationships are forbidden and [it is] agreed on in parliament, we will go with it; if it is rejected, we will not. This is what we mean by a civil government.[9]

There was little sign of the undemocratic instincts and dogmatism that the Hama-centric view of the Brotherhood expected. In fact, when one Brotherhood associate was asked if he thought the group was ideological, he responded:

> I don't think so ... There is not much of ideology. They are pragmatic. This is the most pragmatic Brotherhood ever. Even more than Egypt, more than Tunisia. Just read their statements. We say that if you remove the name of the [Muslim] Brotherhood and you gave it a secular name it wouldn't make much of a difference.[10]

To some, the Brotherhood's positions were so unremarkable that it was viewed as no different to its secular competitors.

---

[7] Anonymous interview.
[8] Ali Al-Bayanouni, 'The Muslim Brotherhood Wants a Future for all Syrians', *The Guardian* (7 August 2012), www.theguardian.com/commentisfree/2012/aug/06/syria-middleeast.
[9] Cited in Tam Hussein, 'The Brotherhood's Man in London', *Majalla* (23 April 2013), https://web.archive.org/web/20171129085905/http://eng.majalla.com/2013/04/article55240699. At the time of writing in 2018, this article was only available online through archive.org.
[10] Anonymous interview.

Although this ideological flexibility and pragmatism is historically consistent, the programmes were seen as so flexible that they stood for nothing. The first Syrian National Council (SNC) President, Burhan Ghalioun, observed:

They have a very uninspired ideology ... [There is nothing to it other than to] be very religious and to pray. This is not a project. The Salafists speak about an Islamic state. This can be a utopia ... But the Muslim Brotherhood does not have [a compelling idea like] this.[11]

He added that 'Their project is to participate and to be relevant. Nothing more.'[12] Former Brotherhood member Mohammed Sarmini criticised the group's decision to cling to its history, arguing that it prevented political innovation. After working closely with the Brotherhood's leadership, he concluded that 'the Muslim Brotherhood doesn't have a clear plan and clear goals ... I believe in this idea [of Hassan al-Banna]. I believe in the thinkers, but it is not enough. I want a restructure and a rethink ... Because 2015 is very different to 1927.'[13] Indeed, while the group viewed its congruence with the path of Mustafa al-Sibai as a sign of its ideological integrity, to some this unwavering commitment to the founding fathers is a source of stagnation that relegates it to the past and prevents innovation. The message had already had its time. Lund noted that in the 2011 uprising, 'the Brotherhood remained aloof from mass politics, and stubbornly held to its moderate Islamist programme instead of trying to curry favour with the rising militant and sectarian fringe'.[14] Although this speaks to the irrelevance of Hama-centric narratives for the group, this perceived intellectual stagnation did little to win it friends among the radicalising opposition landscape. In a context where groups on both sides of the conflict were providing increasingly radical and creative solutions to Syria's worsening problems,[15] the Brotherhood could not compete, although it is worth noting that this failure to put forward a compelling alternative was common across the exiled opposition.

The success of the Brotherhood's message was further complicated by the political diversity that remained a core group feature throughout the uprising. Although such internal ideational pluralism is the mark of a healthy organisation, in the context of the Brotherhood's poor track record it was often interpreted as sinister. It also diluted the Brotherhood's

[11] Interview with Burhan Ghalioun, Paris (3 August 2015).   [12] Ibid.
[13] Interview with Mohammed Sarmini, Istanbul (31 August 2015).
[14] Aron Lund, 'The Syrian Brotherhood: On the Sidelines', *Middle East Institute* (24 September 2013), www.mei.edu/content/syrian-muslim-brotherhood-sidelines.
[15] Benjamin Isakhan, 'The Islamic State Attacks on Shia Holy Sites and the "Shrine Protection Narrative": Threats to Sacred Space as a Mobilization Frame', *Terrorism and Political Violence*, DOI: 10.1080/09546553.2017.1398741, p. 7.

official messages. Some Brotherhood insiders recognised these issues and criticised the group for being 'inconsistent in its positions and uncommitted to principles'.[16] One senior Brotherhood figure complained that such diversity often looks bad for the Brotherhood, saying: non-Brotherhood members 'meet people like Nazir Hakim or Farouq Tayfour [whose disposition differs from other members of the group], which gives them a bad taste and makes the Brotherhood look inconsistent'.[17]

This author's discussions with senior Brotherhood members revealed diversity even on key issues. When asked about anything more than surface-level political issues, senior leaders give varied responses. A discussion with one senior member revealed discrepancies on the type of political system that would be best for Syria, even though the 2005 Political Project document had examined the issue in detail.[18] He explained: 'we don't have a clear-cut view, we are leaving this to later to discuss with our partners in the homeland ... We do not cling to those details. We are flexible.'[19] It seemed quite remarkable that to some leaders, 70 years of preparation had not been long enough to germinate clear ideas. This in many ways exemplified the Brotherhood's political approach: pragmatic, flexible and willing to adapt in any direction to ensure its ongoing relevance. Indeed, Burhan Ghalioun recalled the group's tendency to change positions and political sides on the SNC for expediency: 'Now they are with me, tomorrow they can say that someone else is better. They are very pragmatic. And ... very opportunistic too.'[20] A Brotherhood associate echoed this: 'they are opportunistic people ... they see where the wind is going.' Although this was not the political style of the Brotherhood in its founding decades, such behaviour had characterised its nature in exile and increasingly in the 2011 uprising. Many opposition figures were concerned that this flexibility and opportunism would know no bounds should it end up in power one day.

Internal ideological diversity extended to the role of Islam in the group's ideal state, which remained unresolved even at the highest echelons of the group. When asked about the role that Islam would play in the Brotherhood's ideal state, one senior leader declared: 'Religion will be a general reference ... it is a reference that we will refer to, and we do not deviate from.'[21] But another senior leader complained that he did not

---

[16] Riad Durrar, 'Letter from a Group of the Sons of the Muslim Brotherhood', Facebook (12 January 2014), www.facebook.com/riaddrar/posts/337902093014536.
[17] Anonymous interview.
[18] 'A Summary of the Political Project for the Future Syria: A Vision of the Muslim Brotherhood Group in Syria' (London: Syrian Muslim Brotherhood, 2004), pp. 18–19.
[19] Anonymous interview.   [20] Interview with Burhan Ghalioun, Paris (3 August 2015).
[21] Ibid.

agree with Islam being a point of reference at all; he saw no role for Islam in Syria's political future.[22] An extension of this is the group's position on personal status laws. Syria's existing personal status laws make issues such as marriage and divorce, inheritance and the custody of children the responsibility of local religious courts. Any change to personal status laws are therefore not only significant for Syria's Sunni Muslim majority, but would be of interest to Syria's substantial minority groups who have historically managed their own affairs. Samir abu Laban opined, 'we do not deviate from the Islamic teaching'.[23] Another senior Brotherhood member said that 'we will use all of the Sharia. Islam is not just a penal law, it is justice, freedom and rights. [Although] Sharia and the civil constitution will be separate.'[24] Yet when pressed, he could not specify where the gap between Sharia courts and civil courts would lie. This represented a major challenge for the group's credibility, and drew some legitimate questions about whether the Brotherhood's political goals could be subject to dramatic change if certain members rose to senior office.

This ongoing plurality of ideas within the Brotherhood's ranks demonstrates the group's internal vibrancy and gestures on some level to its internal democratic processes, but these voices are often seen to speak for the organisation, rather than themselves. This means that even though the Brotherhood's official political platforms have not wavered for decades, the contradictory comments made by members are often interpreted as official organisational policy. Rightly or wrongly, this erodes the Brotherhood's otherwise consistent line, and represents a barrier to it conveying a clear message to the Syrian population, who may one day exercise definitive judgement on whether the Brotherhood deserves a role in the country's future.

The 2011 uprising also revealed the hollowness of the group's claim to have strong connections inside Syria. The confrontation in the 1980s and the persistence of Law No. 49 meant that most of the Brotherhood's grassroots supporters had been forced either into exile or to sever all contact with the group. Others disappeared in the Syrian prison system, including at the 1980 Palmyra massacre, or were killed during the 1980s confrontation. This was exacerbated by the group's mismanagement of its relationship with the regime and the regime's co-optation of parts of its base, which damaged its reputation and cost it supporters. Senior members privately acknowledge that the group had very few active members on the ground in the lead-up to 2011. One member close to

---

[22] Ibid.   [23] Interview with Samir Abu Laban, Istanbul.   [24] Anonymous interview.

the leadership acknowledged that this figure could have been as low as in the 'tens',[25] but Brotherhood figures were publicly optimistic, with Zuhair Salem explaining that the Brotherhood 'leads with thoughts, not members'.[26] Nonetheless, it was clear that the group's return would have to be largely executed via import, disseminating its ideological material and employing its significant resources and skills from outside the country as it would be unable to rely on the organic rekindling of old relationships to spur the process.

The Brotherhood would also face a challenge in expanding its base beyond its traditional membership, as the group had suffered severe reputational damage in Ba'thist Syria. The regime had controlled the narrative on the Brotherhood for the 30 years of its exile, meaning that most Syrians' only exposure to the group came through anti-Brotherhood content in the Syrian state media. Because of this the Brotherhood would have to prove to the Syrian population that it was not the totalitarian extremist organisation depicted by the al-Assad regimes and in Hama-centric accounts of the group. This was compounded by the reality that while many Syrians had been initially sympathetic to the group's anti-authoritarian agenda as seen in the large numbers on the streets in the early 1980s, the group's actions and inaction had inflicted an impossibly high price on the Syrian population. One woman imprisoned after her son was linked to the Brotherhood was reported to have complained: 'Damn the Ikhwan [Brotherhood]. Damn your rise to power. Why don't you come here [to the prison] and see what is happening to us. You're out there. You do whatever you want. But we're in here. And we're the ones being squeezed in [*sic*] graves.'[27] This thinking was reflected in comments made by former Brotherhood member Ali al-Ahmad, who explained:

In Syria people blame them [the Brotherhood]. They say: 'look, you started the problem with the regime, but we paid the price'. The people think like this. Normal people say: 'you started [the conflict but] you couldn't finish [it] and we had to pay the price'. So people in Syria don't like them.[28]

In the absence of members or sympathisers inside the country, and without legitimacy or a base that it could easily harness and rebuild, the Brotherhood would face a serious problem in convincing the Syrian population that history did not define the group.

---

[25] Ibid. [26] Interview with Zuhair Salem, London.
[27] Heba Dabbagh, *Just Five Minutes: Nine Years in the Prisons of Syria*, trans. Bayan Khatib (Toronto: Unknown, 2007).
[28] Interview with Ali al-Ahmad, London (parenthesis added).

Significant socio-political shifts had also taken place in Syria since the Brotherhood's exile, leading to the emergence of a new underclass. Many of those who took to the streets in 2011 were not from the Brotherhood's historical support base in Syria's middle merchant classes who had revolted in the 1970s, but were country-dwellers and the urban poor.[29] President Bashar al-Assad's haphazard liberalisation of the country's economy over the previous decade had caused the key indicators of economic health – that is, unemployment, inflation and poverty rates – to skyrocket, and was one of several factors that saw people take to the streets. But the Brotherhood offered few solutions for those worst impacted by these grievances, which were not acknowledged or addressed at all in the 2012 Covenant and Charter. This represented a missed opportunity to engage with one of the root causes of the 2011 conflict. In fact, the Brotherhood had given its last official word on economics in the 2004 Political Project's 17-point economic policy plan.[30] The project promised: 'new investment laws which attract Syrian capital abroad'; 'Gradual and calm transformation from the public sector economy to the open market economy'; 'Encouraging the private sector and enforcing the role and initiatives of producers', as well as banking and tax reform.[31] But these promises reflected the same neoliberal economic principles that the Ba'th had attempted to implement in the 2000s. Aside from a vague commitment to '[p]roviding equal opportunities for all citizens to participate in public and private economic ventures, whilst ensuring the minimum standard of dignified living for all', such an approach would do little to address the issues that formed the backbone of popular dissent in 2011.[32] Again, the Brotherhood's political platforms fell short in providing compelling solutions for the new crisis that Syria had found itself in by 2011.

The group thus primarily sought to rebuild its connections with the Syrian population through humanitarian aid, an aspect of the Syrian conflict that was 'highly politicised' regardless of whether the Brotherhood was involved.[33] The Brotherhood's humanitarian contributions were significant in the early stages of the conflict but were subsequently

---

[29] Dara Conduit, 'The Patterns of Syrian Uprising: Comparing Hama in 1980–1982 and Homs in 2011', *British Journal of Middle Eastern Studies* 44, no. 1 (2017), pp. 2–3.

[30] The Brotherhood's 2012 Covenant and Charter did not address economic policy. The group's last official word on economics was seen in the group's Political Project – 'A Summary of the Political Project for the Future Syria', pp. 20–2.

[31] Ibid., pp. 21–2.   [32] Ibid., p. 21.

[33] Marika Sosnowski, 'Violence and Order: The February 2016 Cease-fire and the Development of Rebel Governance Institutions in Southern Syria', *Civil Wars* 20, no. 3 (2018), p. 317.

dwarfed by Gulf state contributions. The group leveraged the international connections that its members had developed in exile to facilitate this work. As the group's then media chief Omar Mushaweh explained:

> Syrian Muslim Brotherhood members who lived in Saudi Arabia, Qatar and Gulf states ... [used their existing relationships to contact] the respective [humanitarian] organisations in their countries and explained to them our situation and facilitated their entrance into the country.[34]

By 2012, Ali al-Bayanouni estimated that the group was funnelling US$1–2 million per month into Syria for humanitarian aid.[35] This included medical aid and support for schools. After being elected in 2014, the group's new leader Muhammad Walid expressed a commitment to spending 75 percent of the group's financial resources inside the country.[36] By 2015, the group had offices in Idlib and Aleppo, distributed its professionally designed newspaper *al-Ahd* online and in hard copy across these areas, and was one of the biggest humanitarian aid providers in the refugee camps in southern Turkey.[37] Fakher and Weiss wrote in 2012 that 'at present, only the Muslim Brotherhood reportedly has uncontested access to the camps', facilitated by its connections to the highest echelons of power in Turkey.[38] The group also announced the establishment of a multi-faith and multi-ethnic political party called Waad, although the accelerating nature of the conflict soon meant that there was little use for political parties.

The role played by the group's members in their individual capacities was crucial. The son of a former Brotherhood cell leader from central Syria reported being asked to reactivate his father's network by senior Brotherhood members: 'They want me to rebuild the Muslim Brotherhood's group through a charity network by helping poor families, jailed activists and by paying for medical aid ... If we could present good services and policies to all Syrians, we will be elected.'[39] He estimated

---

[34] Interview with Omar Mushaweh, Skype, 2017.
[35] Neil MacFarquhar, 'Trying to Mold a Post-Assad Syria from Abroad', *The New York Times* (5 May 2012), www.nytimes.com/2012/05/06/world/middleeast/from-abroad-trying-to-mold-a-post-assad-syria.html?_r=0.
[36] Yusra Ahmed, 'Syria's Muslim Brotherhood Leader Highlights Reforms, Future Plans – Interview', *Zaman Al Wasl* (20 March 2015), https://en.zamanalwsl.net/news/9402.html.
[37] Raphaël Lefèvre, 'Islamism within a Civil War: The Syrian Muslim Brotherhood's Struggle for Survival', Brookings Institute (2015), www.brookings.edu/wp-content/uploads/2016/07/Syria_Lefevre-FINALE-1.pdf, p. 7.
[38] Hamza Fakher, Michael Weiss and Brian Milne, 'Revolution in Danger: A Critical Appraisal of the Syrian National Council with Recommendations for Reform', The Henry Jackson Society (2012), http://henryjacksonsociety.org/wp-content/uploads/2012/02/SNC.pdf, p. 14.
[39] Cited in MacFarquhar, 'Trying to Mold a Post-Assad Syria'.

in 2012 that the Brotherhood had spent millions of dollars in his local area over the previous year. Yet the group struggled in other areas to win a presence on the ground. One senior Damascene activist noted that the group's 'existence and presence in Damascus was weak ... they don't have any influence in Damascus, and so in the southern area, Damascus and its suburbs and Deraa and even Qunietra, they don't have any impact'.[40]

The Brotherhood's reach into Syria was undermined by the same problematic political decision-making seen on the SNC and the SOC. The Brotherhood's provision of humanitarian aid, which could have formed the key to the group accessing the Syrian population, was initially carried out through a decentralised process, where, as described by Lefèvre:

> Members from each of Syria's regions became responsible for organizing charity and military activities at their local levels. At first, this policy gave members a great degree of autonomy and stoked enthusiasm, but soon it also led to a duplication and fragmentation of Brotherhood efforts, unhealthy competition between regional branches, and confusion about the group's ultimate goals across Syria.[41]

The group was criticised for favouring Brotherhood supporters and the districts associated with their leadership group. According to SNC member Abdulrahman al-Haj, 'the Ikhwan focused only on Hama and Idlib at first, because its leaders came from this area'.[42] This pattern was apparently so pronounced that it filtered down into the group's intercity factional divide. The group did not even begin making serious efforts in Syria's largest city Aleppo until power was reshuffled within the group away from the Hama faction in 2014, suggesting that infighting was having a tangible impact on political performance.[43] Such short-term strategies also created a perception that the Brotherhood only supported its own, which represented a significant barrier to winning hearts and minds beyond the Brotherhood's extended family members and former constituents. Molham Aldrobi acknowledged that, while the Brotherhood distributed humanitarian aid universally on the basis of need,

> [w]hen it comes to supporting our people in Syria, the members of the Muslim Brotherhood, of course we give our organisation's members what they need.

---

[40] Anonymous interview.
[41] Raphaël Lefèvre, 'Syria in Crisis: A New Leader for Syria's Muslim Brotherhood?', *Carnegie Middle East Center* (6 May 2014), http://carnegie-mec.org/diwan/55512.
[42] Aron Lund, 'Struggling to Adapt: The Muslim Brotherhood in a New Syria' (Washington, DC: Carnegie Endowment for International Peace, 2013), p. 16.
[43] Ibid.

Their dues. And we don't give others because like any other organisation like any other company, we have obligations towards our members.[44]

Although this may be the rational behaviour of a political organisation, it won the group few friends.

The reputations of many Brotherhood members as elite and out of touch with the Syrian population proved a further deterrent. As one senior Brotherhood figure said: 'we regard ourselves as an elite party. We have quality and active members that serve the masses and work amongst the people. So the group is elite and at the same time is for the people.'[45] A significant gap emerged between its comparatively wealthy and educated leaders and members in exile, and those who were starving and fighting in Syria, which widened as the conflict unfolded. Although many Syrians acknowledged the Brotherhood's historical suffering, the group was seen as too far removed from the events leading up to 2011 – including the socio-economic pressures that contributed to the uprising. Many of the youth protesters and fighters were not alive during the Brotherhood's original struggle. This thinking was encapsulated in the comments of a Damascus activist, who stated: 'We won't let people living outside the country come here and tell those of us who made the revolution what to do.'[46] In many ways, this marked a continuation of the inside–outside politics that had emerged between the Fighting Vanguard and the Brotherhood during the Brotherhood's first confrontation with the regime. But the history of the chasm between political leaders and activists on the ground goes back even further. Ironically, Brotherhood founder Mustafa al-Sibai himself once complained about the Arab governments' 'fruitless policy of conferences' in attempting to resolve the Palestinian issue.[47]

As a result, the Brotherhood's popular outreach during the Syrian uprising did not appear to have translated into significant new membership numbers. Although its political programmes remained consistent and the Brotherhood made significant efforts to make sure its vision was heard, when asked if the group had many new members, Ali al-Bayanouni avoided a direct response in 2015 and conceded that 'we are still reconstructing'.[48] This sense was echoed by a Brotherhood associate who suggested that the group has not

---

[44] Interview with Molham Aldrobi. [45] Anonymous interview.
[46] Liz Sly, 'Syria's Muslim Brotherhood is Gaining Influence over Anti-Assad Revolt', *Washington Post* (22 May 2012), www.washingtonpost.com/world/syrias-muslim-brotherhood-is-gaining-influence-over-anti-assad-revolt/2012/05/12/gIQAtIoJLU_story.html.
[47] Cited in Umar F. Abd-allah, *The Islamic Struggle in Syria* (Berkeley: Mizan Press, 1983), p. 95.
[48] Interview with Ali al-Bayanouni, London.

gained members in the sense that they have gained people who had nothing to do with Muslim Brotherhood … [but] you had people who used to be Muslim Brotherhood members, but became deactivated … it was like they pressed the activation button and these guys were motivated to come to Turkey and run NGOs and armed opposition groups. So I don't think they've gained new members from scratch. All they've done is reactivate some of the old people.[49]

In this regard, the group's new political platforms, newspapers and humanitarian outreach did not appear to have substantially improved the group's prospects on the ground.

Realistically, the limited success of the group's return to Syria implied that the Brotherhood would struggle to ever earn a significant electoral mandate should free and fair elections ever come back to the country. Although one senior Brotherhood figure told Lefèvre that the group could garner 25 percent of the vote,[50] this seems unlikely given that it received less than 6 percent of the national vote at the peak of its political life under Issam al-Attar in 1961. Given Syria's heterogeneous population and the group's mixed track record, characterised also by violence, a reputation for sectarianism and political opportunism, and long exile, it would be difficult for it to secure a significant position in the future should an election be held. In this regard, while the Brotherhood's strength in the SNC, the SOC and at the various early opposition conferences gave the impression of the group's scale, popularity and even omnipresence in the Syrian political arena, when looking inside Syria it was clear that very little lay beneath a flurry of Brotherhood political activity. History exacted a heavy toll on the Brotherhood's base, and continued to impede its ability to rebuild.

Silencing the Internal Demons

The second area in which the Syrian Muslim Brotherhood would need to attain mastery was over its internal disputes, which were still present in the group in the years leading up to 2011. Many had hoped that the uprising would silence the Brotherhood's historical factionalism and for a short time this seemed to have happened.

By 2011, the Brotherhood's factional issues had changed shape. In the 1970s these had reflected very real geographic and socio-economic divides in Syria, but during the 2011 crisis few members that were interviewed strongly identified with either of the factions, and many denied

---

[49] Anonymous interview.
[50] Raphaël Lefèvre, '*The Muslim Brotherhood Prepares for a Comeback in Syria*' (Washington, DC: Carnegie Endowment for International Peace, p. 3).

that there was any divide at all. What remained of the factional disputes was largely an outdated personality conflict between senior members. Indeed, as one senior Brotherhood member privately acknowledged:

> The revolution did help build bridges and bring people more together, but I think that those who come from the old and historic background are not ready to get rid of the factional tension completely. Those who are coming from a much younger background are more capable of cooperating.[51]

When asked whether the Brotherhood would enjoy greater internal harmony if the head of the Aleppo faction Ali al-Bayanouni and the head of the Hama faction Farouq Tayfour retired, he added:

> Yes, it would be different. And a better organisation today. Because the problem is that you still have this historic background ... But certainly, if you were to give it [power] to the younger generation, the group would move on.[52]

Ironically, the very existence of this tired intercity factionalism among the group's leaders has fuelled a new divide between generations. This challenge had emerged prior to 2011 in the creation of the youth-led Movement for Justice and Development and the National Action Group, discussed in Chapter 3. By 2011, this rift centred around the persistence of petty factionalism, the underperformance of senior leaders and the failure of the Brotherhood's old guard to hand over power.

The Brotherhood's leadership team has rotated at fixed intervals throughout its lifespan, including in 2010, 2014 and 2018, which again differentiates it remarkably from the Baʿth regime and most of its opposition competitors in terms of intra-party democracy. Nevertheless, the leadership tends to rotate between a select few, mostly leaders from the Hama era. As former member Mohammed Sarmini complained: 'The Muslim Brotherhood are all old men. Like [Ali] al-Bayanouni and Zuhair Salem and [Farouq] Tayfour and [Riad al-] Shaqfeh and so on. This is where the power lies. The youth does not have power.'[53] Several high profile 'young' members explained their ongoing support for the Brotherhood 'idea', but accused the older generation in the leadership of failing to do it justice after 2011. In interviews, members of the group's middle generation such as Molham Aldrobi and Hassan al-Hachimi also demonstrated a markedly different approach to the uprising and the group's history. Although both were strong advocates of the group, they were frank about the group's role in both uprisings, and about the contemporary challenges it faced. This stood in stark contrast to many

---

[51] Anonymous interview.   [52] Ibid.
[53] Interview with Mohammed Sarmini, Istanbul (31 August 2015).

older generation members, who often denied involvement in violence or historical wrongdoing. But by 2019, both Aldrobi and al-Hachimi had left the leadership.

To some extent, the failure to transition power is a legacy of the Brotherhood's historical need to close ranks to protect itself, as well as the result of the group's suffering. There is also a sense among the leaders that those at the top had paid the highest price for their membership, and therefore deserved to remain, although the author interviewed many young Muslim Brotherhood members who had never even set foot in Syria prior to 2011: the Brotherhood's fight had forced them to grow up entirely detached from their homeland.

Some of the Brotherhood's leaders also appeared to lack respect for the younger generation, which is a serious problem given how important Syria's youth were to the events that sparked the 2011 uprising. Although there were hopes that the group's leadership would transfer to younger members during the 2014 Brotherhood election, as Samir abu Laban explained:

We had a change [of leadership in 2014] between Mr Riad al-Shaqfeh and Muhammad Walid because Riad believed that this was the time for the revolution we needed a young man who was fearless. So when he resigned and refused to be re-nominated, the Shura Council discussed this point and they reached a conclusion that the current situation in Syria is very serious and we need a wise person and we will not choose a young man.[54]

This led to the election of the septuagenarian Muhammad Walid as leader in 2014. Although Walid was seen as a consensus figure that was approved by and would ratify the existing powers, his election hardly represented a moment of intergenerationalism for the group. One associate was particularly critical of the decision:

He [Walid] is a complete nobody. I mean, when I say nobody, he has zero charisma. He is a poet. He is not someone that is suited ... he is not a charismatic leader. And he was voted in as a compromise.[55]

These feelings were even echoed by Zuhair Salem: 'He [Walid] has written a lot of very nice poems and I love poetry, but the political world has no mercy.'[56] There were some early efforts at dealing with the Brotherhood's youth problem under Walid's leadership. The leader of the Brotherhood's youth wing, Hosam Ghadban, was appointed deputy leader when Walid was elected, and 50 percent of the staff in the group's institutional structure were purportedly youth members, although this

[54] Interview with Samir Abu Laban, Istanbul.   [55] Anonymous interview.
[56] Interview with Zuhair Salem, London (parenthesis added).

figure was not reflected in the leadership.[57] However, Walid was never expected to significantly alter the old tactical power dynamics within the group, meaning that one of the key sources of the intergenerational divide remained unaddressed, further delaying the group's much needed-reconciliation with its history.

Consistent with this, former Brotherhood member Mohammed Sarmini complained that he was not considered mature enough to take on significant responsibilities in the Brotherhood organisation, even though people of similar age (in their 30s) in other countries often did so. Sarmini claimed that the elders' attitude to his resignation from the Brotherhood went along the lines of: 'These young people don't know they're going the wrong way. They'll be back!'[58] Soon after leaving, Sarmini became a senior advisor to the Syrian Interim Government. However, while this attitude of the leaders is pervasive, it is not universal; some senior leaders will privately acknowledge that 'the organisation has struggled with a generation gap'.[59]

It wasn't just the younger generation that was left behind during the uprising: women in the Brotherhood too failed to make any significant strides. Although the 2005 Political Project had recognised the right of women to hold public office, and made a commitment to a limited sort of gender equality 'apart from a very few number of exceptions,' the 2012 Covenant and Charter made no mention of gender.[60] The make-up of the Brotherhood's uprising era leadership group (see Appendix 3) underlined this sense that gender equality was not a major priority: the head of the women's office Kitam al-Adhab, the wife of Farouq Tayfour, was the only female leadership member. Women did not appear to have a significant role outside of this specifically women-focused domain, although others are believed to sit on the Shura Council. Some senior members were not even aware that al-Adhab was a member of the leadership team.[61] When the author asked for referrals to female members, the only women recommended were the wives of senior leaders, giving a sense that the estimated 100 or so female members[62] struggled to rise up the group's ranks in their own right. There was some awareness of this challenge among senior members: Ali al-Bayanouni

---

[57] Ahmed, 'Syria's Muslim Brotherhood Leader highlights reforms'.
[58] Interview with Mohammed Sarmini, Istanbul (31 August 2015).
[59] Anonymous interview.
[60] 'A Summary of the Political Project for the Future Syria' (London: Syrian Muslim Brotherhood, 2004), pp. 24–5; 'Covenant and Charter'.
[61] Anonymous interview.
[62] This figure is an estimate provided by Mohammad Sarmini. Interview with Mohammed Sarmini, Istanbul (31 August 2015).

acknowledged in 2015 that 'There are efforts to make women more prominent, but it is not as we hope.'[63]

These challenges are a significant issue for the group, representing a barrier to the broadening of its future base. The author met with a number of male and female Brotherhood youth and family members who are among the group's most vocal critics. Such critics pose a serious threat to the movement, because as Brotherhood members they are often educated and articulate, and know intimately the inner workings of the group. Previously, such frustration only manifested in minor splinter groups such as the Movement for Justice and Development or the National Action Group, but the scale of the frustration in conjunction with the group's underperformance in the 2011 uprising could have catastrophic consequences. This was seen in comments made by the Shaam News Network's founder Bilal Attar, who had grown up in a Brotherhood family but was not a member himself. He was scathing of the Brotherhood, explaining: 'we were the sons of the Brotherhood but not Brotherhood. In fact, we didn't like them ... we felt very strongly that we didn't want to work with anybody over the age of forty ... They had their turn in the last era. They failed. We wanted to be different.'[64] The youth have many choices. Even one senior middle-generation Brotherhood member made it clear that he would only remain in the Brotherhood for as long as he was convinced that it was the best vehicle for Syria's future. Once this calculus changes, he too would leave the group.[65]

Leveraging International Resources

The final indicator of the Brotherhood's political rehabilitation was its ability to build international relationships in the context of an uprising that was being increasingly shaped by the interests of foreign states. The Brotherhood had a history of forming pragmatic, non-ideological alliances with regional actors, but its most enduring state supporter during the 1980s confrontation, Saddam Hussein, was executed in 2006, and Jordan was never a significant powerbroker in Syria's civil war, particularly for machinations in the country's north. This meant that when the Arab uprisings unfolded, Qatar, Turkey and Saudi Arabia filled the new regional power vacuum, requiring the Brotherhood to build new friendships among the Syrian opposition's international benefactors. The full

---

[63] Interview with Ali al-Bayanouni, London.
[64] Rania Abouzeid, *No Turning Back: Life, Loss and Hope in Wartime Syria* (London: Oneworld Publications, 2018).
[65] Anonymous interview.

extent of these ties are sometimes difficult to elucidate because the Brotherhood's members consistently deny formal links with states.[66]

Qatar was the biggest supporter of the Syrian opposition in the early days of the uprising. According to estimates of those close to the Qatari government, Qatar had spent as much as US$3 billion on the uprising by 2013.[67] The Brotherhood and Qatar had a close relationship, although both parties denied a significant connection. When asked if the Brotherhood receives money from Qatar, Ali al-Bayanouni said, 'no not from the government ... They have humanitarian aid that they collect and distribute away from the political parties.'[68] Qatar for its part also denied a connection; the Qatari Foreign Minister told al-Hayat that 'Qatar does not support the Muslim Brotherhood, full stop'.[69] This was echoed by Qatar's Prime Minister Hamad bin Jassim al-Thani at a Brookings Institute dinner, when he argued that claims of a Qatar–Brotherhood relationship were mere rumours spread by Qatar's regional detractors.[70] As a result, it is difficult to quantify the Qatar–Brotherhood relationship, although Lefèvre suggests that Qatari support for the group came 'mainly through political and material support for the Brotherhood-dominated Syrian National Council'.[71] It is clear that Qatar has provided the group extensive political and diplomatic support at the very least.

Qatar had long had close relations with the Muslim Brotherhood movement as a whole. Yusuf al-Qaradawi, who is often depicted as the international Brotherhood's spiritual guide, has lived in Qatar for decades and gives his high-profile Friday sermons from the Omar Bin al-Khattab Mosque in Doha. Qaradawi also hosts a television programme on the Qatari government-linked Al Jazeera network titled *al-Sharia wa-al-Ḥayat* (Sharia and Life), which has an estimated 60 million weekly viewers.[72]

---

[66] Interview with Omar Mushaweh, Skype, 2017; interview with Molham Aldrobi, 2017.
[67] Roula Khalaf and Abbie Fielding-Smith, 'How Qatar Seized Control of the Syrian Revolution', *Financial Times* (17 May 2013), www.ft.com/cms/s/2/f2d9bbc8-bdbc-11e2-890a-00144feab7de.html.
[68] Interview with Ali al-Bayanouni, London.
[69] Jamil al-Ziabi, 'Qatari FM: We Do not Support the Muslim Brotherhood (translated by Kamal Fayad)', *Al-Monitor (originally published in Al-Hayat)* (22 February 2015), www.al-monitor.com/pulse/politics/2015/02/qatar-foreign-minister-gulf-hezbollah-brotherhood.html.
[70] Michele Kelemen, 'U.S. Wary as Qatar Ramps up Support of Syrian Rebels', *NPR* (26 April 2013), www.npr.org/2013/04/26/179248222/u-s-wary-as-qatar-ramps-up-support-of-syrian-rebels.
[71] Raphaël Lefèvre, 'Saudi Arabia and the Syrian Brotherhood', *Middle East Institute* (27 September 2013), www.mei.edu/content/saudi-arabia-and-syrian-brotherhood.
[72] Alexander Smoltczyk, 'Islam's Spiritual "Dear Abby": The Voice of Egypt's Muslim Brotherhood', *Der Spiegel* (15 February 2011), www.spiegel.de/international/world/islam-s-spiritual-dear-abby-the-voice-of-egypt-s-muslim-brotherhood-a-745526.html.

Qatar's reputation as a Brotherhood sympathiser reached new levels after the Arab uprisings, when it backed the Brotherhood movements in Egypt and Tunisia. This support was so extensive that one Arab politician accused the Qatari Emir of attempting to position himself as an 'Islamist [Gamal] Abdel Nasser'.[73]

Yet, ideologically, the Qatari ruling family and the Brotherhood have little in common, with the monarchs historically avoiding Islamist activism.[74] The Qatari Muslim Brotherhood movement dissolved itself in 1999 and the group's former leader Jassem Sultan declared four years later that the Qatari state was upholding its religious responsibilities.[75] An absence of ideological or political compatibility, however, has never been a barrier to the Brotherhood's state relationships. Individual Syrian Brothers historically resettled across the Gulf following their forced exile, including in Qatar. These members had an almost immediate impact on their host country, purportedly influencing the Qatari Brotherhood's decision to publish the short-lived magazine, *al-Umma al-Qatariyya* (the Qatari Umma) in the 1980s.[76] The magazine was published under the guidance of Syrian Brotherhood member Amr Adib Husna.[77] Dickenson estimated that the gulf state hosted 'many' Syrian Brotherhood members, but exact numbers are not available.[78]

With the spread of the Arab uprisings to Syria, Qatar–Brotherhood relations strengthened significantly alongside Qatar's parallel support for the Muslim Brotherhood regime in Egypt. Qatar was the second-largest backer (behind Libya) of the SNC, donating US$15 million, or almost half of the body's total revenue.[79] Practically, this meant that Qatar and the Brotherhood developed a close relationship early in the conflict. According to Lefèvre, the relationship

---

[73] Khalaf and Fielding-Smith, 'How Qatar Seized Control'.
[74] Kristian Coates Ulrichsen, *Qatar and the Arab Spring* (Oxford: Oxford University Press, 2014), p. 101.
[75] Layla Al-Shoumari, 'Muslim Brotherhood Paves Way for Qatar's Ascent', *Al-Akhbar* (12 April 2013), http://english.al-akhbar.com/node/15508.
[76] Courtney Freer, 'Rentier Islamism: The Role of the Muslim Brotherhood in the Gulf', *LSE Middle East Center* (2015), http://eprints.lse.ac.uk/64446/1/RentierIslamism.pdf, p. 9.
[77] Courtney Freer, *Rentier Islamism: The Influence of the Muslim Brotherhood in Gulf Monarchies* (Oxford: Oxford University Press, 2018), p. 88.
[78] Elizabeth Dickinson, *Godfathers and Thieves, Part Four: How the Syrian Revolution was Crowdfunded* (DECA, 2014), available at: www.decastories.com/godfathers/.
[79] 'Libya Helps Bankroll Syrian Opposition Movement', *The Washington Post* (5 November 2012), www.washingtonpost.com/world/middle_east/libya-helps-bankroll-syrian-opposition-movement/2012/11/05/98cd728a-2764-11e2-b2a0-ae18d6159439_story.html.

has been one of converging interests and mutual trust ... Qatar has surfed on the wave of the Arab Spring by supporting the Brotherhood which was quite popular when Arab autocrats fell. Doha hoped its policy would earn it friends in high places and thus make it a regional power to be reckoned with.[80]

The Brotherhood offered Qatar a network of connections and local knowledge that proved crucial in navigating the emerging opposition environment, particularly through bodies such as the Istanbul Room, which became the major early clearinghouse for foreign materiel.[81] O'Bagy argued that this relationship was key to directing Qatari money into Syria, and choosing which rebel battalions to back.[82] Omar Mushaweh acknowledged that the Brotherhood played a key role in facilitating connections between states and causes inside Syria in the first two years of the uprising, although he maintained that the support never went to Brotherhood projects.[83]

In return, the Brotherhood received significant political and diplomatic support, particularly through Al Jazeera, which is often viewed as the soft power wing of Qatar's government. Al Jazeera gave the Syrian Muslim Brotherhood favourable coverage long before the Arab uprisings. Al Jazeera Arabic screened numerous long interviews with Brotherhood leaders, exemplified in an eight-part interview with former leader Adnan Saadeddine on *Shahad ala al-Asr* (Witness to the Age), which in total spanned more than six hours.[84] The interview was conducted by the high-profile Al Jazeera personality Ahmad Mansour, who is widely suspected of being a Brotherhood sympathiser.[85] The interview was undertaken with Saadeddine as his health declined and not released until after he died, affording Saadeddine the privilege of having the last word on the Brotherhood's history. Although Saadeddine was a controversial figure, Brotherhood leaders responded positively to the interview, which

---

[80] Cited in Lauren Williams, 'Inside Doha, at the Heart of a GCC Dispute', *The National* (19 March 2014), www.thenational.ae/world/qatar/inside-doha-at-the-heart-of-a-gcc-dispute.
[81] Dickinson, *Godfathers and Thieves*.
[82] Cited in Khalaf and Fielding-Smith, 'How Qatar Seized Control'
[83] Interview with Omar Mushaweh, Skype, 2017.
[84] For example, see Ahmed Mansour, 'Adnan Saadeddine – the Brotherhood's Time in Syria, Episode 4', Al Jazeera (12 September 2012), www.aljazeera.net/programs/centurywitness/2012/10/3/%D8%B9%D8%AF%D9%86%D8%A7%D9%86-%D8%B3%D8%B9%D8%AF-%D8%A7%D9%84%D8%AF%D9%8A%D9%86-%D8%B9%D8%B5%D8%B1-%D8%A7%D9%84%D8%A5%D8%AE%D9%88%D8%A7%D9%86-%D9%81%D9%8A-%D8%B3%D9%88%D8%B1%D9%8A%D8%A7-%D8%AC4.
[85] Ahmad Mansour is often seen as supportive of the Muslim Brotherhood; 'Who Is Mansour, Journalist Sought by Egypt?', BBC (24 July 2015), www.bbc.co.uk/monitoring/who-is-ahmad-mansour-journalist-sought-by-egypt.

is hosted on both the Al Jazeera website and on the Brotherhood's YouTube channel.[86] Other Al Jazeera programmes have also run lengthy interviews with Brotherhood figures, including *bi-la-hudood* (Without Borders), in which Mansour interviewed Ali al-Bayanouni at length.[87] The group's website has published glowing editorials of the group. Following the release of the Brotherhood's Covenant and Charter in 2012, one commentator and regular Al Jazeera guest wrote that the Brotherhood's

> organisation and their historic presence in the fabric of Syrian society as the victim of the Hama incident in 1982 [means that] it is able to gather the majority of the independent Islamic figures with its program. Because it bears moderate thought that is fully consistent with the religiosity of most of the Syrian people.[88]

This scale of this support was so extensive that Sultan Sooud al-Qassemi accused Al Jazeera of refusing to cover negative stories on the group.[89]

The impact of Qatar's support for the Brotherhood across the region proved diplomatically costly, with Gulf Cooperation Council (GCC) states withdrawing their diplomats from Doha in 2014, cutting all ties and announcing an economic embargo against the oil and gas-rich state in 2017. This, along with the change of leadership in Qatar, led to the scaling back of support for the uprising in 2014 and the handover of the GCC's 'Syria file' to Saudi Arabia. The rivalry between Saudi Arabia and Qatar was felt among the Syrian opposition, with the head of the Aleppo Revolutionary Council, Abdul Jabbar Akaidi complaining that Qatar and Saudi Arabia were 'playing out their rivalries here; they are dividing people'.[90] This had important implications for the Brotherhood and

---

[86] Ahmed Mansour, 'Witness to Time – with Adnan Saadeddine', YouTube (Ikhwan Syria channel) (2012), www.youtube.com/watch?v=bCTf65YZRnU.

[87] 'Without Borders: The Muslim Brotherhood and Political Reform in Syria (an Interview with Ali al-Bayanouni)', Al Jazeera (21 August 2005), www.aljazeera.net/programs/withoutbounds/2005/8/21/%D8%A7%D9%84%D8%A5%D8%AE%D9%88%D8%A7%D9%86-%D8%A7%D9%84%D9%85%D8%B3%D9%84%D9%85%D9%88%D9%86-%D9%88%D8%A7%D9%84%D8%A5%D8%B5%D9%84%D8%A7%D8%AD-%D8%A7%D9%84%D8%B3%D9%8A%D8%A7%D8%B3%D9%8A-%D8%A8%D8%B3%D9%88%D8%B1%D9%8A%D8%A7.

[88] Mohammad Alloush, 'Reflections on the Syrian Brotherhood's document', Al Jazeera (2012), www.aljazeera.net/knowledgegate/opinions/2012/4/2/%D8%AA%D8%A3%D9%85%D9%84%D8%A7%D8%AA-%D9%81%D9%8A-%D9%88%D8%AB%D9%8A%D9%82%D8%A9-%D8%A5%D8%AE%D9%88%D8%A7%D9%86-%D8%B3%D9%88%D8%B1%D9%8A%D8%A7#2.

[89] Sultan Sooud Al-Qassemi, 'Morsi's Win is Al Jazeera's Loss', *Al-Monitor* (1 July 2012), www.al-monitor.com/pulse/originals/2012/al-monitor/morsys-win-is-al-jazeeras-loss.html.

[90] Khalaf and Fielding-Smith, 'How Qatar Seized Control'.

would require a recalibration of Brotherhood alliances if its position in the uprising was going to be sustained long term.

The transfer of the GCC's Syria file from Qatar to Saudi Arabia represented a considerable challenge for the Brotherhood as the Saudi government had long taken a hard line against Brotherhood groups across the region. The Syrian Brotherhood was sufficiently pragmatic to realise that it needed to overcome this hurdle to survive.

On the surface, rapprochement with Saudi Arabia would prove difficult for the Brotherhood. Saudi Arabia had backed the military regime of Abdel Fattah al-Sisi that overthrew Egypt's elected Muslim Brotherhood government in 2013, and proscribed the Brotherhood in its entirety as 'a terrorist group' in March 2014.[91] Saudi officials are purported to have privately expressed objections to the Brotherhood's leading role in the Syrian uprising,[92] while a member of the Aleppo military council explained that, on the ground, the Saudis 'don't want any ties to anything called Muslim Brothers'.[93] This is corroborated by a number of Brotherhood officials who reported that groups on the ground linked to the Muslim Brotherhood suffered financially and materially because of their affiliation.[94]

As Molham Aldrobi explained, however, the relationship was not so simple: 'we (the Brotherhood and Saudi Arabia) have common enemies like Iran, like Bashar al-Assad. [And] we have common objectives in Syria.'[95] The Brotherhood had extensive personal links to Saudi Arabia for decades, with the Saudi government possibly providing a small amount of funding to the Brotherhood during its previous confrontation with the Baʿth. Several of the group's senior leaders continue to live in Saudi Arabia.[96] Aldrobi, who is based between Jeddah, Istanbul and Toronto, added:

---

[91] Mustapha Ajbaili, 'Saudi: Muslim Brotherhood a Terrorist Group', *Al-Arabiya*, (7 March 2014), http://english.alarabiya.net/en/News/middle-east/2014/03/07/Saudi-Arabia-declares-Muslim-Brotherhood-terrorist-group.html.
[92] Sultan Sooud Al-Qassemi, 'Qatar's Brotherhood Ties Alienate Fellow Gulf States', *Al-Monitor* (23 January 2013), www.al-monitor.com/pulse/originals/2013/01/qatar-muslim-brotherhood.html.
[93] Rania Abouzeid, 'Syria's Secular and Islamist Rebels: Who Are the Saudis and the Qataris Arming?', *Time* (18 September 2012), http://world.time.com/2012/09/18/syrias-secular-and-islamist-rebels-who-are-the-saudis-and-the-qataris-arming/.
[94] Interview with Molham Aldrobi, 2017; interview with Hassan al-Hachimi, Istanbul, 2015.
[95] Interview with Molham Aldrobi (parenthesis added).
[96] Abouzeid, 'Syria's Secular and Islamist Rebels'; 'Mohammad Farouk Tayfour', *Carnegie Europe* (1 February 2012), http://carnegieeurope.eu/publications/?fa=48371.

Many of our leaders and our known key figures have been in Saudi Arabia since the 1970s, and since then we had no issues in Saudi Arabia, and none of us has violated the laws and regulations of Saudi Arabia. We do not operate inside Saudi Arabia. We do not get involved in anything that is internal to Saudi Arabia. We respect the laws wherever we go including Saudi Arabia, and as such we do appreciate that and we do thank them for the support that they give to the Syrian people.[97]

For a long time, Saudi Arabia 'turned a blind eye to private Saudi donations' to the Brotherhood,[98] which continued during the uprising. One Brotherhood associate alleged in 2015 that a Syrian family based in Saudi Arabia had donated US$12 million to the Brotherhood since the uprising began, although the claim could not be verified.[99]

Ever the pragmatic actor, the Brotherhood attempted to build its relationship with Saudi Arabia after Qatari influence dwindled. Lefèvre noted that Farouq Tayfour spared 'none of his own political capital to court Riyadh and to support the Saudi agenda' on the SOC, even though these moves were initially met with some opposition within the Brotherhood.[100] As noted in Chapter 6, in 2013, Tayfour backed the Saudi candidate for SOC presidency, Ahmad al-Jarba, over Qatar's preferred candidate, Mustafa al-Sabbagh. Some analysts believe the Brotherhood secured Farouq Tayfour's SOC Vice Presidency in return.[101] Tayfour had purportedly also met with the Saudi Foreign Minister Saud al-Faisal in May 2013 to offer assurance that the Syrian Brotherhood would behave differently to their Egyptian counterparts.[102] A senior Brotherhood member later explained the Brotherhood's decision to appease Saudi Arabia: 'We all realized that we don't stand to gain anything from confronting Saudi Arabia.'[103]

The scale of the group's pivot towards Saudi Arabia was seen in comments made by Riad al-Shaqfeh in 2014, when he declared that 'Saudi Arabia is the best country to lead the Arab and Islamic world and it must act and play a bigger role in confronting the Iranian project in line with its size and religious status'.[104] However, the group's

---

[97] Interview with Molham Aldrobi.
[98] Sonoko Sunayama, *Syria and Saudi Arabia: Collaboration and Conflicts in the Oil Era* (London: I.B.Tauris, 2007), p. 92.
[99] Anonymous interview. [100] Cited in Lefèvre, 'Islamism within a Civil War', p. 2.
[101] 'SYRIA: Muslim Brotherhood's impact depends on Riyadh' (Oxford: Oxford Analytica, 2013).
[102] Hassan Hassan, 'Saudis Overtaking Qatar in Sponsoring Syrian Rebels', *The National* (15 May 2013), www.thenational.ae/saudis-overtaking-qatar-in-sponsoring-syrian-rebels-1.471446.
[103] Lefèvre, 'Islamism within a Civil War', p. 2.
[104] Wa'il Isam, 'Syria's MB Leader Stresses Need to Get Al-Qa'idah-Linked Group out of Country', *Al-Quds al-Arabi* (London: BBC Monitoring Middle East, 28 January 2014).

enthusiasm was short lived, and the relationship with Saudi Arabia bore the Brotherhood little fruit. While Tayfour's success on the SOC suggested that Saudi Arabia was amenable to working with the Brotherhood, its terrorist proscription of the group took place less than a year later. One member of the political office later reflected: 'We are very surprised by Riyadh's announcement; if nothing is done to reach a compromise, it's of course going to affect our relationship in a negative way.'[105] Another remarked:

> If the Saudi agenda in Syria is similar to that of Egypt and aims at bringing in a 'Syrian el-Sisi', things will not go down well with many of us … We do share the same short-term goals with the Kingdom … but our long-term relationship is currently being re-evaluated.[106]

Indeed, while the Brotherhood's interests temporarily overlapped with Saudi Arabia, the group was reminded of the precariousness of exile politics. Events in the international arena had again intervened to threaten the Brotherhood's goals. By 2016, its Gulf relations were significantly weaker, and the group no longer had substantive diplomatic or financial support from the GCC. In 2017, the group's then media chief Omar Mushaweh explained that the Saudi-led regional crackdown on the Muslim Brotherhood was also influencing the ability of its own members to make financial contributions to the Brotherhood:

> Because everybody now is fighting the Muslim Brotherhood there is a lot of pressure on us. So if there was for example a merchant from the Muslim Brotherhood [living abroad that wishes to send money], nowadays his situation is in jeopardy, he could be classified as a terrorist and so on.[107]

At that point, the group's funding situation was purportedly so tight that the hard-copy distribution of its newspaper *al-Ahd* was cancelled, with the magazine becoming an online-only publication. The *al-Ahd* website was also no longer operational.[108]

Nonetheless, the Brotherhood also enjoyed the backing of Turkey during the Syrian uprising. As with Qatar and Saudi Arabia, the Brotherhood has long had informal links to Turkey, particularly through its Islamist community. Many Syrian Brothers settled or studied in Turkey and some developed relations with the ruling Adalet ve Kalkınma Partisi

---

[105] Raphaël Lefèvre, 'Can Syria's Muslim Brotherhood Salvage its Relations with Riyadh?', *Carnegie Middle East Center* (28 March 2014), http://carnegie-mec.org/diwan/55052?lang=en.
[106] 'Saudi Arabia and the Syrian Brotherhood', *Middle East Institute* (27 September 2013), www.mei.edu/content/saudi-arabia-and-syrian-brotherhood.
[107] Interview with Omar Mushaweh, Skype, 2017.   [108] Ibid.

(Justice and Development Party or AKP). The highest profile of these connections came through Ghazwan Masri (Nurettin Gazi Misirli), a Brotherhood member who fled Aleppo in the early 1980s and became a successful business figure in Turkey. Masri went on to marry a Turkish woman, whose father was a parliamentarian and close associate of the Turkish President Recep Tayyip Erdoğan.[109] Masri is apparently no longer a Brotherhood member, but was a senior figure in MUSIAD, the Turkish Islamist business association and the official liaison between Turkey and the Syrian refugee camps in the country's south. He often acted as a Turkish interpreter and advisor to the Syrian opposition on matters related to Turkey,[110] and he had close ties to President Erdoğan and the AKP. Masri was probably the conduit through which the Brotherhood accessed the refugee camps,[111] although Molham Aldrobi, a friend of Masri's, claimed that 'he does not treat the Muslim Brotherhood differently from any other Syrian group. He gives support to everybody, including us of course.'[112]

Brotherhood–AKP ties were purportedly so close prior to the uprising that the Turkish government was rumoured to have pressured al-Assad to accommodate the Syrian Muslim Brotherhood in Syria's political arrangements since 2009.[113] This is despite the fact that Turkey and Syria had a close and productive relationship at the time. However, the Syrian–Turkish relationship collapsed after 2011 when Turkey saw an opportunity in the Arab uprisings to increase its regional prestige, particularly once the protests spread to neighbouring Syria. Ankara took on a key role in the uprising, with all of the significant Syrian opposition bodies formally establishing centres in Istanbul and Gaziantep. This included the SNC, the SOC, the Syrian Interim Government and the Syrian Muslim Brotherhood's head office and administrative offices. Many of the group's leaders moved to Turkey. As Riad al-Shaqfeh explained:

We think positively about Turkey's approach towards Syria. Turkey has always stood by the Syrian people, hosted the opposition, and provided them with full freedom. Of course, I would like to extend my thanks to Turkey on this subject.[114]

---

[109] Interview with Molham Aldrobi, 2017.   [110] Ibid.
[111] Oytun Orhan, 'An Interview with Syrian Businessman Gazi Misirli (Gazwan Masri)', ORSAM (25 January 2013), www.orsam.org.tr/index.php/Content/Convs/326?s=orsam%7Cenglish. For further detail, see Fakher, Weiss and Milne, 'Revolution in Danger', p. 14.
[112] Interview with Molham Aldrobi, 2017.
[113] Christopher Phillips, 'Into the Quagmire: Turkey's Frustrated Syria Policy', Chatham House (2012), www.chathamhouse.org/sites/files/chathamhouse/public/Research/Middle%20East/1212bp_phillips.pdf.
[114] 'An Interview with Mohammad Riad Al-Shaqfa, Leader of the Muslim Brotherhood', ORSAM (16 January 2013), www.orsam.org.tr/index.php/Content/Analiz/3464?s=orsam%7Cenglish.

This was echoed by Ali al-Bayanouni:

> Turkey has been the most supportive, both materially and morally, in the revolution. They continue to support the revolution without an agenda. They have suffered difficulties inside their own borders as a result, but they continue to help Syria. They recognize the danger of this regime remaining, and have tried in the past to encourage Assad to join the democratization process, but to no avail.[115]

Turkey is thought to have exercised influence on the Brotherhood's response to the early uprising. Erdoğan purportedly convinced the Brotherhood's leaders to take a soft line on al-Assad, including avoiding calling for his permanent departure. In return, Turkey would pressure al-Assad to accept the Brotherhood's political return.[116] Although this report is difficult to corroborate, a number of diplomats claim that Ankara demanded significant concessions from al-Assad, including ministerial positions for Brotherhood members. According to one Western diplomat: 'in June [2011], Turkish Prime Minister Recep Tayyip Erdogan [sic] offered, if Syrian President Bashar al-Assad ensured [that] between a quarter and a third of ministers in his government were members of the Muslim Brotherhood, to make a commitment to use all his influence to end the rebellion'.[117] This was no small ask, and suggests that Turkey thought the Brotherhood had serious weight and bargaining power. The claim was corroborated by a European diplomat, who reported that 'the Turks proposed at first that the Muslim Brotherhood occupy four major ministries and explained that they are part of the political components of this country'.[118] As the uprising wore on, Phillips argued that Ankara's 'disproportionately favourable support for the Muslim Brotherhood within the SNC contributed to its alienation of other key Syrian groups'.[119] Brotherhood members and associates have also worked closely with Ankara in Operation Euphrates Shield and through Faylaq al-Sham and the National Front for Liberation.

The Brotherhood reciprocated Turkey's support, as evidenced by its response to the July 2016 attempted coup in Turkey that was widely

---

[115] Tam Hussein, 'A Brotherhood Vision for Syria: In Conversation with the Former Leader of the Syrian Muslim Brotherhood', *The Majalla* (2013), http://eng.majalla.com/2013/11/article55247035. At the time of writing in 2018, this page was only availableonline through archive.org.

[116] Piotr Zalewski, 'Islamic Evolution: How Turkey Taught the Syrian Muslim Brotherhood to Reconcile Faith and Democracy', *Foreign Policy* (11 August 2011), http://foreignpolicy.com/2011/08/11/islamic-evolution-2/.

[117] 'Turkey "Offered Syria Support" if Brotherhood Given Posts', *Agence France-Presse* (29 September 2011).

[118] Ibid.   [119] Phillips, 'Into the Quagmire'.

blamed on the Gülen movement. The Turkish government responded by rounding up thousands of people in the weeks following in a manner that eerily echoed Hafez al-Assad's response to the Brotherhood's challenge in the 1980s. Ignoring those parallels, the Brotherhood condemned the attempted coup, with one of its Twitter accounts broadcasting comments attributed to deputy leader Hosam Ghadban:

> The counter-revolution continues its war on the Muslim brotherhood by comparing it to @FGulenTR [Gulen] movement ... both #MB & #Gulen mvmnt. support social service, but #MB considers it as a tool to serve the society not to control it.[120]

This position was not surprising given the group's long-standing policy of avoiding criticism of their host states, although it could prove politically damaging in the future should the Turkish regime's credentials be called into question by the Syrian opposition. However, as of 2019, Turkey remained a key actor in funding and supporting groups on the ground, and increasingly as a peace broker with Iran and Russia.

Nonetheless, the challenges for the Brotherhood in securing reliable state partners bear many of the hallmarks of those it faced in the uprising more broadly. Although the group enjoyed every advantage in terms of resources, skills and political know-how when the uprising broke out, it failed to translate this into a substantially improved standing. Conversations with non-Brotherhood members and Brotherhood youth members revealed that the group's leaders were widely perceived as arrogant, out of touch and out of their depth. Its political vision, although historically consistent and moderate, failed to mobilise Syrians en masse. Indeed, the short-term advantage that the Brotherhood enjoyed on exiled political bodies during the uprising proved largely superficial, and reflected the weakness of the opposition more broadly, rather than being an indication of the Brotherhood's strength. As the uprising proceeded, it became clear that the Brotherhood's primacy rested on a narrow foundation of limited support, volatile international relations and internal divisions.

History coloured every decision that the Brotherhood made after 2011. The memory and fear of past mistakes, the dispersed leadership and organisational structures, the ongoing internal paralysis that prevented the group's regeneration, its closeness to foreign states but not to its own people on the ground – these are all conditions of its history. Thus, while the group did not overtly waver from its democratic promises, it demonstrated itself to be deeply scarred by its history. It was a shadow of its former self.

---

[120] MuslimBrotherhood Sy (@IkhwanSyriaEn), Twitter (26 July 2016), https://twitter.com/IkhwanSyriaEn/status/757335387337592834.

8 Military Uprising

The Syrian uprising started as a non-violent protest movement that called for political reform, but it began taking on violent characteristics during the summer of 2011. Following a harsh response by the al-Assad regime, some protesters began to acquire defensive arms, while defections from the Syrian armed forces led to the creation of the Free Syrian Army (FSA).[1] The militarisation was further spurred by the al-Assad regime's announcement of two amnesties in the first months of the unrest, which saw the release of hundreds of political prisoners from jail.[2] The decision was ostensibly aimed at placating protesters, although has since been seen as a sinister move, as many of the detainees were veteran jihadists or Salafists with substantial combat experience released from the notorious Sednaya prison's jihadist wing. These individuals would eventually leverage the chaos to their advantage.[3] That same August, the Iraqi al-Qaeda franchise, the Islamic State of Iraq, sent its governor of Ninewa province Abu Mohammad al-Golani and six others into Syria to activate small cells across the country, marking the entrance into Syria of Jabhat al-Nusra (later known as Jabhat Fateh al-Sham and Hayat Tahrir al-Sham, but referred to as Jabhat al-Nusra here for the sake of simplicity) and the Islamic State (IS) group.[4] This combination of forces gave momentum to the rapidly changing Syrian uprising and solidified its transition into armed conflict.

The militarisation of the uprising provided a new challenge for the Brotherhood because, over the preceding decades, the group's leadership

---

[1] 'Syrian Army Colonel Defects Forms Free Syrian Army', *Asharq al-Awsat* (1 August 2011), http://english.aawsat.com/2011/08/article55245595/syrian-army-colonel-defects-forms-free-syrian-army.
[2] 'Syrian Authorities Release 260 Prisoners – Lawyer', *Reuters* (26 March 2011), www.reuters.com/article/syria-prisoners-idUSLDE72P06120110326; Hamid Dabashi, *The Green Movement in Iran* (London: Transaction Publishers, 2011).
[3] Charles L. Lister, *The Syrian Jihad: Al-Qaeda, The Islamic State and the Evolution of an Insurgency* (London: Hurst, 2015), p. 56.
[4] Ibid.

had demobilised and disbanded its fighting capacity, and politically distanced itself from events involving violence. The group repeatedly stated its non-violent credentials both before and during the uprising as it continued to repair its reputation and position itself as a political player in the governance of a possible new state. The Brotherhood's position was further motivated to garner support from the international community as well as those inside Syria not aligned to the combatant groups.

Reconciling the Conflict with the Brotherhood's Past and Future

The Syrian Muslim Brotherhood had not entered the Syrian conflict with a blank slate; the al-Assad narrative about the group and the memory of 1982 was present in the minds of many Syrians and is a standard by which the Brotherhood is measured. This is the sort of challenge that many oppositions face when re-entering politics under authoritarian conditions.[5] In such a context, any armed activity would be compared to and analysed through the historical lens of Hama. Any oversteps on the battlefield would be interpreted as indicative of the group's brutality, a power-grab and confirmation of their reputed unsuitability for political leadership. These considerations limited the Brotherhood's response to the Syrian civil war and underlined the continued relevance of the Hama event three decades on. But this rigid philosophy of non-violence became problematic as the uprising thrust the country deeper into conflict.

Ironically, while the Brotherhood had gone to considerable lengths to avoid reviving the memory of 1982, its past was deployed symbolically by others throughout the uprising. This was first seen in the 2011 protests in Hama when protesters chanted 'Damn your soul, Hafez (al-Assad)' and erected placards with motifs including 'No repeat of 1982'.[6] In addition, Marwan Hadid, the controversial late Hamawi Fighting Vanguard/Brotherhood figure discussed at length in Chapter 4, who represents a raw nerve for the group's leaders, was lionised by hardline and jihadist groups. This was evident in the name of the Jabhat al-Nusra-affiliated Saraya Marwan Hadid (Marwan Hadid Brigades) and in

---

[5] For further discussion of this, see Alanna Claire Van Antwerp, 'Legacies of Repression: The Revival of Political Participation in the Shadow of Authoritarian Rule' (PhD thesis, George Washington University, 2014).

[6] Phil Sands, 'Government and Protesters both Invoke Hama Massacre of 1982', *The National* (7 July 2011), www.thenational.ae/news/world/middle-east/government-and-protesters-both-invoke-hama-massacre-of-1982 (parenthesis added); Alain Gresh, '"The Bullets Killed our Fear": Syria Waits for Ramadan', *Le Monde Diplomatique* (1 August 2011), http://mondediplo.com/2011/08/03syria.

August 2016 when the jihadist Jund al-Aqsa (Soldiers of al-Aqsa) declared the beginning of 'Ghazwah Marwan Hadid' (Operation Marwan Hadid) in northern Hama province.

Hardline groups' appropriation of the Brotherhood's past was most pronounced in August 2016 when an opposition operation near the artillery academy in southern Aleppo was named 'Ghazwah Ibrahim al-Youssef' (Operation Ibrahim al-Youssef) in honour of the Brotherhood/Vanguard army captain responsible for the massacre at the Aleppo Artillery Academy in 1979. Jabhat Fatah al-Sham later released a video in which the speaker explained that in 1979 al-Youssef had separated Sunnis from Alawites at the academy and slaughtered the Alawites, and chillingly pledged to 'complete what Ibrahim al-Youssef started'.[7] As the battle unfolded in 2016, Ibrahim al-Youssef's widow, Aziza Jalloud, tweeted:

> Abu Khleif (Ibrahim al-Youssef), how long you dreamed of these crowds ... These resilient, long-suffering crowds of *mujahideen* have come to you! Today the martyr returned to life in the souls of the devout *mujahideen*.[8]

Ahrar al-Sham's former Foreign Relations chief Labib al-Nahas purportedly also sent a message to Ibrahim al-Youssef's son during the operation, which said:

> Today is your day, our day, the day of the father (may God have mercy on him). Those who fought as strangers and who were wronged from near and far, today, we give them the respect and regard that they deserve.[9]

The battle name was also used by mainstream groups such as the Brotherhood-linked Faylaq al-Sham.[10]

By contrast, the Brotherhood itself made scant reference to Ibrahim al-Youssef or its own connection to the artillery school in its many public communications about the 2016 operation, tweeting innocuous photos with comments such as: '#JayshAlfath operations room: taking over the artillery college in Ramouseh, southern #Aleppo city.'[11] The one time it acknowledged al-Youssef was in a retweet of an Ahrar al-Sham

---

[7] See Jabhat Fateh al-Sham, 'The Start of the Third Stage of the Operation to Break the Siege of Aleppo, Operation Ibrahim al-Youssef (in Arabic)', YouTube (13 August 2016), www.youtube.com/watch?v=C23ZlPnJlBo.

[8] Aziza Jaloud, Twitter (in Arabic) (4 August 2016), https://twitter.com/azizajalloud/status/761197889863442432 (parenthesis added).

[9] Yaser Ibrahim Al-Youssef, Twitter (in Arabic) (6 August 2016), https://twitter.com/AlyousefYasser/status/761597701993660416.

[10] Faylaq al-Sham (@ShamLegion), Twitter (5 August 2016), https://twitter.com/ShamLegion/status/761546905038053376.

[11] MuslimBrotherhood Sy (@IkhwanSyriaEn), Twitter (26 July 2016), https://twitter.com/IkhwanSyriaEn/status/757335387337592834.

post.¹² The text celebrated the 'martyrs' of the recent operation and declared that Ibrahim al-Youssef would not be forgotten.¹³ This was a stark contrast to much of the opposition's response.

This single incident exemplified the dilemma that the Brotherhood faced throughout the armed component of the uprising. As the uprising became bloodier, a claim to sacrifice became the currency on which many opposition actors traded. Although the Brotherhood had arguably the strongest track record in confronting the Baʿth of any Syrian group pre-2011, it was reticent to stake a claim in this violence because it faced a significant quandary – how could it demonstrate its political prowess and claim a mandate from its historical glory and sacrifices, without resurrecting the ghosts of the past? In addition, given that the Brotherhood had never gained a full understanding of why its previous campaign had gone so wrong nor of its future vulnerabilities, it could not decide on a clear policy response. So, the Brotherhood became paradoxically criticised by some Syrians as 'out of touch' with the suffering going on within the country.¹⁴ It seemed that the Brotherhood's failure to come to terms with its past and produce a compelling narrative to explain events would also have a tangible impact on its prospects in the 2011 war.

Forming a Response

The Brotherhood maintained publicly that it had no connection to the armed events on the ground in Syria, but it was verbally supportive of the revolution's armed actors, frequently celebrating their achievements across its social media platforms. In a statement in 2013, the group declared its commitment to

> stopping the hand of criminality from damaging Syrian life, isolating it from positions of authority and influence, and enabling the forces of the revolution and the Free Syrian Army to confront it by changing the balance of power to their favor is the practical approach to reaching the political solution and the desired national dialogue.¹⁵

---

[12] Labib Al-Nahas (@LabibAlNahhas), Twitter (3 August 2016), https://twitter.com/LabibAlNahhas/status/760559439749476352.
[13] Ibid.
[14] Neil MacFarquhar, 'Trying to Mold a Post-Assad Syria from Abroad', *The New York Times* (5 May 2012), www.nytimes.com/2012/05/06/world/middleeast/from-abroad-trying-to-mold-a-post-assad-syria.html?_r=0.
[15] 'Statement of the Muslim Brotherhood in Syria on Current Developments', *Syrian Observer* (9 May 2013), http://syrianobserver.com/EN/Resources/24756/Statement+of+the+Muslim+Brotherhood+in+Syria+on+current+Developments.

The group's then media chief Omar Mushaweh explained: 'We should not forget that this revolution is the revolution of the Syrian people. When an armed struggle is imposed upon us, we as part of the Syrian people are forced to join the resistance to defend ourselves.'[16] The Brotherhood was therefore supportive of the mainstream armed effort on the ground, but the question of whether it would contribute to the military effort proved significantly more challenging.

The Syrian Muslim Brotherhood had developed substantial resources in exile and therefore had a choice to make early in the uprising about whether it would use these resources militarily. Although the group had few roots left in Syria, it had the option to pursue the military uprising through the same means as its political outreach: by importing influence and using money to buy loyalty. But the group's memory of its prior mobilisation acted as a significant encumbrance when it came to making that decision, with the 1982 Hama uprising remaining a central aspect of the Brotherhood's thinking. Although it does not play the role proscribed by the Hama-centric descriptor of the group, the memory of the uprising and its catastrophic consequences acted as a significant constraint throughout the Brotherhood's engagement.

Accordingly, the Brotherhood's leadership responded to the military uprising with caution, aware of the need to be seen to take a stand, while ensuring that they remained on the right side of history this time. In Europe, memories of repression such as 1953 in Germany and 1968 in Czechoslovakia shaped the way later movements calculated opportunities and risks and such memories often acted as deterrents to the future adoption of violence.[17] The Brotherhood had already paid a significant price for its opposition to the Baʿth and remilitarisation was not a decision that it would take lightly. At the same time, the cost of not responding was also great.

The Brotherhood's approach was initially formalised in late 2011 at a meeting in Saudi Arabia, when it decided against forming militias (although this decision was revised in mid-2012).[18] The leadership also decided to endorse a decentralised approach, which allowed members the freedom to respond on their own accord, with their leadership's implicit sanction. This meant that the Brotherhood's response to the armed uprising was characterised by two tiers: formal decisions made

---

[16] Interview with Omar Mushaweh, Skype, 2017.
[17] Donatella Della Porta, *Mobilizing for Democracy: Comparing 1989 and 2011* (Oxford: Oxford University Press, 2014), p. 157.
[18] Nir Rosen, 'Islamism and the Syrian Uprising', *Foreign Policy* (8 March 2012), http://foreignpolicy.com/2012/03/08/islamism-and-the-syrian-uprising/.

by the central Muslim Brotherhood leadership and informal activities undertaken by the group's base. A Brotherhood member involved in funding armed activities described the process:

> Given that the notion of armed struggle was still, at the time, rather controversial in opposition circles, the Brotherhood's leadership decided to temporarily decentralise decisions on this matter and leave it up to individuals to decide whether to engage or not in those types of activities.[19]

This mirrored the Brotherhood's individualist initial response to the political side of the uprising, where the Brotherhood youth independently ran the 'Syrian Revolution Against Bashar al-Assad' Facebook page, while senior members organised opposition conferences and participated in political bodies as independents. Although this gave the perception that the Brotherhood was attempting to monopolise the Syrian opposition movement, it was in many ways the natural behaviour of a group that had spent decades as a decentralised political network. When it came to the military uprising, such strategies proved useful in increasing the Brotherhood's chances of exerting influence on the ground.

Official Involvement in the Uprising

The Brotherhood's official response to the conflict had many parts. Given it did not have a constituency on the ground that it could easily mobilise for another war against the Ba'th, it turned to its superior fundraising abilities, particularly its ties to wealthy Brotherhood members in the Gulf, as well as deploying its skilled cadre to support, influence and educate those on the ground. As one Hamawi shaykh observed, 'the Brotherhood does not have a presence on the ground but it gave some money and communication devices to some groups. They give you money now so they can ride on your shoulders in the future.'[20]

Senior Brotherhood members are reticent about the Brotherhood's official military involvement in the conflict, implying that the group has an ongoing difficulty in reconciling the current situation in Syria with its own past and future. One senior figure, Samir abu Laban, asserted that the Brotherhood's support for those on the ground was 'mainly relief aid for the families and also health and medical assistance for the fighters,

---

[19] Raphaël Lefèvre, 'The Syrian Muslim Brotherhood's Alawi Conundrum', in *The Alawis of Syria: War, Faith and Politics in the Levant*, ed. Michael Kerr and Craig Larkin (Oxford: Oxford University Press, 2015), p. 134.

[20] Rosen, 'Islamism'.

[the purchase of] ambulance cars, building hospitals. Things like that.'[21] Nonetheless, it would be incorrect to say that the central Brotherhood leadership has had no relationship to violent players in the Syrian uprising. It has on a number of occasions attempted to foster both direct and indirect ties with parties on the ground. According to former leader Riad al-Shaqfeh:

> Those 40 years outside Syria distanced us from the interior. But we are acting in accord with all the factions and trends. Militarily, we have some brigades that we support directly like shields. There are brigades that are close to us and their ideology is close to us, such as the Protection of Civilians Body (the Commission for Protection of Civilians, CPC) and Al-Tawhid Brigade. We have a good relationship and their ideology is moderate. In general, we have good relations with all factions.[22]

The Brotherhood's main contribution in this regard was financial, because the group did not have substantial military connections or resources. As Molham Aldrobi explained: 'The Muslim Brotherhood doesn't have arms, we don't manufacture arms, we don't buy or sell arms ... [the leaders of armed groups on the ground] do so. We were giving them financial support and advisors'.[23] He added that 'we [also] don't have facilities to provide military training. The militants themselves, they do. They have that inside Syria. We do not have that either inside Syria or outside Syria, so we were not in a position to provide that.'[24] At least one Brotherhood member was involved in the Istanbul Room, the outfit based near Ataturk airport in Istanbul that acted as the main clearinghouse for Turkish, Saudi and Qatari materiel in the early stages of the uprising.[25] This bought it indirect influence.

The Brotherhood first became involved in the armed uprising by funding and supporting existing armed groups. An FSA member explained that this decision was often mutually beneficial:

> We benefitted obviously from the money and funding while they benefitted by being able to say that they were involved in operations on the ground and the struggle to bring down Bashar al-Assad, which increased their clout within their own circles.[26]

---

[21] Interview with Samir Abu Laban, Istanbul.
[22] Wa'il Isam, 'Syria's MB Leader Stresses Need to Get Al-Qa'idah-Linked Group Out of Country', *Al-Quds al-Arabi* (London: BBC Monitoring Middle East, 28 January 2014) (parenthesis added).
[23] Interview with Molham Aldrobi, 2017.   [24] Ibid.
[25] David Ignatius, 'Foreign Nations' Proxy War in Syria Creates Chaos', *The Washington Post* (2 October 2014), www.washingtonpost.com/opinions/david-ignatius-foreign-nations-proxy-war-creates-syrian-chaos/2014/10/02/061fb50c-4a7a-11e4-a046-120a8a855cca_story.html?utm_term=.c1b29ac1fd2e.
[26] Noura al-Hourani, 'Former FSA Fighter Recounts Why He Left', *Syria: Direct* (6 May 2015), http://syriadirect.org/news/former-fsa-fighter-recounts-why-he-left/.

The Brotherhood chose to support groups on cautious and pragmatic criteria, that is, mainstream groups with some level of ideological commonality with the Brotherhood, and with significant influence on the ground. In short, it had an interest in backing winners to build a stake in both the conflict and the country's future, while avoiding potential controversy. Its memory of its damaging past association with the Fighting Vanguard may have served as a guiding light, preventing it from overreaching or backing too many groups.

Liwa al-Tawhid (the Tawhid Brigade) was one of the most important early groups to receive Brotherhood funding. The group formed on the outskirts of Aleppo in 2012, and at its peak was the largest group operating in Aleppo governorate. Liwa al-Tawhid was affiliated with the FSA, and its leader Abdul Qadir al-Saleh was a member of the FSA Joint Chiefs.[27] At times, the Brotherhood–Liwa al-Tawhid relationship was viewed as so close that some believed the brigade was the Brotherhood's 'armed wing', although this overstates the Brotherhood's influence.[28] According to a non-Brotherhood opposition member involved in the funding of some armed groups, this was a largely pragmatic decision on Liwa al-Tawhid's behalf: 'at a certain point they [Liwa al-Tawhid] took aid from the Muslim Brotherhood, but they also took it from Salafis, they took from everybody. Their motivation was not to create alliances, they just figured that whoever gives aid, we'll take it.'[29]

The Brotherhood's backing bought it some political influence over Liwa al-Tawhid. In November 2012, just weeks after the formation of the National Coalition, a number of parties including Liwa al-Tawhid released a declaration:

We, the fighting squads of Aleppo city and province, unanimously reject the conspiratorial project called the National Coalition (SOC) and announce our consensus to establish an Islamic state ... We reject any external coalitions or councils imposed on us at home from any party whatsoever.[30]

Within days, Liwa al-Tawhid retracted the statement, releasing a video where the group's commander Abdul Qadir al-Saleh declared: 'we

---

[27] 'The Killing of the Commander of the Tawhid Brigade, One of the Main Leaders of the Armed Opposition in Syria', *Rai al-Youm* (18 November 2013), www.raialyoum.com/?p=22455.

[28] Sahib Anjarini, 'The Story of Al-Tawhid Brigade: Fighting for Sharia in Syria', *Al-Monitor (originally published in al-Safir)* (22 August 2013), www.al-monitor.com/pulse/security/2013/10/syria-opposition-islamists-tawhid-brigade.html.

[29] Aron Lund, '*Struggling to Adapt: The Muslim Brotherhood in a New Syria*' (Washington, DC: Carnegie Endowment for International Peace, 2013, p. 19).

[30] 'In New Blow to Assad, EU Recognizes New Syrian Opposition Bloc', *Al-Arabiya* (19 November 2012), http://english.alarabiya.net/articles/2012/11/19/250551.html.

confirm that Free Syria is a civil state where the basis of legislation is the Islamic faith, with consideration for all the [minority] groups of Syria'.[31] He backed the SOC, while calling for it to 'increase the representation of revolutionary forces'.[32] Al-Saleh's vision bore remarkable similarities to the Brotherhood's 2012 Covenant and Charter, including calling for a 'civil state', which is a hallmark of Brotherhood political thought.[33] Liwa al-Tawhid struggled after Abdul Qadir al-Saleh's death in November 2013 and is no longer operational, but the relationship bore some fruit for the Brotherhood as many of its members joined other groups.[34] The Brotherhood's early financial assistance therefore broadened its connections in other parts of the conflict landscape.

The Brotherhood backed important actors throughout the uprising, with Lefèvre reporting that the group is also thought to have provided 'generous' support to Suqour al-Sham, Ahrar al-Sham and the Farouq Brigades.[35] According to Hassan, the Brotherhood financially supported Ajnad al-Sham Islamic Union, Shabab al-Huda Brigades, Jaysh al-Mujahideen and Liwa al-Moataz.[36] It may also have funded Harakat Hazm.[37] With time, the Brotherhood's financial ties to groups on the ground became dwarfed by the efforts of states such as Saudi Arabia, but it is worth noting that many of the groups linked to the Brotherhood later received the highly coveted CIA-vetted status, which gave them access to US training and comparatively modern and powerful weaponry including anti-tank missiles. This underlined the success of the Brotherhood's strategy of choosing both important and internationally palatable groups.

The Brotherhood's support for groups was not without controversy, with it accused of trying to buy loyalty from those it backs. As opposition figure, Malik al-Abdeh, observed: 'I know of guys who wanted to go to the Muslim Brotherhood to get a slice of the pie, and found out that you

---

[31] Aron Lund, 'Aleppo and the Battle for the Syrian Revolution's Soul', *Carnegie Europe* (4 December 2012), http://carnegieeurope.eu/publications/?fa=50234.
[32] Ibid.
[33] 'Covenant and Charter' (Istanbul: The Muslim Brotherhood in Syria, 2012), p. 1.
[34] Jennifer Cafarella and Genevieve Casagrande, 'Syrian Armed Opposition Forces in Aleppo', *Institute for the Study of War* (13 February 2016), www.understandingwar.org/sites/default/files/Syrian%20Armed%20Opposition%20Forces%20in%20Aleppo_0.pdf, p. 13.
[35] Raphaël Lefèvre, 'The Syrian Brotherhood's Armed Struggle', *Carnegie Middle East Centre* (14 December 2012), http://carnegie-mec.org/publications/?fa=50380&lang=en.
[36] Hassan Hassan, 'In Syria, the Brotherhood's Influence Is on the Decline', *The National* (1 April 2014), www.thenational.ae/thenationalconversation/comment/in-syria-the-brotherhoods-influence-is-on-the-decline.
[37] Suhaib Anjarini, 'Harakat Hazm: America's New Favorite Jihadist Group', *al-Akhbar* (22 May 2014), http://english.al-akhbar.com/node/19874.

have to swear an oath of allegiance to them.'[38] This appeared to have mixed success. One FSA member recalled:

> We received financial support from the Muslim Brotherhood, and in theory, our commanders took up the banner of fighting to restore a modicum of Islamist rule in Syria. However in reality, we never really fought under their banner or adopted the ideologies they advocated, and they were probably aware of this.[39]

Such demands were not unique to the Brotherhood; money from other donors, particularly from the Gulf, often came with ideological strings attached.[40]

Some senior Brotherhood members acknowledge that the group's attempt to buy support through funding had limited success. As a Brotherhood member close to the leadership proffered:

> When you talk about military and this kind of support, you are talking about millions [of dollars]. Hundreds of millions. And the Muslim Brotherhood doesn't have that kind of money.[41]

In the end, this limited strategy may have backfired, as a senior Brotherhood figure reflected: 'Many of them [the groups] are not so satisfied about the Muslim Brotherhood. They say that we were expecting more from you, to be more active, to be more supportive. But there is nothing we can do.'[42]

The Brotherhood also attempted to form its own groups following frustration at the lack of success of the FSA and allegations of rampant looting and corruption.[43] This may also have been an effort to mitigate the risk of associating with groups that were not under complete Brotherhood control. In August 2012, senior Brotherhood figure Molham Aldrobi told *Asharq al-Awsat* that the Brotherhood had formed its own militias in Syria:

> The Muslim Brotherhood for some three months have formed armed battalions within Syria whose mission is self-defence and security protection for the wronged ... This is a legitimate right, and a Shari'ah duty that bestows honour on all ... These battalions are spread in most Syrian regions and governorates, especially the hot spots ... These battalions are affiliated to the Free Syrian Army, and they cooperate and coordinate with it.[44]

---

[38] Cited in Lund, 'Struggling to Adapt', p. 18.
[39] Cited in al-Hourani, 'Former FSA Fighter Recounts Why He Left'. [40] Cited in ibid.
[41] Anonymous interview. [42] Ibid.
[43] Lefèvre, 'The Syrian Muslim Brotherhood's Alawi Conundrum'.
[44] Paula Astih, 'Muslim Brotherhood to Al-Sharq Al-Awsat: We Have Formed Armed Battalions to Defend Ourselves and the Wronged', *Al-Sharq al-Awsat* (Beirut: BBC Monitoring Middle East, 2012).

While Aldrobi was a member of the group's leadership who acted as a regular spokesperson, the comment was disputed by other members of the Brotherhood leadership.[45] Ali al-Bayanouni himself later categorically told the author that the group 'took the decision not to have any militias'.[46] Yet, it transpired that the Brotherhood had assisted the formation of the Hayat Duru al-Thawra (the Shields of the Revolution Council). The group's then-political chief Hassan al-Hachimi acknowledged: 'the Muslim Brotherhood was involved in the establishment of the Shields ... [We] provided endorsement, political support and *tarbiyya* [education].'[47] Aldrobi later explained how the decision had been taken:

For a year after the revolution had started – so from March 2011 to June 2012 – the Muslim Brotherhood refused to use arms in the revolution. We were totally peaceful ... But sometime around June 2012 the Shura Council of the Muslim Brotherhood assessed the situation, and that was a few months after Bashar al-Assad went to Bab al-Amr and destroyed Bab al-Amr in Homs. We assessed the situation and we found that there is no way now to be isolated from what is taking place. We had to protect our people, we had to protect ourselves.[48]

The Shields was an umbrella alliance of 43 groups predominantly based in Idlib and Hama provinces, which at its peak may have totalled 5,000–7,000 fighters, although it was never a major faction.[49] It might be better categorised as a Brotherhood client or employee rather than an organic Brotherhood body. As Aldrobi explained: 'the Muslim Brotherhood initiated the Duru, although the Duru were not technically speaking members of the Muslim Brotherhood, but the Muslim Brotherhood sponsored them and they blessed them'.[50] The Brotherhood had a close working relationship with the Shields, inferred by the attendance of all of the Brotherhood's senior leaders, including Riad al-Shaqfeh, Ali al-Bayanouni and Farouq Tayfour at the Shields' first conference in December 2012.[51] A senior Brotherhood member claimed that the Shields 'believed in our ideology', with members required to 'be good Muslims, and [having to] comply with international law on military conflicts'.[52]

---

[45] Ahmad Da'dush, 'Al-Shaqfah: There Is No Armed Organization for the Syrian Muslim Brotherhood', *Al Jazeera* (Doha: BBC Monitoring Middle East, 10 April 2013).
[46] Interview with Ali al-Bayanouni, London.
[47] Interview with Hassan al-Hachimi, Istanbul (parenthesis added).
[48] Interview with Molham Aldrobi, 2017.
[49] Raphaël Lefèvre and Ali El-Yassir, 'Militias for the Syrian Muslim Brotherhood?', *Carnegie Endowment for International Peace* (29 October 2013), http://carnegieendowment.org/sada/?fa=53452.
[50] Interview with Molham Aldrobi, 2017.   [51] Lund, 'Struggling to Adapt', p. 19.
[52] Cited in Hanlie Booysen, 'Explaining the Moderate Platform of the Syrian Muslim Brotherhood: Against the Inclusion-Moderation Hypothesis', PhD Thesis (Wellington: Victoria Univeristy of Wellington, 2018), p. 195.

The Shields' logo, depicting the famous Brotherhood-like crossed swords, also bore remarkable similarity to that of the Brotherhood. The Shields described itself as 'Islamic-democratic moderate alliance'.[53] According to Lund, it claimed to be 'an independent alliance of moderate Islamists and a responsible actor that seeks to uphold human rights while fighting the al-Assad regime'.[54]

The Brotherhood's decision to form the Shields was consistent with its conservative choices on which groups to fund. It took no chances on radicalism. In this way, Hama's legacy was clear in the risk-averse manner that the Brotherhood interacted with bodies under its control. The Brotherhood attempted to slowly incorporate the organisation into its official framework, taking gradual steps to manage challenges that arose. According to one Brotherhood leader: 'Until now we have given them general instructions, but they have their own structure and merely coordinate with us – ideally we would like to have a proper chain of command and a more centralized decision-making process, but it's going to take time.'[55] This cautious process attempted to mitigate a risk of the Brotherhood being blamed for any oversteps that took place on the battlefield under the Shields' banner, such as what had happened in the past because of the Brotherhood's association with the Fighting Vanguard. In this the Brotherhood's characteristic pragmatism was evident: it was playing a long game and it did not intend to be tarnished by the activities of its partners.

The Shields eventually collapsed, following a lack of support on the ground. Hassan al-Hachimi acknowledged: 'in the end, it became one of the least supported groups, probably because they were close to us, they didn't get other support. Many of them ended up joining Faylaq al-Sham.'[56] Such failures appear to have further weakened the support for armed intervention within the Brotherhood. As another senior leadership figure recalled:

Some argue that we should not get involved in military activities since we are first and foremost an organization focused on *da'wa* [proselytization] and politics. Others are disappointed by the performance of the fighters on the ground. And most of us find that the whole enterprise costs too much money.[57]

---

[53] Ahmed Eleiba, 'A Tapestry of War', *Al-Ahram* (10 April 2014), http://weekly.ahram.org.eg/News/5913/32/A-tapestry-of-war.aspx.
[54] Lund, 'Struggling to Adapt', p. 18. [55] Cited in Lefèvre and El-Yassir, 'Militias'.
[56] Interview with Hassan al-Hachimi, Istanbul.
[57] Cited in Raphaël Lefèvre, 'Islamism within a Civil War: The Syrian Muslim Brotherhood's Struggle for Survival', Brookings Institute (2015), www.brookings.edu/wp-content/uploads/2016/07/Syria_Lefevre-FINALE-1.pdf, p. 8 (parenthesis added).

The collapse of the Shields ended the Brotherhood's experiment with militias, implying a self-acknowledgement of the failure of its efforts. Al-Hachimi explained however that the approach to militias was regularly reviewed and may be subject to change in the future.[58]

Perhaps an area where the Brotherhood remained most active and enjoyed some success was in its provision of training resources to other groups on the ground. This role stemmed from the Brotherhood's recognition that its strengths lay in its political and media skills, and its highly educated membership base. This was something that the group could do without dredging up the ghosts of its past. In many ways, it was an extension of its political activities outside the country.

From the beginning of the uprising, the group deployed members inside Syria to work with armed groups to provide political and religious education and to assist them to formulate political goals that may one day assist groups to work together at a negotiating table.[59] This work did not include military or combat training. In fact, Hassan al-Hachimi saw the Brotherhood's 'moderate Islam as a changing factor in Syria'. He argued that by teaching the precepts of moderate Islam the group was capable of uniting people and marginalising those radical Islamist groups that could not be drawn back to the centre.[60] Many Brotherhood members saw it as their responsibility to educate others in the lessons of moderate Islam, with a view to quelling the appeal of extremism.[61] Another Brotherhood associate explained that the Brotherhood's activities aimed to build understanding of the role of Islam in a civil state.[62]

Senior Brotherhood members are candid about their involvement in this aspect of the armed uprising. According to Samir abu Laban:

[In] our role in the revolution currently, the most important thing that we have succeeded with is to facilitate the relationships between the various rebel groups, and to give them the right ideology. So when the revolution started, afterwards we had more than 1,500 groups and none of them trusted the other. So it needed a lot of work to make those people know each other and they started to unite and form bigger groups.[63]

Another Brotherhood member who had spent most of the uprising inside Syria described his work in attending meetings with armed factions and providing training:

---

[58] Interview with Hassan al-Hachimi, Istanbul.
[59] Anonymous interview.
[60] Interview with Hassan al-Hachimi, Istanbul.
[61] Ibid.
[62] Cited in Lauren Williams, 'Brotherhood Seeks to Fill Post-Assad Vacuum', *The Daily Star* (10 August 2012), www.dailystar.com.lb/News/Middle-East/2012/Aug-10/184107-brotherhood-seeks-to-fill-post-assad-vacuum.ashx.
[63] Interview with Samir Abu Laban, Istanbul.

Inside Syria this is my job. To train [armed groups] about basic politics and how to work as a political group, [including] strategy, political analysis, how to talk to the media and how to understand geopolitics.[64]

The late father of the founder of the 'Syrian Revolution Against Bashar al-Assad' Facebook page and veteran Brotherhood member Tarif al-Sayyid Issa remarked of his own experience:

Part of my job now, as I see it, is to convince people of the need for a civilian leadership. I go around mosques and other places, meeting people and trying to explain to them that the country will never get up on its feet again without a strong civil society. I have met with all the workers' unions in Idlib, with the professional associations, and so on.[65]

The Brotherhood's attempt to be a neutral arbiter on the ground had success. For al-Hachimi, it earned the Brotherhood some influence over the moderate groups: 'in a sense we have influence on the ground we have good relationships',[66] although the group had no relationship with Jabhat al-Nusra or IS. This was backed by a Brotherhood associate, who agreed that the group managed to acquire some influence.

But not by itself. It has to gain consensus from other groups. But for instance, it can derail stuff, or torpedo stuff. More than create stuff. It is better at destroying than creating. That's usually the way. But generally speaking, that's the kind of influence they have.[67]

Indeed, it appeared that Brotherhood had finally understood that its strengths lay in political rather than military activities. The group was never well placed for military action; it had neither the skills, resources nor drive to undertake such activity. This reality was ignored in the 1980s with catastrophic consequences, but appeared to be recognised in the context of the Syrian uprising. Senior Brotherhood members believed that this was the right path for the Brotherhood to take. According to al-Hachimi in 2015:

I think looking at the situation today and the history of it, I think it was a successful strategy that benefited our organisation in this messy battlefield that is full of contradictions and problems. Staying as we are today at equal distance, being contributors and keeping good relationships with everyone enabled us to play our true leadership role.[68]

---

[64] Anonymous interview.
[65] Aron Lund, 'Going Home: An Interview with Tarif al-Sayyed Issa,' *Carnegie Middle East Center* (22 October 2015), http://carnegie-mec.org/diwan/61724?lang=en.
[66] Interview with Hassan al-Hachimi, Istanbul. [67] Anonymous interview.
[68] Interview with Hassan al-Hachimi, Istanbul.

The Brotherhood's direct influence on the conflict was therefore reasonably muted. Although it verbally supported the uprising and backed some winning groups, as the years passed by it was almost universally acting as a political body without having made a serious push to affect change on the ground. The group had the capacity to do much more, as evidenced by the significant amount of money that it poured into aid in Syria over the same period. Yet in contrast to the Hama-centric description of the Brotherhood as innately violent, the group demonstrated itself to be cautious to the point of indecisive. This passivity could be a serious barrier to the group in the future as it may not be able to claim a significant mandate as a contributor to the military effort. On the other hand, as a political player with broad relationships across the armed opposition, the possibilities post-conflict could be enhanced. The Brotherhood leadership appeared to be backing this second strategy and outcome.

Informal Brotherhood Involvement in the Uprising

The Brotherhood's influence on the uprising was augmented by the activities of its members and associates on the ground. As noted above, many Brotherhood members used the leadership's silence in the early days of the uprising to formulate their own response. Ali al-Bayanouni explained: 'many people from the Brotherhood joined [groups] ... But we support all the groups. And we deal with the revolution as a national movement, not as a party.'[69] Brotherhood members were present in a number of groups. Liwa al-Tawhid was rumoured to have several 'senior leadership figures who are members of the Brotherhood',[70] while a number of Brotherhood families were involved in Ahrar al-Sham, which according to Lund, 'created a web of personal links between the exiled Ikhwan (Brotherhood) cadre and Ahrar al-Sham fighters'.[71] Brotherhood member Tarif al-Sayyed Issa was active in Faylaq al-Sham in Idlib. He recalled:

> I began working with an armed group in the Fath [*sic*] Army called Faylaq al-Sham, which contains some people from the Muslim Brotherhood. They made me field commander of a small unit. I had already received military training in the 1980s when we in the Muslim Brotherhood first rose up against Hafez al-Assad. Now, I took a short refresher course in a training camp that had been set up before the Idlib operation.[72]

---

[69] Interview with Ali al-Bayanouni, London.   [70] Anonymous interview.
[71] Lund, 'Struggling to Adapt', p. 20 (parenthesis added).
[72] Cited in Lund, 'Going Home'.

Such activity was facilitated by the group's network structure and individualist tendencies, which meant that individual members had extensive and important ties outside the group. When it came to responding to the military conflict, the group's members took immediate and tangible steps themselves without leadership direction to support and participate in the uprising while the Brotherhood's leadership deliberated over how to formally respond. This has been a long-term trend for the Brotherhood, where its leadership is unable to engage fully with its grassroots and is too slow and deliberative to make a timely response on military strategies that they also do not understand. In such circumstances, Brothers have often taken matters into their own hands.

As one Brotherhood figure close to the leadership noted, many members 'have their own relationships inside Syria, like their families, their friends. And they try to support them because as you know the situation inside Syria is so bad'.[73] This pattern was also explained by Rosen early in the conflict:

The SMB [Syrian Muslim Brotherhood] does not have cadres on the ground, nor does it have much ideological influence. Most people I spoke to admitted that their role was limited to sending money but they were not sending it as the SMB, only as individuals who happened to belong to the SMB. In Homs some leaders view their role as positive but they did not see it as the SMB acting as an organization, which it did not have the capacity to do anymore. Homs receives help only from members of the Syrian wing of the M[uslim] B[rotherhood] who are based in the Gulf, Lebanon, or Jordan. Most of the money has gone to aid and medical support.[74]

This was echoed by a Homs Revolutionary Council leader who received money from the Brotherhood: 'there are Muslims Brothers in groups of two or three and they are giving support to people inside Syria. They are not organized like they were before.'[75]

The group's inability to respond empowered the entrepreneurial and individualistic nature of the Brotherhood's base, many of whom fundraised for or privately funded their own activities within Syria. One Brotherhood member close to the leadership and who worked extensively in Syria in an individual capacity remarked:

I work in Syria by myself. Not as a representative of the Brotherhood. But people know that I am a member of the Muslim Brotherhood, but I say that I am not. But for a short time, one to two months, I was yes. I represented the Muslim Brotherhood at some small meetings.[76]

---

[73] Anonymous interview. [74] Rosen, 'Islamism' (parenthesis added).
[75] Cited in ibid. [76] Anonymous interview.

The lines between Brotherhood individuals and official Brotherhood activities are often blurred.

The impact of individual Brotherhood members became evident early in the uprising, particularly through their financial contributions. As noted in Chapter 5, many members were financially successful, with some gathering significant wealth running businesses in exile. In this manner, history empowered Brotherhood members to be able to respond to the conflict in a way that its leaders could not do. This pattern was described by a Brotherhood associate:

> We have a lot of Homsi businessmen, especially in the beginning who invested a lot of their own money in the armed uprising, supporting groups in Homs. These guys were all Muslim Brotherhood affiliated. Not just affiliated. They began their business careers and they've made money on the back of start-up cash that was given by the Brotherhood back in the 1980s, so now the Brotherhood is calling in the favour.[77]

The Brotherhood's ability to call on and direct exile capital that went into Homs goes some way to explaining the group's influence in the city early in the conflict. One estimate in 2012 suggested that the Brotherhood supported 60–65 percent of groups operating in Homs and Idlib.[78] Hossam Abu Habil, the son of a late Brotherhood member, claimed to receive US$40,000–50,000 per month from wealthy Brotherhood members based in Kuwait and Qatar for salaries and to purchase weapons and medical equipment for two brigades near Homs.[79] At times, this support is thought to have been definitive; Hamawi Brotherhood member Basil Haffar, who is Riad al-Shaqfeh's son-in-law, is rumoured to have been a major independent funder of Liwa al-Tawhid in the early days of the conflict alongside his father, who is a Syrian Brotherhood branch leader.[80] One Brotherhood associate reported that Haffar 'is very respected' among those on the ground as a result.[81]

Brotherhood members were also involved in founding groups. This was most pronounced through the CPC, an organisation established by current and former Brothers to support the armed uprising. Its key members include Haitham Rahma and Nazir Hakim. Rahma was part of the Brotherhood in the 1980s and in the past also deputy head of the League of Muslim Scholars, which is seen as a Brotherhood front group.[82] Hakim is an Aleppan, who, as noted, purportedly claims loyalty

---

[77] Ibid. [78] Williams, 'Brotherhood Seeks to Fill Post-Assad Vacuum'. [79] Ibid.
[80] Anonymous interview. [81] Ibid.
[82] Aron Lund, 'The Curious Case of the Commission for the Protection of Civilians', *Carnegie Middle East Center* (6 November 2013), http://carnegie-mec.org/diwan/53518?lang=en.

to the international Muslim Brotherhood, rather than the Syrian branch. He is nonetheless a member of the Brotherhood's Syrian National Coalition alliance and is seen as close to the group.

The Brotherhood officially claimed no relationship to the CPC, while the CPC maintained that it was not a Brotherhood front group.[83] The relationship appeared to be informal, but one of close proximity, highlighting the scope of the group's network structure and cross-over between members and non-members. Molham Aldrobi explained the relationship:

[The CPC] was established by members who were historically from the Muslim Brotherhood, and when they established it they talked to us about it ... and we told them if this is going to be part of the Muslim Brotherhood, it needs to be under our control, and they refused to do so, they said no, and we agreed that 'yes fine, it's ok, you are by yourselves. God bless you.'[84]

Thus, even though many of these individuals were members or associates who were Brotherhood supporters, the CPC was formed without the backing or support of the central Brotherhood. Nonetheless, Lund argued that the 'CPC's establishment may have been encouraged by hardliners within the Muslim Brotherhood, including Tayfour and Hakim, as a way to test a military option while retaining plausible deniability'.[85] Individual Brotherhood members may have therefore also acted as the long arm of senior leaders who were unable to achieve goals directly through the group.

The CPC played an important role early in the uprising by funnelling exile capital into Syria, especially around Homs. It was later involved in arms smuggling, purportedly via Libya. The group officially began sending arms and money to armed groups in Syria in March 2012, although this may have begun informally in the autumn of the previous year.[86] Haitham Rahmeh has faced investigation in Sweden (where he is a citizen) for arms smuggling.[87] The CPC later merged into Faylaq al-Sham (The Sham Legion), a newer opposition coalition that emerged in March 2014.[88] According to one Syrian activist, this was largely 'a marketing change. They wanted a sexier name. CPC was boring in Arabic.'[89]

Faylaq al-Sham amalgamated 19 groups. Ali al-Bayanouni acknowledged that 'some of the founders of Faylaq al-Sham are Ikhwan',[90]

---

[83] Lund, 'Struggling to Adapt', p. 17.   [84] Interview with Molham Aldrobi.
[85] Lund, 'Struggling to Adapt', p. 17.   [86] Ibid.
[87] 'Swedish Ex-Imam Formed Militia Group in Syria', Radio Sweden (1 November 2013), http://sverigesradio.se/sida/artikel.aspx?programid=2054&artikel=5691854.
[88] Interview with Molham Aldrobi.   [89] Anonymous interview.
[90] Interview with Ali al-Bayanouni, London.

although Molham Aldrobi maintained that Faylaq al-Sham required recruits to give up their Brotherhood membership.[91] The group obtained US government-vetted status, which may have given it access to US training and powerful weaponry.[92] But the relationship with the Brotherhood is not clear-cut. As Aldrobi explained:

There is no relationship between the Muslim Brotherhood and Faylaq Sham. None behind the table, and none above the table. They are by themselves. They are good people by the way. We have nothing to say against them.[93]

The relationship has been at times antagonistic. One CPC leader reported that 'Brotherhood leaders criticized our calls for Shields brigades to defect and join the new legion, which is not subject to them even in appearance – they were affected negatively by our move'.[94] Yet, Lister called the Faylaq al-Sham, 'Muslim Brotherhood aligned',[95] and it remained an important group in Syria. It was a member of key functional opposition coalitions, including Jaysh al-Fateh (The Army of Conquest) within which it worked with Ahrar al-Sham and Jabhat Fatah al-Sham, as well as in the National Front for Liberation in Idlib. In August 2016, it was one of the handful of FSA-linked groups to work alongside Turkish forces in pushing IS from the Jarablus on the Syrian–Turkish border.[96]

Decentralised activities boosted the reputation of the Brotherhood. As one Syrian activist who was otherwise very critical of the Brotherhood said:

The Brotherhood are on the moderate side so if you compare Faylaq al-Sham, and I've spent [time with them] ... if you compare them to Daesh [IS] or Nusra or those nutters, you think 'Please I want the whole uprising to be Muslim Brotherhood run if that's what it's going to be like.'[97]

In fact, the activities of Brotherhood members were remarkable for the lack of controversy they attracted. Unlike in the previous uprising when the Brotherhood youth were seen as the radical harbingers of violence, Brotherhood members since 2011 have been depicted mostly as responsible conflict actors. In this regard, the informal activities of Brotherhood members

---

[91] Interview with Molham Aldrobi.
[92] Charles Lister, Twitter (24 May 2016), https://twitter.com/charles_lister/status/734836962847133696.
[93] Interview with Molham Aldrobi.
[94] Raphaël Lefèvre and Ali El-Yassir, 'The Sham Legion: Syria's Moderate Islamists', *Carnegie Middle East Center* (14 April 2014), http://carnegie-mec.org/diwan/55344?lang=en.
[95] Lister, *The Syrian Jihad*, p. 216.
[96] William Gourlay, 'Kurdayetî: Pan-Kurdish Solidarity and Cross-Border Links in Times of War and Trauma', *Middle East Critique* 27, no. 1 (2017), pp. 25–42.
[97] Anonymous interview (parenthesis added).

enhanced the group's reputation as a whole, by providing it with tangible connections on the ground and indirectly implementing the Brotherhood message. Thus, while the Brotherhood's leaders were paralysed from action, its proactive members afforded the group a second tier of interaction with the armed conflict, which may bring it benefits in time. The group's characteristic individualism once again proved a valuable asset.

Former Brotherhood Members and Associates in Groups

The Brotherhood's history facilitated further links to the conflict by way of the involvement of former members or Brotherhood family members on the ground, mostly participating in Islamist groups. Some retained productive ties with the Brotherhood, while others were the group's sworn enemies, reflecting the rift that developed historically between both the Brotherhood and Fighting Vanguard, as well as the Brotherhood and parts of its base. This makes the impact of such engagement difficult to quantify.

Examples of family members of key Brothers who participated in the 2011 uprising included Yassar al-Youssef, the son of the Aleppo Artillery Massacre's Ibrahim al-Youssef, who was a member of the political office of the Harakat Nour al-Din al-Zinki (the Zinki Movement) and participated in the Levant Front.[98] The Zinki Movement was a US-vetted group that attracted condemnation in July 2016 after beheading a child soldier.[99] Al-Youssef did not appear to have active connections to the Brotherhood, although would have closely associated with Brotherhood members and officials through the Levant Front. In another instance, Mahmoud al-Hamid, the elderly son of the Hamawi cleric and founding Brotherhood member Muhammad al-Hamid, and a former associate of Marwan Hadid, was a member of Ahrar al-Sham.[100] Eyad Shaar (Abu al-Hassan al-Tabuki) was part of a Brotherhood family that was forced to leave Jisr al-Shughour in the 1970s. Although it is unclear whether he was ever a Brotherhood or Vanguard member, he fought in Afghanistan and was an Ahrar al-Sham commander before becoming the chief aide to the movement's then political leader, Moneer al-Sayyal (Abu Khalid).[101]

---

[98] 'Clashes between al-Nusra and al-Zinki in Aleppo' (6 October 2015), www.zamanalwsl.net/news/64774.html.

[99] 'Syria Conflict: Boy Beheaded by Rebels "Was Fighter"', *BBC News* (21 July 2016), www.bbc.com/news/world-middle-east-36843990.

[100] Muzmajer Al-Sham (@saleelalmajd1), Twitter, (4 August 2014), https://twitter.com/saleelalmajd1/status/495977025984008192.

[101] Charles Lister, 'Why Assad Is Losing', *Foreign Policy* (5 May 2015), http://foreignpolicy.com/2015/05/05/why-assad-is-losing-syria-islamists-saudi/.

Bilal Attar and Abulhassan Abazeed both grew up in Brotherhood families in Jordan, and became senior members of the Farouq Brigades, and were key players in the Istanbul Room arms clearing house. The Farouq Brigades were one of the most important groups in the early uprising, controlling smuggling and transit routes across the country, and the Bab al-Hawa border crossing between Syria and Turkey, although Attar has been very critical of the Brotherhood.[102]

Some members of Brotherhood families have had a significant influence on the conflict, including Ahmad Issa al-Shaykh (Abu Issa), who was released from prison in the years prior to the 2011 uprising. Abu Issa adopted an important role in the armed conflict in his hometown of Jabal al-Zawiya in Idlib province, with his brothers Daoud, Abou al-Fadl and Yahya Zakaria (this may also be Abu Yahya).[103] Their father, Zakaria, was a Brotherhood member who was purportedly involved in the Hama uprising. He was executed in Syrian regime custody, apparently after being found to have carried out assassinations on behalf of the Brotherhood.[104] Abu Issa founded Suqour al-Sham, another group that enjoyed some Brotherhood funding, and his brother Yahya Zakaria became a senior commander.[105] The group later merged into Ahrar al-Sham, with Abu Issa remaining a key commander. Ahrar al-Sham's former leader Ali al-Omar (Abu Ammar or Babi Ammar Taftanaz) purportedly grew up in a Brotherhood family that had fled Idlib for Iraq in the late 1970s.[106]

The nature of Abu Issa's historical Brotherhood ties underline the complexity of the Brotherhood's relationship with its associates and former members. Suqour al-Sham's ideology bore remarkable similarity to that of the Brotherhood, including calling for a state with an 'Islamic reference'. As Abu Issa described:

---

[102] Rania Abouzeid, *No Turning Back: Life, Loss and Hope in Wartime Syria* (London: Oneworld Publications, 2018).

[103] Asher Berman, 'Rebel groups in Jabal al-Zawiyah', Institute for the Study of War (26 July 2012), www.understandingwar.org/sites/default/files/Backgrounder_RebelGroupsJebelAlZawiyah_31July.pdf.

[104] Rasha Abu Haidar, 'Islamic Front Shura Chief: Our Brothers Are in the Lap of Saudi Arabia and America (in Arabic)', *Al-Akhbar* (17 January 2014), http://al-akhbar.com/node/198815.

[105] Charles Lister, 'Jihadology Podcast: Syria Status Update with Charles Lister', *Jihadology* (23 June 2015), https://jihadology.net/2015/06/23/jihadology-podcast-syria-status-update-with-charles-lister/; Dania Akkad, Nadine Dahan and Zouhir Al-Shimale, 'Jaish al-Islam Says it Inflated Hostage Numbers, Leaving Syrian Families in the Dark', *Middle East Eye* (13 April 2018), www.middleeasteye.net/news/revealed-thousands-missing-syrians-not-jaish-al-islam-1492653856.

[106] Nicholas A. Heras, 'In Brief: A Snapshot of Two Rebel Commanders Vying for Survival in Damascus Governorate', *Militant Leadership Monitor* 7, no. 12 (2017), n.p.

We are proud of our Islamism and we are Islamists. But we do not want to show it in a slogan because we might not live up to the responsibility of Islam … But we want a state with Islamic reference and we are calling for it.[107]

Such a vision could be coincidental or it may be a legacy of Abu Issa's socialisation in a Brotherhood family. Abu Issa later joined the CPC, creating a closer tie to the Brotherhood. Yet this relationship was not easy. Abu Issa left the CPC, purportedly after refusing to pledge allegiance to the Brotherhood.[108] He also worked with direct Brotherhood competitors, such as Emad al-Din al-Rashid, a popular centrist cleric who has competed with the Brotherhood in the Syrian political opposition, and was purportedly critical of the Brotherhood.[109]

The return of several Fighting Vanguard members to the theatre further highlighted old Brotherhood links, although did not appear to have direct ramifications for the Brotherhood. This included Abu Khalid al-Suri (Mohammed al-Bahaiy), who was a close associate of Abu Musab al-Suri and an Afghan veteran, released from prison during the 2011 amnesties. Abu Khalid became a founding member of Ahrar al-Sham along with a host of others, including the former Fighting Vanguard member Mohamed Ayman Aboul-Tout (Abul-Abbas a-Shami).[110] Abu Khaled later became the al-Qaeda leader Ayman Zawahiri's appointed emissary to Syria to mediate the conflict between Jabhat al-Nusra and IS. A handful of non-Afghan war Vanguard veterans such as Abu Basir al-Tartusi and Zuay al-Zubi also joined militias.[111] Perhaps the most sinister case was that of Radwan Nammous (Abu Firas al-Suri),[112] an army officer who trained Vanguard members from 1977 to 1980 and was involved in anti-government operations from 1979 to 1980. He left for Afghanistan in 1981. Until his death in a drone strike in April 2016, Abu Firas was the spokesperson for al-Qaeda's Syrian franchise, Jabhat al-Nusra.

The Brotherhood's former members and associates nonetheless indirectly extended the group's links into the conflict and provided a further

---

[107] Mariam Karouny, 'Syria's Islamist Rebels Join Forces against Assad', *Reuters* (11 October 2012), www.reuters.com/article/us-syria-crisis-rebels-idUSBRE89A0Y920121011.
[108] Raphaël Lefèvre, '*The Muslim Brotherhood Prepares for a Comeback in Syria*' (Washington DC: Carnegie Endowment for International Peace, p. 14).
[109] Rania Abouzeid, 'Syria's Secular and Islamist Rebels: Who Are the Saudis and the Qataris Arming?', *Time* (18 September 2012), http://world.time.com/2012/09/18/syrias-secular-and-islamist-rebels-who-are-the-saudis-and-the-qataris-arming/.
[110] Kyle Orton, 'Al Qaeda Central in Syria', *The Syrian Intifada* (14 September 2015), https://kyleorton1991.wordpress.com/2015/09/14/al-qaeda-central-in-syria/.
[111] Lefèvre, 'The Syrian Brotherhood's Armed Struggle'.
[112] Hassan Abu Haniyeh, 'Who's Who in the Nusra Front?', *The New Arab* (15 December 2014), www.alaraby.co.uk/english/politics/2014/12/15/whos-who-in-the-nusra-front.

channel through which the Brotherhood's history played out there. This was particularly clear in the role of former Vanguard members, whose return to Syria marked the continuation of the legacy of the group's first confrontation with the Ba'th.

Overall, however, the Brotherhood's response to the armed uprising highlighted the depths to which the ghosts of Hama continued to haunt the group. It did not want an armed confrontation in 2011, and may have enjoyed greater success if the unrest had remained in the political sphere. As violence in Syria became inevitable, the group took a strong rhetorical stand on the need for self-defence and the protection of civilians, but the risk-adverse leadership struggled to take any tangible steps towards supporting these ideals. History, and especially the memory of the Brotherhood's past violence, deeply influenced the group.

The Syrian war posed a significant challenge for the Syrian Muslim Brotherhood because the group had spent three decades trying to convince the Syrian population that it was a non-violent movement. Although the 2011 civil war enjoyed broader popular support than its 1980s confrontation, the group was constrained by its fear of repeating past mistakes. The scale of this strain was evident in the Brotherhood's reticence to acknowledge its history, or to overtly use its history as an asset in the conflict. Had the group made the effort to come to terms with its past during its time in exile, including taking responsibility for its mistakes, learning how it went so wrong and developing a compelling narrative to explain its 1980s-era tactical choices, it may have been better equipped to respond. But in practice, these lingering questions meant that while the Brotherhood had the financial capability and the connections necessary to mount a cohesive but limited response to the conflict, its piecemeal reaction and inability to make strong decisions out of fear of repeating history prevented it from playing a decisive or even a significant role in the conflict. In the end, the group's greatest contribution to the armed conflict was its efforts at mediating various groups, but this may not be enough to earn it the respect and position in craves.

The Brotherhood's network structure to some extent compensated for its limitations, giving the group tentacles and influence across a broad range of players in the conflict. This took place through both card-carrying Brotherhood members and former associates, and represented the most substantial Brotherhood contribution to the conflict. This caution and restraint represents a stark contrast to the group defined in the Hama-centric descriptors of one that is violent by definition, but could prove the right strategy longer term – depending on how the history of the Syrian uprising is written.

Conclusion
The Past Remains the Syrian Muslim Brotherhood's Present

The Syrian Muslim Brotherhood was one of Syria's most resilient opposition movements. Since the 1940s, the group has transitioned from parliamentary party to an opposition group under authoritarianism, to a banned movement, to an organisation in exile. But it still emerged on the eve of the 2011 uprising as Syria's most capable opposition actor. History influenced every move that the Brotherhood made throughout the 2011 uprising, but not in the way that the Hama-centric understanding of the group anticipated. Ultimately, it stood in the way of the Brotherhood's widely anticipated political comeback.

The Hama-centric understanding of the group depicted the Hama uprising as proof of the Syrian Muslim Brotherhood's violent, undemocratic and dogmatic nature. Hama was seen as the centre of gravity in the Brotherhood's history: everything before and after 1982 was a ruse. While the period of violence sheds some light on the group, its character is the sum of parts acquired over decades of political life. When looking from a wider aperture, it was clear that the group's defining features were pragmatism, ideological flexibility and individualism – features built into the group during its founding decades that shaped the way that it has responded to every political challenge since. In this regard, the Syrian Muslim Brotherhood in 2011 bore little resemblance to the group seen in the Hama uprising. It was also nowhere near as significant an actor as observers had expected.

On the eve of the 2011 uprising, the Brotherhood carried the substantial weight of history on its shoulders, some of which facilitated its strong early performance in the unrest. It easily echoed the emerging opposition's democratic promises because it had long spoken about democracy itself. Democratic ideas were enshrined in its being in the 1940s when its most senior figures ran for election, implicitly signalling their approval of the Brotherhood's involvement in the secular state. The Brotherhood was a minor political player, but it took the opportunity seriously. In 2011 the group's members joined the chorus of those calling for the restoration of the Syrian democratic system. Although there would always be undemocratic voices or opportunists within the movement, there were reasons for optimism: its leadership and Shura Council rotated at fixed intervals, while the group tolerated some internal ideational pluralism, making it at the very least more internally democratic than many parties in the uprising, including the Syrian regime. Further, while its status as an Islamist group seemed to imply a level of ideological affiliation, the Brotherhood was never dominated by ideological considerations. Pragmatism consistently guided the group, giving it the ideological flexibility necessary to navigate the changing political landscape. Its stated ambitions were no more presumptuous than the language and goals used by political parties in other parts of the world.

History, by way of its long exile, also gave the Brotherhood an organisational tradition and resources far superior to any opposition group. Exile bestowed the Brotherhood with safety, financial security and the space to advance new programmes. Moreover, the group developed political connections that linked it to the major centres of power in Washington DC, New York, London and Brussels. This meant that on the eve of the uprising, the group had a paid secretariat, financial resources and the political know-how to maximise the effectiveness of its response.

These historical experiences proved an asset for the group, endowing it with the resources and political connections to engage the opposition, create relations with international powers, and guarantee it an important role in the SNC and SOC. Its moderate credentials enabled it to collaborate with secular players to work at restoring democracy to Syria. Noteworthy is that the Brotherhood's political and economic principles held steadfast even in the face of the radicalising opposition landscape where it may have been politically expedient to emphasise its Islamist credentials. A further asset of history was the Brotherhood's individualist tendencies, which enabled the group to mount a multi-fronted campaign across the political and armed uprising that amplified its influence and maximised its chances of being involved in the carving of Syria's political future. This pattern was accentuated by the comparative weakness of the other opposition political groups.

At the same time, history proved an encumbrance for the Syrian Brotherhood. It underwent significant change after the 1963 Ba'th coup, losing much of the political and strategic refinement that had been the hallmark of its existence. Although it is common for opposition groups facing authoritarian conditions to endorse violent tactics, the Brotherhood had survived periods of authoritarianism in its founding decades, persevering without resorting to arms. The new Ba'th regime, however, proved a merciless foe, inflicting years of repression, arrests, executions and expulsions on members of the Brotherhood. Ultimately, the polarisation of the Syrian political landscape, power shifts within its leadership and competing pressures from the Fighting Vanguard led the Brotherhood to acquiesce and endorse violent aggression against the Baʿth in 1979. Such a policy would have seemed unfathomable 30 years before in view of the group's heritage, and while it lasted for only a short period, it had devastating consequences that would scar the Brotherhood, its supporters and the Syrian people up to the present day. The Baʿth proved a brutal enemy with scant regard for people or property and it was willing to stop at nothing to ensure the destruction of the rebels. And so a massacre at Hama ensued.

Associations with violence diminished substantially after Hama in 1982 and largely ceased over the next few years, returning the Brotherhood to its non-violent roots. But the pressure of authoritarianism and its cumulative political failures continued to distort the group's behaviour. Thus, maintaining ambitions to return to Syria, the Brotherhood was desperate to maximise any opportunity, no matter how small or incongruous. In practice, this saw the group prepared to accept the political boundaries defined by the Baʿth – leading it to unilaterally suspending opposition to the regime in 2009, undermining its decades-long opposition credentials. Opportunism thereby became the norm as the Brotherhood repeatedly sold its opposition counterparts short, privileging its own short-term gains over long-term strategy. This would represent the Brotherhood's weakness going forward.

This political baggage had a stunting effect throughout the 2011 uprising, as the Brotherhood was unable to jettison its authoritarian survival techniques. While the group entered the uprising on strong footing, history led it often to act in a perceived opaque or underhanded manner, and it overplayed its hand when collaborating with opposition players in the SNC. The group was no longer the finely tuned political organisation that it had been under Mustafa al-Sibai, but increasingly appeared clumsy and lacking the political aptitude necessary to build genuine influence over the Syrian opposition and population. Furthermore, history had robbed the group of its large popular membership base, and thus while its tentacles stretched far and wide, the Brotherhood organisation had become endowed with weak command and control capacity, which restricted its ability to act on the ground in Syria. Its moderate liberal economic message no longer resonated with many of those inside the country. Syria's 2000s-era haphazard economic liberalisation and corruption created the new underclass that took to the streets in 2011, to whom the Brotherhood had few links or appeal. Consequently, as time progressed, the group struggled to rebuild the trust of the Syrian population, which augured poorly for the Brotherhood's ultimate political relevance and contribution to a final settlement in Syria. Many worried that the group's opportunism would morph into something more sinister should the Brotherhood one day get its hands on the reins of power.

Perhaps the most unexpected element of the group's historical burden, however, was the ongoing relevance of Hama. The memory of Hama had distorted the view of the Syrian Muslim Brotherhood from the outside, and as a result early in the project there seemed little value in discussing Hama when talking about the contemporary group. Yet, while the group found it difficult to escape the reputational issue related to Hama, perhaps the most unexpected finding was the way in which the events continued to affect the group's internal calculus. As interviews were conducted and the uprising unfolded, it became clear that the memory of the event continued to haunt the movement in many ways. Hama today generates a number of core questions for the Brotherhood's ongoing reflection: How did we drift so far from our original path? Who is to blame? How do we prevent history from repeating? and How do we take ownership of our record of largely non-violent opposition and bury our short history and reputation for violence? The group has been unwilling to discuss these questions frankly either internally or externally, and has therefore never fully cognised what went wrong and what it needs to do in the future to prevent a repeat of history. This means that the Brotherhood has taken few steps towards rebuilding its position in the eyes of its potential stakeholder base, and is often crippled by the indecision and fear that comes from not understanding its own past. In this regard, the 1996 Evaluation Report's failure to prompt change represents a missed opportunity. Today, little short of a full generational handover and the retirement of the Hama-era leaders will be sufficient to finally exorcise the demons. But if anything, the group's actions after 2011 only exacerbated intergenerational divisions.

The Syrian Muslim Brotherhood's past, particularly its history of violence, therefore still affected the group strongly following the 2011 uprising. This is significant, because it provides context and precedent for the role that the Brotherhood might attempt to play in a future Syria. Although many commentators have suggested that the Brotherhood could not possibly interact fairly or genuinely in a democratic environment, history tells us that the group has a long track record of calling for democracy, playing within the rules of the game and participating in a secular political system in partnership with secular parties. Moreover, while some might expect that its track record of violence signals a future propensity to the same, the uprising has shown that the Brotherhood has largely sought to avoid violence and bury that history, even when others lionised this radical past. Conversely, its own history appears to have deterred it from such radical tactics.

The Syrian Muslim Brotherhood by 2019 was therefore neither as violent nor as undemocratic as the conventional narrative purported. Indeed, the Brotherhood's return to Syria was constrained by mundane organisational flaws such as internal dissent, poor political decision-making and lack of mechanisms for command and control of its cadre. It is an understanding of these organisational flaws and its history that illuminates the true character of the movement, as these organisational deficiencies are likely to ensure that the group finds a glass ceiling that will prevent it achieving either a dominant or prominent role in the exercise of power in Syria in the future. It is simply not well placed to harness any such opportunity.

In the end, the Syrian Muslim Brotherhood was but a single opposition party within a broad and fragmented opposition environment. By 2019 the war looked to be reaching an end, on terms almost universally opposed by the Syrian opposition. This meant that even if open warfare ends, the root causes of the conflict remain unresolved. It may be a long time before the Syrian people see peace in the fullest sense of the word.

Groups such as the Brotherhood will have to remain on the side-lines waiting for the time when politics returns to Syria. As the Brotherhood's then media chief Omar Mushaweh surmised:

> This revolution is not a Brotherhood revolution. The Muslim Brotherhood if they worked alone providing humanitarian relief or politically, then they will never succeed. The Muslim Brotherhood are a fraction or a small part [of the Syrian population], and a revolution depends on a movement of the whole people to make this revolution succeed.[1]

But proving to the majority of stakeholders in Syria that they are deserving of trust will be key to the Brotherhood's emancipation.

---

[1] Interview with Omar Mushaweh, Skype, 2017.

Appendix 1 Brotherhood Electoral Details 1947–1963[1]

	Total seats	Seats won	Ba'th won	Notable candidates	Successfully elected	Responsibilities
1947	136	≤ 3	0[2]	Independent Brotherhood candidates: Mahmud al-Shaqfeh (Hama) Maruf al-Dawalibi (Aleppo) *Note: The above list may not be complete* Damascus Rabitat al-Ulama list[3]: Brotherhood members: Abd al-Hamid al-Tabba Arif al-Taraqji Muhammad al-Mubarak Ahmad Mazhar al-Azma Non-Brotherhood Muslims: Zaki al-Khatib, Hassan al-Hakim Nuri al-Ibish Ali Buzzo (Kurd) Mohammad Akbik Sami Kabbara Saidi Kaylani Ali al-Tantawi Subhi al-Khatib. Non-Muslims: Fares al-Khury (Protestant) Constantine Mensi (Greek Orthodox) Farid Arsalanian (Armenian) Elias Dummar (Roman Catholic) Wahid Mezrahi (Jewish).	Brotherhood: Mahmud al-Shaqfeh[4] Muhammad al-Mubarak[5] Maruf al-Dawalibi[6] Non-Brotherhood: Wahid Mizrahi[7] Zaki al-Khatib[8] Nuri al-Ibish[9] Faris al-Khuri[10] *Note: this list may not be complete*	Nuri al-Ibish – Minister of Agriculture[11] Faris al-Khuri – Parliamentary Speaker (1947-9), Head of Syrian delegation to UNGA 1947, Syrian Representative on UNSC 1946-8.[12] (both non-Brotherhood)

Year						
1949	114	3 (2.6%)[13]–4[14]	1	Islamic Socialist Front (Damascus) Mustafa al-Sibai, Muhammad al-Mubarak, Arif al-Taraqji, Subhi al-Umari (not a member, but 'affiliated in some way')[15], Georges Shalhub (Catholic)[16]; Aleppo Baha al-Din al-Amiri, Maruf al-Dawalibi	Mustafa al-Sibai, Muhammad al-Mubarak, Arif al-Taraqji[17], Subhi al-Umari, Georges Shalhub	Mustafa al-Sibai (Constitutional committee), Muhammad al-Mubarak (Minister of Public Works December 1949–May 1950)[18], Maruf al-Dawalibi (Minister of National Economy December 1949–May 1950,[19] Parliamentary Speaker June–September 1951. Prime Minister, 28–9 November 1951)
1954	141	5 (3.5%)	22	Muhammad al-Mubarak, Maruf al-Dawalibi[20]		*Did not directly contest elections, but endorsed candidates.* Maruf al-Dawalibi (Minister of Defence) March – June 1954[21]
1961	173	10 (5.8%)[22]	18[23]	Damascus:[24] Issam al-Attar, Hussein Khattab, Umar Awdat al-Khatib, Zuhayr al-Shawish, Abd al-Rauf Abu Tawq (variously described as either MB or ulama)[25], Muhammad Said al-Abbar, Bashir Ramadan (both variously described as either MB or independent)[26]		Mustafa al-Zarqa (Minister of Justice, Minister of Awqaf), Maruf al-Dawalibi – Prime Minister (December 1961-March 1962), Four members in Khalid al-Azm's 1962 cabinet (names unknown)[29]

(cont.)

Total seats	Seats won	Ba'th won	Notable candidates	Successfully elected	Responsibilities
				Homs: Muhammad Ali Mashal (either Brotherhood or People's Party) Tayyib al-Khoja (either Brotherhood or independent) Aleppo: Abd al-Fatah abu Ghudda Mustafa al-Zarqa ('close to Brotherhood,' ulama)[27] Lattakia Nabil al-Tawil (Brotherhood or ulama)[28] People's Party – Maruf Dawalibi	

[1] Owing to the lack of complete electoral data and the need to harvest information from multiple sources, entries in this table may be inaccurate, or missing.
[2] John F. Devlin, *The Ba'th Party: A History from its Origins to 1966* (Stanford: Hoover Institution Press, 1976), p. 48.
[3] 'The List of the Umma', *Al-Manar* (7 July 1947).
[4] Robert G. Rabil, 'The Syrian Muslim Brotherhood', in *The Muslim Brotherhood: The Organization and Policies of a Global Islamist Movement*, ed. Barry Rubin (New York: Palgrave Macmillan, 2010), p. 74.
[5] Ibid.
[6] Ibid.
[7] 'Letter dated January 12', American Minister at Damascus (1949).
[8] Sami M. Moubayed, *Steel & Silk: Men and Women who shaped Syria 1900–2000*. (Seattle: Cune Press, 2006), p. 275.
[9] M.C. Man, 'E 11904/1012/89 No. 16 – Leading Personalities in Syria', UK Foreign Office (1949).
[10] Ibid.
[11] Ibid.

12 Ibid.
13 Hanna Batatu, 'Syria's Muslim Brethren', *MERIP Reports*, no. 110 (1982), p. 17.
14 Patrick Seale, *The Struggle for Syria: A Study of Post-War Arab Politics, 1945–1958* (Oxford: Oxford University Press, 1965), p. 182.
15 Raphaël Lefèvre, *Ashes of Hama: The Muslim Brotherhood in Syria* (London: Hurst, 2013), p. 28.
16 Joshua Teitelbaum, 'The Muslim Brotherhood and the "Struggle for Syria", 1947–1958: Between Accommodation and Ideology.' *Middle Eastern Studies* 40, no. 3 (2004), p. 141.
17 Lefèvre, *Ashes of Hama*, p. 29.
18 W. Montagu-Pollock, 'EY 1012/1 – Leading Personalities in Syria', *British Embassy Damascus*, 2 July 1951.
19 Ibid.
20 Lefèvre, *Ashes of Hama*, p. 39.
21 John Gardener, 'NY 1012/1 - Leading personalities in Syria', UK Foreign Office (15 January 1955).
22 Eyal Zisser, 'Syria', in *Elections in Asia and the Pacific: A Data Handbook: Volume I: Middle East*, ed. Dieter Nohlen, Florian Grotz and Christof Hartmann (Oxford: Oxford University Press, 2001), p. 225.
23 Yitzhak Oron, *Middle East Record*, vol. 2 (Jerusalem: Tel Aviv University, 1961), p. 505.
24 Ibid., pp. 503–5.
25 Ibid., p. 503.
26 Ibid.
27 Oron, *Middle East Record*, p. 505.
28 Ibid.
29 Thomas Mayer, 'The Islamic Opposition in Syria 1961–1982', *Orient* 24, no. 4 (1983), p. 591.

Appendix 2 Reported Syrian Brotherhood/Vanguard Members and Syrians Who Travelled to Afghanistan

The author has collated every report she found of Syrians in Afghanistan in the table below, but this list may not be exhaustive. Owing to the nature of the Syrian/Afghan conflicts, the widespread use of *kunya* (nom de guerre) and the difficulty of verifying reports, some information may be incorrect or individuals may be counted twice.

Name	Location	Affiliation	Description	2011 uprising status
Farouk Abdul Rahman (Bilal al-Dimashqi)[1]	Damascus	Brotherhood and Fighting Vanguard	Armed activities 1979–89, travelled to Afghanistan mid-1986.	In Damascus, possibly jailed?
Mustafa bin abd al-Qadir Sitt Maryam Nasar (Abu Musab al-Suri, Omar Abdul Hakim)[2]	Aleppo	Brotherhood and Vanguard. Joined Vanguard June 11, 1980	Armed activities inside Syria, travelled to Afghanistan late 1986–mid 1987 with five other Syrians, one of whom died in Jalalabad, another died in Khost. One left Afghanistan.[3]	Military instructor and lecturer in the Afghan-Arab training camps from 1987–92[4] In jail in Syria?[5]
Mohammed al-Bahaiya[6] **(Abu Khaled al-Suri)**	Aleppo	Fighting Vanguard[7]	Travelled to Afghanistan late 1986–mid 1987. Linked to attacks in Spain.	Founding member of Ahrar al-Sham. Al-Qaeda intermediary between Jabhat al-Nusra and IS. Dead. Lister: 'no evidence' that he was ever an official AQ member.[8]
Abu Burhan[9]		Ex-Syrian army officer, Muslim Brotherhood	In Afghanistan 1986–1993 (active until 1992). Commander in the Khaldan camp, trained Arabs. Ran Maktab al-Khadimat's Sadda and Khaldan camps, and alleged founding member of al-Qaeda.[10]	Unknown

(cont.)

Name	Location	Affiliation	Description	2011 uprising status
Radwan Nammous[11] (Abu Firas al-Suri)	Rif Damascus	Ex-army, apparently left after the Aleppo Artillery massacre. Trained Fighting Vanguard members from 1977–80, involved in operations 1979–80	Left for Afghanistan 1981. Bin Laden envoy involved in the establishment of Lashkar-e Taiba.[12]	Spokesman of Jabhat al-Nusra. Killed 2016.[13]
Mohamed Ayman Aboul-Tout (Abul-Abbas a-Shami)[14]	Idlib	Fighting Vanguard		Founding member of Ahrar al-Sham, later served as the Islamic Front's top-ranking sharia official.[15]
Mohammed Haydar Zammar[16]	Syria/Germany	Attempted to join the Fighting Vanguard	Travelled from Germany to Jordan in 1982 to join the Fighting Vanguard, but was "turned back by the Jordanian authorities."[17] Travelled to Afghanistan many times after 1991, fought in Bosnia Alleged to have recruited the 9/11 hijackers Arrested in Morocco 2001, transferred to Syria	Released from Syrian prison in 2012 following a prisoner swap negotiated by Abu Khalid Joined Islamic State group. In Kurdish custody in Qamishli as of late 2018.
Abu Talha[18]		Fighting Vanguard	Founding member of Maktab al-Khidimat	

Abu Bakr		Fighting Vanguard	Founding member of Maktab al-Khadimat
Abu Hussein		Fighting Vanguard	Founding member of Maktab al-Khadimat
Abu Asteef		Unknown	
Abu Talha al-Suri		Unknown	
Muhammad Amin[19]	From Syria, but lived in Kuwait.	Unknown	
Abu Aseed[20] Aztyar	Damascus	Unknown	
Abu al-Hassan al-Suri[21]		Unknown	
Abu Az al-Suri[22]		Unknown	
Abu Saef al-Suri[23]		Unknown	
Abu al-Rida al-Suri[24]		Unknown	
Arsalan Jamblat (Shamil Sharksi)[25]	Syria 1966, brought up in the US	Unknown (unlikely)	Entered Afghanistan in 1989, trained at the Saadi camp. Killed 1990
Abu Hamid Zabeeh Ullah[26]	Syria	Unknown	First Syrian killed in Afghanistan
Muhammad Usman (Abu Asim)[27]	Unknown	Unknown	Fought with Ahmad Shah Masoud Deceased

(*cont.*)

Name	Location	Affiliation	Description	2011 uprising status
Abu Anas Palestinian[28]	Syria (Palestinian background)	Unknown		Deceased
Abu Ahmad al-Aleebi[29]	Aleppo	Unknown	Spent three months in Afghanistan before being killed. Date unknown	Deceased
Abu Muhammad al-Suri[30]	Syria	Unknown, although was forced into exile from Syria	Joined Afghan jihad in 1988	Killed in Jalalabad
Mustafa al-Hajj Khalil (Abu Hamid Marwan/ Zabeeh Ullah)	Syria	Unknown, but spent time in jail in Syria		Killed near Mazar-e Sharif

[1] Sami Moubayed, *Under the Black Flag: At the Frontier of the New Jihad* (London: I.B.Tauris, 2015), pp. 46–7.
[2] Brynjar Lia, *Architect of Global Jihad: The Life of Al-Qaida Strategist Abu Mus'ab al-Suri* (London: Hurst & Company, 2007), p. 30.
[3] Ibid., p. 75.
[4] Ibid., p. 2.
[5] Bill Roggio, 'Abu Musab al Suri Released from Syrian Custody: Report', *The Long War Journal* (6 February 2012), www.longwarjournal.org/archives/2012/02/abu_musab_al_suri_re.php.
[6] Lia, *Architect of Global Jihad*, p. 123.
[7] Charles L. Lister, *The Syrian Jihad: Al-Qaeda, The Islamic State and the Evolution of an Insurgency* (London: Hurst, 2015), p. 107.
[8] Ibid.
[9] Leah Farrall and Mustafa Hamid, *The Arabs at War in Afghanistan* (London: Hurst, 2015), p. 84.
[10] Mark Long, 'Ribat, al-Qa'ida, and the Challenge for US Foreign Policy', *Middle East Journal* 63, no. 1 (2009), pp. 31–47 at 39.
[11] Hassan Abu Haniyeh, 'Who's Who in the Nusra Front?', *The New Arab* (15 December 2014), www.alaraby.co.uk/english/politics/2014/12/15/whos-who-in-the-nusra-front.

12 Thomas Joscelyn, 'Al Qaeda Veteran Appears in Al Nusrah Front Video, Criticizes Rival', *Long War Journal* (20 March 2014). www.longwarjournal.org/archives/2014/03/al_qaeda_veteran_app.php

13 Phil Stewart, 'U.S. behind Strike That Killed Nusra Front's Abu Firas: Officials', *Reuters* (4 April 2016), www.reuters.com/article/us-mideast-crisis-syria-usa-idUSKCN0X11R3.

14 Kyle Orton, 'Al Qaeda Central in Syria', *The Syrian Intifada* (14 September 2015), https://kyleorton1991.wordpress.com/2015/09/14/al-qaeda-central-in-syria/.

15 Aron Lund, 'Syria in Crisis: Who and What Was Abu Khalid al-Suri? Part II', *Carnegie Middle East Center* (25 February 2014), http://carnegie-mec.org/diwan/54634?lang=en.

16 Liz Sly, "This is the Man Who Recruited the 9/11 Hijackers," *The Washington Post* (30 November 2018), www.washingtonpost.com/news/world/wp/2018/11/30/feature/this-is-the-man-who-recruited-the-9-11-hijackers/?utm_term=.cb85d2780e28.

17 Ibid.

18 Lefèvre, *Ashes of Hama*, p. 143.

19 Basil Muhammad, *The Arab Supporters in Afghanistan* (Riyadh: Lajnat al-Birr al-Islamiyya, 1991), p. 103.

20 Ibid.

21 Ibid, p. 111.

22 Ibid, p. 113.

23 Ibid, p. 112.

24 Ibid.

25 Muhammad Amir Rana and Mubashar Bukhari, *Arabs in Afghan Jihad* (Lahore: Pakistan Institute for Peace Studies, 2007), p. 143.

26 Ibid. p. 144.

27 Ibid.

28 Ibid.

29 Ibid.

30 Ibid., p. 145.

Appendix 3 Relationships between Current and Past Leaders

The Leadership of the Syrian Muslim Brotherhood as of September 2017[1]

Position	Name	History
Leader	Muhammad Walid	Unknown
Political Office		
Deputy Leader	Hosam Ghadban	Nephew of Munir Ghadban, former-Comptroller General
Relief Office		
Financial Office		
Organisational Office	Osama Homsi	Unknown
Administrative Office	Ahmed al-Bayanouni	Unknown
Media office	Omar Mushaweh*	From prominent Brotherhood family in Deir al-Zor
Strategic Planning	Molham Aldrobi*	
Organisation inside Syria	Undisclosed	Unknown
Women	Kitam al-Ahdab	The wife of Farouq Tayfour
General Secretariat	Samir (surname unknown)	Unknown
Security	UNDISCLOSED	Unknown
Youth	Aamer	Unknown
***Shura* Council chief**	Ali al-Bayanouni	Past leader

* **Left leadership in the 2018 election**
[1] The list of the Brotherhood's leadership was kindly given to the researcher by Molham Aldrobi.

Non-executive and former members

Former head of the Istanbul office	Basil Haffar	Son in law of Riad al-Shaqfeh. Haffar's father is a leader of a local Brotherhood branch
Brotherhood representative in the Syrian Islamic Council	Ahmad Hawwa	Son of Said Hawwa
Political Office	Hassan al-Hachimi	Father was former deputy Brotherhood leader and senior figure in Aleppo wing, brother is on *Shura* Council, uncle was former-Comptroller General Abd al-Fatah abu Ghuddah, former-deputy leader Amin Yegen was married to his cousin.
Organisational Office	Ahmed al-Bayanouni	Son of Ali al-Bayanouni

Bibliography

'3 in Syria Sentenced to Life for an Article Attacking Religion.' *New York Times*, 12 May 1967.
Al-Nadhir no. 11 (in Arabic), 20 February 1982.
Al-Nadhir no. 10 (in Arabic), 19 February 1982.
Al-Nadhir no. 43 (English edition), 4 February 1982.
Al-Nadhir no. 49 (English edition), 15 February 1982.
Al-Nadhir no. 1 (in Arabic), 9 September 1979.
Abd-allah, Umar F. *The Islamic Struggle in Syria*. Berkeley: Mizan Press, 1983.
Abdo, Geneive. 'Salafists and Sectarianism: Twitter and Communal Conflict in the Middle East'. Brookings Institute, 2015. www.brookings.edu/~/media/research/files/papers/2015/03/26-sectarianism-salafism-social-media-abdo/abdo-paper_final_web.pdf.
Abed, Shukri B. 'Syria: Muslim Brotherhood Pressure Intensifies', Defense Intelligence Agency report, 1982.
 'Islam and Democracy.' In *Democracy, War and Peace in the Middle East*, edited by David Garnham and Mark Tessler. Bloomington: Indiana University Press, 1995, pp. 116–34.
Abedin, Mahan. 'The Battle within Syria: An Interview with Muslim Brotherhood Leader Ali Bayanouni'. *Terrorism Monitor*, 21 July 2005, www.jamestown.org/single/?no_cache=1&tx_ttnews%5Bswords%5D=8fd5893941d69d0be3f378576261ae3e&tx_ttnews%5Bany_of_the_words%5D=bayanouni&tx_ttnews%5Btt_news%5D=551&tx_ttnews%5BbackPid%5D=7&cHash=a3596e18cae2d132225d7cfe253aa2cf.
Abouzeid, Rania. 'Syria's Secular and Islamist Rebels: Who Are the Saudis and the Qataris Arming?', *Time*, 18 September 2012. http://world.time.com/2012/09/18/syrias-secular-and-islamist-rebels-who-are-the-saudis-and-the-qataris-arming/.
 'Syrian Opposition Groups Stop Pretending'. *New Yorker*, 26 September 2013. www.newyorker.com/news/news-desk/syrian-opposition-groups-stop-pretending.
 'The Jihad Next Door: The Syrian Roots of Iraq's Newest Civil War'. *Politico*, 23 June 2014. www.politico.com/magazine/story/2014/06/al-qaeda-iraq-syria-108214.
 No Turning Back: Life, Loss and Hope in Wartime Syria. London: Oneworld Publications, 2018.

Bibliography

Abu Haidar, Rasha. 'Islamic Front Shura Chief: Our Brothers Are in the Lap of Saudi Arabia and America (in Arabic)'. *Al-Akhbar*, 17 January 2014. http://al-akhbar.com/node/198815.

Abu Haniyeh, Hassan. 'Who's Who in the Nusra Front?', *The New Arab*, 15 December 2014. www.alaraby.co.uk/english/politics/2014/12/15/whos-who-in-the-nusra-front.

AFP (Agence France-Presse). 'Syria Opposition Commemorates Hama Massacre'. *The Telegraph*, 2 February 2012. www.telegraph.co.uk/news/world news/middleeast/syria/9056350/Syria-opposition-commemorates-Hama-massacre.html.

Ahmed, Yusra. 'Syria's Muslim Brotherhood Leader Highlights Reforms, Future Plans-Interview'. *Zaman Al Wasl*, 20 March 2015. https://en.zamanalwsl.net/news/9402.html.

Ajbaili, Mustapha. 'Saudi: Muslim Brotherhood a Terrorist Group'. *Al-Arabiya*, 7 March 2014. http://english.alarabiya.net/en/News/middle-east/2014/03/07/Saudi-Arabia-declares-Muslim-Brotherhood-terrorist-group.html.

Akkad, Dania, Dahan, Nadine and Al-Shimale, Zouhir. 'Jaish al-Islam Says it Inflated Hostage Numbers, Leaving Syrian Families in the Dark'. *Middle East Eye*, 13 April 2018. www.middleeasteye.net/news/revealed-thousands-missing-syrians-not-jaish-al-islam-1492653856.

al-Amine, Hazim. 'Leader of Syrian Muslim Brotherhood Discloses Secret Offer from Iran'. *Al-Monitor* (originally published in *al-Hayat*, translated by Naria Tanoukhi), 20 January 2012. www.al-monitor.com/pulse/politics/2012/01/tayfour-to-al-hayat-iran-offered.html#ixzz47rSW2vW2.

Al-Assad, Hafez. 'Asad's Remarks about the Moslem Brotherhood'. *Damascus Home Service*. Damascus: BBC Monitoring Middle East, 30 June 1979.

'Excerpts from Recording of Speech Made at Graduation of Paratroopers in Latakia'. *Damascus Home Service*. Damascus: BBC Monitoring Middle East, 1 October 1981.

Al-Attar, Issam. 'Statement from the Muslim Brotherhood in Syria'. 9 July 1980, in Umar abd Al-Hakim, *The Islamic Jihadi Revolution in Syria* (in Arabic). Peshawar: n.p., 1991, p. 574.

'Untitled Letter in Response to the Artillery Massacre, Translated by the British Embassy Damascus'. 28 June 1979.

Words, vol. 2, Aachen: Dar al-Islamiya l-l-Alam, 2008.

Al-Bayanouni, Ali. 'The Muslim Brotherhood Wants a Future for All Syrians'. *The Guardian*, 7 August 2012. www.theguardian.com/commentisfree/2012/aug/06/syria-middleeast.

'No One Owns Syria's Uprising'. *The Guardian*, 16 April 2011. www.theguardian.com/commentisfree/2011/apr/16/syria-uprising-assad-blames-extremists.

Al-Fagali, Badra Bakhus. 'Dissent Continues among Syrian Opposition.' *Al-Diyar*. London: BBC Monitoring Middle East, 6 April 2006.

Al-Hakim, Umar abd. The Islamic Jihadi Revolution in Syria *(in Arabic)*. Peshawar: Unknown, 1991.

al-Hourani, Noura. 'Former FSA Fighter Recounts Why He Left'. *Syria: Direct*, 6 May 2015. http://syriadirect.org/news/former-fsa-fighter-recounts-why-he-left/.

al-Jaza'iri, Mahmud. 'Al-Jazeera Interviews Syria's Muslim Brotherhood Official on Recent Protests', in *Al-Jazeera*. Doha: BBC Monitoring Middle East, 13 April 2011.

Al-Khalidi, Suleiman. 'Syrian Forces Kill Three Protesters in Southern City'. *Reuters*, 19 March 2011.

Al-Majd. 'Jordan Reportedly Bans Syrian Muslim Brotherhood Leaders from Returning'. London: BBC Monitoring Middle East, 24 July 2000.

Al-Masri, Ahmad. 'Al-Banayuni [sic] Rejects Foreign Help Despite Opposition to Regime in Syria'. *Al-Quds al-Arabi* (London: BBC Monitoring Middle East, 15 November 2008.

Al-Masri, Fahd al-Argha. 'Muslim Brotherhood Chief Announces End of "Truce" with Syria'. *Free Syria*. London: BBC Monitoring Middle East, 15 August 2010.

Al-Mujahideen in Syria. 'News'. *Abstracts from Al-Nazeer no. 36*, 14 July1980.

1981 'The News'. *Abstracts from Al-Nazeer, no. 38*.

Al-Nahas (@LabibAlNahhas), Labib. Twitter, 3 August 2016. https://twitter.com/LabibAlNahhas/status/760559439749476352.

Al-Nahas, Labib. 'I'm a Syrian and I Fight Isil Every Day. It Will Take More than Bombs from the West to Defeat this Menace'. *The Telegraph*, 21 July 2015. www.telegraph.co.uk/news/worldnews/islamic-state/11752714/Im-a-Syrian-and-I-fight-Isil-every-day.-We-need-more-than-bombs-from-the-West-to-win-this-battle.html.

Al-Qassemi, Sultan Sooud. 'Morsi's Win Is Al Jazeera's Loss'. *Al-Monitor* (1 July 2012), www.al-monitor.com/pulse/originals/2012/al-monitor/morsys-win-is-al-jazeeras-loss.html.

'Qatar's Brotherhood Ties Alienate Fellow Gulf States'. *Al-Monitor*, 23 January 2013, www.al-monitor.com/pulse/originals/2013/01/qatar-muslim-brotherhood.html.

Al-Sham (@saleelalmajd1), Muzmajer. Twitter, 4 August 2014, https://twitter.com/saleelalmajd1/status/495977025984008192.

Al-Shoumari, Layla. 'Muslim Brotherhood Paves Way for Qatar's Ascent'. *Al-Akhbar*, 12 April 2013, http://english.al-akhbar.com/node/15508.

Al-Siba'i, Mustafa. 'Mutual Responsibility', in *Islamism: A Documentary and Reference Guide*, edited by John Calvert. Westport: Greenwood Press, 2008, pp. 83–7.

Al-Sibai, Mustafa. 'Al-Takaful al-Ijtimai', in *Arab Socialism. [al-Ishtirakīyah Al-'Arabīyah]: A Documentary Survey*, edited by Sami Ayad Hanna and George H. Gardner. Leiden: Brill, 1969, pp. 149–71.

'The Establishment of Islam as the State Religion of Syria', *The Muslim World* 44, nos 3–4 (1954): 217–26.

Al-Suri, Abu Musab. 'Lessons Learned from the Armed Jihad Ordeal in Syria'. Translated and published by the Combatting Terrorism Centre (CTC), West Point, www.ctc.usma.edu/v2/wp-content/uploads/2013/10/Lessons-Learned-from-the-Jihad-Ordeal-in-Syria-Translation.pdf.

al-Tamimi, Aymenn J. Twitter, 29 August 2016, https://twitter.com/ajaltamimi/status/770171683244244993.

Al-Youssef, Yaser Ibrahim. Twitter (in Arabic), 6 August 2016, https://twitter.com/AlyousefYasser/status/761597701993660416.

Bibliography

al-Ziabi, Jamil. 'Qatari FM: We Do not Support the Muslim Brotherhood (translated by Kamal Fayad)'. *Al-Monitor* (originally published in *Al-Hayat*), 22 February 2015, www.al-monitor.com/pulse/politics/2015/02/qatar-foreign-minister-gulf-hezbollah-brotherhood.html.

Albrecht, Holger. *Raging against the Machine: Political Opposition under Authoritarianism in Egypt*. Syracuse: Syracuse University Press, 2013.

Alloush, Mohammad. 'Reflections on the Syrian Brotherhood's Document'. *Al-Jazeera* (2012), www.aljazeera.net/knowledgegate/opinions/2012/4/2/%D8%AA%D8%A3%D9%85%D9%84%D8%A7%D8%AA-%D9%81%D9%8A-%D9%88%D8%AB%D9%8A%D9%82%D8%A9-%D8%A5%D8%AE%D9%88%D8%A7%D9%86-%D8%B3%D9%88%D8%B1%D9%8A%D8%A7#2.

Anjarini, Sahib. 'The Story of Al-Tawhid Brigade: Fighting for Sharia in Syria'. *Al-Monitor* (originally published in *al-Safir*), 22 August 2013, www.al-monitor.com/pulse/security/2013/10/syria-opposition-islamists-tawhid-brigade.html.

Anjarini, Suhaib. 'Harakat Hazm: America's New Favorite Jihadist Group', *al-Akhbar*, 22 May 2014, http://english.al-akhbar.com/node/19874.

Anonymous interview. 2015.

AP. 'Syria Cuts Off Iraqi Pipeline', *The Globe and Mail*, 20 April 1982.

As-Sibaa'ie, Mustafa. *The Life of the Prophet Muhammad: Highlights and Lessons*. Translated by Nasiruddin Al-Khattab. Riyadh: International Islamic Publishing House, 2003.

Associated Press. 'Bomb Explosion in Syria Kills 64 and Hurts 135 in Crowded Area', *The New York Times*, 30 November 1981, www.nytimes.com/1981/11/30/world/bomb-explosion-in-syria-kills-64-and-hurts-135-in-crowded-area.html.

1985 'Syria Offering Amnesty to Underground Group', *The New York Times*, 27 January 1985.

Astih, Paula. 'Muslim Brotherhood to Al-Sharq Al-Awsat: We Have Formed Armed Battalions to Defend Ourselves and the Wronged'. *Al-Sharq al-Awsat*. Beirut: BBC Monitoring Middle East, 5 August 2012.

'Attack at Syrian Army Barracks, Text of Statement by Syrian Interior Minister and Deputy Martial Law Governor, Adnan Dabbagh'. *Damascus Home Service*. Damascus: BBC Monitoring Middle East, 22 June 1979.

Azzam, Abdullah. 'The Defence of Muslim Lands: The Most Important Individual Duties', *c.* 1985, https://archive.org/stream/Kklkkkk/20#page/n0/mode/2up.

'The Soul Shall Rise Tomorrow: The Story of Marwan Hadid'. From Dhilal Surat at-Tawbah, published on *Milestones on the Road to Firmness in Faith*, https://iskandrani.wordpress.com/2008/02/09/the-soul-shall-rise-tomorrow-the-story-of-marwan-hadid/.

Barnard, Anne. 'Syria Opposition Group Is Routed and Divided', *The New York Times*, 14 March 2012, www.nytimes.com/2012/03/15/world/middleeast/syria-torture-report-military-maintains-assaults.html.

Batatu, Hanna. 'Some Observations on the Social Roots of Syria's Ruling Military Group and the Causes for Its Dominance', *Middle East Journal* 35, no. 3 (1981): 331–44.

'Syria's Muslim Brethren', *MERIP Reports*, no. 110 (1982): 12–36.
Syria's Peasantry: the Descendants of Its Lesser Rural Notables, and Their Politics. Princeton: Princeton University Press, 1999.
'The Bayanouni–Khaddam Link-up: Is the Opposition Real Now?', *Syria Comment*, 17 March 2006, http://faculty-staff.ou.edu/L/Joshua.M.Landis-1/syria blog/2006/03/bayanouni-khaddam-link-up-_114264946582158617.htm.
Bayly-Winder, R. 'Islam as the State Religion a Muslim Brotherhood View in Syria', *The Muslim World* 44, nos 3–4 (1954): 215–17.
Beach, Stephen W. 'Social Movement Radicalization: The Case of the People's Democracy in Northern Ireland'. *The Sociological Quarterly* 18, no. 3 (1977): 305–18.
Beaumont, Peter. 'Mohammed Bouazizi: The Dutiful Son Whose Death Changed Tunisia's Fate'. *The Guardian*, 21 January 2011, www.theguardian.com/world/2011/jan/20/tunisian-fruit-seller-mohammed-bouazizi.
Becker, Petra. 'Syrian Muslim Brotherhood: Still a Crucial Actor', *SWP Comments 34*. Berlin: German Institute for International and Security Affairs, 2013.
Bellin, Eva. 'The Robustness of Authoritarianism in the Middle East: Exceptionalism in Comparative Perspective'. *Comparative Politics* 36, no. 2 (2004): 139–57.
Bergan, Peter and Cruickshank, Paul. 'Revisiting the Early Al Qaeda: An Updated Account of its Formative Years', *Studies in Conflict and Terrorism* 35, no. 1 (2012): 1–36.
Berman, Asher. 'Rebel Groups in Jabal al-Zawiyah', *Institute for the Study of War*, 26 July 2012, www.understandingwar.org/sites/default/files/Backgrounder_RebelGroupsJebelAlZawiyah_31July.pdf.
Bermeo, Nancy. 'Democracy and the Lessons of Dictatorship', *Comparative Politics* 24, no. 3 (1992): 273–91.
Berrebi, Claude. 'Evidence about the Link between Education, Poverty and Terrorism among Palestinians', *Peace Economics, Peace Science and Public Policy* 13, no. 1 (2007): 1–36.
Bhatia, Shyam. 'Situation in Syrian Town Fluid Despite Army Step', *The Times of India*, 29 April 1980.
Bilyakov, Vladimir. 'Muslim Brotherhood's "Aggressive Campaign against Syrian Regime".' London: BBC Summary of World Broadcasts, 1980.
Bin-Qinnah, Khadijah. 'Syrian Muslim Brotherhood leader interviewed on proposed reform plan.' In *Al-Jazeera TV*. Doha: BBC Summary of World Broadcasts, 2004.
Black, Ian.'Homs: The Story behind Mani's Extraordinary Images from the Frontline', *The Guardian*, 25 November 2011, www.theguardian.com/world/2011/nov/25/homs-mani-images-frontline.
Block, Melissa. 'In Syria, Homs Emerges as Center of Protest', *NPR*, 30 August 2011, www.npr.org/2011/08/30/140070135/in-syria-homs-emerges-as-center-of-protest-movement.
Booysen, Hanlie. 'Surviving the Syrian Uprising: The Syrian Muslim Brotherhood', in *New Opposition in the Middle East*, edited by Dara Conduit and Shahram Akbarzadeh. New York: Palgrave Macmillan, 2018, pp. 151–76.

'Explaining the Moderate Platform of the Syrian Muslim Brotherhood: Against the Inclusion-Moderation Hypothesis', PhD Thesis, Wellington: Victoria Univeristy of Wellington, 2018.

Borger, Julian. 'Arab Monitors Visit Restive Syrian City: Protest in Homs Over Fears of 'Whitewash Inspection' Claims of Tanks Hidden after Army Withdrawal'. *The Guardian*, 28 December 2011.

Boudreau, Vincent. *Resisting Dictatorship: Repression and Protest in Southeast Asia*. Cambridge: Cambridge University Press, 2004.

Brady, Thomas F. 'Syrians Using Force to Break a Protest Strike by Merchants', *The New York Times*, 9 May 1967.

Brand, Laurie A. 'Economics and Shifting Alliances: Jordan's Relations with Syria and Iraq, 1975–81', *International Journal of Middle East Studies* 23 (1994): 393–413.

Broadmead, Philip. 'E 15809/2603/89 no. 136: Disturbances in Syria'. *British Embassy Damascus*, 1948.

Brotherhood, The Media Office of the Fighting Vanguard of the Muslim. 'Untitled letter', 11 May 1979.

Brown, Nathan J. *When Victory Is Not an Option: Islamist Movements in Arab Politics*. Ithaca: Cornell University Press, 2012.

Amr Hamzawy and Marina Ottaway. 'Islamist Movements and the Democratic Process in the Arab World: Exploring the Grey Zones'. Washington, DC: Carnegie Endowment for International Peace/Herbert-Quandt-Stiftung, 2006.

Cafarella, Jennifer and Casagrande, Genevieve. 'Syrian Armed Opposition Forces in Aleppo', *Institute for the Study of War*, 13 February 2016, www.understandingwar.org/sites/default/files/Syrian%20Armed%20Opposition%20Forces%20in%20Aleppo_0.pdf.

Carmichael, Lachlan. 'US Hedges Its Bets on Syria: Analysts', *Agence France Presse*, 3 April 2011.

Cavatorta, Francesco. '"Divided They Stand, Divided They Fail": Opposition Politics in Morocco', *Democratization* 16, no. 1 (2009): 147–56.

'Clashes between al-Nusra and al-Zinki in Aleppo', 6 October 2015, www.zamanalwsl.net/news/64774.html.

Cobb, Sara. *Speaking of Violence: The Politics and Poetics of Narrative in Conflict Resolution*. Oxford: Oxford University Press, 2013.

Commins, David. *Historical Dictionary of Syria*. London: The Scarecrow Press, 1996.

Islamic Reform: Politics and Social Change in Late Ottoman Syria. New York: Oxford University Press, 1990.

Conduit, Dara. 'The Patterns of Syrian Uprising: Comparing Hama in 1980–82 and Homs in 2011', *British Journal of Middle Eastern Studies* 44, no. 1 (2017): 73–87.

'The Syrian Muslim Brotherhood and the Spectacle of Hama', *The Middle East Journal* 70, no. 2 (2016): 211–26.

'Constitution of the Republic of Syria', *Middle East Journal* 7, no. 4 (1953).

Cook, Steven A. 'Unholy Alliance: How Syria Is Bringing Israel, Iran, and Saudi Arabia Together', *The Atlantic*, 9 May 2011, www.theatlantic.com/inter

national/archive/2011/05/unholy-alliance-how-syria-is-bringing-israel-iran-and-saudi-arabia-together/238084/.
'Court in Syria Dooms 21 for Part in Riots in Hama', *The New York Times*, 3 May 1964.
'Covenant and Charter'. Istanbul: The Muslim Brotherhood in Syria, 2012.
Da'dush, Ahmad. 'Al-Shaqfah: There Is No Armed Organization for the Syrian Muslim Brotherhood'. *Al-Jazeera*. Doha: BBC Monitoring Middle East, 10 April 2013.
Dabashi, Hamid. *The Green Movement in Iran*. London: Transaction Publishers, 2011.
Dabbagh, Heba. *Just Five Minutes: Nine Years in the Prisons of Syria*. Translated by Bayan Khatib. Toronto: Unknown, 2007.
'The Damascus Declaration for Democratic National Change (translated by Joshua Landis)', *Syria Comment*, 1 November 2005, http://faculty-staff.ou.edu/L/Joshua.M.Landis-1/syriablog/2005/11/damascus-declaration-in-english.htm.
'Damascus Radio Broadcast: Syrian Allegation of Jordanian Aid for Muslim Brotherhood'. London: BBC Monitoring Middle East, 20 November 1980.
'The Damascus Spring', *Carnegie Middle East Center* (1 April 2012), http://carnegie-mec.org/diwan/48516?lang=en.
'Damascus Suffering War Nerves: Hama Rebellion Fans Discontent in Syrian Capital', *The Washington Post*, 20 April 1964.
Damascus, US Embassy. 'The Muslim Brothers in Syria; Part 1: Could They Win an Election Here?', *Wikileaks*, 8 February 2006, www.wikileaks.org/plusd/cables/06DAMASCUS517_a.htm.
  'The Syrian Muslim Brotherhood', *Wikileaks*, 16 February 1985, www.wikileaks.org/plusd/cables/85DAMASCUS1314_a.html.
'Deaths in Syria as Protests Continue', *Al Jazeera*, 2 April 2011, www.aljazeera.com/news/middleeast/2011/04/201141132440493496.html.
'Declaration of Program of the Islamic Revolution in Syria'. Damascus: The Higher Command of the Islamic Revolution in Syria, 1980.
Dean, Aiman, Cruickshank, Paul and Lister, Tim, *Nine Lives: My Time as MI6's Top Spy Inside al-Qaeda*, London: Oneworld, 2018.
Dekmejian, R. Hrair, *Islam in Revolution: Fundamentalism in the Arab World* (2nd edn), Syracuse: Syracuse University Press, 1985.
Della Porta, Donatella. *Mobilizing for Democracy: Comparing 1989 and 2011*. Oxford: Oxford University Press, 2014.
Devlin, John F. *The Ba'th Party: A History from Its Origins to 1966*. Stanford: Hoover Institution Press, 1976.
Dickinson, Elizabeth. *Godfathers and Thieves, Part Four: How the Syrian Revolution Was Crowdfunded*. DECA, 2014. Available at: www.decastories.com/godfathers/.
Djerejian, Edward P. and Martin, William. *Danger and Opportunity: An American Ambassador's Journey through the Middle East*. New York: Simon & Schuster, 2008.
Drysdale, Alasdair. 'The Asad Regime and Its Troubles', *MERIP Reports*, no. 110 (1982): 3–11 + 36.

Dukhan, Haian. 'Tribes and Tribalism in the Syrian Uprising.' *Syria Studies* 6, no. 2 (2014): 1–28.

State and Tribes in Syria: Informal Alliances and Conflict Patterns, New York: Routledge, 2019.

Durrar, Riad. 'Letter from a Group of the Sons of the Muslim Brotherhood', Facebook, 12 January 2014, www.facebook.com/riaddrar/posts/337902093014536.

Duverger, Maurice. *Political Parties*. Translated by Barbara North and Robert North (3rd edn). Paris: Methuen & Co Ltd., 1967.

'E 2101/171/89 – Syria: Weekly Summary no. 7', UK Foreign Office, Week ending 18 February 1947.

'E 2507/171/89 – Correspondence Respecting Syria Part 1', *British Embassy Damascus*, week ending 25 February 1947.

'E 7787/171/89 – Syria: Political Summary no. 5 for July 1947', *British Embassy Damascus*, received by UK Foreign Office, 25 August 1947.

'E 9383/213/89: Extract from the Weekly Political Summary no 230 Syria and Lebanon (Secret)', *British Embassy Damascus*, 1946.

'E 10404/171/89 – Syria Political Summary no 7 for September 1947', *British Embassy Damascus*, received 7 November 1947.

'E 12267/213/89 – Weekly Political Summary no. 241', UK Foreign Office, Week ending 3 December 1947.

'E 15809/2603/89 – Further Correspondence Respecting Syria Part 2', *British Embassy Damascus*, 1948.

Edgar, Adrienne. 'The Islamic Opposition in Egypt and Syria: A Comparative Study', *Journal of Arab Affairs* 6, no. 1 (1987): 82–108.

'Editorial', *Al-Nadhir no. 42* (English edition), 8 January 1982.

'Editorial: The Declaration of the National Alliance for the Liberation of Syria', *Al-Nadhir no. 45* (English edition), 27 March 1982.

El-Gamal, Rania and Hammond, Andrew. 'Mistrust of Syria's Muslim Brotherhood lingers', *Reuters*, 12 November 2012, www.reuters.com/article/us-syria-crisis-brotherhood-idUSBRE8AB1CQ20121112.

Eleiba, Ahmed. 'A Tapestry of War'. *Al-Ahram*, 10 April 2014, http://weekly.ahram.org.eg/News/5913/32/A-tapestry-of-war.aspx.

Eliassen, Kjell A. and Svaasand, Lars. 'The Formation of Mass Political Organizations: An Analytical Framework', *Scandinavian Political Studies* 10, no. A10 (1975): 95–121.

Esposito, John L. *Islam: The Straight Path* (3rd edn). New York: Oxford University Press, 2005.

'EU Recognises Syria Opposition Bloc', *Al-Jazeera*, 20 November 2012, www.aljazeera.com/news/europe/2012/11/20121119195737909518.html.

'Explosions in Aleppo Work of Muslim Brotherhood', *Damascus Home Service*. Damascus: BBC Summary of World Broadcasts, 1980.

Fakher, Hamza, Weiss, Michael and Milne, Brian. 'Revolution in Danger: A Critical Appraisal of the Syrian National Council with Recommendations for Reform', The Henry Jackson Society, 2012, http://henryjacksonsociety.org/wp-content/uploads/2012/02/SNC.pdf.

Farrall, Leah. 'Revisiting al-Qaida's Foundation and Early History', *Perspectives on Terrorism* 11, no. 6 (2017): 17–37.

Farrall, Leah and Hamid, Mustafa. *The Arabs at War in Afghanistan*. London: Hurst, 2015.
Faylaq al-Sham (@ShamLegion). Twitter, 5 August 2016, https://twitter.com/ShamLegion/status/761546905038053376.
'FCO 93/2253: Letter from From CJS Rundle, FCO Research Department', *British Embassy Damascus*, 1 October 1979.
'FCO 93/2253: Letter from From Vincent Fean', *British Embassy Damascus*, 18 September 1979.
'FCO 93/2253: Letter from Vincent Fean to Douglas Gordon on Husni Abo's Televised Confession', British Embassy, 7 September 1979.
'FCO 93/2943: Leading Personalities in Syria.' *British Embassy Damascus*, 1981.
'FCO 93/2944: Syria Internal: Muslim Brotherhood – Damascus Telno 404', *British Embassy Damascus*, December 3 1981.
'FCO 93/3280: FM Damascus 081040Z FEB 82: TELNO u25/43', *British Embassy Damascus*, 8 February 1982.
Fean, Vincent. 'FCO 93/2253: 014/1 Correspondence to Douglas Gordon titled "Moslem Brothers"', *British Embassy Damascus*, 15 August 1979.
  'FCO 93/2253: Syria Internal: Moslem Brotherhood', *British Embassy Damascus*, 14 November 1979.
'First Hama "Plotter" Sentenced to Death', *The Jerusalem Post*, 21 April 1964.
Ford, P.W. 'FCO 93/301 – Letter to MLH Hope – Disturbances in Syria', *British Embassy Beirut*, 26 February 1973.
Freer, Courtney. 'Rentier Islamism: The Role of the Muslim Brotherhood in the Gulf', *LSE Middle East Center* (2015), http://eprints.lse.ac.uk/64446/1/RentierIslamism.pdf.
  Rentier Islamism: The Influence of the Muslim Brotherhood in Gulf Monarchies, Oxford: Oxford University Press, 2018.
Friedman, Thomas. *From Beirut to Jerusalem*. London: HarperCollins, 1995.
Gardener, John. 'NY 1012/1 – Leading Personalities in Syria', UK Foreign Office, 15 January 1955.
Gause, Gregory F. 'Why Middle East Studies Missed the Arab Spring: The Myth of Authoritarian Stability', *Foreign Affairs* 90, no. 4 (2011): 81–90.
George, Alan, *Syria: Neither Bread Nor Freedom*. London: Zed Books, 2003.
Ghadbian, Najib. 'New Syrian Brotherhood Leader: Continuity or Change?', *Carnegie Endowment for International Peace*, 8 September 2010, http://carnegieendowment.org/sada/?fa=41527.
Ghusheh, Ibrahim. *The Red Minaret: Memoirs of Ibrahim Ghusheh (Ex-spokesman of Hamas)*. Beirut: Al-Zaytouna Centre, 2013.
Goldstone, Jack A., and Tilly, Charles. 'Threat (and Opportunity): Popular Action and State Responses in the Dynamics of Contentious Action', in *Silence and Voice in the Study of Contentious Politics*, edited by Ronald R. Aminzade, Jack A. Goldstone, Doug McAdam, Elizabeth J. Perry, William H. Sewell, Sidney Tarrow and Charles Tilly. Cambridge: Cambridge University Press, 2001, pp. 179–95.
Gourlay, William. 'Kurdayetî: Pan-Kurdish Solidarity and Cross-Border Links in Times of War and Trauma', *Middle East Critique* 27, no. 1 (2017): 25–42.

Gresh, Alain. '"The Bullets Killed Our Fear": Syria Waits for Ramadan', *Le Monde Diplomatique*, 1 August 2011, http://mondediplo.com/2011/08/03syria.

'Hafez Meets Hama Citizens', *The Jerusalem Post*, 19 April 1964.

Hajjar, Roula and Daragahi, Borzou. 'At Least 18 Killed in Syrian Crackdown; An Assault Is Launched in the City of Homs, Activists Say, to End Demonstrations and Detain Protest Leaders', *Los Angeles Times*, 12 May 2011, http://articles.latimes.com/2011/may/11/world/la-fg-syria-protests-20110512.

Hassan, Hassan. 'How the Syrian Muslim Brotherhood Hijacked Syria's Revolution', *Foreign Policy*, 13 March 2013, www.foreignpolicy.com/articles/2013/03/13/how_the_muslim_brotherhood_hijacked_syria_s_revolution.

'Saudis Overtaking Qatar in Sponsoring Syrian Rebels', *The National*, 15 May 2013, www.thenational.ae/saudis-overtaking-qatar-in-sponsoring-syrian-rebels-1.471446.

'In Syria, the Brotherhood's Influence Is on the Decline', *The National*, 1 April 2014, www.thenational.ae/thenationalconversation/comment/in-syria-the-brotherhoods-influence-is-on-the-decline.

Hatina, Meir. 'Appendix: Translation of Muṣṭafā l-Sibāʿī's Essay "ʿUlamāʾ and Politics" in an Earlier Sunnī Version of Khomeini's Rule of the Jurist: Mustafā l-Sibāī on Ulamā and Politics', *Arabica* 57, no. 4 (2010): 470–6.

'Restoring a Lost Identity: Models of Education in Modern Islamic Thought', *British Journal of Middle Eastern Studies* 33, no. 2 (2006): 179–97.

Hawwa, Said. This Is My Experience and This Is My Testimony *(in Arabic)*. Cairo: Maktabat Wahba, 1987.

Hegghammer, Thomas. *Jihad in Saudi Arabia: Violence and Pan-Islamism since 1979*. Cambridge: Cambridge University Press, 2010.

'The Rise of Muslim Foreign Fighters: Islam and the Globalization of Jihad', *International Security* 25, no. 3 (2010): 53–94.

Heras, Nicholas A. 'In Brief: A Snapshot of Two Rebel Commanders Vying for Survival in Damascus Governorate', *Militant Leadership Monitor* 7, no. 12 (2017). Available at: https://jamestown.org/brief/brief-snapshot-two-rebel-commanders-vying-survival-damascus-governorate-free/.

Hider, James and Blanford, Nicholas. 'There Was a Massacre in the Streets but We Are not Afraid, Say Witnesses', *The Times*, 25 March 2011.

Hijazi, Ihsan A. 'Jordan, Joining Trend, Curbs Islamic Militants', *The New York Times*, 9 December 1985, p. 6.

'Jordanian Prime Minister to Visit Syria', *The New York Times*, 12 November 1985, p. A3.

Hinnebusch, Raymond. *Authoritarian Power and State Formation in Bathist Syria: Army, Party and Peasant*. Boulder: Westview Press, 1990.

'Syria', in *The Politics of Islamic Revivalism: Diversity and Unity*, edited by Shireen T. Hunter. Bloomington: Indiana University Press, 1988.

Syria: Revolution from Above. London: Routledge, 2001.

Hourani, Albert. *A History of the Arab Peoples*. London: Faber and Faber, 1991.

Howe, Marvine. 'Syria Concedes Wide Unrest Over Policies', 28 March 1980.

Hudson, John. 'U.N. Envoy Revises Syria Death Toll to 400,000', *Foreign Policy*, 22 April 2016, http://foreignpolicy.com/2016/04/22/u-n-envoy-revises-syria-death-toll-to-400000/.
Husaini, Ishak Musa. *The Muslim Brethren: The Greatest of Modern Islamic Movements*. Beirut: Khayat's College Book Cooperative, 1956.
Hussein, Tam. 'A Brotherhood Vision for Syria: In Conversation with the Former Leader of the Syrian Muslim Brotherhood', *The Majalla* (2013), http://eng.majalla.com/2013/11/article55247035.
'The Brotherhood's Man in London', *Majalla*, 23 April 2013, https://web.archive.org/web/20171129085905/http://eng.majalla.com/2013/04/article55240699.
Ibrahim, Youssef M. 'Syria and Jordan Still Poised on Border', *The New York Times*, 8 December 1980.
Ignatius, David. 'Foreign Nations' Proxy War in Syria Creates Chaos', *The Washington Post*, 2 October 2014, www.washingtonpost.com/opinions/david-ignatius-foreign-nations-proxy-war-creates-syrian-chaos/2014/10/02/061fb50c-4a7a-11e4-a046-120a8a855cca_story.html?utm_term=.c1b29ac1fd2e.
'IJMES Translation and Transliteration Guide', *International Journal of Middle East Studies* (2013), http://ijmes.chass.ncsu.edu/IJMES_Translation_and_Transliteration_Guide.htm.
'IJMES Word List', *International Journal of Middle East Studies*, 5 October 2010, https://ijmes.chass.ncsu.edu/docs/WordList.pdf.
'In New Blow to Assad, EU Recognizes New Syrian Opposition Bloc', *Al-Arabiya*, 19 November 2012, http://english.alarabiya.net/articles/2012/11/19/250551.html.
'Internal Syrian Opposition Claims No Ties to Exile Group', *The Daily Star*, 21 March 2006, www.dailystar.com.lb/News/Middle-East/2006/Mar-21/69201-internal-syrian-opposition-claims-no-ties-to-exile-group.ashx.
'An Interview', *Abstracts from al-Nazeer no. 38* (English edition), 9 September 1981.
'An Interview with Issam al-Attar, Leader of Syria's Muslim Brothers', *An-Nahar Arab Report and Memo*, 18 February 1980, pp. 3–5.
'An Interview with Mohammad Riad Al-Shaqfa, Leader of the Muslim Brotherhood', *ORSAM*, 16 January 2013, www.orsam.org.tr/index.php/Content/Analiz/3464?s=orsam%7Cenglish.
'Iraq's Chemical Warfare Program', *CIA* (2004), www.cia.gov/library/reports/general-reports-1/iraq_wmd_2004/chap5.html.
Isakhan, Benjamin. 'The Islamic State Attacks on Shia Holy Sites and the "Shrine Protection Narrative": Threats to Sacred Space as a Mobilization Frame', *Terrorism and Political Violence*, DOI: 10.1080/09546553.2017.1398741.
Isam, Wa'il. 'Syria's MB Leader Stresses Need to Get Al-Qa'idah-Linked Group out of Country', in *Al-Quds al-Arabi*. London: BBC Monitoring Middle East, 28 January 2014.
Ismael, Tareq Y. and Ismael, Jacqueline S. *The Communist Movement in Syria and Lebanon*. Gainesville: University Press of Florida, 1998.

Ismail, Salwa, *The Rule of Violence: Subjectivity, Memory and Government in Syria*. Cambridge: Cambridge University Press, 2018.

Jabhat Fateh al-Sham. 'The Start of the Third Stage of the Operation to Break the Siege of Aleppo, Operation Ibrahim al-Youssef (in Arabic)', YouTube, 13 August 2016, www.youtube.com/watch?v=C23ZlPnJlBo.

Jaloud, Aziza. Twitter (in Arabic), 4 August 2016, https://twitter.com/azizajaloud/status/761197889863442432.

Jocelyn, Thomas. 'Osama bin Laden on the Muslim Brotherhood', *The Long War Journal: Threat Matrix*, 10 May 2012, www.longwarjournal.org/archives/2012/05/osama_bin_laden_on_the_muslim.php.

'Jordanian Islamist Leader Denies Mediating between Syria and Muslim Brotherhood', *Al-Sharq Al-Awsat*. London: BBC Summary of World Broadcasts, 1999.

Joscelyn, Thomas. 'Al Qaeda Veteran Appears in Al Nusrah Front Video, Criticizes Rival', *Long War Journal*, 20 March 2014, www.longwarjournal.org/archives/2014/03/al_qaeda_veteran_app.php.

Kaczmarski, Marcin. *Russia–China Relations in the Post-Crisis International Order*. Abingdon: Routledge, 2015.

Karouny, Mariam. 'Syria's Islamist Rebels Join Forces against Assad', *Reuters*, 11 October 2012, www.reuters.com/article/us-syria-crisis-rebels-idUSBRE89A0Y920121011.

Kelemen, Michele. 'U.S. Wary as Qatar Ramps up Support of Syrian Rebels.' *NPR*, 26 April 2013, www.npr.org/2013/04/26/179248222/u-s-wary-as-qatar-ramps-up-support-of-syrian-rebels.

Khadduri, Majid 'Constitutional Development in Syria: With Emphasis on the Constitution of 1950', *Middle East Journal* 5, no. 2 (1951): 137–60.

Khalaf, Roula and Fielding-Smith, Abbie. 'How Qatar Seized Control of the Syrian Revolution', *Financial Times*, 17 May 2013, www.ft.com/cms/s/2/f2d9bbc8-bdbc-11e2-890a-00144feab7de.html.

Khatib, Line. 'Islamic and Islamist Revivalism in Syria: The Rise and Fall of Secularism in Ba'thist Syria', PhD thesis, McGill University, 2010.

Islamic Revivalism in Syria: The Rise and Fall of Ba'thist Secularism. Abingdon: Routledge, 2011.

Khoury, Philip S. *Syria and the French Mandate: The Politics of Arab Nationalism, 1920–1945*. Princeton: Princeton University Press, 1987.

Urban Notables and Arab Nationalism: The Politics of Damascus 1860–1920. Cambridge: Cambridge University Press, 1983.

Kifner, John. 1980 'Syria Starts Drive to Curb Terrorism: Guard Said to Fall on Grenade Assad Introduced Death Bill "New Chapter of the Conspiracy"', *The New York Times*, 4 July 1980.

'The Killing of the Commander of the Tawhid Brigade, one of the Main Leaders of the Armed Opposition in Syria', *Rai al-Youm*, 18 November 2013, www.raialyoum.com/?p=22455.

Kindy, Steve K. 'Unrest Mounts in Syria against Assad's Regime', *Boston Globe*, 28 March 1980.

Kirkpatrick, David D. 'Concerns about Al Qaeda in Syria Underscore Questions about Rebels', *The New York Times*, 21 August 2012, http://thelede.blogs

.nytimes.com/2012/08/21/concerns-about-al-qaeda-in-syria-underscore-questions-about-rebels/.
'Knocking on the Doors of Freedom: The Founders of the Syrian Revolution Facebook Pages Speak to al-Ahd,' *Al-Ahd no. 2*, 15 March 2013.
Kutschera, Chris. 'Syria: Muslim Brothers: The Question of Alliances', *The Middle East* 103 (May) (1983): 25–8.
'When the Brothers Fall Out', *The Middle East Magazine* 162 (1988): 21.
Lacroix, Stéphane. *Awakening Islam: The Politics of Religious Dissent in Contemporary Saudi Arabia*. Cambridge: Harvard University Press, 2011.
Lahoud, Nelly, Caudill, Stuart, Collins, Liam, Koehler-Derrick, Gabriel, Rassler, Don and al-`Ubaydi, Muhammad. 'Letters from Abbottabad: Bin Ladin Sidelined?', Combatting Terrorism Center at West Point, 3 May 2012, www.ctc.usma.edu/v2/wp-content/uploads/2012/05/CTC_LtrsFromAbottabad_WEB_v2.pdf.
Landis, Joshua. 'Khaddam Damns Bashar al-Asad', *Syria Comment*, 1 January 2006, http://faculty-staff.ou.edu/L/Joshua.M.Landis-1/syriablog/2006/01/khaddam-damns-bashar-al-asad.htm.
'The Man behind "Syria Revolution 2011" Facebook-Page Speaks Out', *Syria Comment*, 24 April 2011, www.joshualandis.com/blog/the-man-behind-syria-revolution-2011-facebook-page-speaks-out/.
'Syrian Revolution 2011 Facebook Page Administrator, Fidaaldin Al-Sayed Issa, Interviewed by Adam Almkvist', *Syria Comment*, 11 May 2011, www.joshualandis.com/blog/syrian-revolution-2011-facebook-page-adminis trator-fidaaldin-al-sayed-issa-interviewed-by-adam-almkvist/.
Landis, Joshua M. and Pace, Joe. 'The Syrian Opposition', *The Washington Quarterly* 30, no. 1 (2006–7): 45–68.
Laqueur, Walter Z. *Communism and Nationalism in the Middle East*. London: Routledge & Paul, 1956.
Lawson, Fred H. *Global Security Watch: Syria*. Denver: Praeger, 2013.
'Social Bases for the Hamah Revolt', *MERIP Reports*, no. 110 (1982): 24–8.
Why Syria Goes to War: Thirty Years of Confrontation, Ithaca: Cornell University Press, 1996.
Lee, Jenna. 2011 'Interview with Jonathan Schanzer', *Fox News: Live Event*, 1 April 2011.
Lefèvre, Raphaël. *Ashes of Hama: The Muslim Brotherhood in Syria*. London: Hurst, 2013.
'Can Syria's Muslim Brotherhood Salvage its Relations with Riyadh?', *Carnegie Middle East Center*, 28 March 2014, http://carnegie-mec.org/diwan/55052?lang=en.
'Islamism within a Civil War: The Syrian Muslim Brotherhood's Struggle for Survival', *Brookings Institute* (2015), www.brookings.edu/wp-content/uploads/2016/07/Syria_Lefevre-FINALE-1.pdf.
'*The Muslim Brotherhood Prepares for a Comeback in Syria*', Washington DC: Carnegie Endowment for International Peace, 2013.
'POMEPS Conversations 46 with Raphaël Lefèvre ~ 2/10/15 [Video]', *POMEPS*, 10 February 2015, http://pomeps.org/2015/02/10/pomeps-conversations-46-with-raphael-lefevre-21015/.

'A Revolution in Syria's Muslim Brotherhood?', *Carnegie Middle East Center*, 23 January 2014, http://carnegie-mec.org/diwan/54287?lang=en.
'Saudi Arabia and the Syrian Brotherhood', *Middle East Institute*, 27 September 2013, www.mei.edu/content/saudi-arabia-and-syrian-brotherhood.
'Syria in Crisis: A New Leader for Syria's Muslim Brotherhood?', *Carnegie Middle East Center*, 6 May 2014, http://carnegie-mec.org/diwan/55512.
'The Syrian Brotherhood's Armed Struggle', *Carnegie Middle East Centre*, 14 December 2012, http://carnegie-mec.org/publications/?fa=50380&lang=en.
'The Syrian Muslim Brotherhood's Alawi Conundrum', in *The Alawis of Syria: War, Faith and Politics in the Levant*, edited by Michael Kerr and Craig Larkin. Oxford: Oxford University Press, 2015, pp. 125–40.
Lefèvre, Raphaël and El-Yassir, Ali. 'Militias for the Syrian Muslim Brotherhood?', *Carnegie Endowment for International Peace*, 29 October 2013, http://carnegieendowment.org/sada/?fa=53452.
'The Sham Legion: Syria's Moderate Islamists', *Carnegie Middle East Center*, 14 April 2014, http://carnegie-mec.org/diwan/55344?lang=en.
Legum, Colin and Shaked, Hakim. *Arab Relations in the Middle East: The Road to Realignment*. London: Holmes & Meier Publishers, 1979.
Lerner, Daniel. *The Passing of Traditional Society: Modernizing the Middle East*. Glencoe: Free Press, 1958.
Lesch, David W. *Syria: The Fall of the House of Assad*. New Haven: Yale University Press, 2012.
'Letter Dated January 12', *American Minister at Damascus*, 1949.
Leverett, Flynt. *Inheriting Syria: Bashar's Trial by Fire*. Washington, DC: Brookings Institute, 2005.
Li, Darryl. '"Afghan Arabs", Real and Imagined', *Middle East Report* 41 (2011): 2–7.
Lia, Brynjar. *Architect of Global Jihad: The Life of Al-Qaida Strategist Abu Mus'ab al-Suri*. London: Hurst & Company, 2007.
'Libya Helps Bankroll Syrian Opposition Movement', *The Washington Post*, 5 November 2012, www.washingtonpost.com/world/middle_east/libya-helps-bankroll-syrian-opposition-movement/2012/11/05/98cd728a-2764-11e2-b2a0-ae18d6159439_story.html.
'The List of the Umma', *Al-Manar*, 7 July 1947.
Lister, Charles. Twitter, 24 May 2016, https://twitter.com/charles_lister/status/734836962847133696.
   Twitter, 24 August 2016, https://twitter.com/Charles_Lister/status/768428963127369728.
   Twitter, 28 August 2013, https://twitter.com/charles_lister/status/372427476682555392.
'Why Assad Is Losing', *Foreign Policy*, 5 May 2015, http://foreignpolicy.com/2015/05/05/why-assad-is-losing-syria-islamists-saudi/.
The Syrian Jihad: Al-Qaeda, The Islamic State and the Evolution of an Insurgency. London: Hurst, 2015.
'Jihadology Podcast: Syria Status Update with Charles Lister', *Jihadology*, 23 June 2015, https://jihadology.net/2015/06/23/jihadology-podcast-syria-status-update-with-charles-lister/.

Lobmeyer, Hans Gunter. 'Al-dimuqratiyya hiyya al-hall? The Syrian Opposition at the End of the Asad Era', in *Contemporary Syria: Liberalization between Cold War and Cold Peace*, edited by Eberhard Kienle. London: British Academic Press, 1994.

'Islamic Ideology and Secular Discourse', *Orient* 32, no. 3 (1991): 395–415.

Lodge, Tom. 'State of Exile: The African National Congress of South Africa, 1976–86', *Third World Quarterly* 9, no. 1 (1987): 1–27.

Long, Mark. 'Ribat, al-Qa'ida, and the Challenge for US Foreign Policy', *Middle East Journal* 63, no. 1 (2009): 31–47.

Love, Kennett. 'Moslem Brothers Faithful to Chief', *New York Times*, 27 February 1955.

Lund, Aron. 'Aleppo and the Battle for the Syrian Revolution's Soul', *Carnegie Europe*, 4 December 2012, http://carnegieeurope.eu/publications/?fa=50234.

'The Curious Case of the Commission for the Protection of Civilians', *Carnegie Middle East Center*, 6 November 2013, http://carnegie-mec.org/diwan/53518?lang=en.

'Going Home: An Interview with Tarif al-Sayyed Issa', *Carnegie Middle East Center*, 22 October 2015, http://carnegie-mec.org/diwan/61724?lang=en.

'Struggling to Adapt: The Muslim Brotherhood in a New Syria', Washington DC: Carnegie Endowment for International Peace, 2013.

'Syria in Crisis: Who and What Was Abu Khalid al-Suri? Part II', *Carnegie Middle East Center*, 25 February 2014, http://carnegie-mec.org/diwan/54634?lang=en.

'The Syria Muslim Brotherhood: Leadership Transition from Bayanouni to Shaqfa', *Syria Comment*, 21 August 2010, www.joshualandis.com/blog/the-syria-muslim-botherhood-leadership-transition-from-bayanouni-to-shaqfa-by-aron-lund/.

'The Syrian Brotherhood: On the Sidelines', *Middle East Institute*, 24 September 2013, www.mei.edu/content/syrian-muslim-brotherhood-sidelines.

Lust-Okar, Ellen. *Structuring Conflict in the Arab World: Incumbents, Opponents and Institutions*. Cambridge: Cambridge University Press, 2005.

MacFarquhar, Neil. 'Syrian Opposition Meets to Seek Unity', *The New York Times*, 8 November 2012, www.nytimes.com/2012/11/09/world/middleeast/syria-war-developments.html.

'Trying to Mold a Post-Assad Syria from Abroad', *The New York Times*, 5 May 2012, www.nytimes.com/2012/05/06/world/middleeast/from-abroad-trying-to-mold-a-post-assad-syria.html?_r=0.

Man, M.C. 'E 11501/1018/89 – Syrian Electoral Law', UK Foreign Office, 19 September 1949.

'E 11904/1012/89 no. 16 – Leading Personalities in Syria', UK Foreign Office, 1949.

'EY 1015/18 no. 5 – Formation of a Cabinet under Nazim al-Qudsi', UK Embassy Damascus, 5 June 1950.

Mansour, Ahmed. 'Adnan Saadeddine – The Brotherhood's Time in Syria, Episode 4', *Al-Jazeera*, 3 October 2012, www.aljazeera.net/home/print/0353e88a-286d-4266-82c6-6094179ea26d/2c67f0e3-02ac-4bd9-b2c5-d050bad6ab5d.

'Adnan Saadeddine – The Brotherhood's Time in Syria, Episode 4', *Al-Jazeera*, 12 September 2012, www.aljazeera.net/programs/centurywitness/2012/10/3/%D8%B9%D8%AF%D9%86%D8%A7%D9%86-%D8%B3%D8%B9%D8%AF-%D8%A7%D9%84%D8%AF%D9%8A%D9%86-%D8%B9%D8%B5%D8%B1-%D8%A7%D9%84%D8%A5%D8%AE%D9%88%D8%A7%D9%86-%D9%81%D9%8A-%D8%B3%D9%88%D8%B1%D9%8A%D8%A7-%D8%AC4.

'Without Borders: The Muslim Brotherhood and Political Reform in Syria (an Interview with Ali al-Bayanouni)', *Al-Jazeera*, 21 August 2005, www.aljazeera.net/programs/withoutbounds/2005/8/21/%D8%A7%D9%84%D8%A5%D8%AE%D9%88%D8%A7%D9%86-%D8%A7%D9%84%D9%85%D8%B3%D9%84%D9%85%D9%88%D9%86-%D9%88%D8%A7%D9%84%D8%A5%D8%B5%D9%84%D8%A7%D8%AD-%D8%A7%D9%84%D8%B3%D9%8A%D8%A7%D8%B3%D9%8A-%D8%A8%D8%B3%D9%88%D8%B1%D9%8A%D8%A7.

'Witness to Time – With Adnan Saadeddine', YouTube (Ikhwan Syria channel) (2012), www.youtube.com/watch?v=bCTf65YZRnU.

Marsh, Katherine and Chulov, Martin. 'Assad Blames Conspirators for Syrian Protests', *The Guardian*, 30 March 2011, www.theguardian.com/world/2011/mar/30/syrian-protests-assad-blames-conspirators.

Martin, Kevin W. *Syria's Democratic Years: Citizens, Experts, and Media in the 1950s*. Bloomington: University of Indiana Press, 2015.

Martin, Susanne and Perliger, Arie. 'Turning to and from Terror: Deciphering the Conditions under which Political Groups Choose Violent and Nonviolent Tactics', *Perspectives on Terrorism* 6, no. 4–5 (2012): 21–45.

Mayer, Thomas. 'The Islamic Opposition in Syria 1961–82', *Orient* 24, no. 4 (1983): 589–609.

McDonnell, Patrick J. 'Syria Says Troops Have Overrun Rebel Enclave in Homs', *Los Angeles Times*, 2 March 2012, http://articles.latimes.com/2012/mar/02/world/la-fg-syria-opposition-20120302.

'A Meeting with the Comptroller General Mohammad Riad al-Shaqfeh (in Arabic)', The Association of Syrian Writers, 30 October 2010, www.odabasham.net/%D9%85%D9%82%D8%A7%D8%A8%D9%84%D8%A7%D8%AA/43355-%D9%84%D9%82%D8%A7-43355.

'Members', Syrian National Council, 11 February 2012, http://web.archive.org/web/20120207234952/www.syriancouncil.org/en/members.html.

Middle East Watch. *Syria Unmasked*. New Haven: Yale University Press, 1991.

Mitchell, Richard P. *The Society of the Muslim Brothers*. Oxford: Oxford University Press, 1991.

'Mohammad Farouk Tayfour', *Carnegie Europe*, 1 February 2012, http://carnegieeurope.eu/publications/?fa=48371.

Montagu-Pollock, William. 'EY1015/31 no. 11 – Political Situation', *British Embassy Damascus*.

'EY1011/1: Syria: Annual Review for 1950', *British Embassy Damascus*, 6 January 1951.

'EY 1012/1 – Leading Personalities in Syria', *British Embassy Damascus*, 2 July 1951.

'EY 1016/1 – Political Situation in Syria', *British Embassy Damascus*, 8 January 1952.

Moore, Cerwyn. 'Foreign Bodies: Transnational Activism, the Insurgency in the North Caucasus and "Beyond"', *Terrorism and Political Violence* 27, no. 3 (2015): 395–415.

Morton, Michael. 'Foreign Capital Vital to Syria's Economic Boom', *The Jerusalem Post*, 10 May 1977.

Moubayed, Sami. 'The History of Political and Militant Islam in Syria', *Terrorism Monitor* 3, no. 15 (2005), www.jamestown.org/programs/tm/single/?tx_ttnews%5Btt_news%5D=550&tx_ttnews%5BbackPid%5D=180&no_cache=1#.VhJ-QI9Viko.

Under the Black Flag: At the Frontier of the New Jihad. London: I.B.Tauris, 2015.

Moubayed, Sami M. *Steel & Silk: Men and Women Who Shaped Syria 1900–2000*. Seattle: Cune Press, 2006.

Mouline, Nabil. *The Clerics of Islam: Religious Authority and Political Power in Saudi Arabia*. Translated by Ethan S. Rundell. New Haven: Yale University Press, 2014.

Moussalli, Ahmad S. 'The Geopolitics of Syrian-Iraqi Relations', *Middle East Policy* 7, no. 4 (2000): 100–9.

Mouton, Johann and Marais, H. C. *Basic Concepts in the Methodology of the Social Sciences* (Pretoria: HSRC, 1996).

Muhammad, Basil. *The Arab Supporters in Afghanistan*. Riyadh: Lajnat al-Birr al-Islamiyya, 1991.

Muslim Brotherhood, 'Text of the Project Offered by Adnan Saad al-Din and Ali Sadr al-Din al-Bayanouni as Part of a National Alliance with Opposition Political Parties and Groups for Rule in Syria (in Arabic)', 1981, 598. Available in: Umar abd Al-Hakim, *The Islamic Jihadi Revolution in Syria* (in Arabic). Peshawar: Unknown, 1991, p. 574.

Muslim Brotherhood. Hama: The Tragedy of the Times *(in Arabic)*. Beirut: al-Maktab al-Ilami, 1982.

'Muslim Brotherhood Leader Molham al-Droubi Exclusively Opens Up his Papers to al-Ahd', *al-Ahd no. 1*, 1 March 2013.

MuslimBrotherhood Sy (@IkhwanSyriaEn). Twitter, 26 July 2016, https://twitter.com/IkhwanSyriaEn/status/757335387337592834.

'National Charter of Syria', London: Syrian Muslim Brothehrood, 2002.

'New Coup in Syria'. *The New York Times*, 15 August 1949.

'New Violence Erupts in Two Syrian Cities Despite Assad Action', *The Globe and Mail*, 10 April 1980.

'News', *Al-Nadhir no. 77–78* (English edition), 3 February 1985.

Olmert, Yosef. 'The Syrian Arab Republic', in *Middle East Contemporary Survey, Vol. X 1986*, edited by Itamar Rabinovich and Haim Shaked. Boulder: Westview Press, 1988.

Orhan, Oytun. 'An Interview with Syrian Businessman Gazi Misirli (Gazwan Masri)', *ORSAM*, 25 January 2013, www.orsam.org.tr/index.php/Content/Convs/326?s=orsam%7Cenglish.

Oron, Yitzhak. *Middle East Record*, vol. 2, Jerusalem: Tel Aviv University, 1961.

Orton, Kyle. 'Al Qaeda Central in Syria', *The Syrian Intifada*, 14 September 2015, https://kyleorton1991.wordpress.com/2015/09/14/al-qaeda-central-in-syria/.
Oweis, Khaled Yacoub. 'Syria's Muslim Brotherhood Rise from the Ashes', *Reuters*, 6 May 2012, www.reuters.com/article/us-syria-brotherhood-idUSBRE84504R20120506.
Pace, Eric. 'Shift in Syria Is Setback for Extremists', *The New York Times*, 22 November 1970.
Pace, Joe. 'Riad al-Turk Interviewed by Joe Pace on Mehlis, the Opposition, Ghadry', *Syria Comment*, 8 September 2005, http://faculty-staff.ou.edu/L/Joshua.M.Landis-1/syriablog/2005/10/riad-al-turk-interviewed-by-joe-pace.htm.
Panebianco, Angelo. *Political Parties: Organization & Power*. Translated by Marc Silver. Cambridge: Cambridge University Press, 1988.
Pargeter, Alison. *The Muslim Brotherhood: The Burden of Tradition*. London: Saqi Books, 2010.
The Muslim Brotherhood: From Opposition to Power, London: Saqi books, 2013.
Perthes, Volker. *The Political Economy of Syria Under Assad*. London: I.B.Tauris, 1995.
Pettitt, Robin T. *Contemporary Party Politics*. New York: Palgrave Macmillan, 2014.
Phillips, Christopher. 'Into the Quagmire: Turkey's Frustrated Syria Policy', Chatham House (2012), www.chathamhouse.org/sites/files/chathamhouse/public/Research/Middle%20East/1212bp_phillips.pdf.
'Sectarianism and Conflict in Syria', *Third World Quarterly* 25, no. 2 (2015): 357–76.
Pierret, Thomas. *Religion and State in Syria: The Sunni Ulama from Coup to Revolution*. Cambridge: Cambridge University Press, 2011.
Pierret, Thomas. 'Syria: Old-Timers and Newcomers', in *The Islamists Are Coming: Who They Really Are*, edited by Robin Wright. Washington DC: Woodrow Wilson Center Press, pp. 71–80.
Pinto, Paulo G. 'Sufism, Moral Performance and the Public Sphere in Syria', *Revue des mondes musulmans et de la Méditerranée* (December 2006): 115–16.
'Political Committee', *National Coalition of Syrian Revolution and Opposition Forces* (2017), http://en.etilaf.org/coalition-components/general-body/political-committee.html.
Powers, Thomas. 'Burdened in Proof in Claiming Detailed Knowledge of Iraq's Illegal Weapons, US Officials May Have Jeopardized the Credibility of American Intelligence and Policy-Making for Years to Come', *Boston Globe*, 15 June 2003.
'Protests and Shooting in Syria as the Death Toll Climbs', *Al-Arabiya*, 25 March 2011.
Published by the Freedom Fighters in Syria Damascus. 'Commmunique no. 1 Issued by the Syrian Liberation Army', 1 September 1985.
Rabil, Robert G. 'The Syrian Muslim Brotherhood', in *The Muslim Brotherhood: The Organization and Policies of a Global Islamist Movement*, edited by Barry Rubin. New York: Palgrave Macmillan, 2010.

Rabinovich, Itamar. 'The Syrian Arab Republic (al-Jumhuriyyat Suriyya al-'Arabiyya)', in *Middle East Contemporary Survey, Vol. IX 1984–5*, edited by Itamar Rabinovich and Haim Shaked. Boulder: Westview Press, 1987.

Raja, Abdullah. 'Syrian National Coalition Official Comments on Muslim Brotherhood', *Zaman al-Wasl*. Doha: BBC Monitoring Middle East, 14 October 2013.

Rana, Muhammad Amir and Bukhari, Mubashar. *Arabs in Afghan Jihad*. Lahore: Pakistan Institute for Peace Studies, 2007.

Rassas, Mohammad Saied. 'Syria's Muslim Brotherhood: Past and Present', *Al-Monitor*, 5 January 2014, www.al-monitor.com/pulse/politics/2014/01/syria-muslim-brotherhood-past-present.html#.

Rathmell, Andrew. *Secret War in the Middle East: The Covert Struggle for Syria 1949–1961*. London: I.B.Tauris, 2013.

Reuters. 'Big Arab Army under Training to "Save Palestine"', *The Times of India*, 21 September 1947.

'Syria Opposition Forms United Front to Oust Assad', *Hurriyet Daily News*, 18 March 2006, www.hurriyetdailynews.com/syria-opposition-forms-united-front-to-oust-assad.aspx?pageID=438&n=syria-opposition-forms-united-front-to-oust-assad-2006-03-18.

'Wife of Syrian Dissident Is Slain in West Germany', 18 March 1982.

Riedel, Bruce. 'The 9/11 Attacks' Spiritual Father', *Brookings Institute* (2011), www.brookings.edu/research/opinions/2011/09/11-riedel.

Rinehart, Christine Sixta. *Volatile Social Movements and the Origins of Terrorism: The Radicalization of Change*. Lanham: Lexington Books, 2013.

Roded, Ruth. 'Lessons by a Syrian Islamist from the Life of the Prophet Muhammad', *Middle Eastern Studies* 42, no. 6 (2006): 855–72.

Roggio, Bill. 'Abu Musab al Suri Released from Syrian Custody: Report', *The Long War Journal*, 6 February 2012, www.longwarjournal.org/archives/2012/02/abu_musab_al_suri_re.php.

Rosen, Nir. 'Islamism and the Syrian Uprising', *Foreign Policy*, 8 March 2012, http://foreignpolicy.com/2012/03/08/islamism-and-the-syrian-uprising/.

Rouhani, Hassan (@HassanRouhani). 'Evening, @Jack. As I told @camanpour, my efforts geared 2 ensure my ppl'll comfortably b able 2 access all info globally as is their #right', Twitter, 1 October 2013, https://twitter.com/hassanrouhani/status/385138174822850560?lang=en.

Rubin, Barnett R. 'Arab Islamists in Afghanistan', in *Political Islam: Revolution, Radicalism, or Reform?*, edited by John L. Esposito. London: Lynne Rienner, 1997, pp. 179–207.

Saadeddine, Adnan. The Muslim Brotherhood in Syria: Notes and Memories *(in Arabic)*, vol. 1. Dar al-Amar, 2006.

The Muslim Brotherhood in Syria: Notes and Memories *(in Arabic)*, vol. 3. Dar al-Amar, 2006.

The Muslim Brotherhood in Syria: Notes and Memories *(in Arabic)*, vol. 4. Dar al-Amar, 2006.

'Said Hawwa Speech on the "Voice of Arab Syria" Radio (Transcript, in Arabic)', *Al-Nadhir no. 7*, 17 February 1982.

Saleh, Yassin al-Haj. 'From Damascus, an Appeal for Salvation', *The Daily Star* (2005), www.dailystar.com.lb/Opinion/Commentary/2005/Oct-28/98244-from-damascus-an-appeal-for-salvation.ashx.
Impossible Revolution: Making Sense of the Syrian Tragedy. London: Hurst, 2017.
Sands, Phil. 'Government and Protesters both Invoke Hama Massacre of 1982', *The National*, 7 July 2011, www.thenational.ae/news/world/middle-east/government-and-protesters-both-invoke-hama-massacre-of-1982.
Seale, Patrick, *The Struggle for Syria: A Study of Post-war Arab Politics, 1945–1958.* Oxford: Oxford University Press, 1965.
Schmidt, Dana Adams. 'Nasserite Riots in Syria Quelled by Martial Law', *The New York Times*, 2 April 1963.
Schrivener, Mr. 'E 7037/388/89 – The Syrian Elections', UK Foreign Office, 28 July 1947.
Schwedler, Jillian. *Faith in Moderation: Islamist Parties in Jordan and Yemen.* Cambridge: Cambridge University Press, 2006.
Schwedler, Jillian. 'The Islah Party in Yemen: Politics Opportunities and Coalition Building in a Transitional Society', in *Islamic Activism: A Social Movement Theory Approach*, edited by Quintan Wiktorowicz. Bloomington: University of Indiana Press, 2004.
Asad of Syria: The Struggle for the Middle East. Berkeley: University of California Press, 1988.
The Struggle for Syria. London: Oxford University Press, 1965.
Shadid, Anthony. 'Inside and Outside Syria, a Debate to Decide the Future', *The Washington Post*, 9 November 2005, www.washingtonpost.com/wp-dyn/content/article/2005/11/08/AR2005110802070_pf.html.
Shain, Yossi. *The Frontier of Loyalty: Political Exiles in the Age of the Nation-State.* Ann Arbor: University of Michigan Press, 2005.
Sharro, Karl. 'Did the Muslim Brotherhood Hijack Syria's Revolution?', *Karl reMarks*, 14 March 2013, www.karlremarks.com/2013/03/did-muslim-brotherhood-hijack-syrias.html.
Sharrouf, Ayman. 'The Destructive Ascendancy of Syria's Muslim Brotherhood', *Now*, 3 December 2014, https://now.mmedia.me/lb/en/commentaryanalysis/564483-the-destructive-ascendancy-of-syrias-muslim-brotherhood.
Shorbaji, Ayman. *The Diary of a Vanguard Combatant in Syria* (in Arabic). Unknown: Unknown, ND.
Sly, Liz. 'Syria's Muslim Brotherhood Is Gaining Influence Over Anti-Assad Revolt', *Washington Post*, 22 May 2012, www.washingtonpost.com/world/syrias-muslim-brotherhood-is-gaining-influence-over-anti-assad-revolt/2012/05/12/gIQAtIoJLU_story.html.
'This is the Man Who Recruited the 9/11 Hijackers,' *The Washington Post* (30 November 2018), www.washingtonpost.com/news/world/wp/2018/11/30/feature/this-is-the-man-who-recruited-the-9-11-hijackers/?utm_term=.cb85d2780e28.
Smoltczyk, Alexander. 'Islam's Spiritual "Dear Abby": The Voice of Egypt's Muslim Brotherhood', *Der Spiegel*, 15 February 2011, www.spiegel.de/international/world/islam-s-spiritual-dear-abby-the-voice-of-egypt-s-muslim-brotherhood-a-745526.html.

Soloman, Jay and Spindle, Bill. 'Syria Strongman: Time for "Reform"', *The Wall Street Journal*, 31 January 2011, http://online.wsj.com/articles/SB10001424052748704832704576114340735033236.

Sosnowski, Marika. 'Violence and Order: The February 2016 Cease-fire and the Development of Rebel Governance Institutions in Southern Syria', *Civil Wars* 20, no. 3 (2018): 309-32.

Sprinzak, Ehud. 'The Process of Delegitimation: Towards a Linkage Theory of Political Terrorism', *Terrorism and Polical Violence* 3, no. 1 (1991): 50-68.

'A Statement from the Muslim Brotherhood, Issued on June 24 (in Arabic)', 3 July 1979.

'Statement of the Muslim Brotherhood in Syria on Current Developments', *Syrian Observer*, 9 May 2013, http://syrianobserver.com/EN/Resources/24756/Statement+of+the+Muslim+Brotherhood+in+Syria+on+current+Developments.

Stearns, Scott. 'Clinton: SNC No Longer Leads Syrian Opposition', *VOA*, 31 October 2012, www.voanews.com/a/brahimi-seeks-chinese-support-for-syria-solution/1536429.html.

Stewart, Phil. 'U.S. behind Strike that Killed Nusra Front's Abu Firas: Officials', *Reuters*, 4 April 2016, www.reuters.com/article/us-mideast-crisis-syria-usa-idUSKCN0X11R3.

'A Summary of the Political Project for the Future Syria: A Vision of the Muslim Brotherhood Group in Syria', London: Syrian Muslim Brotherhood, 2004.

Sunayama, Sonoko. *Syria and Saudi Arabia: Collaboration and Conflicts in the Oil Era*. London: I.B.Tauris, 2007.

Swami, Praveen. 'Family in Power for 40 Years; Assad's Dynasty', 25 March 2011.

'Swedish Ex-Imam Formed Militia Group in Syria', *Radio Sweden*, 1 November 2013, http://sverigesradio.se/sida/artikel.aspx?programid=2054&artikel=5691854.

'Syria Averts Protest by Jailing Writer of an "Atheistic" Article', *New York Times*, 7 May 1967.

'Syria Conflict: Boy Beheaded by Rebels "Was Fighter"', *BBC News*, 21 July 2016, www.bbc.com/news/world-middle-east-36843990.

'Syria Crackdown Leaves 15 Dead, Activists Say', 24 March 2011.

'Syria Cuts off Iraqi Pipeline', *The Globe and Mail*, 20 April 1982.

'Syria Hangs 2 Alleged Iraqi Agents', *The New York Times*, 14 June 1977, p. 4.

'Syria in a Period of Economic Growth', *The New York Times*, 16 November 1976.

'Syria in Crisis – The Damascus Declaration', *Carnegie Middle East Center*, 1 March 2012, http://carnegie-mec.org/diwan/48514?lang=en.

'Syria Isolates City Following Uprising', *The New York Times*, 17 April 1964.

'Syria Live Blog – April 23', *Aljazeera*, 23 April 2011, https://web.archive.org/web/20110426120021/http://blogs.aljazeera.net/live/middle-east/syria-live-blog-april-23.

'Syria Ousts 2 Saudi Diplomats as Active in "Anti-State Plot"', *The Jerusalem Post*, 10 May 1967.

'Syria Quells Revolt, Arrests 19', 16 April 1964.

'Syria Sheiks See Bloodshed in U.N. Partitioning Proposal', *The Washington Post*, 11 September 1947.
'SYRIA: Muslim Brotherhood's Impact Depends on Riyadh', Oxford: Oxford Analytica, 2013.
'Syria: Muslim Brotherhood Pressure Intensifies (U)', US Defense Intelligence Agency, May 1982.
'Syrian Army Colonel Defects Forms Free Syrian Army', *Asharq al-Awsat*, 1 August 2011, http://english.aawsat.com/2011/08/article55245595/syrian-army-colonel-defects-forms-free-syrian-army.
'Syrian Authorities Release 260 Prisoners – Lawyer', *Reuters*, 26 March 2011, www.reuters.com/article/syria-prisoners-idUSLDE72P06120110326.
'The Syrian Constitution – 1973–2012', *Carnegie Middle East Center*, 5 December 2012, http://carnegie-mec.org/diwan/50255?lang=en.
'Syrian Leader Must Adapt or Go', *The Australian*, 2 April 2011. Available at : www.theaustralian.com.au/opinion/editorials/syrian-leader-must-adapt-or-go/news-story/ab29258aaecef4c74e8b614a832e4266.
'Syrian MB: Uprising Will not Stop until Demands Are Met', *Asharq al-Awsat*, 23 March 2011, https://english.aawsat.com/theaawsat/news-middle-east/syrian-mb-uprising-will-not-stop-until-demands-are-met.
'Syrian Muslim Brotherhood Claims Damascus Bombings', Agence France Presse, 24 December 2011.
'Syrian Navy Base Reported Seized by Rebel Troops', *Christian Science Monitor*, 26 February 1982.
'The Syrian Opposition Coalition Accuses Sides of Thwarting the Interim Government, and 13 Military Factions Withdraw from it', *Al-Sharq al-Awsat*. Beirut: BBC Monitoring Middle East, 26 September 2013.
'Syrian Opposition Coalition Formed Without the SNC', *Al-Akhbar*, 17 March 2012, http://english.al-akhbar.com/node/5319.
'Syrian Pressure Continues', *The New York Times*, 29 April 1963.
'Syrian Violence Escalates', *Financial Times*, 24 March 2011.
Taleghani, R. Shareah. 'Breaking the Silence of Tadmor Military Prison', *Middle East Report* 45, no. 275 (2015). Available at: https://merip.org/2015/06/breaking-the-silence-of-tadmor-military-prison/.
Talhami, Ghada Hashem. 'Syria: Islam, Arab Nationalism and the Military', *Middle East Policy* 8, no. 4 (2001): 110–27.
Talhamy, Yvette. 'The Muslim Brotherhood Reborn: The Syrian Uprising', *Middle East Quarterly Spring* (2012): 33–40.
Tamimi, Azzam. 'Democracy in Islamic Political Thought', *Encounters: Journal of Inter-Cultural Perspectives* 3, no. 1 (1997): 21–44.
Teitelbaum, Joshua. 'The Muslim Brotherhood and the "Struggle for Syria", 1947–1958: Between Accommodation and Ideology', *Middle Eastern Studies* 40, no. 3 (2004): 134–58.
   'The Muslim Brotherhood in Syria, 1945–1958: Founding, Social Origins, Ideology', *The Middle East Journal* 65, no. 2 (2011): 213–33.
The Syrian Brotherhood Media Office. Facebook, 14 October 2016, www.facebook.com/IkhwanSyriaMedia/posts/1111832078869231:0.

Facebook, 13 November 2016, www.facebook.com/IkhwanSyriaMedia/photos/a.581223625263415.1073741826.555454591173652/1318636824855421/?type=3&theater.

The Thawra Foundation. 'The Antalya Conference – A Brief Report', *POMED*, 23 June 2011, http://pomed.org/wp-content/uploads/2011/06/The-Antalya-Conference.pdf.

The voice of the Islamic Revolution in Syria. 'Editorial: Army and People Unite against the Tyrant', *Al-Nadhir no. 44* (English edition), 27 February 1982.

'Letter to the Freedom Fighters in Afghanistan', *Al-Nadhir no. 75–6* (English edition), 1 December 1984.

Thompson, Elizabeth. *Colonial Citizens: Republican Rights, Paternal Privilege and Gender in French Syria and Lebanon*. New York: Columbia University Press, 2000.

Tilly, Charles, and Tarrow, Sidney. *Contentious Politics*. Oxford: Oxford University Press, 2015.

'Top Syrian Officers Confess Plot to Murder Jordan's PM', *The Jerusalem Post*, 26 February 1981.

Tripp, Charles. *A History of Iraq*. Cambridge: Cambridge University Press, 2007.

The Power and the People: Paths of Resistance in the Middle East. Cambridge: Cambridge University Press, 2013.

'Turkey "Offered Syria Support" if Brotherhood Given Posts', Agence France-Presse, 29 September 2011.

Ulrichsen, Kristian Coates. *Qatar and the Arab Spring*. Oxford: Oxford University Press, 2014.

'United States v. Osama Bin Laden – Day 2 Transcript', *United States District Court: Southern District of New York*, 6 February 2001.

Unknown author. ND 'SOCOM-2012–0000017-HT – Letter found in Osama bin Laden's Abbottabad, translated by the Combatting Terrorism Center at West Point, thought to be written by Osama bin Laden', ND.

Uqlah, Adnan. 'Letter from Adnan Uqlah', 11 June 1980.

Van Antwerp, Alanna Claire. 'Legacies of Repression: The Revival of Political Participation in the Shadow of Authoritarian Rule', PhD thesis, George Washington University, 2014.

Van Dam, Nikolaos. 'Middle Eastern Political Cliches "Takriti" and "Sunni" Rule in Iraq; "Alawi" Rule in Syria. A Critical Appraisal', *Orient* 21, no. 1 (1980): 42–57.

The Struggle for Power in Syria. London: I.B.Tauris, 1996.

The Struggle for Power in Syria: Politics and Society Under Asad and the Ba'th Party (4th edn). London: I.B.Tauris, 2011.

VanderVeen, Mark A. 'Showdown in Syria: An Examination of Islamist Repression and Rebellion in 1982 Hama', PhD thesis, American University of Paris, 2009.

Wallace, Charles P. 'Visit to Damascus Moves Jordan, Syria Closer', *Los Angeles Times*, 13 November 1985, p. 22.

Wedeen, Lisa. *Ambiguities of Domination: Politics, Rhetoric and Symbols in Contemporary Syria*. Chicago: University of Chicago Press, 1999.

Weinberg, Leonard, Pedahzur, Ami and Perliger, Arie. *Political Parties and Terrorist Groups* (2nd edn). London: Routledge, 2009.

Weismann, Itzchak. 'Between Ṣūfī Reformism and Modernist Rationalism: A Reappraisal of the Origins of the Salafiyya from the Damascene Angle', *Die Welt des Islams* 41, no. 2 (2001): 206–37.

——— 'Democratic Fundamentalism? The Practice and Discourse of the Muslim Brothers Movement in Syria', *The Muslim World* 100, no. 1 (2010): 1–16.

——— 'The Hidden Hand: The Khalidiyya and Orthodox-Fundamentalist Cooperation in Aleppo', *Journal of the History of Sufism* 5 (2006): 1–18.

——— 'The Politics of Popular Religion: Sufis, Salafis, and Muslim Brothers in 20th-Century Hamah', *International Journal of Middle East Studies* 37, no. 1 (2005): 39–58.

——— 'Sa'id Hawwa: The Making of a Radical Muslim Thinker in Modern Syria', *Middle Eastern Studies* 29, no. 4 (1993): 601–23.

——— 'Sa'id Hawwa and Islamic Revivalism in Ba'thist Syria', *Studia Islamica* 85 (1997): 131–54.

——— 'Sufi Fundamentalism between India and the Middle East', in *Sufism and the Modern in Islam*, edited by Martin Van Bruinessen and Julia Day Howell. London: I.B. Tauris, 2007, pp. 115–48.

——— 'Sufism and Salafism in Syria', *Syria Comment*, 11 May2007, www.joshualandis.com/blog/sufism-and-salafism-in-syria-by-itzchak-weismann/.

——— *Taste of Modernity: Sufism, Salafiyya, and Arabism in Late Ottoman Damascus*. Leiden: Brill, 2001.

Whitaker, Brian. 'Syria to Free 600 Political Prisoners', *The Guardian*, 17 November 2000, www.theguardian.com/world/2000/nov/17/brianwhitaker.

Williams, Lauren. 'Brotherhood Seeks to Fill Post-Assad Vacuum' *The Daily Star*, 10 August 2012, www.dailystar.com.lb/News/Middle-East/2012/Aug-10/184107-brotherhood-seeks-to-fill-post-assad-vacuum.ashx.

——— 'Inside Doha, at the Heart of a GCC Dispute', *The National*, 19 March 2014, www.thenational.ae/world/qatar/inside-doha-at-the-heart-of-a-gcc-dispute.

'World Illiteracy at Mid-Century', Geneva: UNESCO, 1957.

Yassin-Kassab, Robin and al-Shami, Leila, *Burning Country: Syrians in Revolution and War*, London, Pluto Press, 2016.

Yazbeck, Natacha. 'Syria Accuses Fundamentalists of Stirring Unrest', *Agence France Presse*, 28 March 2011.

Yemma, John. 'Both Sides Seek Face-Saving Device in Syria-Jordan Confrontation', *The Christian Science Monitor*, 4 December 1980.

Zahr-al-Din, Lina. 'Interview with Ali Sadr-al-Din al-Bayanuni, Controller General of the Syrian Muslim Brotherhood Movement, Via Satellite from London', *Al-Jazeera*. London: BBC Monitoring Middle East, 4 April 2009.

Zalewski, Piotr. 'Islamic Evolution: How Turkey Taught the Syrian Muslim Brotherhood to Reconcile Faith and Democracy', *Foreign Policy*, 11 August 2011, http://foreignpolicy.com/2011/08/11/islamic-evolution-2/.

Ziadeh, Radwan. *Power and Policy in Syria: Intelligence Services, Foreign Relations and Democracy in the modern Middle East*. London: I.B.Tauris, 2011.

Zidan, Ahmad. 'Issam al-Attar ... The Islamic Movement in Syria (in Arabic)'. *Today's Meeting, Al-Jazeera Arabic*, 1 July 2007, www.aljazeera.net/programs/today-interview/2007/7/1/%D8%B9%D8%B5%D8%A7%D9%85-%D8%A7%D9%84%D8%B9%D8%B7%D8%A7%D8%B1-%D8%A7%D9%84%D8%AD%D8%B1%D9%83%D8%A9-%D8%A7%D9%84%D8%A5%D8%B3%D9%84%D8%A7%D9%85%D9%8A%D8%A9-%D9%81%D9%8A-%D8%B3%D9%88%D8%B1%D9%8A%D8%A7.

Zisser, Eyal. 'Syria', in *Elections in Asia and the Pacific: A Data Handbook: Volume I: Middle East*, edited by Dieter Nohlen, Florian Grotz and Christof Hartmann. Oxford: Oxford University Press, 2001.

'The Syrian Army: Between the Domestic and the External Fronts', *Middle East Review of International Affairs* 5, no. 1 (2001): 1–12.

Index

Page numbers in italics refer to tables

Abu Musab al-Suri, 148–9
Abu, Husni, 98, 110, 112, 114
activism, 26, 37–8, 159
Afghanistan, 146–51, *232–6*
al- Houeidi, Hassan, 119
al-Abdeh, Anas, 84
al-Ahmad, Ali, 119, 127, 179
al-Assad, Bashar, 5–6, 37, 60–1, 83
  and economy, 180
  and Syrian uprising, 155–7
al-Assad, Hafez, 31, 109, 115
  assassination attempt on, 35, 114
  and coup, 33–4
  death of, 37, 60
  and negotiations with Brotherhood, 80–1
  and secularism, 78–9, 94
  see also Ba'th Party
al-Assad, Rifaat, 77, 114, 117
al-Attar, Issam
  on Aleppo Artillery Academy massacre, 113
  and exile, 32, 52, 76
  leadership, 74, 78, 108
  and non-violence, 32, 97, 103–4
  in parliament, 66, *229*
Alawites, 31, 57, 104
  and Aleppo Artillery Academy massacre, 112, 201
al-Bayanouni, Abu Nasr, 56, 119, 122, 135, 142
al-Bayanouni, Ali, 25–7, 59–62, 88–9, *239*
  and Ba'th negotiations, 80–2
  and Damascus Declaration, 88, 116
  on democracy, 40, 175
  on Hama uprising (1982), 125, 127, 132
  on Syrian protests, 157, 161
al-Dawalibi, Maruf, 43, 68, 72, 74, 142, 144, *228–30*

Aldrobi, Molham, 168–70, *238*
  on arms funding, 205
  on Commission for the Protection of Civilians, 216–17
  on humanitarian aid, 168, 182
  on Saudi Arabia, 193
  and Shields of the Revolution Council, 208–9
  on Syrian uprising (2011), 1, 157, 173
Aleppo, 104, 117–18
  faction of Brotherhood, 104–6, 108, 128–9
  see also Fighting Vanguard: Aleppo Artillery Academy massacre *see also* Liwa al-Tawhid
al-Fatah abu Ghuddah, Shaykh, 32, 67, 82, 108, 142, *239*
al-Hachimi, Hassan, 132, 164, 209–12, *239*
al-Hachimi, Mohammad, 132
al-Haj Saleh, Yassin, 6, 31, 88, 171
al-Hamid, Muhammad, 26, 53, 72, 97
al-Jazeera, 191–2
al-Khaddam, Abdul Halim
  and Hama riots (1964), 96
  on Law no. 49, 115
  and National Salvation Front, 38, 88
  on negotiations with the Ba'th Party, 82
al-Mubarak, Muhammad, 51, 70, 72–4, 142, *228–9*
al-Qaeda, 100, 146, 150, 199, 220, *233*
al-Sayyid Issa, Fida, 158
al-Sayyid Issa, Tarif, 212
al-Shaqfeh, Riad, 84, 99, 137, 186, 194, 196, 205, *239*
al-Shishakli, Adib, 12, 28–9, 69, 73, 93, 141
al-Sibai, Mustafa, 25, 27–30, 41, 43, *229*
  death, 52, 64, 103
  and democracy, 62, 64
  and elections, 68–9

265

Index

al-Sibai, Mustafa (cont.)
  on Islamic state, 45–9, 54
  and non-violence, 59
  and religious tolerance, 49–51
  and socialism, 71–2
al-Suri, Abu Musab, 100–2, 118–21, 126, *233*
al-Youssef, Ibrahim, 101, 112–13, 201–2
al-Zaim, Abd al-Sattar, 98–9, 101
Arab Uprisings, 1, 155, 188, 196 *see also* Hama uprising (1982) *see also* Syrian uprising (2011)
army, 2, 29, 36, 75
  and factionalism, 104
  and Fighting Vanguard, 101
  and Hama riots (1964), 96
  and Jordan, 139
  Syrian Liberation Army, 129
  see also Fighting Vanguard *see also* Free Syrian Army
assassinations. *See under* Fighting Vanguard
authoritarianism
  and Ba'th Party, 66, 76, 89, 94, 111, 223
  and contentious politics, 12–13
  and Syrian political system, *28*

Batatu, Hannah, 7, 42, 46, 49
Ba'th Party, 30
  as Alawite, 31, 50
  and Aleppo Artillery Academy massacre, 112–15
  arrests, 76, 156
  and authoritarianism, 18, 94, 111
  and class, 45, 70
  coup, 2, 29, 52, 76, 78, 89, 94–5, 223
  and economy, 32–4, 109, 180
  and elections, 73, *228*
  and Hama riots (1964), 95
  and Hama uprising (1982), 107, 124
  and Iraq, 135
  and Law no. 49, 35
  and negotiations with Brotherhood, 80–2
bin Laden, Osama, 9, 96, 131, 149
bourgeoisie. *See* class
Burhan, Abu, 150

Christianity, 22, 45, 49–52
class, 24, 41–3, 105, 110–11, 142, 180
  and Ba'th Party, 31, 33–4, 70
Commission for the Protection of Civilians (CPC), 215–17, 220
Communist Party, 29, 31–2, 69–70, 86
Constitution, Syrian, 30, 33, 55, 72
  and al-Assad, Hafez, 78–9

  and al-Sibai, Mustafa, 47–8, 70
  and democratic era, 28
  and *Salafiyya* movement, 24
constructionism, 8
contentious politics, 12–15

Damascus, 21–4, 104–5
  faction of Brotherhood, 15, 32, 35, 42, 51, 78
  and *jamiyat*, 24–5
Damascus Declaration, 87, 162
Damascus Spring, 37, 61
democracy
  al-Bayanouni, Ali on, 41
  and Aldrobi, Molham, 1
  and al-Mubarak, Muhammad, 51
  and al-Sibai, Mustafa, 47–9
  and Brotherhood ideology, 14, 44, 66, 222–3
  and Damascus Declaration, 87
  and Declaration and Program of the Islamic Revolution in Syria, 55–7
  democratic era, 2, 27–9, 67, 69, 76
  and Hawwa, Said, 54–5, 57
  and Islam, 6–7, 47, 49, 51
  and National Honour Charter, 61
  and Political Project for the Future Syria, 63–4
  and *Salafiyya*, 26
  and Salem, Zuhair, 175
  and Syrian political system, *28*
  see also elections

economy
  and oil boom, 33
  see also class *see also* ideology (Brotherhood): economic liberalism *see also under* Ba'th Party *see also under* Hama
education, 14, 71, 142, 211
  and al-Hamid, Muhammad, 26
  of Brotherhood members, 43–5, 142
  and Hawwa, Said, 53
Egypt, 1, 29, 34, 56, 73, 120
Egyptian Muslim Brotherhood, 26–7, 34, 41, 52, 134, 162
elections, 27–32, 67–70, 73–6, *227–9*

factionalism, 103–9, 184–5 *see also* Aleppo: faction of Brotherhood *see also* Damascus: faction of Brotherhood *see also* Hama: faction of Brotherhood
Fighting Vanguard, 34–7, 80–1, 98–101, 109–10, 120–1, 220–1

Index 267

in Afghanistan, 145–7, *232–6*
and Aleppo Artillery Academy massacre, 112–14
and assassinations, 34, 80, 101–2, 110
and Hama uprising (1982), 123–4, 130–1
and Syrian Islamic Front, 85–6
see also al-Suri, Abu Musab *see also* Uqlah, Adnan
Free Syrian Army, 199, 202, 206, 208

Ghadban, Hosam, 186, 198, *238*
Ghalioun, Burhan, 141, 145, 151, 163, 165, 169, 171, 176–7

Hadid, Marwan, 34, 96–103, 200
Hama, 107, 117
  faction of Brotherhood, 26, 34, 53, 82, 105, 109
  riots (1964), 96
  see also Hama uprising (1982)
Hama uprising (1982), 2–7, 59, 123–7, 222
  aftermath, 128–31
  and Evaluation Committee, 132
  and Iraq, 136
  legacy of, 200–1, 203, 225
Hawwa, Said, 27, 48, 52–5, 57–9, *239*
  and the constitution, 78–9
  on Hama riots (1964), 96
  JundAllah, 54, 110, 142
humanitarian aid, 168, 180, 182

ideology (Brotherhood), 26
  and al-Bayanouni, Ali, 60
  in 'Covenant and Charter', 174–5
  and Declaration and Program of the Islamic Revolution in Syria, 55–7
  and democracy, 44
  diversity of, 51–2, 72, 177
  and economic liberalism, 14, 42, 53, 224
  flexibility of, 14, 48, 71
  and Hawwa, Said, 55, 59, 111
  and Iraq, 135, 138
  and National Honour Charter, 60–2
  and Political Project for the Future Syria, 62–4
  pragmatism of, 48, 72, 175, 206
  and Salem, Zuhair, 40, 45, 59
  and socialism, 70–2
  and violence, 15, 30
  see also democracy: and Brotherhood ideology
internationalism, 134–5, 141, 145, 151–2, 188
  and Afghhanistan, 147–8

Iraq, 123, 135–8
  military camps, 36–7, 120, 126–8
Islam
  and Brotherhood ideology, 15, 30, 175, 220
  and democracy, 6–7, 47, 49, 51
  Islamist groups, 6–7, 11, 63
  Orthodox, 22, 26
Israel, 50, 76, 83

jamiyat, 21, 24–7, 41–2
  Jamiyat al-Gharra, 51, 67, 105
jihad
  and Hawwa, Said, 58
  jihad movement, 145–51
Jordan, 61, 98, 123, 138–41
Jordanian Muslim Brotherhood, 98
Judaism, 45, 49

Laban, Samir abu, 106, 144, 165, 186, 211
Liwa al-Tawhid (the Tawhid Brigade), 206–7

militarism, 60, 77, 94, 118–20
  and al-Attar, Issam, 75
  and Fighting Vanguard, 34–6
  and *Futuwwa*, 92–3
  and Hadid, Marwan, 97–9
  and Saadeddine, Adnan, 37
  and Shields of the Revolution Council, 209–11
  and Syrian uprising (2011), 199
  see also Fighting Vanguard *see also* Hama uprising (1982) *see also* Iraq: military camps *see also* Shields of the Revolution Council *see also* Syrian uprising (2011): arms funding

National Action Group (NAG), 84, 185, 188
National Coalition for Syrian Revolution and Opposition Forces (SOC), 3, 38, 163, 166–7, 194
National Party, 69, 104
nationalism, 31, 94

Ottoman Empire, 21, 24, 26, 104

Palestine, 73, 82–3, 93–4
parliament, 2, 27–30, 66–76
People's Party, 30, 69, 104–5, *230*

Qatar, 188–93
Quran, 23, 48, 64, 174

radicalisation, 15, 58, 110
reform
　and al-Bayanouni, Issa, 27
　and al-Hamid, Muhammad, 26
　economic, 33–4
　Islamic, 21–3
　and *jamiyat*, 24
research methodology, 8–11

Saadeddine, Adnan, 34, 37, 102, 108–9, 191–2
　on Aleppo Artillery Academy massacre, 113
　and Hama uprising (1982), 128–30, 132
　and Iraq, 137–8
　on negotiations with Ba'th Party, 82
Salafiyya, 23–4, 26–7
Salem, Zuhair, 40, 59–60
　on democracy, 49, 175
　on Egyptian Muslim Brotherhood, 162
　on Hama uprising (1982), 129
　on Hawwa, Said, 59
　on Islamic state, 45
　on National Honour Charter, 61
Sarmini, Mohammed, 176, 185, 187
Saudi Arabia, 142, 144, 192–5
secularism, 7, 31, 78–9, 85, 94, 175
Sharia, 64, 175, 178
Shields of the Revolution Council, 209–11
Shorbaji, Ayman, 93, 98–9, 101–2, 109, 131
Shura, 54, 56, 64
SOC *see* National Coalition for Syrian Revolution and Opposition Forces (SOC – Syrian Opposition Coalition)
socialism, 31, 70–3
Socialist Party, 69, 86
Sufism, 22–7
　and Hawwa, Said, 58
Sunnis, 4, 22, 26, 77, 201
Syrian Islamic Front (SIF), 27, 35, 56, 85–6

Syrian Muslim Brotherhood
　characteristics of, 13–14, 48–9, 66, 71, 170
　formation of, 21, 41
　outlawed, 32, 52, 76
Syrian National Council (SNC), 3, 163–5 *see also under* Tayfour, Farouq
Syrian uprising (2011), 1–7, 17–18, 40, 155–63, 173, 222–6
　arms funding, 215
　and militarism, 199–204
　see also Commission for the Protection of Civilians *see also* Shields of the Revolution Council

Tayfour, Farouq, 106, 163, 168, 194, *238*
　on democracy, 66
　on Hama uprising (1982), 130
　on Iraq, 138
Turkey, 195–8

United Arab Republic, 12, 29, 73, 78, 80
Uqla, Adnan, 35–7, 86, 100–1, 120
　and Hama uprising (1982), 123–4, 130

violence
　under Ba'th Party regime, 94–5, 115–17
　and Brotherhood ideology, 30–6
　and *Futuwwa*, 92–3
　and Hawwa, Said, 58–9
　and Islamism, 6–7
　scholarship on, 14–15, 91
　see also Fighting Vanguard *see also* Hama: riots (1964) *see also* Hama uprising (1982) *see also* militarism *see also* Syrian uprising (2011)

Walid, Muhammad, 181, 186–7, *238*
women, 25, 51, 63, 117, 175, *238*

youth, 92–3, 96, 118, 131, 185–8, *238*

Books in the Series

1. Parvin Paidar, *Women and the Political Process in Twentieth-Century Iran*
2. Israel Gershoni and James Jankowski, *Redefining the Egyptian Nation, 1930–1945*
3. Annelies Moors, *Women, Property and Islam: Palestinian Experiences, 1920–1945*
4. Paul Kingston, *Britain and the Politics of Modernization in the Middle East, 1945–1958*
5. Daniel Brown, *Rethinking Tradition in Modern Islamic Thought*
6. Nathan J. Brown, *The Rule of Law in the Arab World: Courts in Egypt and the Gulf*
7. Richard Tapper, *Frontier Nomads of Iran: The Political and Social History of the Shahsevan*
8. Khaled Fahmy, *All the Pasha's Men: Mehmed Ali, His Army and the Making of Modern Egypt*
9. Sheila Carapico, *Civil Society in Yemen: The Political Economy of Activism in Arabia*
10. Meir Litvak, *Shi'i Scholars of Nineteenth-Century Iraq: The Ulama of Najaf and Karbala*
11. Jacob Metzer, *The Divided Economy of Mandatory Palestine*
12. Eugene L. Rogan, *Frontiers of the State in the Late Ottoman Empire: Transjordan, 1850–1921*
13. Eliz Sanasarian, *Religious Minorities in Iran*
14. Nadje Al-Ali, *Secularism, Gender and the State in the Middle East: The Egyptian Women's Movement*
15. Eugene L. Rogan and Avi Shlaim, eds., *The War for Palestine: Rewriting the History of 1948*
16. Gershon Shafir and Yoar Peled, *Being Israeli: The Dynamics of Multiple Citizenship*
17. A. J. Racy, *Making Music in the Arab World: The Culture and Artistry of Tarab*
18. Benny Morris, *The Birth of the Palestinian Refugee Crisis Revisited*
19. Yasir Suleiman, *A War of Words: Language and Conflict in the Middle East*
20. Peter Moore, *Doing Business in the Middle East: Politics and Economic Crisis in Jordan and Kuwait*
21. Idith Zertal, *Israel's Holocaust and the Politics of Nationhood*
22. David Romano, *The Kurdish Nationalist Movement: Opportunity, Mobilization and Identity*
23. Laurie A. Brand, *Citizens Abroad: Emigration and the State in the Middle East and North Africa*
24. James McDougall, *History and the Culture of Nationalism in Algeria*
25. Madawi al-Rasheed, *Contesting the Saudi State: Islamic Voices from a New Generation*

26. Arang Keshavarzian, *Bazaar and State in Iran: The Politics of the Tehran Marketplace*
27. Laleh Khalili, *Heroes and Martyrs of Palestine: The Politics of National Commemoration*
28. M. Hakan Yavuz, *Secularism and Muslim Democracy in Turkey*
29. Mehran Kamrava, *Iran's Intellectual Revolution*
30. Nelida Fuccaro, *Histories of City and State in the Persian Gulf: Manama since 1800*
31. Michaelle L. Browers, *Political Ideology in the Arab World: Accommodation and Transformation*
32. Miriam R. Lowi, *Oil Wealth and the Poverty of Politics: Algeria Compared*
33. Thomas Hegghammer, *Jihad in Saudi Arabia: Violence and Pan-Islamism since 1979*
34. Sune Haugbolle, *War and Memory in Lebanon*
35. Ali Rahnema, *Superstition as Ideology in Iranian Politics: From Majlesi to Ahmadinejad*
36. Wm. Roger Louis and Avi Shlaim eds, *The 1967 Arab-Israeli War: Origins and Consequences*
37. Stephen W. Day, *Regionalism and Rebellion in Yemen: A Troubled National Union*
38. Daniel Neep, *Occupying Syria under the French Mandate: Insurgency, Space and State Formation*
39. Iren Ozgur, *Islamic Schools in Modern Turkey: Faith, Politics, and Education*
40. Ali M. Ansari, *The Politics of Nationalism in Modern Iran*
41. Thomas Pierret, *Religion and State in Syria: The Sunni Ulama from Coup to Revolution*
42. Guy Ben-Porat, *Between State and Synagogue: The Secularization of Contemporary Israel*
43. Madawi Al-Rasheed, *A Most Masculine State: Gender, Politics and Religion in Saudi Arabia*
44. Sheila Carapico, *Political Aid and Arab Activism: Democracy Promotion, Justice, and Representation*
45. Pascal Menoret, *Joyriding in Riyadh: Oil, Urbanism, and Road Revolt*
46. Toby Matthiesen, *The Other Saudis: Shiism, Dissent and Sectarianism*
47. Bashir Saade, *Hizbullah and the Politics of Remembrance: Writing the Lebanese Nation*
48. Noam Leshem, *Life After Ruin: The Struggles over Israel's Depopulated Arab Spaces*
49. Zoltan Pall, *Salafism in Lebanon: Local and Transnational Movements*
50. Salwa Ismail, *The Rule of Violence: Subjectivity, Memory and Government in Syria*
51. Zahra Ali, *Women and Gender in Iraq: Between Nation-Building and Fragmentation*
52. Dina Bishara, *Contesting Authoritarianism: Labour Challenges to the State in Egypt*
53. Rory McCarthy, *Inside Tunisia's al-Nahda: Between Politics and Preaching*
54. Ceren Lord, *Religious Politics in Turkey: From the Birth of the Republic to the AKP*
55. Dörthe Engelcke, *Reforming Family Law: Social and Political Change in Jordan and Morocco*
56. Dara Conduit, *The Muslim Brotherhood in Syria*